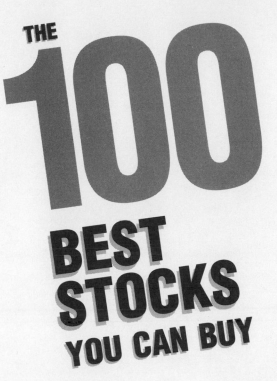

THE

100

BEST
STOCKS

YOU CAN BUY

THE 100 BEST STOCKS YOU CAN BUY

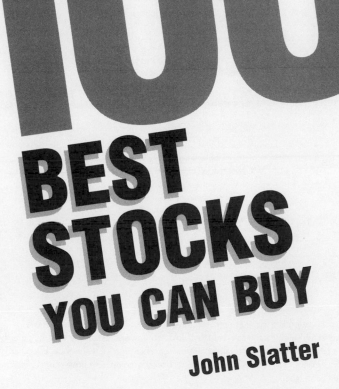

John Slatter

Adams Media Corporation
Holbrook, Massachusetts

To
My wife,
Beverly G. Slatter, RN

Published by
Adams Media Corporation
260 Center Street, Holbrook, MA 02343

ISBN: 1-55850-755-8

Printed in the United States of America.

J I H G F E D C B A

Library of Congress Cataloging-in-Publication Data
Slatter, John, 1924–
100 best stocks you can buy / John Slatter.
p.   cm.
At head of title: 1998.
"Second editon"—Pref.
ISBN 1–55850–755–8
1. Stocks. 2. Investments. 3. Securities—Ratings. I. Title.
HG6041.S579   1998
338.7'4'0973—dc21   97–36929
CIP

This publication is designed to provide accurate and authoritative information with
regard to the subject matter covered. It is sold with the understanding that the publisher
is not engaged in rendering legal, accounting, or other professional advice. If legal advice
or other expert assistance is required, the services of a competent professional person
should be sought.
— From a *Declaration of Principles* jointly adopted by a Committee of the American Bar
Association and a Committee of Publishers and Associations

This book is available at quantity discounts for bulk purchases.
For information, call 1-800-872-5627 (in Massachusetts, 781-767-8100).

Visit our home page at http://www.adamsmedia.com

Table of Contents

Part I
The Art and Science of Investing in Stocks

Part II
100 Best Stocks You Can Buy

Part I

Preface

If you are like me, you are reluctant to buy a book until you examine the credentials of the author. Unfortunately, this is rarely easy—the biographical blurb on the cover is often too skimpy. This preface is my attempt to bridge that gap.

I started in the investment business over thirty-five years ago (at the end of 1960) and operated as a plain-vanilla stockbroker.

To find clients, I made scads of "cold calls." I also taught evening adult-education classes at local high schools. It was hard work, but my teaching skill, coupled with my expanding knowledge of investments, helped me convince people that I was a reliable person to do business with.

When my knowledge of the business progressed still further, I took a stab at becoming an author by writing an article for *Barron's Financial Weekly*. The editor asked me if I had any more bright ideas that might be fashioned into articles. From then on, I wrote regularly for *Barron's* on a free-lance basis, while still working as a stockbroker. Over the years, I may have written as many as one hundred articles for *Barron's*. In addition, I have written for such magazines as *Physician's Management* and *Better Investing*.

Eventually, I wrote my first book, *Safe Investing* (Simon & Schuster, 1991). More recently, my book *Straight Talk About Stock Investing* (McGraw-Hill, 1995) was published. Finally, in late 1996, the first edition of my latest book, *The 100 Best Stocks You Can Buy*, was published by Adams Media.

Because of my writing, I began to be quoted in such periodicals as *The New York Times*, the *Cleveland Plain Dealer*, the *Christian Science Monitor*, the *Toledo Blade*, the *Cincinnati Enquirer*, *Money Magazine*, *The Washington Post*, *Barron's*, *The Kiplinger Magazine*, the *Dick Davis Digest*, *The Buffalo News*, the Gannett chain, as well as numerous syndicated columns and advisory services.

I became a bit more famous when I developed a strategy based on investing in the ten stocks with the highest yield from the thirty stocks that make up the Dow Jones Industrial Average. My scheme was discussed in an article by John Dorfman in the *Wall Street Journal* in August of 1988. Such innovative approaches to stock selection are my specialty and are presented in detail in all of my books.

In the late 1960s, I moved from central New York State to Buffalo to become editor of a publication that promoted mutual funds. At that time, I believed that investors were well served by investing in these professionally managed financial instruments. I have since changed my mind. I am now convinced that you can do better by investing in individual stocks. Mutual funds have some flaws:

- They are too expensive. Even no-load funds have an annual charge that averages 1.5 percent.
- They are difficult to select. There is no good way to determine which of the 8,000 funds is best. Past performance is rarely translated into future performance.
- They saddle you with capital gains taxes. Every year, their profits are paid out at year end. You have no choice in

when the manager buys and sells the fund's holdings. When you own your own stocks, *you* decide when to sell.

- Worst of all, they don't do as well as the general market. Only 20 percent even equal such indexes as the Dow Jones Industrial Average or the Standard & Poor's 500.

By 1972 I had gradually educated myself so that I could assume the title of a securities analyst. I moved from Buffalo, New York, to Cleveland, Ohio, and gave up being a stockbroker (I wasn't exactly a super salesman, being more studious than back-slapping) and worked full time analyzing stocks and writing reports that were distributed to the brokers and clients of that brokerage firm.

After a few years of hard study (and three beastly all-day examinations), I was also able to tack after my name the designation of CFA (which stands for Chartered Financial Analyst).

As I continued to hone my skills as a securities analyst, I became a specialist in certain industries, including public utilities, food processors, and pharmaceuticals.

Somewhat later I developed another skill, that of analyzing investors' portfolios and writing reports that enabled the clients to ascertain which stocks should be sold and which stocks should serve as replacements.

At this point, my firm wanted me to move from Cleveland to Chicago, since it had its headquarters there. Unwilling to leave, I looked for a new job and was employed by a Cleveland-based advisory firm.

Such a firm is entirely different from a brokerage house. Brokers make their living from commissions. Unless you buy or sell a stock, mutual fund, or some other product, stockbrokers don't get paid.

By contrast, an investment advisor charges a fee—typically 1 percent of your portfolio per year—to manage your investments. Such a firm does not benefit from transactions. I liked this idea for two reasons.

First, it seemed to benefit the investor as well as the management firm, since both did well if the portfolio continued to grow. To illustrate: The annual fee on a $300,000 portfolio is $3,000. If the investment advisor can make your portfolio grow to $400,000, the fee expands to $4,000. Obviously, the client is happy, but so is the firm managing the portfolio.

Second, I liked the advisory business because it gave me an opportunity to look at the whole investment scene, not merely one or two industries. I could fashion a portfolio and exercise my skill in stock selection, for which I seem to have considerable talent.

Which brings us up to the present. I am still working as an investment advisor, which means that I manage portfolios for people who have substantial holdings.

In addition, I edit a monthly market letter, called *John Slatter's Investment Commentary*. The 100 stocks that I rank, analyze, and discuss on a continuing basis are the same 100 stocks that are dealt with in this book.

Finally, in May of 1996—to be closer to my family—my wife and I moved to northwestern Vermont, near the largest city in that state, Burlington. You can reach me by addressing your correspondence to me at 70 Beech Street, Essex Junction, Vermont 05452. Or you may call me at (802) 872-0637.

Preface to the Second Edition

When I wrote the first edition of *The 100 Best Stocks You Can Buy*, I was warned by the editor that I might be called upon to update the book if investors in droves bought it. Apparently, that's what happened, so I was ordered back to my computer.

The editor didn't think this would be much of a chore, but he turned out to be wrong. Using the 1996 annual reports—and other information such as *Value Line*, newspaper and magazine articles, and Standard & Poor's reports—I found that about 80 percent of my first write-ups were old news. In some instances I abandoned the entire text and started over.

Equally important, I added a batch of new stocks and dropped an equal number that I decided no longer interested me. Among the twenty-one new stocks are such intriguing companies as Baldor Electric, Pioneer Hi-Bred, Dover, W. W. Grainger, Compaq, and Cedar Fair.

Adding new stocks means dropping old ones. One investor suggested that I give reasons for each stock being eliminated. Although this may seem sensible, I have elected not to comply. On the other hand, I see no reason to sell your shares of the stocks that do not appear in this edition. In most instances, switching from one stock to another doesn't work out. For one thing, every time you replace a stock, you have two commissions to pay. And don't forget the cash you have to ship to the IRS when you sell a stock that has risen in price.

In this edition, I have become somewhat more growth-oriented and aggressive. The number of stocks labeled *aggressive* growth has climbed from twenty-two to twenty-six. This will probably surprise many of the people who know me well. They tend to regard me as a "value investor." They will be shocked that I am recommending such stocks as Compaq, Pioneer Hi-Bred, Pfizer, and Diebold.

And, for heaven's sake, don't fret when you can't find your favorite stock in my list of 100. Some of my own stocks are also missing, such as Royal Dutch Petroleum, British Telecommunications, Houghton Mifflin, Indiana Energy, Lakehead Pipeline, and National Service Industries. What it amounts to is this: There are more than a hundred great stocks. There are probably thousands. Nor is my list necessarily the best one.

On the other hand, my wife and I own 33 of the 100 stocks, which I guess makes us believers. It also makes us believers in the magic of common-stock investing.

It has now been over thirty-five years since I first joined the investment community. My philosophy over that span has not changed drastically, but there are a few fundamental truths that I cling to:

- You can't forecast the market, so quit trying.
- Common stocks are the only place to put your money. Everything else is inferior, such as real estate, bonds, coins, stamps, antiques, baseball cards, certificates of deposit, and money-market funds.
- Trading is the quickest way to the poorhouse. The only sensible strategy is to buy and hold.

- Don't bet the farm on one or two stocks. There are 2,700 stocks listed on the New York Stock Exchange. Surely you can find fifteen or twenty that will help you become rich.
- Don't buy mutual funds. Why? They charge too much; they create unwanted tax liabilities; they are generally inept. Also, there is no way to know which ones are the best. Past history is of little help.
- Don't ask anyone for advice; make up your own mind. That way you won't have anyone to blame if you goof. And you will goof once in a while. But you don't have to be right too often to make a bundle. If the average stock returns 10 percent a year, here is how rich you'll be at age 65. If you invest $5,000 a year beginning at age 45, you'll have $286,375 at age 65. If you start at age 35, you'll have $822,470.

It pays to start early. Here's proof. If you start at age 25 and invest only $2,000 a year, you'll reach age 65 with $885,185.

- Don't put off investing because you are saving for a car, saving for education, saving for a house, saving for a vacation. Put aside at least 10 percent of every paycheck. Even better, make it 15 or 20 percent. But don't do this unless you are prepared to reach retirement with stocks worth hundreds of thousands of dollars.
- Don't make the mistake of avoiding high-priced stocks such as Royal Dutch Petroleum, Exxon, Intel, Compaq, or Pfizer. Investors often tell me, "I am just a small investor; I can't afford a high-priced stock. Don't you have something under $30 a share?" Rubbish. Buy 10, 20, or 30 shares if you can't afford 100.
- Don't buy a stock simply because my write-up appeals to you. Call the company and get a copy of the annual report. Study it as if your life depended on it. It does.

Why Invest in Stocks?

Investing is a complex business. But, then, so is medicine, engineering, chemistry, geology, law, gardening, philosophy, cooking, paleontology, dentistry, photography, history, accounting—you name it.

In fact, investing is so daunting and intimidating that many otherwise intelligent individuals avoid it. Instead, they stash their money in certificates of deposit (CDs), annuities, bonds, or mutual funds.

Apparently they can't face buying common stocks. This is too bad, because common stocks are precisely where the money is made. To be sure, you don't make money every day, every week, or even every year. But over the long term, you will make the most out of your investment dollars in stocks.

Look at the Facts

One persuasive study, for instance, contends that common stocks will make money for you in most years. This study, which was done by the brokerage firm Smith Barney, looked at the thirty-five one-year periods between 1960 and 1995.

The study computed total return, which adds together capital gains and dividends. Over that span, stocks (as represented by the Standard & Poor's 500 index) performed unsatisfactorily in only eight of those thirty-five years. In other words, you would have been better off in money-market funds during those eight years. That's not a bad track record. Common stocks would have been more successful in twenty-seven of those thirty-five years.

Investing for the Long Term

Investing, however, is not a one-year endeavor. Most investors start their programs in their forties and fifties, which means they could be investing over a twenty-, thirty-, or forty-year period.

If we look at the relative returns of different investments over five-year periods—rather than one-year periods—the results are even more encouraging. During the years from 1960 through 1994, there were thirty-one such periods. In only two of those five-year periods did the total return of the Standard & Poor's-based portfolio become negative.

Let's move ahead to all ten-year holding periods. There were twenty-six in that span. Exactly 100 percent worked out profitably. Equally important, the returns to the investor were impressive in all of these one-, five-, and ten-year periods. The one-year periods, for instance, gave you an average annual total return of 11.1 percent; for five-year periods, it was 10.5 percent, and for ten-year periods, it was 10.2 percent.

Based on this brokerage house study, then, we can say with a great deal of confidence that over a lifetime of investing, an investor will reap a total annual return of 10 percent or more.

If you compare this with the amount you could earn by owning CDs, annuities, government bonds, or any other conservative investments, the difference is considerable.

Some Profitable Comparisons

Let's see how that difference adds up. Suppose you invested $25,000 in a list of common stocks at the age of forty, and your portfolio built up at a 10 percent compound annual rate. By the time you reached sixty-five, your common stock nest egg would be worth $270,868.

On the other hand, let's say you had invested your money in government bonds, yielding 6 percent. The same $25,000 would be worth only $107,297, which is a difference of $163,571. Neither of these calculations has taken into account income taxes or brokerage commissions.

Now, let's look at the timid soul who invested $25,000 in CDs at age forty and averaged a return of 4 percent. By age sixty-five, that investment would be worth a paltry $66,646.

Why Doesn't Everyone Buy Common Stocks?

That's a good question, and I'm not sure I can provide you with a satisfactory answer. Part of the reason may be ignorance. Not everyone is willing to investigate the field of common stocks. These noninvestors may be too preoccupied with their jobs, sports, reading, gardening, travel, soap operas, hobbies, or whatever. Then there are the people who are heavily influenced by family members who have sold them on the idea that stocks are too speculative and better left to millionaires. (Of course, that's how many of these millionaires became millionaires.)

Even if you are convinced that I may be right about the potential of stocks, you are probably wondering how anyone can possibly figure out which stocks to buy, since there are tens of thousands to choose from. That, in essence, is the purpose of this book—and the subject of the chapter that follows.

How the 100 Best Stocks Were Selected

Within the covers of this book are 100 stocks that make excellent targets if you're hunting for another stock for your portfolio. If you're a beginning or casual investor, 100 may seem like an overwhelming number.

To be sure, no one needs to own 100 stocks. On the other hand, there are thousands of stocks that you could invest in, including 2,600 traded on the New York Stock Exchange, over 1,000 traded on the American Stock Exchange, plus tens of thousands that are traded over the counter, usually referred to as NASDAQ. Stocks in this last category are not traded on an exchange. Instead, they are handled by scores of brokerage firms across the country. These firms actually own the stocks they make markets in, whereas stocks traded on an exchange are not owned by the members who handle these transactions.

As you can see, there is no shortage of stocks. In fact, there are too many for any one person to understand—and that doesn't even take into account the vast number of foreign stocks. Is it any wonder that some investors are confused as to which way to turn?

When I started my research for this book, I began with a "wish list" of nearly 200 stocks. As I pointed out in the preface, stock picking has been my passion for the past thirty-five years. My 200 stocks included the best performers in a broad range of business sectors, ranging from heavy industries to utilities to consumer goods producers to service businesses.

Next, I set up a research file for each stock. Dutifully, I clipped out articles from the *Wall Street Journal*, the *New York Times*, *Barron's*, *Forbes*, *Financial World*, and *Business Week*, among other periodicals. And, of course, I wrote letters to the investor contacts at each company, instructing them to send me the latest annual report and quarterly reports. I also asked them to provide any basic reports they had that had been written by analysts from Wall Street's leading brokerage houses. In addition, I collected write-ups on the stocks from brokerage houses such as Merrill Lynch, Morgan Stanley, Cowen and Company, and Paine Webber. Some of my file folders got pretty full, giving me lots of ammunition for this book.

Once I had whittled down my original "wish list" to the top 100 stocks, I pulled out my files again and examined the clippings and analysts' reports that had been published since my original research. With the new information obtained from these articles, I went back and revised each report in light of recent developments.

Finally, I mailed each entry to the investor contact at the company in question for fact checking and some feedback. Some came back with only minor changes. Others were blue-penciled heavily. And a few were deemed hopeless, requiring a complete rewrite.

If you are looking for a brief idea of how I zeroed in on these 100 stocks, here are some general criteria that I used in my analyses.

Financial Strength

Unless you are a rank speculator, you should invest only in companies that are financially strong. There are a number of ways to recognize such companies.

First, a financially strong company will have a strong balance sheet. This can be determined by checking Value Line, an advisory service available at brokerage houses and libraries (a trial subscription is available for around $55).

On most companies' balance sheets, there is a combination of debt (bonds) and equity (common stock). The larger the percentage of common stock, the stronger the balance sheet. For a nonutility, a balance sheet with 75 percent equity and 25 percent debt would be acceptable. Utilities are more leveraged (heavy in debt) and often have 50 percent of their capitalization in long-term debt, 10 or 15 percent in preferred stock, and 35 or 40 percent in equity. When you find a company that falls below these parameters, you are increasing your risk.

If you don't know how to read a Value Line report, your best bet is to examine the financial strength rating in a Standard & Poor's *Stock Guide*, available at any brokerage house or public library. Sound stocks are rated at least B+, which is an average quality rating. The best rating is A+. Such stocks as Merck, General Electric, McDonald's, and Minnesota Mining are rated A+ by the *Stock Guide*. Most of the stocks in this book are rated at least A- by Standard & Poor's or at least A by Value Line.

Surprisingly, these two publications often disagree. For instance, RPM is rated A+ by Standard & Poor's and only B by Value Line. Similarly, Exxon is rated B+ by Standard & Poor's and A+ by Value Line. Finally, J. P. Morgan is awarded a B+ by the *Stock Guide*, while Value Line thinks J. P. Morgan is worthy of an A+. (It reminds me of the two portfolio managers I listened to at the analysts' lunch one day. The man sitting next to me was convinced that Kmart was close to going

into Chapter 11. The lady across the table was equally sure that Kmart was a great "value at less than $10 a share.")

The Keys to Value

Next, it is important not to pay too much for a stock. There are plenty of great stocks with stupendous records, but they may cost too much to be good investments. I tend to be a value investor, which means that I try to buy stocks that are relatively underpriced, or "cheap," relative to the rest of the market.

A stock's "value" can be determined in a number of ways. The easiest way is to examine the dividend yield, if the company pays a dividend. (Many smaller companies do not.) The dividend yield is the dividend as a percentage of the stock price and can be found in the *Wall Street Journal*. A value stock generally has a higher yield than a growth stock—let's say in the range of 3, 4, or 5 percent.

Perhaps the best way to get a bead on value is to calculate the price–earnings ratio, usually referred to as the P/E or the "multiple." This is calculated by dividing the price of the stock by the earnings per share over the past twelve months. Let's say the price of the stock is $30 and the earnings per share are $2.35. That works out to a P/E of 12.77. Compared to most other stocks, that's a good value, since the average P/E is about 17, as of this writing.

Studies indicate that stocks with low P/E ratios are better investments than those with high P/E ratios. Of course, there are plenty of exceptions to this rule of thumb.

A few people think that it makes sense to calculate the price-to-book ratio. With access to Value Line, this is easy to ascertain. The calculation requires two numbers: the price of the stock and the book value per share. The book value is simply the difference between the assets and the liabilities. After deducting the liabilities from the assets, you divide by the number of shares outstanding. (Fortunately, you don't have to do any calculating, since Value Line provides these numbers for each of the past fifteen years.)

Once you know the book value, the rest is easy. Divide this into the price of the stock. If the stock is selling for $45 and the book value is $18.79, the ratio works out to be 2.39, which is about average these days. However, you won't have to search far to find stocks selling for four, five, and six times book. These are high numbers and indicate a stock that has a good growth record but that is no longer in the value category.

Still another way to recognize value is to calculate the price-to-cash-flow ratio. Here again, Value Line gives you the cash-flow figure on a per-share basis. (Cash flow, incidentally, is determined by adding depreciation to net earnings. In practice, the calculation is much more complicated, so we're lucky that we can just look it up.). This cash-flow figure is then divided into the price of the stock. A stock with a price of $76 and a cash-flow figure of $8 would have a ratio of less than 10. If the ratio is much above 10, true value investors will feel that they are on shaky ground.

How to Recognize Growth

So far, I have talked about quality (or financial strength) and value. Next, let's look at growth. There are plenty of stocks with good yields and low P/E ratios, but not all of them are attractive. They must also exhibit some semblance of growth.

The most obvious way to ascertain growth is to examine the trend of earnings per share. Value Line gives you this information, generally for the past fifteen years. I normally look at the past ten years. Let's say it's 1996. I can go back and see what the company earned in 1985 and compare with 1995, a ten-year period.

Using a financial calculator, I can quickly figure out the compound annual growth rate. Here's an example. Chubb (a great insurance company) earned 83 cents in 1984 and $5.95 in 1994. That's a growth rate of 21.8 percent, which is excellent.

A word of caution: Calculating growth rates using earnings per share can prove inconclusive. Returning to Chubb, let's see what happens when we pick a different ten-year period, such as 1983–1993. Earnings per share in that span climbed from $1.52 to $3.91, a compound annual growth rate of 9.9 percent. What it amounts to is this: Take great care in picking your beginning and ending years, since earnings per share sometimes bounce around.

A much better way to calculate growth is to use the dividend, since most dividends advance steadily upward and are far less volatile. Again, we'll use Chubb. In a recent ten-year stretch, 1984 to 1994, the dividend advanced from 72 cents to $1.84, giving you a compound annual growth rate of 9.8 percent.

To prove my point, let's see how it works if we use a slightly different period, 1983–1993. In that span, the dividend advanced from 68 cents to $1.69, for a growth rate of 9.5 percent. You can quickly see that the two numbers are reasonably close.

Still another way to evaluate growth is to see what book value per share has done in the past ten years. Quite often, this test is even more reliable than the dividend method. In the 1984–1994 period, Chubb's book value per share advanced from $14.19 to $48.92. That works out to be a compound annual growth rate of 13.2 percent.

Finally, to verify this figure, let's see how the 1983–1993 period worked. In that span, the book value rose from $14.06 to

$47.84, giving us a growth rate of 13.0 percent, which confirms the growth rate using the 1984–1994 period.

Putting It All Together

Once you have looked at a company's financial strength, along with its performance on measures of value and growth, you can begin to compare stocks to see which have the best overall numbers. A good first step is to eliminate any stock that is well below average in any one of these three dimensions. For instance, let's look at ten stocks with the following P/E ratios: 13.4, 23.7, 28.5, 18.1, 17.4, 19.9, 13.9, 21.4, 15.3, 21.7. If we make a standard deviation study, we will find that the mean (or average) P/E is 19.3, and the standard deviation is 4.1. This is a statistical gimmick that tells you which readings are at one of the extremes. In this illustration, we add 4.1 to 19.3, which tells us that a P/E of 23.4 is too high. The stocks with P/Es of 23.7 and 28.5 are eliminated from consideration.

The same approach can be given to the growth rate and the Standard & Poor's rating. Again, using the standard deviation, we might look at stocks with compound annual growth rates of 3.4 percent, 7.8 percent, 12.6 percent, 22.8 percent, 8.9 percent, 6.1 percent, 12.8 percent, 6.5 percent, 8.1 percent, and 11.8 percent. The mean of these ten growth rates is 10.1, with a standard deviation of 5.4. Subtract 5.4 from 10.1 and you get 4.7, which tells you to eliminate the stock with a growth rate of 3.4 percent.

Other Factors

To be sure, picking stocks does not depend entirely on a stock's passing all three of these calculated criteria. There are a host of other things to bear in mind. Let me give you a few:

• Are you satisfied that this company has a competitive product or service? This is a bit subjective, to be sure, and can't readily be measured. If you drive General Motors cars and love them, that might be enough reason to consider GM as a stock to purchase. Or you might love shopping in JC Penney because the products are great and the prices are reasonable. Or perhaps you use Healthy Choice foods, which are made by ConAgra. Once again, this might be a stock to consider.

• Does the company have an aggressive marketing arm? This could involve innovative advertising or a well-trained sales force. In this regard, Merck fits the bill. Its army of "detail men" is most persuasive in convincing physicians to prescribe Merck's pharmaceuticals.

In terms of advertising, Procter & Gamble spends a ton of money to promote Tide, Crest toothpaste, Head & Shoulders, Secret, Old Spice, Pampers, and Bounty—to name just a few of its highly successful products. Obviously, this is a great company to bear in mind.

• How does the company stack up when it comes to spending money on research? New products are the lifeblood of many businesses. Hewlett-Packard is an example of a company with hundreds of products that are the by-products of the company's research effort.

• Is the company a low-cost producer? In today's highly competitive arena, it pays to keep your costs under control. Your company may make the best loaf of bread, but if you have to sell it for $8.95 to make a living, you aren't going to sell it to Mr. and Mrs. Average American. Only the carriage trade will use your bread. There aren't many people in this category. Of course, a lot of people pay $8 a pound for superior coffee, rather than the price charged for a supermarket brand. Thus, it's important to keep both quality and costs in mind, not just one or the other. The buying public wants good products, but they also want a low price.

On the other hand, there are certain products of which one brand can't easily be distinguished from another. For instance, gasoline is hard to differentiate. Products from Gulf, Texaco, Amoco, and Mobil are all about equal. In these cases, price becomes even more important, and price is dependent on efficient manufacturing. Keep your manufacturing costs low and you can win over more customers, since your price will be lower. Or, even if it's the same, your margin of profit will be greater.

If you have read thus far, you understand that picking stocks can be a complicated business, unless you prefer the hunch method, which doesn't tax your brainpower.

The point to be made is this: The stocks in this book have already undergone a great deal of analysis and careful scrutiny. To be sure, they may not all turn out to be winners, but there are enough solid performers in this group to give you a superior return on your investment, assuming that you stock your portfolio with at least ten or fifteen of them.

In the next chapter, I will outline a method of picking the individual stocks that are best for your portfolio. After all, you may not be ready to buy all 100!

Picking the Right Stocks for You

If you are a typical reader, it is unlikely that you will read this book straight through. You are more likely to treat it as a reference work, or have it handy on the coffee table for browsing while you munch on an apple or suffer through a lopsided football game.

As you flip through these pages, you'll probably skip over certain stocks that have no appeal. Others, on the other hand, will catch your attention and be read more carefully.

After you have thumbed through the book a few times, you will probably have flagged a "short list" of fifteen or twenty stocks that sound especially interesting to you. Even though this process may sound entirely subjective, you will have taken an important first step in choosing prime candidates for consideration. Here's why.

You may have noticed that the stocks listed in this book are broken down into four categories: aggressive growth, conservative growth, growth and income, and income. Roughly defined, these are:

- *Aggressive growth*: Stocks of companies that are growing fast. These stocks often have a low yield. Their chief shortcoming is their high volatility. They are not for the faint of heart.
- *Conservative growth*: Stocks of companies that are growing, but perhaps not as fast as those on the aggressive growth list. These companies are often more mature, larger, better known. They are generally financially strong, with a good balance sheet and a consistent earnings record. They typically pay a dividend of 2 percent to 4 percent.

- *Growth and income*: These stocks have a moderate dividend, usually 3 percent or more, and a solid record of growth.
- *Income*: Stocks in companies that are more mature. These may have a yield of 4 percent or more. Most of the income stocks I have selected are those of companies that are still growing, but you are not likely to double your money in six weeks.

Each of these four types of stock corresponds to—and is best suited for—a specific investment personality or "temperament." By making subjective choices out of the list of 100 stocks, you have revealed important aspects of *your* investment temperament.

The next step is to list the fifteen or twenty stocks you've chosen, along with the category (income, etc.) listed in the report for each stock. Chances are you will find that most of the stocks you've chosen fall under one or two headings. For instance, you may have picked one aggressive growth stock, seven conservative growth stocks, five growth-and-income stocks, and two income stocks.

Your Investment Temperament

This kind of pattern is a sure indicator of what kind of investment temperament you have. In this case, you are obviously a middle-of-the-road, conservative investor who is not too aggressive. At the same time, it's clear from your choices that you are not urgently in need of income.

Another person might have chosen an entirely different assortment of stocks. For example, he or she may have picked six aggressive growth stocks, seven conservative growth stocks, two growth-and-income stocks, and no income stocks. This person's temperament is obviously different from yours. But at least both of you know where you stand. In effect, you know what kind of investor you are—and what kinds of stock you should be looking at.

At this juncture, it would pay you to review the stocks in the categories for which you have already shown a strong preference. This might result in your selecting as many as five more stocks for evaluation. Now, you have a total of twenty stocks that seem to fit your needs.

Once again, you want to whittle this down to the one, two, or three stocks that you should consider for immediate purchase. Unfortunately, it is not always easy to make up your mind on which ones to buy.

Some Easy-to-Use Formulas

In order to help you pick only the best of these stocks, I have developed some simple formulas that use information found in the Standard & Poor's *Stock Guide*, which is readily available in any brokerage office. These formulas use four basic values that can be determined for each stock you're considering. Here they are:

• The Standard & Poor's *quality rating*. The highest rating—assuming you are a conservative investor—is A+, followed by A, A-, B+, and so on. An average rating would be B+.

• The *dividend yield*, which can be found in the Money & Investing section of the *Wall Street Journal*. As discussed earlier, this is the annualized dividend as a percentage of the stock price—2.7 percent, 5.3 percent, and so on.

• The *price-earnings ratio* is calculated by dividing the price of the stock by the earnings per share for the most recent twelve months. The earnings figure is in the *Stock Guide* under the heading "Last

12 Mos." For instance, as of this writing, Minnesota Mining's last twelve months' earnings were $3.34. The price of the stock in today's paper was $56.25. Dividing this by 3.34, and you get a P/E of 16.8.

• The *dividend payout ratio* is calculated by dividing the annualized dividend by the most recent twelve months' earnings. Let's use 3M again. The dividend in today's *Wall Street Journal* is $1.88. To arrive at the payout ratio, divide this figure by the earnings per share (EPS). You'll get a payout ratio of 0.563, or 56.3 percent. This is *not* especially attractive. A growth investor would prefer a company with a lower payout ratio, since it would indicate a company that believes in plowing back earnings into the business. Income investors, however, might be quite happy with 56.3 percent. But they wouldn't—or shouldn't—be happy with an 85 percent payout.

Now that you understand these four factors, we can look at how to apply them to the stock selection process. A good way to proceed is to list your chosen stocks down the left side of the page and list the relevant factors across the top. (Several of the formulas use only two or three of the factors; one uses all four.)

Stocks for Income
The S&P Rating

To start out, let's look at the formula you should use if you're most interested in income stocks. The first factor to look at for this category is the Standard & Poor's rating. Look for the stocks with the best S&P rating, probably an A+. Give one point to each A+ stock. (As in golf, a low score will be best in these formulas.) Next, find the second-best stocks, which will probably be A stocks. If there were six A+ stocks, each A stock will be given 7 points. (This reflects the fact that the six A+ stocks can be considered "tied," and so the first stock with an A rating is, at best, your seventh-best stock in terms of this factor. If there were only two A+ stocks, each A stock would be given 3 points.) Once you have taken care of the A stocks, rate the two or three A- stocks. The total number of A+ and A stocks will determine the grade for the A- stocks.

To make this rating system crystal clear, here is a list of stocks from the Dow Jones Industrial Average, along with their S&P ratings and the number of points that should be awarded:

Name of Stock	S&P Rating	Point Score
American Express	B	7
Alcoa	B-	12
AlliedSignal	B+	4
Bethlehem Steel	C	15
Chevron	B	7
DuPont	B+	4
Eastman Kodak	B	7
General Electric	A+	1
General Motors	B-	12
International Paper	B+	4
Minnesota Mining	A+	1
Procter & Gamble	A	3
Sears, Roebuck	B-	12
United Technologies	B	7
Westinghouse Electric	B	7

The Dividend Yield

Next, let's grade these same stocks on their dividend yield. The procedure changes somewhat, since there are rarely ties to deal with—particularly if you take the yield out to the second decimal place. Again, a high dividend yield is better for income stocks than for stocks in other categories, but the best stock gets the lowest score in our system. Here is how our stocks looked at the end of 1995, using the year-end 1995 Stock Guide.

Name of Stock	Dividend Yield	Point Score
American Express	2.18%	10
Alcoa	1.70	12
AlliedSignal	1.64	13
Bethlehem Steel	Nil	15
Chevron	3.82	1
DuPont	2.98	2
Eastman Kodak	2.39	6
General Electric	2.56	5
General Motors	2.27	9
International Paper	2.64	4
Minnesota Mining	2.83	3
Procter & Gamble	1.93	11
Sears, Roebuck	2.36	7
United Technologies	2.32	8
Westinghouse Electric	1.22	14

The Price–Earnings Ratio

The final factor in selecting an income stock is the price–earnings ratio, which is calculated by dividing the price of the stock by the latest earnings per share for the past twelve months, which is readily available by consulting the S&P Stock Guide. As noted earlier, a lower P/E is better in this case. Here is a tabulation of the same fifteen stocks.

Name of Stock	Price/Earnings Ratio	Point Score
American Express	13.79x	7
Alcoa	9.36	4
AlliedSignal	15.89	8
Bethlehem Steel	11.19	5
Chevron	17.29	10
DuPont	12.89	6
Eastman Kodak	18.21	11
General Electric	22.22	14
General Motors	7.49	1
International Paper	9.24	3
Minnesota Mining	19.81	12
Procter & Gamble	21.50	13
Sears, Roebuck	8.44	2
United Technologies	17.13	9
Westinghouse Electric	NM*	15

*NM=not meaningful, since there were no earnings.

The Final Score

Our final step is to put these three scores together, as follows:

Name of Stock	S&P Score	Yield Score	PE Score	Final
American Express	7	10	7	24
Alcoa	12	12	4	28
AlliedSignal	4	13	8	25
Bethlehem Steel	15	15	5	35
Chevron	7	1	10	18
DuPont	4	2	6	12
Eastman Kodak	7	6	11	24
General Electric	1	5	14	20
General Motors	12	9	1	22
International Paper	4	4	3	11
Minnesota Mining	1	3	12	16
Procter & Gamble	3	11	13	27
Sears, Roebuck	12	7	2	21
United Technologies	7	8	9	24
Westinghouse Electric	7	14	15	36
	Mean (average)			22.87
	Standard deviation			6.98
	Best buys			15.89

If you add up these scores, the mean (or average) score is just under 23 points. The standard deviation is about 7.

(The standard deviation is a statistical concept that enables you to determine what is very far from the average in either direction. If you don't know how to calculate the standard deviation, you can estimate it by using 16 percent of the total. Thus, if there are twenty-five stocks, the 16 percent best ones amount to four.)

Subtract the standard deviation from the mean, and you get about 16. Any stock with a score less than or equal to this value can be considered top-notch. In this case, the three stocks that are the best choice for income investors are:

DuPont	12
International Paper	11
Minnesota Mining	16

Stocks for Growth and Income

Let's assume that you would prefer to invest in stocks that provide a combination of growth and income. If that's the case, you would go through a similar exercise, using a different set of factors.

The dividend yield would be calculated in the same way, and it would be combined with one other factor, the payout ratio. This is simple to calculate, using the *Stock Guide*. You divide the indicated dividend by the latest twelve months' earnings per share. Thus, if a stock had a dividend of $1.25 and earning of $3.67, the payout ratio would be 0.361, or 36.1 percent. The lower the payout ratio, the better. The theory is that growing companies plow back earnings into new facilities, equipment, research, and so forth. If we examine the same fifteen stocks, here is how they looked at the end of 1995, along with the corresponding point scores.

Name of Stock	Payout Ratio	Point Score
American Express	0.300	6
Alcoa	0.159	1
AlliedSignal	0.261	5
Bethlehem Steel	NM	14
Chevron	0.660	13
DuPont	0.384	7
Eastman Kodak	0.437	10
General Electric	0.568	12
General Motors	0.170	2
International Paper	0.244	4
Minnesota Mining	0.561	11
Procter & Gamble	0.414	9
Sears, Roebuck	0.199	3
United Technologies	0.397	8
Westinghouse Electric	NM	14

If the two scores are combined, they look like this:

Name of Stock	Yield Score	Payout Score	Total
American Express	10	6	16
Alcoa	12	1	13
AlliedSignal	13	5	18
Bethlehem Steel	15	14	29
Chevron	1	13	14
DuPont	2	7	9
Eastman Kodak	6	10	16
General Electric	5	12	17
General Motors	9	2	11
International Paper	4	8	12
Minnesota Mining	3	11	14
Procter & Gamble	11	9	20
Sears, Roebuck	7	3	10
United Technologies	8	8	16
Westinghouse Electric	14	14	28
Mean (or average)			15.93
Standard deviation			6.12
Best buys			9.81

The Final Winners

If we add these up and calculate the mean, it comes to just under 16. We subtract the standard deviation, which is 6.12, and we determine that a stock can be bought for growth and income if the score is 10 or less. These stocks qualify:

DuPont	9
International Paper	8
Sears, Roebuck	10

Stocks for Conservative Growth

If you are looking for stocks that are best for conservative growth, you should go through a similar process, using all four factors discussed earlier: the Standard & Poor's quality rating, the yield, the P/E, and the payout ratio.

Stocks for Aggressive Growth

Now, it's time for a change of pace. Not everyone is conservative. Many are more growth-oriented and are willing to forgo yield if they can get better-than-average growth of capital. I have developed an exceptional method of picking stocks for aggressive growth. It is rather complicated, but let's look at the basics. In this exercise, four factors come into play.

• The P/E ratio using the most recent twelve months' earnings. This is subtracted from 100. Thus, a P/E of 18 would give you a score of 82, a P/E of 32 would result in a score of 68, and so forth.

• The median P/E ratio. In this instance, you use the median earnings per share for the past five years. For instance, let's say the company earned $2.57, 3.02, 1.78, 2.80, and 1.92. These figures come from the *Stock Guide*. To arrive at the median, simply discard the two lowest numbers and use the next lowest. The two lowest in this illustration are $1.78 and $1.92. The next lowest is $2.57, which is the one you divide into the current price of the stock. Once again, you subtract the result from 100 to arrive at the score for this factor.

• The payout ratio is now calculated using the most recent earnings per share and the indicated dividend. Let's say the company earned $3.46 and paid out $1.50 in dividends. By dividing $1.50 by $3.46, you find a payout ratio of 43.35 percent. Subtract this from 100, for a final score of 56.65.

• The last factor is the median payout ratio. The earnings figure you will use is calculated in the same way as for the median P/E ratio. Again, subtract this figure from 100 for the score for this factor.

The last step is easy. Add up the first four and divide by 4. Suppose the scores for your four factors were 78.21, 75.90, 65.43, and 43.33. The total is 262.87. After dividing by 4, you get your final score, 65.72. In this system, higher scores are best—not lower, as in my other methods. According to tests I have made with system, it works about 90 percent of the time.

Nothing, of course, is simple. This system will not work on stocks that give you a meaningless score. For instance, if the company had earnings of 35 cents, 10 cents, 2 cents, $3.50, and $2.99, you are going to get a meaningless score with the three low EPS numbers.

One thing more: If the score for a payout ratio is more than 80, reduce it to 80. This will happen with a company that pays a very skimpy dividend, such as Archer Daniels.

Final Summary

Here is a brief recap of my "mechanical" approach, listing the factors to use, depending on what you are trying to accomplish:

Factors for selecting income stocks:
- The S&P quality rating, such as A, B+, or B-.
- The dividend yield, such as 2.78, 3.41, or 5.49.
- The P/E ratio, using the most recent twelve months' earnings, such as 18.89, 21.42, or 29.02.

Factors for selecting growth-and-income stocks:
- The dividend yield, such as 1.43, 3.98, or 4.12.
- The dividend payout ratio, using the most recent twelve months' earnings per share and the indicated dividend.

Factors for selecting stocks for conservative growth:
- The S&P quality rating, such as A+, A, or C.
- The dividend yield, such as 2.89, 4.18, or 3.20.
- The P/E ratio, such as 14.19, 18.38, or 22.47.
- The dividend payout ratio, such as 82.90, 23.87, 34.89, or 78.14.

Factors for selecting stocks for aggressive growth:
- The P/E ratio using the most recent earnings per share. Subtract from 100.
- The P/E ratio using the median EPS. Subtract from 100.
- The dividend payout ratio using the most recent twelve months' EPS. Subtract from 100, but do not use a figure in excess of 80. For instance, if you get a score of 91.39, reduce it to 80.
- The dividend payout ratio using the median EPS. Again, reduce all high scores to 80.

Divide the four factors by 4 and buy the stocks with good scores, normally between 75 and 80.

If all of these calculations seem thoroughly confusing to you, keep in mind that it is possible to use this book without going through these exercises. As I pointed out earlier, these 100 stocks have already been subjected to rigorous analysis. Once you've identified your investment personality and done your homework on the current status and prospects of the stocks that interest you, you're ready to start investing.

One final note: When this book was written, I had 1996 annual reports to refer to. Before you invest, it would be wise to read the company's latest report, which is available at no charge.

Basic Terminology

If you are new to the investment arena, you may have difficulty understanding parts of this book. To get you over the rough spots, I have listed some common expressions that appear frequently in books on investing. You will also encounter them in the *Wall Street Journal, Forbes, Financial World, Business Week, Barron's,* and other periodicals devoted to investing.

This is not a glossary but merely a brief list of terms that are essential for understanding this book. If you would like a more complete glossary, refer to either of my previous books: *Safe Investing* (Simon & Schuster, 1991) or *Straight Talk About Stock Investing* (McGraw-Hill, 1995).

Analyst

In nearly every one of the 100 articles, you will note that I refer to "analysts" and what they think about the prospects for a particular stock. Analysts are individuals who have special training in analyzing stocks. Typically, they have such advanced degrees as M.B.A.s or C.F.A.s. Many of them work for brokerage houses, but they may also be employed by banks, insurance companies, mutual funds, pension plans, or other institutions. Most analysts specialize in one or two industries. A good analyst can tell you nearly everything there is to know about a particular stock or the industry it's part of.

However, analysts can be dead wrong about the future action of a stock. The reason is: surprises. Companies are constantly changing, which means they are acquiring, divesting, developing new products, restructuring, buying back their shares, and so forth. When they make a change and announce this change to Wall Street, the surprise can change the course of the stock. In short, analysts can be helpful, but don't bet the store on what they tell you.

Annual Report

If you own a common stock, you can be certain that you will receive a fancy annual report a couple of months after the close of the year. If the year ends December 31, look for your annual report in March or April. If the fiscal year ends some other time of the year, such as September 30, the annual report will appear in your mailbox two or three months later.

Not all investors read annual reports, but they might be better off if they did. Although most companies will not list their problems, you can usually get a pretty good idea how things are going. In particular, read the report by the president or CEO. It's usually one, two, or three pages long and is written in language you can understand.

If you want detailed information on the company's various businesses, the annual report will often overwhelm you with details that may be difficult to fathom. If you are really curious about what they are trying to say, feel free to call the investor contact. I have provided the name of this person in all 100 stocks listed. Have a list of questions ready, and call during the person's lunch hour, leaving your name and phone number. This sneaky little strategy means the cost of the call back will be paid by the company, not you. By the way, don't assume you will be intimidated by the investor contact. Investor contacts are usually quite personable and helpful.

Asset Allocation

This is not the same as diversification. Rather, it refers to the strategy of allocating your investment funds among different types of investments, such as stocks, bonds, or money market funds. In the long run, you will be better off with all of your assets concentrated in common stocks. In the short run, this may not be true, since the market occasionally has a sinking spell. A severe one, such as that of 1973–74, can cause your holdings to decline in value 20 percent or more. To protect against this, most investors spread their money around. They may, for instance, allocate 50 percent to stocks, 40 percent to bonds, and 10 percent to a money market fund. A more realistic breakdown might be 70 percent in stocks, 25 percent in bonds, and 5 percent in a money market fund.

Balance Sheet

All corporations issue at least two financial statements, the balance sheet and the income statement. Both are important. The balance sheet is a financial picture of the company on a specific date, such as December 31 or at the end of a quarter.

On the left side of the balance sheet are the company's assets, such as cash, current assets, inventories, accounts receivable, and buildings. On the right side are its liabilities, including accounts payable and long-term debt. Also on the right side is shareholders' equity. The right side of the balance sheet adds up to the same value as the left side, which is why it is called a balance sheet.

In most instances, corporations give you figures for the current year and the prior year. By examining the changes, you can get an idea of whether the company's finances are improving or deteriorating.

Bonds

Entire books have been written on the various kinds of bonds. A bond, unlike a stock, is not a form of ownership. A bond is a contractual agreement that means you have loaned money to some entity, and that entity has agreed to pay you a certain sum of money (interest) every six months until that bond matures. At that time, you will also get back the money you originally invested—no more, no less. Most bonds are issued in $1,000 denominations. The safest bonds are those issued by the U. S. government. Not since the War of 1812 has there been a default on government bonds. The two advantages of bonds are safety and income. If you wait until the maturity date, you will be assured of getting the face value of the bond. In the meantime, however, the bond will fluctuate, because of changes in interest rates or the creditworthiness of the corporation. Long-term bonds, moreover, fluctuate far more than short-term bonds. But enough about bonds. This book is about stocks.

Capital Gains

When you buy common stocks, you expect to make money in two ways: capital gains and dividends. Over an extended period of time, about half of your total return will come from each sector. If the stock rises in value and you sell it above your cost, you are enjoying a capital gain. The tax on long-term capital gains is less than it is on dividends—a maximum of 28 percent.

Common Stocks

We might as well define what a common stock is, since this whole book is devoted to them. All publicly owned companies— those that trade their shares outside of a small group of executives or the founding family—are based on common stocks. A common stock is evidence of partial ownership in a corporation. Most of the stocks described in this book have millions of shares of their stock outstanding, and the really large one many have in excess of 100 million shares. When you own common stock, there are no guarantees. If the company is successful, it will probably pay a dividend four times a year. These dividends may be raised periodically, perhaps once a year. If, however, the company has problems, it may cut or eliminate its dividend. This can happen even to a major company, such as Commonwealth Edison, Woolworth, IBM, Goodyear, or General Motors. As I said, there are no guarantees.

Investors who own common stock can sell their shares at any time. All you do is call your broker, and the trade is executed a few minutes later at the prevailing price—which fluctuates nearly every day, sometimes by a sixteenth of a point (a point is a dollar) or sometimes two or three points.

Current Ratio

The current ratio is calculated by dividing current assets by current liabilities. Current assets include any assets that will become cash within one year, including cash itself. Current liabilities are those that will be paid off within a year. A current ratio of 2 is considered ideal. Most companies these days have a current ratio of less than 2.

Diversification

Since investments are inherently risky, it pays to spread the risk by diversifying. If you don't, you may be too heavily invested in a stock or bond that turns sour. Even well-known stocks such as Alcoa, International Paper, Eastman Kodak, and American Express can experience occasional sinking spells.

To be on the safe side, don't invest more than 5 percent of your portfolio in any one stock. In addition, don't invest too heavily in any one sector of the economy. A good strategy is to divide stocks among twelve sectors: basic industries, capital goods/technology, capital goods, consumer growth, consumer cyclical, credit cyclical, financial, energy, transportation, utilities, and conglomerates.

Here's a rule of thumb that will keep you out of trouble: Invest at least 4 percent in each sector but not more than 12 percent. That means that you should own at least twelve stocks so that you have representation in all twelve sectors.

Dividends

Unlike bonds, common stocks may pay a dividend. Bonds pay interest. Most dividends are paid quarterly, but there is no set date that all corporations use. Some, for instance, may pay January 1, March 1, July 1, and September 1. Another company may pay February 10, May 10, August 10, and November 10. If you want to receive checks every month, you will have to make sure you buy stocks that pay dividends at different times of the year. The Standard & Poor's *Stock Guide* is a source for this information, as is the Value Line Survey. Most companies like to pay the same dividend every quarter until they can afford to increase it. Above all, they don't like to cut their dividends, since investors who depend on this income will sell their shares, and the stock will decline in price. If you use good judgment in selecting your stocks, you can expect that your companies will increase their dividends nearly every year.

Dividend Payout Ratio

If a company earns $4 per share in a given year and pays out $3 to its shareholders, it has a payout ratio of 75 percent. If it pays out only $1, the payout ratio is 25 percent. A low payout ratio is preferred, since it means that the company is plowing back its profits into future growth.

The Dividend Reinvestment Plan

Unless you are retired, you might like to reinvest your dividends in more shares.

Many companies have a plan (also known as a DRIP) that will allow you to do this, and the charge for this service is often minimal. Most of these companies also allow you to mail in additional cash, which will be used to purchase new shares, again at minimal cost.

This may sound like a good way to avoid paying brokerage commissions, but there are some drawbacks to bear in mind. For one thing, you can't time your purchases, since it may be a week or more before your purchase is made.

Even worse is calculating your cost basis for tax purposes. By the time you sell, you may have made scores of small investments in the same stock, each with a different cost basis. Make sure you keep a file for each company so that you can make these calculations when the time comes. Or, better still, don't sell.

Dollar Cost Averaging

Dollar cost averaging is a systematic way to invest money over a long period, such as ten, fifteen, or twenty years. It entails investing the same amount of money regularly, such as each month or each quarter. If you do this faithfully, you will be buying more stock when the price is lower, and less stock when the price is high. This tends to smooth out the gyrations of the market. Dollar cost averaging is often used with a mutual fund, but it can just as easily be done with a company that has a dividend reinvestment plan (DRIP).

Income Statement

Most investors are more interested in the income statement than they are the balance sheet. They are particularly interested in the progress (or lack of it) in earnings per share. The income statement lists such items as net sales, cost of sales, interest expense, and gross profit. As with the balance sheet, it makes sense to compare this year's numbers with those of the prior year.

Investment Advisor

Investors who do not have the time or inclination to manage their own portfolios may elect to employ an investment advisor. Most advisors charge 1 percent a year. Thus, if you own stocks worth $300,000, your annual fee would be $3,000. Advisors differ from brokers, since they do not profit from changes. Brokers, by contrast, charge a commission on each transaction, which means they profit from changes in your portfolio. Advisors profit only when the value of your holdings increases. For instance, if the value of your portfolio increases to $500,000, the annual fee will be $5,000. You, of course, will be $200,000 richer.

Preferred Stock

The name sounds impressive. In actual practice, owning preferred stocks is about as exciting as watching your cat take a bath. A preferred stock is much like a bond. It pays the same dividend year in and year out. The yield is usually higher than a common stock. If the company issuing the preferred stock does well, you do not benefit. If it does poorly, however, you may suffer, since the dividend could be cut or eliminated. My advice is: Never, never buy a preferred stock.

Price–Earnings Ratio

This is a term that is extremely important. Don't make the mistake of overlooking it. Whole books have been written on the importance of the P/E ratio, which is sometimes referred to as "the P/E" or "the multiple."

The P/E ratio tells you whether a stock is cheap or expensive. It is calculated by dividing the price of the stock by the company's earnings per share over the most recent twelve months. For instance, if you refer to the *Stock Guide*, you will see that Leggett and Platt had earnings of $1.52. At the time, the stock was selling for $24.62. Divide that figure by $1.52 and you get a P/E of 16.86.

In most instances, a low P/E indicates a stock that Wall Street is not too excited about. If they like a stock, they will bid it up to the point where its P/E is quite high, let's say 25 or 30. Coca-Cola is such a stock. In this same *Stock Guide*, Coca-Cola had annual earnings per share of $2.20. Based on the price of the stock at that time (it was $69) that works out to a P/E ratio of 31.36. Of course, Coca-Cola is extremely well regarded by investors and is expected to do well in the future—but is it really worth 31 times earnings?

Stock Split

Corporations know that investors like to invest in lower-priced stocks. Thus, when the price of the stock gets to a certain level, which varies with the company, they will split the stock. For instance, if the stock is $75, they might split it three-for-one. Your original 100 shares now become 300 shares. Unfortunately, your 300 shares are worth exactly the same as your original 100 shares. What it amounts to is this: Splits please small investors, but they don't make them any richer. One company, Berkshire Hathaway, has never been split. It is now worth a huge amount per share: well over $30,000. It also pays no dividend. The company is run by the legendary Warren Buffett. He has made a lot of people very wealthy without a stock split or dividend.

Yield

If your company pays a dividend, you can relate this dividend to the price of the stock in order to calculate the yield. A $50 stock that pays a $2 annual dividend (which amounts to 50 cents per quarter) will have a yield of 4 percent. You arrive at this figure by dividing $2 by $50. Actually, you don't have to make this calculation, since the yield is given to you in the stock tables of the *Wall Street Journal*. Here are some typical yields from mid-1997. Coca-Cola, 0.8 percent; Exxon, 2.8 percent; General Electric, 1.7 percent; Illinois Tool Works, 1.0 percent; Kimberly-Clark, 1.8 percent; and Minnesota Mining and Manufacturing, 2.3 percent. Although the yield is of some importance, you should not judge a stock by its yield without looking at many other factors.

Part II

100 Best Stocks You Can Buy

The following table lists the 100 stocks discussed in this book. A brief description of each stock appears here.

The ticker symbol is given so that you can use the quote machine in your broker's office. Or, if you call your broker on the phone, it makes it easier if you know the ticker symbol, since your broker may not.

The second column in the table, "Industry," describes one of the company's main businesses. This is not always easy to express in one or two words.

For instance, United Technologies is involved in a variety of industries, such as aircraft engines, elevators, and air conditioning equipment. To describe the company succinctly, I arbitrarily picked the designation "aircraft engines."

Similarly, General Electric owns NBC and makes appliances, aircraft engines, medical devices, and a host of other things.

The designation "Sector" indicates the broad economic industry group that the company operates in, such as Transportation, Capital Goods, Energy, Consumer Cyclicals, and so forth. As described elsewhere, a properly diversified portfolio should include at least one stock in each of the twelve sectors. However, I see no problem in having stocks in nine or ten sectors.

"Category" identifies the stock as belonging to one of the following: (1) income (Income), (2) growth and income (Gro inc), (3) conservative growth (Con grow), or (4) aggressive growth (Aggr gro).

An income stock may have a yield that is well above average, such as 4 percent or 5 percent. Typical yield stocks are public utilities.

A growth-and-income stock often yields 2 percent or 3 percent. Banks and oil stocks may fall into this category.

A conservative growth stock often has a small yield, such as less than 2 percent. To be deemed "conservative," it should have a strong balance sheet, be reasonably priced, and have a steady string of dividend increases.

An aggressive growth stock may pay no dividend, or only a small percentage of earnings. Such stocks tend to be more volatile than conservative growth stocks.

It might make sense to have some representation in each category, even if you have a strong preference for only one.

I have not included the page numbers because of space limitations. In any event, it is easy enough to find a particular stock, since they appear alphabetically in the book.

Company	Symbol	Industry	Sector	Category	
—A—					
Abbott Laboratories	ABT	Med supplies	Cons staples	Con grow	✓
Air Products	APD	Chemical	Basic ind	Con grow	✓
Alberto-Culver	ACV	Cosmetics	Cons staples	Con grow	✓
Albertson's	ABS	Grocery	Cons staples	Con grow	✓
Alcoa	AA	Metals	Basic ind	Aggr gro	
AlliedSignal	ALD	Diversified	Conglomerates	Aggr gro	
American Brands	AMB	Diversified	Cons staples	Income	✓
American Greetings	AGREA	Cards	Cons services	Aggr gro	

Company	Symbol	Industry	Sector	Category
American Home Prod.	AHP	Drugs	Cons staples	Gro inc
American Water Works	AWK	Water	Utilities	Gro inc
Ameritech	AIT	Telephone	Utilities	Gro inc
Amoco	AN	Oil	Energy	Gro inc
AMP, Inc.	AMP	Switches	Cap goods-tech	Con grow
Applied Ind. Tech.	APZ	Components	Capital goods	Aggr gro
Archer Daniels Mid.	ADM	Foods	Cons staples	Aggr gro
Automatic Data Proc.	AUD	Comp software	Cap goods-tech	Aggr gro
—B—				
Baldor Electric	BEZ	Elect equip	Capital goods	Con grow
Banc One	ONE	Bank	Financial	Income
Bank of New York	BK	Bank	Financial	Gro inc
Becton Dickinson	BDX	Med supplies	Cons staples	Aggr gro
BellSouth	BLS	Telephone	Utilities	Income
Bristol-Myers Squibb	BMY	Drugs	Cons staples	Gro inc
—C—				
Campbell Soup	CPB	Foods	Cons staples	Con grow
Caterpillar	CAT	Machinery	Capital goods	Aggr gro
Cedar Fair	FUN	Entertainment	Cons staples	Income
Chevron	CHV	Oil	Energy	Gro inc
Cincinnati Fin'l	CINF	Insurance	Financial	Aggr gro
Clorox	CLX	Household pd	Cons staples	Gro inc
Coca-Cola	KO	Beverages	Cons staples	Aggr gro
Colgate-Palmolive	CL	Household pd	Cons staples	Con grow
Compaq Computer	CPQ	Computers	Cap goods-tech	Aggr gro
ConAgra	CAG	Foods	Cons staples	Con grow
CPC International	CPC	Foods	Cons staples	Con grow
—D—				
Deere	DE	Machinery	Capital goods	Aggr gro
Diebold	DBD	Auto teller	Capital goods	Aggr gro
Dover	DOV	Machinery	Capital goods	Aggr gro
Duke Energy	DUK	Elect util	Utilities	Income
Du Pont	DD	Chemicals	Basic ind	Gro inc
—E—				
Edwards, A. G.	AGE	Broker	Financial	Con grow
Emerson Electric	EMR	Elect equip	Capital goods	Con grow
Energen	EGN	Natural gas	Utilities	Income
Enron	ENE	Nat gas pipe	Energy	Gro inc
Exxon	XON	Oil	Energy	Gro inc
—F—				
Federal Signal	FSS	Elect equip	Capital goods	Aggr gro
Fifth Third Bancorp	FITB	Bank	Financial	Gro inc
Fleetwood Enter	FLE	Man housing	Credit cyclic	Gro inc
FPL Group	FPL	Elect util	Utilities	Gro inc
—G—				
Gannett	GCI	Newspapers	Cons services	Con grow
General Electric	GE	Elect equip	Capital goods	Con grow
Genuine Parts	GPC	Parts distrib	Cons cyclical	Con grow
Goodyear Tire	GT	Auto tires	Cons cyclical	Aggr gro
Grainger, W. W.	GWW	Elect equip	Cap goods-tech	Con grow

Company	Symbol	Industry	Sector	Category
—H—				
Hannaford Brothers	HRD	Grocery	Cons staples	Con grow
Hewlett-Packard	HWP	Computers	Cap goods-tech	Aggr gro
Hubbell	HUB.B	Elect equip	Capital goods	Gro inc
—I—				
Illinois Tool Works	ITW	Machinery	Capital goods	Aggr gro
Ingersoll-Rand	IR	Machinery	Capital goods	Gro inc
Int'l Business Mach	IBM	Computer	Cap goods-tech	Aggr gro
Int'l Flavors	IFF	Fragrances	Cons staples	Income
—J—				
Jefferson-Pilot	JP	Insurance	Financial	Gro inc
Johnson & Johnson	JNJ	Med supplies	Cons staples	Con grow
—K—				
Kimberly-Clark	KMB	Tissues	Basic Ind	Gro inc
—L—				
Leggett & Platt	LEG	Furniture cmp	Credit cyclic	Con grow
Lilly, Eli	LLY	Drugs	Cons staples	Gro inc
Lubrizol	LZ	Oil additives	Basic ind	Gro inc
—M—				
MDU Resources	MDU	G&E utility	Utilities	Income
Merck	MRK	Drugs	Cons staples	Con grow
Minnesota Mining	MMM	Diversified	Cap goods-tech	Con grow
Morgan, J. P.	JPM	Bank	Financial	Income
—N—				
National City	NCC	Bank	Financial	Income
Newell	NWL	Cons durables	Cons staples	Con grow
NICOR	GAS	Natural gas	Utilities	Income
Nordson	NDSN	Machinery	Capital goods	Cons gro
Norfolk Southern	NSC	Railroad	Transportation	Con grow
—P—				
Pfizer	PFE	Drugs	Cons staples	Aggr gro
Philip Morris	MO	Tobacco	Cons staples	Gro inc
Piedmont Nat'l Gas	PNY	Natural gas	Utilities	Income
Pioneer Hi-Bred	PHB	Seeds	Cons staples	Aggr gro
Pitney Bowes	PBI	Postage mtrs	Cap goods-tech	Gro inc
PPG Industries	PPG	Glass	Basic ind	Aggr gro
Praxair	PX	Indust gases	Basic ind	Aggr gro
Procter & Gamble	PG	Household pd	Cons staples	Con grow
—R—				
Russell	RML	Apparel	Cons cyclical	Con grow
—S—				
Sara Lee	SLE	Foods, app'l	Cons staples	Con grow
Sherwin-Williams	SHW	Paint	Credit cyclic	Con grow
SIGCORP	SIG	G&E utility	Utilities	Income
Snap-on	SNA	Tools	Credit cyclic	Cons gro

Company	Symbol	Industry	Sector	Category
—T—				
Texaco	TX	Oil	Energy	Income
Textron	TXT	Diversified	Conglomerates	Con grow
TRW	TRW	Auto, elect	Cap goods-tech	Gro inc
—U—				
United Technologies	UTX	Aircraft eng	Cap goods-tech	Aggr gro
—V—				
Varian Associates	VAR	Electronics	Cap goods-tech	Aggr gro
VF Corporation	VFC	Apparel	Cons cyclical	Aggr gro
Vulcan Materials	VMC	Const materi	Credit cyclic	Gro inc
—W—				
Wachovia	WB	Bank	Financial	Income
Walgreen	WAG	Drug stores	Cons staples	Con grow
Wash. Gas Light	WGL	Natural gas	Utilities	Income
Weyerhaeuser	WY	Forest prod	Basic ind	Gro inc
Winn-Dixie	WIN	Grocery	Cons staples	Con grow
Worthington Ind.	WTHG	Steel fabri	Basic ind	Aggr gro

65 selected in
American Forest Corp.

Abbott Laboratories

100 Abbott Park Road, Abbott Park, Illinois 60064-6100 □ Investor contact: Catherine Babington (847) 937-3931 □ Dividend reinvestment plan available: (617) 575-2900 □ Ticker symbol: ABT □ S&P rating: A+ □ Value Line financial strength rating: A++

Abbott Laboratories is one of the largest diversified healthcare manufacturers in the world, with 1996 revenues of $11 billion. The company's products are sold in more than 130 countries, with nearly 40 percent of sales derived from those international operations.

Abbott's major business segments include Pharmaceuticals and Nutritionals (prescription drugs, medical nutritionals, and infant formulas) and Hospital and Laboratory Products (intravenous solutions, administrative sets, drug delivery devices, and diagnostic equipment and reagents).

Although revenue growth in Abbott's infant formula and diagnostics businesses has slowed in recent years, new drugs (such as the antibiotic clarithromycin), new indications (diseases or conditions a drug can be prescribed for), the launch of disease-specific medical nutritionals, and cost-cutting (in diagnostics and hospital supplies) continue to boost the company's profits.

Brand names include Erythrocin, Similac, Isomil, and Selsun Blue. What's more, Ensure (an over-the-counter medical nutritional for adults) is an important cornerstone of the company's nutritional products franchise and one of the largest over-the-counter health-care and nutritional products sold in the United States.

Several new drugs that are crucial to Abbott's outlook continue to do well, and analysts expect that new indications will sustain the business's earnings growth over the next three to five years. One of the most important of these drugs is Biaxin.

Clarithromycin (Biaxin), an antibiotic used to treat respiratory infection, is a second-generation macrolide antibiotic similar to erythromycin. Introduced in the United States in 1992, the drug generated worldwide sales of $1 billion in 1996—up more than 20 percent from the prior year.

Biaxin is sold under other trade names, such as Klacid and Klaricid. Factors contributing to this record growth include Abbott's strong commercial execution, a heavy flu season that caused more prescriptions to be written for respiratory tract infections, and regulatory clearance for new treatment indications.

In October 1996, clarithromycin received approval in the United Kingdom for a once-a-day tablet indicated for respiratory tract and soft-tissue infections. Once-a-day dosing simplifies the treatment regimen, offering patients greater convenience. The company expects additional European approvals and regulatory filings for these indications in 1997.

Clarithromycin also has been approved for the treatment and prevention of Mycobacterium avium complex (MAC). MAC is an opportunistic infection that occurs in AIDS patients and may be fatal to those in the advanced stages of the disease. Sales for MAC indications grew steadily during 1996.

In most countries, including the United States, clarithromycin has now been approved for combination therapy for the elimination of *Helicobacter pylori*, a bacterium that causes ulcers. It is now the consensus among physicians that *H. pylori* infection, rather than stress or dietary factors as previously believed, is the leading cause of peptic ulcers. Abbott will increase sales for this indication through an aggressive physician education campaign that highlights the efficacy of using a combination of anti-infectives and acid suppressants to eliminate ulcers.

Shortcomings to Bear in Mind

■ Like all drug companies, Abbott is encountering increased market competition and increased pressure on prices throughout the world. What's more, the company is competing in a healthcare environment characterized by maturing markets.

Well aware of what it faces, Abbott has an imaginative and aggressive growth strategy. The four basic drivers of this strategy underscore Abbott's commitment to innovation as well as to product and geographic diversification. The first two of these drivers—internal research and development and market expansion—are complemented by the second two—external collaboration and acquisitions.

Reasons to Buy

■ Like most healthcare companies, Abbott devotes a large percentage of its sales dollar to research. In the past five years, for instance, research and development spending has grown at a 12.5 percent pace, reaching $1.2 billion in 1996, or 10.9 percent of sales.

Abbott is committed to scientific research because the company is seeing high productivity from this investment. A team of Abbott scientists, for instance, developed the company's AIDS drug, Norvir (its chemical name is ritonavir) in less than four years. Clinical results show that Norvir, taken with another protease inhibitor or other anti-viral drugs, can reduce HIV in the blood to undetectable levels.

Norvir received approval from the United States Food and Drug Administration (FDA) in a record seventy-two days after the filing of its new drug application (NDA). A typical drug approval in the United States takes about twenty months. Norvir is also approved in key countries in Europe and Latin America.

■ In December of 1996, Zyflo, Abbott's innovative asthma drug, received approval from the FDA. Zyflo (for children over the age of twelve) helps control asthma symptoms by inhibiting the formation of leukotrienes. Leukotrienes contribute to the symptoms of asthma, including inflammation, swelling, and mucous secretion in the airways, as well as the tightening of muscles around the outside of the airways. Abbott began marketing Zyflo in the United States in January 1997.

■ In 1996 FDA advisory committees also recommended approval of two Abbott neuroscience compounds:

Serlect (sertindole) is an antipsychotic drug licensed for marketing in the United States, Canada, and Latin America from H. Lundbeck A/S of Denmark. Serlect treats both the positive and negative symptoms of schizophrenia. In clinical trials, Serlect was shown to be as effective as haloperidol, the traditional therapy. However, Serlect was no different from a placebo (an inert substance) in producing a movement disorder known as extrapyramidal syndrome, a significant side effect in haloperidol therapy.

Gabitril (tiagabine) is an add-on epilepsy treatment licensed from Novo-Nordisk A/S of Denmark. Gabitril offers a new alternative for the more than 200,000 epilepsy sufferers in the United States who do not respond to existing therapies. Once approved, the addition of Gabitril will enhance Abbott's already strong epileptic drug business.

In January of 1997, Abbott's epilepsy drug business was enhanced by the FDA approval of Depacon IV (valproate sodium injection). Depacon IV in an intravenous drug used for epileptic patients who are unable to receive drugs orally.

- Growth has been steady and impressive. Earnings per share climbed from $.58 in 1986 to $2.41 in 1996, a compound annual growth rate of 15.3 percent. In the same ten-year period, dividends per share advanced from $.21 to $.96, a growth rate of 16.4 percent.

- In the area of animal health, Abbott's patented anti-infective product, sarafloxacin, is under U.S. FDA review for use in poultry and fish. Abbott is also developing sarafloxacin internationally for use in aquaculture. The drug currently is pending approval in Latin America for use in shrimp.

- In the growing adult medical nutritional business, Abbott offers the broadest portfolio of products in the industry. The company's line of disease-specific nutritionals was expanded with the introduction of Advera, a new product designed for the dietary management of patients with HIV infection or AIDS. Advera has been launched in the United States and the United Kingdom. The product will be rolled out in other international markets over the next several years.

- Abbott remains the U.S. leader in the overall retail market for infant formula. In 1996 Wyeth-Ayerst, with a market share of about 10 percent, exited the U.S. infant formula market. This created an opportunity for Abbott, and the company gained a major portion of Wyeth-Ayerst's market share. Similac and Isomil are Abbott's two principal infant formula products.

In 1996 Abbott's research and development focus was most clearly illustrated with the launch of Similac Advance in Canada, Italy, Spain, and Latin America. This improved infant formula is the result of a long-term program to bring infant formula closer to the effects of breast milk. Similac Advance is the only infant formula with added nucleotide levels and ratios patterned after the total potentially available nucleotides from breast milk. Nucleotides are compounds that are found in most living cells and in breast milk. Similac Advance also contains a unique blend of fats and proteins. Abbott has been test marketing this improved formulation in the United States since mid-1996. A national launch took place in 1997.

- In 1996, Abbott acquired MediSense, Inc., of Waltham, Mass., for about $876 million. MediSense is the biosensor technology leader in blood glucose self-testing, the fastest-growing segment of the diagnostics business, and an area in which Abbott had no previous presence.

- In April of 1997, Abbott acquired Alcyon Analyzer S.A., a French manufacturer of low-volume, benchtop clinical chemistry analyzers. Alcyon, based in Saint Mathieu de Treviers, France, manufactures and sells a family of three low-volume, clinical chemistry instruments. The acquisition strengthens Abbott's presence in the clinical chemistry market, estimated to be $3.7 billion. This low-volume segment accounts for more than $500 million of the total.

- Sevorane (sevoflurane), Abbott's newest inhalation anesthetic, has been launched in 45 countries. Sevorane has broad applicability for both induction and maintenance of anesthesia and can be used for both pediatric and adult patients, strengthening the company's existing franchise in general anesthesia.

Total assets: $11,126 million
Current ratio: 1.00
Common shares outstanding: $777 million
Return on 1996 shareholders' equity: 40.8%

	1996	1995	1994	1993	1992	1991	1990	1989
Revenues (millions)	11,014	10,012	9,156	8,408	7,852	6,877	6,159	5,380
Net income (millions)	1,882	1,689	1,517	1,399	1,198	1,089	966	860
Earnings per share	2.41	2.12	1.87	1.69	1.42	1.28	1.11	.96
Dividends per share	.96	.84	.76	.68	.60	.50	.42	.35
Price: High	57.4	44.8	33.9	30.8	34.2	34.9	23.2	17.6
Low	38.1	30.8	25.4	22.6	26.1	19.6	15.6	11.6

CONSERVATIVE GROWTH

Air Products and Chemicals, Inc.

7201 Hamilton Boulevard, Allentown, PA 18195-1501 ▫ Investor contact: Brennen M. Arndt (610) 481-6747 ▫ Dividend reinvestment plan available: (800) 526-0801 ▫ Listed: NYSE ▫ Fiscal year ends September 30 ▫ Ticker symbol: APD ▫ S&P rating: A ▫ Value Line financial strength rating: A+

Air Products and Chemicals, Inc., with operations in thirty countries and annual revenues in excess of $4.0 billion, is a leading supplier of industrial gases and related equipment, specialty and intermediate chemicals, and environmental and energy systems.

Air Products's industrial gas and chemical products are used by a diverse base of customers in manufacturing, process, and service industries.

In the environmental and energy businesses, Air Products and its affiliates own and operate facilities to reduce air and water pollution, dispose of solid waste, and generate electric power.

Industrial Gases
• APD is the fourth-largest supplier in the world.
• Its products are essential in many manufacturing processes.
• Gases are produced by cryogenic, adsorption, and membrane technologies.
• They are supplied by tankers, on-site plants, pipelines, and cylinders.

• International sales, including the company's share of joint ventures, represent more than half of Air Products' gas revenues.

The markets served by Industrial Gases include chemical processing, metals, oil and gas production, electronics, research, food, glass, healthcare, and pulp and paper. Principal products are industrial gases, such as nitrogen, oxygen, hydrogen, argon, and helium, and various specialty, cutting, and welding gases.

Chemicals
• APD has a leadership position in over 80 percent of the markets served.
• Markets include a wide range of attractive, diversified end uses that reduce overall exposure to economic cycles.
• World-scale, state-of-the-art production facilities and process technology skills ensure consistent, low-cost products while enhancing long-term customer relationships.
• International sales, including exports to over one hundred countries, represent a quarter of the business.

The markets served by Chemicals include adhesives, agriculture, furniture, automotive products, paints and coatings, textiles, paper, and building products. Principal products are emulsions, polyvinyl alcohol, polyurethane and epoxy additives, surfactants, amines, and polyurethane intermediaries.

Environmental and Energy Systems
• Facilities, owned and operated with partners, dispose of solid waste, reduce air pollution and generate electrical power.
• Strong positions are built by extending core skills developed in the industrial gas business.
• Forces driving this market are environmental regulation, demand for efficient sources of electrical power, utility deregulation, and privatization. Principal products are waste-to-energy plants, electric power services, and air pollution control systems.

The markets served by Environmental and Energy Systems include solid waste disposal, electrical power generation, and air pollution reduction.

Equipment and Services
• Cryogenic and noncryogenic equipment is designed and manufactured for various gas-processing applications.
• Equipment is sold worldwide or manufactured for Air Products's industrial gas business and its international network of joint ventures.

The markets served by Equipment and Services include chemicals, steel, oil and gas recovery, and power generation.

Shortcomings to Bear in Mind
■ In 1996, APD's industrial gases business had a difficult year. Its major reengineering programs took longer, cost more, and delivered fewer benefits than expected. Costs from aggressive investment over the past few years also hurt near-term earnings. Finally, the company experienced a few unusual, but significant, contract changes and expirations, and new business signings produced slower-than-expected volume growth.

Reasons to Buy
■ Demand for industrial gas has been strong. This high demand is more than a cyclical phenomenon and is being fueled by new applications and new industrial gas production technology.
■ In Eastern Europe, Air Products was awarded a contract to design, build, and operate the largest and most modern air separation plant in that region. It will serve the growing markets of the Czech and Slovak republics and the highly industrialized regions of southern and eastern Germany.
■ Air Products also acquired the polymer emulsions business of Dale Quimica, S.A. de C.V., one of Mexico's leading suppliers, to strengthen the company's position in that emerging market.
■ In 1996, the company moved to decrease equity as a percentage of total capitalization. This move is expected to lower Air Products' cost of capital and maintain the financial flexibility required in a capital-intensive industry.

The company began a two-year program to acquire about 10 percent of its outstanding shares, financed primarily by debt and proceeds from asset sales, notably APD's 50 percent interest in American Ref-Fuel.
■ Today, some 60,000 customers in North America—once served by eighty different locations—are now managed from the company's Single-Point-Of-Contact Center, using state-of-the-art information technology systems. The number of error-free deliveries is improving, customer runouts are significantly lower, and APD's customers are increasingly positive about the changes made.

- Air Products is well positioned to benefit from increased demand from new plants being built in the chemical, paper, and other basic industries. In particular, the company is seeing an acceleration in bidding for new gas contracts in the electronics market and in gaseous hydrogen for oil refineries.
- APD's margins should expand further as the company continues to realize savings from its cost-reduction efforts.
- Air Products' electronics business has grown 20 percent annually over the past five years, enabling the company to maintain its position as the industry's leading supplier. Its MEGASYS Total Gas Management Program is one reason why. Under this program, the company operates and manages virtually every aspect of gas supply for semiconductor manufacturers. What's more, the company won twenty major orders at new semiconductor manufacturing facilities or expansions of existing ones in nine countries around the world, including an order to provide all gases and gas-handling equipment for Motorola's leading-edge wafer fabrication facility in northern China. It was APD's fortieth MEGASYS contract overall, its twenty-first with the semiconductor manufacturer, and the company's first MEGASYS contract in China.
- In the glass industry, Air Products won ten new contracts for its CLEANFIRE Oxy-Fuel Burner, which helps glass producers reduce nitrogen oxide and particulate emissions. The majority of those new contracts will require on-site oxygen plants.
- In the medical market, the company signed a seven-year contract extension to supply liquid helium, nitrogen, and on-site services to General Electric's magnetic resonance imaging customers around the world. To further

strengthen Air Products' position as the number one supplier of helium, the company formed a joint venture company to market helium in China and completed construction of a new plant in Algeria.
- Air Products continues to be among the lowest-cost, highest-quality manufacturers in the chemicals industry. To maintain that leadership, the company implemented a systematic process for setting productivity goals and monitoring progress throughout its operations. Management also instituted a manufacturing incentive program that rewards employees for suggesting process improvements or cost reduction measures.
- In its first year of operation, APD's 120-megawatt cogeneration plant in Orlando, Florida received one of *Power* magazine's prestigious "Powerplant of the Year" awards for efficiency and superior environmental performance.
- Pure Air, a company Air Products formed to develop and market air pollution-control systems, continued to achieve over 99 percent operating availability at its plant in Indiana. In addition, the company signed a contract to build, own, and operate two air-emission control facilities for a Florida utility that is converting a power plant from burning oil to Orimulsion, a less expensive fuel. APD expects these facilities to be onstream by 1998 and to generate revenues of $1 billion over the life of the contract. Finally, there are several additional candidates for conversion to Orimulsion, each representing an opportunity for Pure Air.
- Air Products recently won important new hydrogen/carbon monoxide/syngas (HYCO) business, building on APD's leadership position for the worldwide chemical process industries. The company effectively doubled capacity along

the Texas/Gulf Coast pipeline system, expanded its Louisiana pipeline, and increased output at its Avon, California, facility by 40 percent. What's more, the company began construction of large HYCO facilities in Brazil and the United Kingdom.

- Earnings and dividends have been advancing at a healthy clip. Earnings per share (EPS) climbed from $1.17 in 1986 to $3.27 in 1996, a compound annual growth rate of 11.2 percent. In the same ten-year stretch, dividends expanded from $.39 to $1.07, a growth rate of 10.6 percent.
- Investors seem pleased with the change in executive compensation. It

is designed to align management's interests with those of stockholders. The company established a bonus plan tied to achieving compound annual earnings growth in excess of 12 percent by 1998 and authorized options exercisable after two years at a strike price of $73.

In addition, APD's officers are required to own two to five times their annual salary in company stock, based on the level of responsibility. Finally, a minimum of 25 percent of board members' fees will be paid in deferred stock units, payable after the end of their board service.

Total assets: $6,522 million
Current ratio: 1.09
Common shares outstanding: 111 million
Return on 1996 shareholders' equity: 16.6%

	1996	1995	1994	1993	1992	1991	1990	1989
Revenues (millions)	4,008	3,865	3,485	3,328	3,217	2,931	2,895	2,642
Net income (millions)	416	368	264	268	235	216	212	214
Earnings per share	3.37	3.23	2.06	2.32	2.37	2.10	1.96	1.93
Dividends per share	1.07	1.01	.95	.88	.83	.74	.69	.63
Price: High	80.62	59.5	50.4	48.5	49.5	37.1	30.5	24.4
Low	50.38	43.9	37.5	36.4	25.6	21.4	20.0	18.3

CONSERVATIVE GROWTH

Alberto-Culver Company

2525 Armitage Avenue, Melrose Park, Illinois 60160 □ Investor contact: Daniel B. Stone (708) 450-3005 □ Dividend reinvestment plan not available □ Fiscal year ends September 30 □ Listed: NYSE □ Ticker symbols: ACV and ACVA □ S&P rating: A □ Value Line financial strength rating: B++

Alberto-Culver is a leading developer and manufacturer of personal care products, primarily for hair care, retail food products, household items, and health and hygiene products.

Alberto-Culver is comprised of three strong businesses built around potent brands and trademarks:

- Alberto-Culver USA develops innovative brand name products for the

retail, professional beauty, and institutional markets. Personal use products include: hair fixatives, shampoos, hair dressings, and conditioners sold under such trademarks as Alberto VO5, Bold Hold, Alberto, Alberto Balsam, Consort, TRESemme, and FDS.

Retail food product labels include SugarTwin, Mrs. Dash, Molly McButter, Baker's Joy, and Village Saucerie.

Household products include Static Guard (antistatic spray) and Kleen Guard (furniture polish).

• Alberto-Culver International has carried the Alberto VO5 flag into more than a hundred countries and from that solid base has built products, new brands, and businesses focused on the needs of each market.

• Sally Beauty Company is the engine that drives Alberto-Culver. With 1,656 outlets in the United States and the United Kingdom, Sally is the largest cash-and-carry supplier of professional beauty products in the world.

The typical Sally Beauty store averages 1,800 square feet and is situated in a strip shopping center. It carries more than 3,000 items. About three-quarters of Sally Beauty's sales are to small beauty salons and barber shops, with the rest to retail customers.

In fiscal 1996, this fast-growing business was responsible for three-quarters of ACV's operating profits.

Sally is the only national player in the United States in cash-and-carry beauty supplies sold primarily to professionals. It is the market leader by a wide margin. Sally capitalizes on its dominance in that niche, which gives beauty professionals the opportunity to purchase products from a wide selection of vendors at wholesale prices without having to manage and carry inventory in their stores.

The company's products do not have a common origin. They have come to Alberto-Culver in diverse ways. For instance, the original Alberto VO5 Hairdressing was a small, regional brand that the company acquired because it felt it had national sales potential.

In another instance, the feminine deodorant spray products and mousse products had counterparts in the marketplace in Europe. Consequently, ACV brought the ideas to the United States and introduced these products to an American audience.

In another realm, Mrs. Dash, Static Guard, and Consort were all developed internally by the company's research and development team because its customers identified a need that these products met. SugarTwin and TRESemme were acquired by the company as tiny brands and grown to the strong positions they hold today.

Perhaps the company's most important acquisition—after the original purchase of Alberto VO5 Conditioning Hairdressing—was the purchase of the Sally Beauty Company, originally a chain of twelve stores, many of which were franchised.

Today, the chain has 1,656 company-owned stores, with 40 in Great Britain and the balance in the United States. Sally is the largest distributor of professional beauty supplies in the world.

The primary customer for Sally is the salon and barber professional, who can find at Sally an unmatched selection of professional beauty supplies available at discount prices. In addition to the supplies they need, these professionals find in Sally a valuable source of information about trends and products that they can take back to their customers.

One of the keys to Sally's success is the ability to quickly get product from warehouse to shelf. This process starts with proprietary point-of-sale registers in each Sally store that record and report each sale. Sally is now investing millions of dollars to add a second POS register to each store to enhance its ability to serve customers.

Sally greatly improved its inventory control ability with the opening of a new computer-controlled, state-of-the-art warehouse in northern Nevada. The company has a similar distribution center in Columbus, Ohio.

Shortcomings to Bear in Mind

- In 1997, the company introduced a new product line, Cortexx, a premium-priced group of shampoos and conditioners containing gelatin to retard hair breakage. Advertising expenses may hurt earnings in the third quarter of 1997. A major product introduction can be risky. In the past, Alberto-Culver has experienced a negative impact on earnings when a new line went on sale. However, the company's considerable size now provides more of a buffer than it might have a few years earlier.

Reasons to Buy

- In fiscal 1996 (ended September 30, 1996), Alberto-Culver completed its fifth consecutive year of record sales and earnings. Sales for the year increased 17.1 percent. Net earnings jumped 19.2 percent.

  Each of the company's three operating units—Alberto-Culver USA, Alberto-Culver International, and Sally Beauty Company—achieved double-digit sales and profit increases. Alberto-Culver USA's operating earnings shot up more than 70 percent on a sales increase of 23 percent. Alberto-Culver International had an operating increase of 24 percent. Sally Beauty continued its superb growth. The chain ended the year with 1,656 units, a sales increase of 11 percent and a profit increase of 13 percent.

  To put those numbers in perspective: In 1990, the company's corporate sales were just under $800 million, which means ACV has doubled its sales since then. What's more, Alberto-Culver also doubled its sales between 1985 and 1990. At the same time, Sally, which had about 800 units in 1990, has nearly doubled its units during the '90s, as well.

- Perhaps the most significant event in 1996 was the acquisition of St. Ives Laboratories. This was the largest acquisition in the company's history. With the St. Ives Swiss Formula products, Alberto-Culver has a very potent brand name that strengthens its market position in hair care and, more important, the company now has a substantial presence in the skin-care category for the first time. In addition to the domestic impact, St. Ives adds to ACV's sales in some of the company's current international markets, as well as some additional countries.

- However, Alberto-Culver is aware that growth cannot come from acquisitions alone. The company must also develop new products internally. ACV has made significant progress on that front recently. In the United States, the company introduced significant additions to its major lines in 1996, such as Alberto VO5 Hot Oil Aromatherapy, Alberto VO5 Naturals Plus Hair & Body Shampoo, FDS with Baking Soda, TRESemme Naturals, and TCB Naturals. Toward the end of 1996, the company announced three more products:

  - Cortexx, a shampoo-and-conditioner line based around a patented formula that includes gelatine to strengthen hair and reduce hair breakage.
  - The Consort Hair Regrowth System—a minoxidil product.
  - TCB Relax & Color, an innovative product that combines a hair relaxer and a hair color for the ethnic market.
  - St. Ives has introduced a new line of hair care products, Swiss Formula Botanicals Plus.
  - In the United Kingdom, the company launched a line of semipermanent hair color products under the name Alberto VO5 Select and extended its successful Andrew

Collinge line with the launch of Thickening Solutions.

■ Alberto-Culver has taken steps to strengthen its new product capabilities. Management has established a New Business Development Group that will coordinate new product development for both the United States and International. With creative research and development labs in several of its facilities, Alberto-Culver is in an excellent position to accelerate its new product efforts and is committed to making the investments necessary in development and marketing to bring these products to market successfully.

■ Alberto VO5 Conditioning Hairdressing remains by far the number one brand in its category and the best-selling hairdressing in the world. VO5 is among the market leaders in the United States, Great Britain, Scandinavia, Canada, Mexico, Australia, and Japan.

Total assets: $909,266,000
Current ratio: 1.79
Common shares outstanding: 56 million
Return on 1996 shareholders' equity: 14.8%

	1996	1995	1994	1993	1992	1991	1990	1989
Revenues (millions)	1,590	1,358	1,216	1,148	1,091	874	796	717
Net income (millions)	62.7	52.7	44.1	41.3	38.6	30.1	35.0	29.4
Earnings per share	1.06	.94	.79	.72	.68	.53	.65	.56
Dividends per share	.18	.16	.14	.14	.12	.11	.10	.09
Price: High	25.0	18.3	13.7	14.1	16.0	17.1	16.6	13.3
Low	16.3	12.9	9.7	10.1	10.6	10.3	9.6	8.2

CONSERVATIVE GROWTH

Albertson's, Inc.

P.O. Box 20, Boise, Idaho 83726 ☐ Investor contact: Renee Bergquist (208) 395-6622 ☐ Dividend reinvestment plan available: (800) 982-7649 ☐ Fiscal year ends Thursday nearest January 31 ☐ Listed: NYSE ☐ Ticker symbol: ABS ☐ S&P rating: A+ ☐ Value Line financial strength rating: A+

In terms of sales volume, Albertson's is the fourth-largest retail food-drug chain in the United States. Although Albertson's operates in twenty states, its greatest concentration is in two states: California (170 stores) and Texas (167), with Florida (95) and Washington (75) also having a large number of outlets. By contrast, the number of stores in several states is low, such as South Dakota (1 store), Arkansas (1) and Kansas (5).

Overall, the company operates 826 stores located in 20 western, midwestern and southern states. At the end of 1996, the average store size was 48,200 square feet, and the average weekly sales per store was $335,000.

Combination food and drug stores range in size from 35,000 to 75,000 square feet. Conventional supermarkets range from 15,000 to 35,000 square feet and offer a full line of grocery items and, in many locations, feature in-store bakeries and delicatessens.

Retail operations are supported by eleven company-owned distribution centers. About 78 percent of all products purchased by the stores are supplied from facilities operated by Albertson's. Distribution facilities operate as profit centers. Profits earned by a distribution center are rebated to each store, based on merchandise purchased from the center.

Shortcomings to Bear in Mind

- Food retailing is a competitive business and is often subject to price wars.
- Supermarkets have to compete with each other (usually with nearly identical products priced competitively). They also have to be concerned with the inroads being made by warehouse clubs like Sam's and Costco and with supercenters that sell food and general merchandise, like those being rolled out by Wal-Mart and Kmart.

Reasons to Buy

- Albertson's retail square footage grew at a record pace during 1996. The company opened sixty-six newly constructed stores and acquired four stores, bringing the total store openings in 1996 to seventy. To keep Albertson's stores up-to-date, the company completely remodeled forty-two stores, including six that were expanded. Eight units were closed during 1996, of which five were replaced with larger stores. Net square footage expanded by 9.6 percent in 1996 (excluding acquisitions) to 39.8 million square feet of retail space.
- Albertson's distribution system continues to keep pace with the rapid growth of its retail stores. The company's distribution centers encompass nearly 7.4 million square feet and are situated strategically throughout the twenty-state operating region. Albertson's newest distribution center, covering 698,000 square feet, opened in the spring of 1996.
- In-store pharmacies and in-store banks continue to add value for Albertson's customers. During 1996, the company worked with local banks to install 174 in-store banks for a total of 256 in-store units at the year's end. Albertson's puts pharmacies in nearly all supermarkets; it ended 1996 with 544 in-store pharmacies.
- In March of 1997, ABS increased its quarterly dividend from $.15 a share to $.16; it was the twenty-sixth consecutive annual dividend increase.
- Albertson's Quick Fixin' Ideas give shoppers exactly what they want—meals that can be prepared quickly and conveniently at home. Since it was first introduced in southern California in February of 1996, Quick Fixin' has been a success. By December of 1996, all company stores were featuring Quick Fixin' Ideas throughout the aisles.

  Albertson's provides solutions for meals at home through sampling stations in the grocery department, heat-and-serve entrees in the service deli and complete meal recipes and value-added products in the produce, meat, and frozen food departments.
- Albertson's has been able to increase sales through an everyday-low-pricing strategy, coupled with strong in-store merchandising programs and increased efficiencies from its expanded distribution system.
- As one of the most conservative food retailers in the business, Albertson's prefers to let others test-market new products and services. If they work for other retailers, Albertson's is content to jump on their train.
- In the past ten years, earnings per share climbed from $.38 to $1.96, a compound annual growth rate of 17.8 percent. In the same 1986–1996 period, dividends per share advanced from $.11 to $.60, an 18.5 percent growth rate.
- The company believes good retail site selection is the foundation of its success. Unlike grocery chains that cluster their stores, Albertson's is careful to place each store far enough away from

another Albertson's store so they do not compete with each other.

- Albertson's is one of the main beneficiaries within the food retailing group of the improved drug store industry fundamentals. The key factors are:
  - Re-negotiated third-party prescription drug margins (in favor of the retailer);
  - Burgeoning generic drug sales (which have higher profit margins);
  - Reformatted/remerchandised stores with more focused general merchandise;
  - Stabilized prescription drug inflation.
- Albertson's is well organized when it comes to property development. Here are some highlights of its strategy:
  - Cross-functional teams were created to increase efficiency and continuity on new store construction projects. Each team is comprised of store planners, real estate specialists, economic analysts, lawyers, architects, engineers, and construction supervisors.
  - A new single-entrance store format that is more employee- and customer-friendly was implemented in 1994.
  - A micromarket approach is used to select store sites that maximize sales and profits within individual trade areas.
  - All prospective store sites are personally visited by top management before approval.
  - Combination food–drug stores of 50,000 square feet are constructed primarily, with only a limited number of 40-000-square-foot stores for smaller cities. A limited number of Max warehouse stores are built as needed.
  - All stores are continually reviewed and marginal performers eliminated; surplus stores are sold, leased, or subleased.

- In-house design and construction departments enhance speed and efficiency on new store and remodeling projects using computer-aided design equipment.
- Stores are located in eighteen of the twenty fastest-growing domestic metropolitan areas as identified by Market Metrics.
- All potential acquisitions are reviewed to ensure that they meet the company's tough criteria.
- An efficient, phased remodeling process minimizes shopper disruption.
- About 90 percent of Albertson's square footage is "combo stores" (essentially a complete drug store under the same roof as a complete supermarket), with about 80 percent of these actually having a pharmacy.
- The company's distribution centers service Albertson's stores exclusively.
- Information systems and technology play a key role in the ability of the company to grow and prosper by providing information across all boundaries of the organization.
- The company's gross margin is expanding modestly. The improvement, moreover, is largely the result of distribution efficiencies, such as savings realized from buying in larger quantities and gains resulting from spreading out fixed costs over a larger sales base. A more profitable sales mix is another plus. Analysts believe that Albertson's can expand gross margins even further over the next four or five years.
- Computer Guided Training is going online at Albertson's. New computers that help entry-level employees learn their jobs better and faster are being installed in all Albertson's stores. They will make learning fun and easy through a simple touch-screen interface. Behind the simplicity are sophisticated software

programs designed exclusively for Albertson's. Computer Guided Training will add structure and consistency to the hands-on training already provided by management. The combined methods of instruction will teach employees how to do their jobs better and more effectively while providing top-notch customer service.

- A private data communications network links all retail stores, distribution centers, division office, and the corporate office. This network, along with the large-scale computers, in-store processors, and numerous personal computers, provides the infrastructure for companywide messaging and information access.

- A fully computerized demographic and lifestyle-based site selection and neighborhood mapping system is used for real estate site evaluation, merchandising, and advertising.

- All stores with pharmacies have computers that provide information on drug interaction, initiate third party billings, and enhance customer service.

Total assets: $4,715 million
Current ratio: 1.35
Common shares outstanding: 251 million
Return on 1996 shareholders' equity: 23.5%

	1996	1995	1994	1993	1992	1991	1990	1989
Revenues (millions)	13,777	12,585	11,894	11,284	10,174	8,680	8,219	7,423
Net income (millions)	494	465	417	352	276	258	234	197
Earnings per share	1.96	1.84	1.65	1.39	1.05	.97	.88	.73
Dividends per share	.60	.52	.42	.36	.32	.28	.24	.20
Price: High	43.8	34.6	30.9	29.6	26.7	25.7	18.9	15.1
Low	31.5	27.3	25.1	23.4	18.4	16.3	12.2	9.2

AGGRESSIVE GROWTH

Aluminum Company of America

425 Sixth Avenue, Pittsburgh, PA 15219-1850 ◻ Investor contact: Edgar M. Cheely, Jr. (412) 555-4498 ◻ Dividend reinvestment plan available: (412) 553-4431 ◻ Listed: NYSE ◻ Ticker symbol: AA ◻ S&P rating: B- ◻ Value Line financial strength rating: A

Alcoa, founded in 1888, is the world's leading integrated producer of aluminum products. These products are used worldwide by packaging, transportation, building, and industrial customers. In addition to components and finished products, Alcoa produces alumina, alumina-based chemicals, as well as primary aluminum for a multitude of applications.

Alcoa competes against such companies as Alcan Aluminium (note the Canadian spelling of aluminum) and Reynolds Metals. Alcoa, with 1996 revenues of $13.1 billion, is the largest factor in the aluminum industry. The company has 178 operating and sales locations in 28 countries.

Alcoa's operations are broken down into the following segments:

- Alumina and chemicals
- Aluminum processing
- Nonaluminum products

The alumina and chemicals segment includes the production and sale of bauxite, alumina, and alumina chemicals.

Aluminum processing comprises the manufacturing and marketing of molten metal, ingot, and aluminum products that are flat-rolled, engineered, or finished.

The nonaluminum products segment includes the production and sale of electrical, ceramic, plastic, and composite materials products; manufacturing equipment; gold; separations systems; magnesium products; and steel and titanium forgings.

Most of the company's aluminum facilities in the United States are owned by the parent company. The two largest operating subsidiaries are Alcoa of Australia Limited and Alcoa Aluminio S.A. of Brazil.

Since aluminum is expensive and has difficulty competing against steel—even though it has some admirable qualities—it might appear to be a rare element. Not so.

Aluminum is an abundant metal, in fact, it is the most abundant metal in the earth's crust. Of all the elements, only oxygen and silicon are more plentiful. Aluminum makes up 8 percent of the crust. It is found in the minerals of bauxite, mica, and cryolite, as well as in clay.

When aluminum is discussed, two terms are frequently heard: alumina and bauxite. Alumina is an aluminum oxide produced from bauxite by an intricate chemical process. It is a white, powdery material that looks like granulated sugar. Alumina is an intermediate step in the production of aluminum from bauxite and is also a valuable chemical on its own.

Bauxite is an ore from which alumina is extracted and from which aluminum is eventually smelted. Bauxite usually contains at least 45 percent alumina. About four pounds of bauxite are required to produce one pound of aluminum.

Until about 100 years ago, aluminum was virtually a precious metal. Despite its abundance, it was very rare as a pure metal because it was so difficult to extract from its ore. This is because aluminum is a reactive metal, and it cannot be extracted by smelting with carbon.

To solve the enigma, displacement reactions were tried, but metals such as sodium or potassium had to be used, making the cost prohibitive.

Electrolysis of the molten ore was tried, but the most plentiful ore, bauxite, contains aluminum oxide, which does not melt until it reaches 2,050° Celsius.

The solution to the problem of extracting aluminum from its ore was discovered by Charles Hall in the United States and by Paul Heroult in France—both working independently. The method now used to extract aluminum from its ore is called the Hall-Heroult process.

I won't bore you with the steps in this process. The important fact to remember is that it is far from cheap. Even so, it can be done economically enough to make aluminum the second most widely used metal. However, it is not likely to replace iron and steel anytime soon. Iron makes up more than 90 percent of the metals used in the world.

The main cost in the Hall-Heroult process is electricity. So much energy is required that aluminum smelters have to be situated near a cheap source of power, normally hydroelectric.

Alcoa and its handful of competitors may view the intricate and expensive smelting process as a mixed blessing. However, it keeps out the riffraff. The price of entry into the business is so high that it discourages most upstarts from taking the plunge.

On the other hand, this frustrating effort to produce commercial aluminum is worth the cost, since the white metal has a number of valuable attributes:

- It has a low density.
- It is highly resistent to corrosion.
- It is light in weight—one-third the weight of steel.

- It is an excellent reflector of heat and light.
  - It is nonmagnetic.
  - It is easy to assemble.
  - It is nontoxic.
  - It can be made strong with alloys.
  - It can be easily rolled into thin sheets.
  - It has good electrical conductivity.
  - It has good thermal conductivity.
- Aluminum doesn't rust. As one economist commented: "You can sell it as new ten years later. There is no cost of holding it, like steel, where you need a warehouse, or wheat, where you need a silo, or oil, where you need a tank. Aluminum can be stored by just throwing it in your backyard."

Shortcomings to Bear in Mind

- Since aluminum is easy to preserve without costly warehouses, overproduction carries little or no penalty. It becomes a lethal habit. According to Theodor Tschopp, an engineer economist with Alusuisse-Lonza Holding, "I really believe in the future of aluminum in transportation and many other areas, but it is the product of an industry that is killing itself."
- If you are looking for an industry with predictable, steady growth, you had better forget about aluminum. It has plenty of ups and downs. Not long ago, for instance, Russia threw aluminum producers into a frenzy.

  The Soviet Union (before it fell apart) was rich in natural resources, and one of the big resources was aluminum. But its huge military complex used as much as half of its aluminum production. When the Soviet Union collapsed, Russia found herself with a massive surplus of aluminum.

  Cash-starved Russian smelters, freed from government control, could do only one thing with their product:

export it. They began sending aluminum into the world market, undercutting Western prices by as much as 50 percent. By the summer of 1992, ingots of the white metal were stacked high on the docks of Rotterdam, the Netherlands, the main storage site for the global industry.

Meanwhile, the London Metal Exchange inventories soared to 2.5 million metric tons at the end of 1993. Prices plunged: From about 93 cents a pound in September 1990, primary aluminum prices fell to a just under 58 cents in September 1993, close to the break-even level of aluminum producers. Needless to say, red ink was soon evident among such companies as Pechiney SA, Europe's largest producer, Alcoa, and others.

Fortunately, the story has a happy ending. Russian production costs finally climbed to more realistic levels. And in November 1993, the Western producers cut a deal, called "Memorandum of Understanding"— known within the industry as MOU— with the Russians. In a cartel-like move that so far has successfully evaded antitrust laws, Western producers have agreed to roll back production by 877,000 tons a year, while the Russians will honor a 141,000-ton production cutback. On the strength of that agreement, prices began rising on the London Metal Exchange and later hit a thirty-nine-month high.

Reasons to Buy

- Alcoa has a variable dividend policy, currently $.90 a share. If earnings stay strong, the dividend will be supplemented by the company's formula that states that an additional dividend will be paid if earnings exceed $3 a share. Shareholders will be entitled to receive 30 percent of anything over $3. Looking back in recent history, there are several years when this occurred, such as 1988 (earnings were $4.87), 1989 ($5.34), 1990 ($3.30), 1995 ($4.43) and 1996 ($3.17). In early 1997, moreover, analysts were looking for bountiful earnings for 1997 ($5.00) and 1997 ($7.23).

- In 1997, Alcoa announced the acquisition of Spain's state-run aluminum business, Inespal S.A. Based in Madrid, Inespal is an integrated aluminum producer with 1996 revenues of $1.1 billion. This move boosts Alcoa's global aluminum-making capacity by 370,000 metric tons a year, or nearly 17 percent. It also gives Alcoa an additional 1 million metric tons of capacity to make alumina. Before the acquisition, the company's alumina capacity was 11.6 million metric tons.

    For Alcoa, already the world's largest aluminum producer, the move follows other efforts to expand its reach in Europe. In 1996, the company purchased Italy's state-run aluminum business, which boosted its annual aluminum-making capacity by 170,000 metric tons. Alcoa already had aluminum-making operations in the Netherlands and operations in several European countries that fabricate aluminum for specific uses.

- Alcoa is the world's largest producer of alumina (and at low cost). Alumina is the white, powdery substance used to produce aluminum.

- One analyst observes that, "Unlike the boom-and-bust cycles of the 1980s, the aluminum market in the 1990s has been characterized by much steadier growth." Similarly, another analyst points out that "Emerging markets will need aluminum for everything from pots and pans to infrastructure."

- Alcoa has the most geographically diverse bauxite reserves in the industry.

- In 1996, Alcoa Foil Products received its first commercial order from the Trane Corporation for hydrophilic fin stock for their air handler products. This newly developed treatment for aluminum fin stock improves the performance of heat exchangers used in air conditioners and heat pumps.

- Alcoa's revenues from automotive components have more than quadrupled since 1993, to nearly $2 billion in 1996. The Audi A8 is the world's first all aluminum Space Frame production car. The Audi Space Frame is 40 percent sturdier than conventional unit-body structures.

- Alcoa Aluminio won the 1996 Brazil Packaging Award in the Systems and Processes category. Competing against more than 70 companies, Aluminio's new, high-efficiency bottle rinser came out on top as the best project using in-house technology.

- In 1996, the company announced that Alcoa will build a $20 million facility at its Cleveland plant site to make wheels for Chrysler's Dodge Ram pickup truck. Capacity: 900,000 wheels a year. It's the first step in a multi-phase plan to increase production of forged aluminum wheels for the U. S. light truck market.

- According to analysts, greater usage of aluminum in the auto industry, along with improving demand for beverage cans in developing nations, should combine to fuel rapid earnings growth in the years ahead.

Total assets: $13,450 million
Current ratio: 1.67
Common shares outstanding: 174 million
Return on 1996 shareholders' equity: 14.4%

	1996	1995	1994	1993	1992	1991	1990	1989
Revenues (millions)	13,061	12,500	9,904	9,056	9,492	9,884	10,710	10,910
Net income (millions)	555	796	193	67	196	280	570	945
Earnings per share	3.17	4.46	1.08	.40	1.14	1.64	3.30	5.34
Dividends per share	1.33	.90	.80	.80	.80	.89	1.50	1.36
Price: High	66.3	60.3	45.1	39.2	40.3	36.6	38.6	39.8
Low	49.1	36.9	32.1	29.5	30.5	26.9	24.8	27.6

AGGRESSIVE GROWTH

AlliedSignal Inc.

101 Columbia Road, P. O. Box 2245, Morristown, New Jersey 07962-2245 ◻ Investor contact: James V. Gelly (201) 455-2222 ◻ Dividend reinvestment program available: (800) 255-4332 ◻ Ticker symbol: ALD ◻ S&P rating: B+ ◻ Value Line financial strength rating: A++

AlliedSignal is an advanced technology and manufacturing company serving customers worldwide with aerospace and automotive products, chemicals, fibers, plastics, and advanced materials.

For years, the vast majority of AlliedSignal's revenues came from mature or cyclical businesses—as evidenced by the company's erratic earnings and stagnant stock price.

Beginning in 1991, AlliedSignal began to revitalize its business portfolio, selling some businesses, while improving and acquiring others. Today, more than half of the company's revenues are generated by growth businesses, making a solid platform on which to build further sales and earnings gains.

A review of 1996

In 1996, AlliedSignal "made its numbers" for the fifth consecutive year—this time at the high end of its commitment of 13 to 17 percent earnings growth. What's more, ALD passed the billion-dollar earnings milestone for the first time, as net income for 1996 reached a record $1.02 bil-

lion ($3.61 per share), up 17 percent from 1995's $875 million ($3.09 per share).

As a result of the April 1996 divestiture of Allied's passenger car brake business, sales in 1996 were $14.0 billion, compared with $14.3 billion in 1995. Excluding braking sales from both years, sales increased by $1 billion in 1996, or 8 percent.

Operating margin widened to 10.8 percent, from 8.8 percent, as productivity increased 6 percent. Return on equity in 1996 was a most impressive 26.6 percent. Operating cash flow totaled $1.2 billion, and free cash flow was $313 million.

AlliedSignal's Strategy

AlliedSignal is not a "pure play" that commands investor interest, based on spectacular growth of any one hot product line. Rather, the company's attractiveness to the investing public stems from the ability to produce increases in earnings—consistently, year after year, from a host of different product lines.

Consequently, AlliedSignal is harvesting some of the mature businesses in its portfolio and reinvesting the resources in businesses that management regards as future growth platforms. In 1990, only 13 percent of AlliedSignal's sales were derived from businesses that could be characterized as growth businesses. Today, ALD is up to 56 percent. This change was achieved partly through acquisitions and divestitures but also by changing the strategy and market focus of some of its businesses to enable them to grow more rapidly.

Additionally, AlliedSignal is pressing for a better balance of original equipment (OE) and aftermarket offerings, since aftermarkets are more stable and predictable. Aftermarket sales are now 41 percent of the company's total revenues. What's more, management is pushing for more business outside North America in order to expand its participation in faster growing global markets and better equip Allied to weather an economic downturn on any one continent.

Lawrence A. Bossidy, CEO

What has transpired during these past six years can be credited to Larry Bossidy, the CEO of AlliedSignal since mid-1991. It is Mr. Bossidy who is the architect of the changes that have transformed the company in this brief span.

"Six percent forever" continues to serve as AlliedSignal's productivity mantra. Nearly six years have elapsed since Larry Bossidy launched a major set of initiatives designed to dramatically change the way the company operates.

Staff cuts were part of the solution, but by no means was this the bulk of Mr. Bossidy's program. For instance, far-flung networks of data and finance centers were consolidated.

Analysts are most impressed with leverage opportunities for AlliedSignal. Management believes the company can achieve 12 percent margins, 6 percent forever gains in productivity, and working

capital turns of ten times (versus five turns now), which would provide annual cash flows of $400 to $650 million. What's more, analysts look for long-term growth to be enhanced by acquisitions and further joint ventures, as ALD moves to expand its global markets.

AlliedSignal's growth plan includes $1 billion (half of which is completed) in additional deals by the end of 1998 to further strengthen its operations and bolster earnings per share. Strong free cash flow of $300 to $400 million per year give the company the capability to accomplish this goal. On average, the company believes that deals to date have added about $.02 a share for each $100 million invested. Conceivably, these ventures could augment the company's market position and boost its commercial mix.

What's more, the new CEO also centralized materials management. Under the old regime, buying was done by smaller units that couldn't take advantage of the bargaining potential that a company Allied's size ought to enjoy.

While Mr. Bossidy was courted by IBM and Merck, where he's a board member, he declined both overtures and made the unambiguous statement that he "is committed to remaining at AlliedSignal for the remainder of my career."

Aerospace is the largest of ALD's groups. As the broadest supplier of commercial aircraft systems, with strong market positions in auxiliary power units (APUs), wheels and brakes, and environmental controls, ALD should benefit from the early part of the commercial aircraft cycle, as high-margin aftermarket business recovers.

The Automotive segment, which accounts for 38 percent of sales, manufactures safety restraints, air bags, spark plugs, turbochargers, and filters for passenger cars and light trucks.

Finally, Engineered Materials, which accounts for 26 percent of revenues, manufactures nylon and polyester carpet fibers, fluorine products, plastics, refrigerants, solvents, films, and laminates.

Shortcomings to Bear in Mind

- If you look at the price action of AlliedSignal since Larry Bossidy took the helm, you might conclude that you have arrived on the scene too late. Since late 1990, the stock has climbed from a low of $13 to over $74 in 1996. In the 1996 annual report, Mr. Bossidy says, "Despite our progress, most of the people who work at AlliedSignal are convinced that our best days are yet to come—a conviction stemming from the aggressive efforts under way to drive further gains."

Reasons to Buy

- AlliedSignal's strong financial position—it's rated A++ by Value Line—provides the resources and flexibility to respond to opportunities for internal growth and acquisitions. The $1.5 billion of proceeds from the braking divestiture essentially offsets all of the company's long-term debt. Over the next three years, moreover, cash flow from operations, existing cash resources, and additional borrowing capacity will provide $6 billion of resources for acquisitions and investments in business expansion.
- AlliedSignal Aerospace won a contract to provide its parallel approach radar monitor system for the airport in Sydney, Australia. The system allows simultaneous aircraft landings on parallel runways as close as 3,400 feet.
- *Aviation Week & Space Technology* devoted a cover story to AlliedSignal Aerospace, citing the company as a "world-class supplier in an industry in which success is being increasingly defined by responsiveness."

- AlliedSignal has sharply upgraded the quality of its work force by improving the skills and career development opportunities of existing employees and by bringing bright, new talent into the company. An often overlooked benefit of the company's progress is a newfound ability to attract the very best talent that is available in the marketplace.
- In May of 1997, AlliedSignal acquired Prestone Products Corporation for more than $300 million. Prestone makes antifreeze and other car care products. Allied had been looking for ways to increase its presence in the consumer end of the auto parts market and to rely less on sales of components to automakers. It's a less cyclical part of the business.
- AlliedSignal has licensed its Genetron AZ-20 refrigerant to DuPont, helping to establish AZ-20 as the standard non–ozone-depleting refrigerant for new air-conditioning equipment. Manufacturers purchase about 100 million pounds of refrigerant every year for use in new units. In addition to being environmentally safer, AZ-20 also offers greater energy efficiency and capacity than traditional refrigerants.
- AlliedSignal will manufacture and integrate the sophisticated electronic systems of Lockheed Martin's VentureStar X-33, a new single-stage-to-orbit, reusable launch vehicle designed to replace NASA's current fleet of space shuttles.
- AlliedSignal Automotive has become the sole supplier of spark plugs to Ford in North America and Europe, and the preferred supplier for Ford in the rest of the world.
- The company's Aerospace sector has made a significant contribution toward making aircraft safer, with the development of an early-warning system for

wind shear. In addition, the company has developed sophisticated new systems to detect ice on aircraft wings.

- AlliedSignal continues to improve productivity. Many of the improvements are initiated by more than 6,000 work teams throughout the company, using principles learned in Total Quality training. These teams, by attacking cycle time, scrap, defects, and other costs, are generating important results.

- The aerospace unit is benefiting from improving demand for engine spare parts and strong sales of safety equipment, such as wind shear detection instruments, ground proximity warning systems, and collision avoidance systems (which are now required on smaller planes). Repair and overhaul services are proving to be a growth area for this division.

Total assets: $12,829 million
Current ratio: 1.57
Common shares outstanding: 283 million
Return on 1996 shareholders' equity: 26.6%

	1996	1995	1994	1993	1992	1991	1990	1989
Revenues (millions)	13,971	14,346	12,817	11,827	12,042	11,831	12,343	11,942
Net income (millions)	1,020	875	759	659	541	342	462	528
Earnings per share	3.61	3.09	2.68	2.31	1.92	1.25	1.67	1.78
Dividends per share	.90	.78	.65	.58	.50	.80	.90	.90
Price: High	74.4	49.8	40.7	40.1	31.0	22.5	19.0	20.2
Low	47.1	33.4	30.4	28.8	20.5	13.0	12.5	15.9

INCOME

American Brands, Inc.

1700 East Putnam Avenue, P. O. Box 811, Old Greenwich, CT 06870-0811 ▫ **Listed: NYSE** ▫ **Investor contact: Dan Conforti, CFA (203) 698-5132** ▫ **Dividend reinvestment plan available: (203) 698-5461** ▫ **Ticker symbol: AMB** ▫ **S&P rating: B+** ▫ **Value Line financial strength rating: A+**

American Brands has been undergoing a restructuring program. It has already sold its domestic tobacco business, its life insurance company, as well as its chain of United Kingdom optical stores and specialty businesses—Prestige and Forbuoys. In 1997, it spun off its British tobacco operation, Gallaher Limited.

The restructuring dates back to 1994 with the sale of The American Tobacco Company. This was followed in 1995 with the sales of Franklin Life and Gallaher's retailing and housewares operations. In 1996, the company acquired Cobra Golf.

The new nontobacco company calls itself Fortune Brands. It consists of the nontobacco operations of American Brands, which include golf and office products, spirits and hardware.

A Review of 1996

Sales of the Fortune Brands hit $4.7 billion, up 8 percent, excluding businesses sold in 1995. In 1996, about one-third of profits came from distilled spirits, another third from hardware and home improvement. The final third was split between golf and office products.

Record sales and higher contributions were achieved in every category. The golf and office products brands each achieved double-digit profit growth. Profit expansion from the distilled spirits and hardware brands were not as dramatic. But with their powerful cash generation, spirits and hardware both provided substantially faster growth in pretax income.

For the distilled spirits brands, the company made major investments to enhance prospects. Marketing spending, for instance, jumped 17 percent. Jim Beam, the number one bourbon in the world, sold over 5 million cases, and its export sales set a record.

The very profitable Small Batch Bourbon Collection of ultrapremium bourbons posted a 36 percent worldwide case increase, led by a 63 percent gain for Knob Creek. In the fast-growing premium cordial category, After Shock, introduced in 1995, and Avalanche Blue, introduced in June of 1996, together shipped 250,000 cases. In international markets, private label Scotch whisky volume grew 18 percent.

The hardware and home improvement brands are also positioned well. Moen is the number one faucet brand in North America. Aristokraft is the number two kitchen and bath cabinet manufacturer. Both scored double-digit earnings gains, and Moen widened its U.S. market share lead over the number two brand.

Aristokraft had an exceptional year in 1996, with an 18 percent sales gain by the semicustom Decora line. Waterloo, the world's leading maker of tool-storage products, also posted a strong increase. Master Lock, as noted in the "Shortcomings" section, had rough sledding in 1996. Overall, the profit growth for the hardware brands was a modest 3 percent in 1996.

The golf and office products brands, however, achieved strong advances. The company is number one, worldwide, in both categories.

In golf, Fortune Brands has a solid position. Titleist is the number one golf ball and has a fast-growing position in clubs. Foot-Joy is the number one golf shoe and golf glove by a wide margin. And Cobra is a leader in golf clubs. Profits from these brands increased 49 percent in 1996, reflecting continued solid gains for the Titleist, Pinnacle, and Foot-Joy brands, as well as the January 1996 acquisition of Cobra. The company sold a record 231 million golf balls, up 12 percent over 1995. This also represents a significant increase in market share.

Titleist golf clubs posted a strong 22 percent volume increase in 1996, led by a solid gain for Titleist DCI irons and Scotty Cameron by Titleist putters. Some 70 percent of PGA Tour players wore Foot-Joy shoes in 1996, eight times the share of the nearest competitor. Cobra introduced Ti titanium woods and King Cobra II irons. While startup production problems resulted in lower-than-expected profits for Cobra, its innovative reputation is enhanced by the new products, and management is optimistic about this strong brand.

The office products brands had another excellent year. Profits rose 10 percent. Fortune Brands is the world leader. It grew at a robust pace in 1996 in North America, led by substantial growth in the key computer-related products and accessory category.

However, results for Day-Timer in 1996 were hurt by comparison with strong initial sales in 1995 to the retail channel. Internationally, office products scored double-digit sales growth in Ireland as well as Australia, where the company has the number one position and has been achieving sustained share gains. What's more, margins were strengthened in 1996 and are likely to continue that trend in 1997.

Shortcomings to Bear in Mind

- For Master Lock, the world's number one padlock brand, fierce competitive conditions at mass merchants caused a sharp drop in profits in 1996. The company has taken aggressive actions to support this brand, including a 15 percent average price reduction, effective January 1997 on core padlock products. Management concedes that these actions will reduce 1997 profits, but should enhance longer-term prospects.

- In the 1986–1996 period, earnings per share inched ahead, from $2.09 to $3.20, for a compound annual growth rate of 4.4 percent. In the same ten-year span, dividends per share advanced from $1.02 to $2.00, a compound growth rate of 7 percent. For that reason, American Brands seems more like an income stock than a growth stock. On the other hand, with the restructuring that has taken place in recent years, perhaps this picture will improve.

Reasons to Buy

- Long an icon of American culture, Jim Beam bourbon outsells every other bourbon in the world. Worldwide sales in 1996 again surpassed 5 million cases. Jim Beam's bourbon's legendary heritage is backed by powerfully effective advertising and promotion in domestic and international markets.

  Export sales of Jim Beam bourbon reached record levels in 1996, up 3 percent. In Australia, volume of Jim Beam bourbon, the number one spirit brand, rose nearly 5 percent for the year. Jim Beam premixed cocktails jumped 15 percent. Solid gains also came in selected emerging markets, including the Czech Republic, where Jim Beam bourbon volume nearly doubled in 1996.

  Solid marketing strategies helped the company reach new markets, like the bourbon connoisseurs who favor the Small Batch Bourbon Collection of ultrapremium bourbons produced in limited quantities. These four brands—Booker's, Baker's, Basil Hayden's, and Knob Creek—created an entirely new segment of the bourbon category in 1992 and now hold 50 percent of that ultrapremium bourbon segment in the United States. The entire collection was up 36 percent worldwide in 1996, and Knob Creek, the brightest star of the collection, boosted its worldwide sales by 63 percent.

- In the hardware segment, Moen is the leader in faucets in the United States. Its exceptionally popular Monticello line of bathroom faucets has an appealing design, coupled with durability, helping boost sales nationwide. For example, Monticello is a huge hit with commercial contractors who have selected Monticello for major construction projects across the country. The newest twist to Monticello is the state-of-the-art LifeShine polished brass faucet guaranteed not to tarnish or discolor under even the harshest conditions.

- Among the world's top golfers to play the Cobra brand of golf clubs are Greg Norman, one of the leading golfers in the world, and Hale Irwin, the 1996 Senior PGA Tour scoring leader. Others include Steve Jones, the 1996 U. S. Open Champion, Seve Ballesteros, captain of the 1997 Ryder Cup European team, Beth Daniel and Pat Bradley, members of the 1996 Solheim Cup winning team, and Tiger Woods, the sport's latest sensational star.

- The Titleist golf ball, which has been the number one ball in professional golf since 1949, has an equally awesome record of winning, such as Steve Jones at the U. S. Open, Tom Lehman at the British Open, and Mark Brooks at the PGA Championship.

- In 1996, Titleist was the winning ball in over 150 tournaments worldwide. It was used by more players, won more tournaments, and won more money than all other golf balls combined. Such success with golf Tour professionals drives the growth of the Titleist, Cobra, and Foot-Joy brands around the world. Titleist sold a record 231 million golf balls in 1996, up 12 percent from 1995, with market share exceeding 40 percent in the United States and Europe.

- The Titleist DCI is now the number one iron used by golf professionals and was the number one iron at the PGA Club Championship for the fourth consecutive year. Titleist DCI irons were the number one iron at thirty-six of forty-one PGA Club Professional Sectional Championships, and they were used by the winners of the LPGA Tour, Senior PGA Tour, and Nike Tour championships.

- In the office products realm, the company is the leading supplier with category-leading brands such as ACCO paper fasteners; Kensington computer accessories; Day-Timer time management systems; Swingline staplers; and Wilson Jones binders, indexes, and filing supplies in North America; and ACCOdata and Rexel products in Europe.

- The four operating units of MasterBrand Industries, Inc.—Moen, Master Lock, Aristokraft, and Waterloo—have a major presence in the huge North American hardware and home-improvement industry. The companies manufacture and market primarily kitchen, bath, security, and tool-storage products under some of the best-known brand names in the industry.

Total assets: $9,504 million
Current ratio: 1.05
Return on 1996 shareholders' equity: 15.1%
Common shares outstanding: 173 million

	1996	1995	1994	1993	1992	1991	1990	1989
Revenues (millions)	11,579	11,367	13,147	13,701	14,624	14,064	13,781	11,921
Net income (millions)	497	523	618	686	884	806	745	631
Earnings per share	2.80	2.80	3.06	3.39	4.29	3.91	3.76	3.26
Dividends per share	2.00	2.00	1.99	1.97	1.81	1.59	1.40	1.26
Price: High	50.1	47.3	38.4	40.6	49.9	47.6	41.6	40.9
Low	39.9	36.6	29.4	28.5	39.0	35.6	30.9	30.6

AGGRESSIVE GROWTH

American Greetings Corporation

1 American Road, Cleveland, Ohio 44144-2398 ◻ Investor contact: Dale A. Cable (216) 252-7300 ◻ Dividend reinvestment plan available: (216) 252-7300 ◻ Listed: NASDAQ ◻ Fiscal year ends last day of February ◻ Ticker symbol: AGREA ◻ S&P rating: A ◻ Value Line financial strength rating: B++

Founded in 1906 by Jacob Sapirstein, American Greetings is an international manufacturer and marketer of personal expression products, most notably greeting cards, which generate two-thirds of sales. American Greetings holds the number two position in the United States, with close to 40 percent of the greeting card market.

The company is also a leading producer of gift wrap, paper party goods, stationery, and related products, including gift items, picture frames, hair accessories, and nonprescription reading glasses.

American Greetings operates thirty-one plants and facilities throughout the United States, as well as Canada, the United Kingdom, France, and Mexico.

The company's products are distributed through a global network of nearly 100,000 retail outlets. AGREA's primary channels are mass merchandisers, chain drug stores, and supermarkets, which are the fastest-growing outlets. The company also distributes through card and gift shops and other specialty retailers.

Subsidiaries

American Greetings's consumer products are an excellent complement to greeting cards and make the company a more valuable supplier to retail accounts.

Acme Frames is a manufacturer and distributor of high-quality picture frames, marketed through mass retail channels under the brand names of Profile Gallery and Royal Gallery of Frames.

AG Industries is a designer and manufacturer of custom permanent display fixtures and merchandising systems for American Greetings, CreataCard, the company's other subsidiaries, consumer product companies, and retailers.

Magnivision is the world's largest manufacturer and distributor of nonprescription reading glasses sold over-the-counter through mass retail accounts.

Plus Mark is the world's second largest manufacturer and distributor of promotional Christmas gift wrap, boxed cards, and accessories to the mass retail marketplace. Brand names are Plus Mark and Greeneville Press.

Wilhold is a manufacturer and distributor of quality hair accessory products, designed for the mass retail marketplace.

Shortcomings to Bear in Mind

- American Greetings has a spotty record of growth. In the 1986–1996 period, earnings per share advanced from $1.16 to $2.01, which translates into a compound annual growth rate of only 5.6 percent. In the same ten-year span, dividends expanded from $.31 to $.62, a growth rate of 7.2 percent, which is not exceptional.
- While the domestic greeting card industry is a textbook oligopoly (with close to 90 percent of revenues generated by three companies), operating dynamics with this industry continue to become more difficult. According to analysts, the pressures that are in evidence that limit returns in this business are coming primarily from demands of retailers and the aggressiveness of competition.
- According to analysts, Hallmark continues to aggressively pursue business. Meanwhile, consolidation in the drug-store industry (a traditional stronghold of AGREA) could put some of its business at risk.

Reasons to Buy

- The management of American Greetings appears to be increasing its focus on building shareholder value at a time that the domestic greeting card industry continues to become more difficult. Management, however, now seems determined to shed some of its acquired noncore assets in an effort to increase the focus of the company and build greater shareholder value (in part by instituting a share repurchase program).
- AGREA has gained market share over Hallmark primarily as a function of its established presence in mass retail channels. Mass retail has seen a significant market share increase as consumers are doing more of their shopping at these outlets. One reason is because women purchase 90 percent of greeting cards; since many of them work outside the home, they have less time to

shop and are inclined toward one-stop shopping at a mass retailer, supermarket, or drug store.

- The average age of the U.S. population has been increasing in recent years and is certain to continue. Older people tend to buy more cards than younger consumers.
- American Greetings has a strong balance sheet, with 84 percent of its capitalization in shareholders' equity. Coverage of bond interest is also solid, at nine times.
- American Greetings has produced ninety consecutive years of sales growth and eight consecutive years of net income growth.
- American Greetings licenses its greeting cards, verse, and artwork in seventy-three countries and in twenty-three languages worldwide.
- CreataCard is the world's leader in on-demand personalized greeting cards that consumers make at retail.
- Greeting cards are the company's main business. It generates more than 20,000 new designs every year, all pretested to meet the changing needs of consumers. These cards are delivered to retail outlets on a just-in-time basis. The company has wholly owned subsidiaries in five countries, and it licenses its greeting card art and verse throughout the world.
- Americans purchase 7.4 billion greeting cards each year. To continually increase its market share, American Greetings offers programs that appeal to niche and micromarkets. For example, the company's new Love Talk line appeals to men and women in love, while its new Sabor cards target Hispanic males, 30 percent of whom purchase greeting cards.
- Available for everyday occasions and holidays, flags and balloons are the company's hottest new noncard prod-

ucts. This balloon program is like no other because it is supported by superior merchandiser service. Decorative flags offer an increasingly popular way for consumers to commemorate special occasions and to add a festive touch to their homes.

- American Greetings leads the industry with technology that maximizes sales and reduces operating costs for retailers.
  - The company helps retailers increase their productivity through the use of a variety of technologies.
  - Based on American Greetings' sales results and third-party research, retailers are assured of the best-selling products and a product mix that is tailored to their particular customer base.
- American Greetings is the only supplier to offer value-added programs that increase total store productivity.

  The company's Retail Creative Services department creates store-decor packages and seasonal spectaculars that help retailers create holiday excitement in their stores.

- American Greetings delivers superior retail sales performance.
  - The company uses a variety of advanced research techniques to determine how its specific products and entire greeting card department compare to the competition.
  - Through third-party validation, side-by-side testing at retail, and analyzing point-of-sale data, American Greetings continue to prove that the company delivers the very best performance.
- American Greetings is the industry leader with programs that drive customers to the store and create additional sales.
  - In 1996, the company strengthened its position as the birthday company by placing celebrity birthday ads in

such popular consumer magazines as *Redbook* and *People*. Each month the company features new celebrities and makes a donation in their name to the charity of their choice.

- American Greetings continues to offer Store-Smart Marketing signs that direct shoppers to the greeting card department.

■ Over the years, American Greetings has pioneered products that mirror a changing society, including military cards, studio cards, and soft-touch cards. What's more, the company has also created some unforgettable characters such as Holly Hobbie, Strawberry Shortcake, Care Bears, Peppermint Rose, and its newest, Birthday Bear.

In 1996, the company strengthened its leadership position as the premier innovator. Its most exciting new products include the following:

- Mylar Balloons. American Greetings is taking ownership of this expanding product category with unparalleled expertise in creativity, design, and merchandising that has made this a big hit at retail.
- Love Talk is a new card line celebrating romance and the differences between men and women.
- Baobab Tree is an exciting new card line for the growing African-American market.
- Sabor is a new line of humorous cards for the Hispanic market.

- A Wonderful Year is a card line featuring fun facts about the year in which people were born.
- Hey, That's Me is a colorful alternative birthday card line for children featuring pop-up names.

■ With CreataCard, American Greetings pioneered on-demand, personalized greeting cards that consumers make quickly and conveniently in stores. Today, more than three years after the company launched CreataCard, American Greetings is the undisputed leader in this growing business, with 10,000 interactive kiosks operating in stores all over the United States and selected foreign markets. Improved merchandising and marketing, a better product mix, upgrades in the computer software and better positioning of the kiosks at retail should boost the performance of CreataCard as it becomes a profitable business.

■ In the future, consumers may shop more extensively using interactive television, personal computers, and CD-ROMs. American Greetings fully intends to maintain its leadership role in helping people exchange personal sentiment. The company's technology-based businesses will complement its traditional business, attract new consumers, and generate additional growth for American Greetings.

Total assets: $2,319 million
Current ratio: 1.96
Common shares outstanding: 75 million
Return on 1996 shareholders' equity: 9.6%

	1996	1995	1994	1993	1992	1991	1990	1989
Revenues (millions)	2,003	1,869	1,770	1,672	1,554	1,413	1,287	1,253
Net income (millions)	75	149	131	112	98	83	72	44
Earnings per share	2.01	2.00	1.77	1.55	1.40	1.31	1.13	.69
Dividends per share	.62	.53	.48	.42	.38	.35	.33	.33
Price: High	30.5	31.1	34.0	34.3	26.2	20.8	18.7	18.6
Low	23.5	25.8	25.9	22.5	18.6	15.5	13.3	10.2

GROWTH AND INCOME

American Home Products Corporation

Five Giralda Farms, Madison, NJ 07940 ◻ Listed: NYSE ◻ Investor contact: Thomas G. Cavanagh (201) 660-5706 ◻ Dividend reinvestment plan available: (800) 565-2067 ◻ Ticker symbol: AHP ◻ S&P rating: A+ ◻ Value Line financial strength rating: A+

American Home Products is a global leader in discovering and commercializing innovative, cost-effective healthcare and agricultural products.

AHP's broad, growing lines of prescription drugs, vaccines, nutritionals, over-the-counter medications, and medical devices benefit healthcare worldwide. Among the company's leading products are such names as Triphasal, Norplant, Premarin, Cordarone, Redux, Naprelan, Orudis, Advil, Anacin, Dimetap, Robitussin, Preparation H, Centrum vitamins, Primatene, SMA, Lodine, and Effexor.

In 1996, the company achieved record sales and earnings, and the dividend was increased for the forty-fifth consecutive year.

In 1996, sales results were mixed in the company's five divisions. The largest division, Pharmaceuticals (56 percent of total corporate sales), expanded revenues 9 percent. Major products included:

• The new anti-obesity drug Redux, which contributed $132 million.

• The Premarin line of hormonal products, which generated $1 billion in sales.

• Lodine, an anti-inflammatory drug that contributed $308 million.

• Effexor, an antidepressant, with $234 million.

• Consumer Healthcare products (15 percent of sales) reported a 5 percent increase in revenues as contributions from new products, such as Children's Advil, were offset by declines in mature products, such as Anacin. Revenues from Advil, the division's largest-selling product, were down 4 percent to $400 million.

• Medical Devices (9 percent) was flat for the year, reflecting difficult industry conditions.

• Agriculture (14 percent) rose 4 percent.

• Food (6 percent) was down 4 percent. This division, which was turning around its performance, was sold to Hicks Muse for $1.2 billion.

Like most drug stocks, American Home Products has risen in price. This is partly because of the benefits of its acquisition of American Cyanamid in 1994, along with the earnings outlook.

Despite declining sales in many older drug lines, American Home Products is benefiting from new compounds emanating from the research and development (R&D) pipeline. Significant savings are also accruing from Cyanamid, especially in drug production, marketing, and research.

By the end of 1997, the company expects to reduce debt by about $5 billion, including over $2 billion from asset sales, with the balance from internal funds. In 1996, AHP divested its food business.

Shortcomings to Bear in Mind

■ One of the company's important drugs is Premarin, a brew of estrogens used to treat the symptoms of menopause. For nearly a decade, Cincinnati-based Duramed Pharmaceuticals has sought Food and Drug Administration approval for a generic version this widely prescribed drug. Standing in the way is American Home Products (and its subsidiary Wyeth-Ayerst Laboratories, which makes Premarin from the urine of pregnant mares). AHP has blocked Duramed by arguing that its generic version of Premarin lacks a crucial ingredient (delta 8,9-dehydroestrone sulfate) found in the brand-name product, and might therefore be less effective. But there's more to the Premarin fight than just the fate of one blockbuster drug. In a growing trend, brand-name companies are using regulatory and legal tactics to delay the approval of cheaper generics. Their favorite strategy is arguing that a generic differs in some key way from the equivalent brand-name drug. For instance, the generic may lack a trace ingredient. Or it may not exactly mimic the way the brand-name drug delivers its chemicals. On the other hand, generics supporters say these differences are immaterial.

Reasons to Buy

- Positive long-term fundamentals include the nation's insistence on quality healthcare, new drugs and devices spawned by rising R&D spending, and benefits from foreign expansion, especially in developing countries. Prospects for nonprescription medications are enhanced by the large number of potential Rx-to-OTC switches in the years ahead.

- In late 1996, American Home Products purchased the worldwide animal health business of Solvay S.A., a Belgian-based multinational corporation. Solvay's animal health business has been combined with AHP's veterinary division, Fort Dodge Animal Health, headquartered in Overland Park, Kansas. Solvay's product lines complement the Fort Dodge business, giving Fort Dodge a greater market presence in Europe and the Far East, as well as strong entry into the global swine and poultry bio-

logical markets. The acquisition raised the worldwide sales of Fort Dodge Animal Health to about $800 million, which ranks it in the top tier of a worldwide pharmaceutical and biological animal health business that approximated $8.2 billion in 1997.

- Generic substitution risk for American Home Products is below average. One-third of the company's current prescription sales come from Premarin, the estrogen replacement therapy (ERT) for menopause and osteoporosis, and oral contraceptives (OC), such as Triphasil and Lo/Ovral. To be sure, both the estrogen replacement therapy and the oral contraceptive franchises are without patent protection. On the other hand, generic substitution has never been prominent in those gynecological markets.

- In late 1995, American Home Products received approval for Premarin MPA, a single tablet combination of Premarin (an estrogen) and progestin for the treatment of menopause and osteoporosis. Hormone replacement therapy is moving away from single estrogen treatments (such as AHP's Premarin) toward estrogen-progestin combinations. This is because those combinations tend to reduce the occurrence of changes within the endometrial lining of the uterus. Premarin MPA could capture over 50 percent of the Premarin franchise, potentially realizing $1 billion earning in the next century. Premarin MPA single tablet was launched in January 1996.

  The two Premarin MPA products, Prempro (patented until the year 2006) and Premphase, are a continuous, single tablet therapy, including MPA for only the last two weeks of the cycle. Analysts believe the approval of Premarin MPA is significant for two reasons:

1. It diminishes the Premarin generic risk. Analysts expect the company to price Premarin MPA at a slight premium to Premarin (but at a discount to Premarin plus Upjohn's Provera) and to aggressively seek to cannibalize sales.

2. Premarin MPA opens up a potentially significant opportunity by expanding the Premarin franchise to post-menopausal women with an intact uterus. In the PEPI study, women experienced a diminished level of cardiovascular risk that was associated with Premarin. However, in women with an intact uterus, there was an abnormal proliferation of endometrial cells (resulting in a 32 percent dropout rate). Premarin MPA opens up this market segment by offering the Premarin benefit without its liability. Analysts look for Premarin MPA to carve out annual sales of $300 to $500 million by 1998.

■ American Home (combined with Lederle, which was part of American Cyanamid) has the biggest primary physician detail force in the United States. In terms of total prescriptions in the nonhospital segment, the company ranks first by a wide margin. Equally important, American Home will be marketing actively in a therapeutic segment where most of the major drugs are generic and where most competitors, therefore, have a passive posture.

■ Although drug companies tend to rise and fall on the strength of their research departments, some of the older drugs are still important. For instance, American Home Products still does well with Premarin. To be sure, the drug has been on the market since 1942. But it was not until the 1980s that scientists showed that it could ward off bone loss as well as symptoms of menopause. That helped Premarin reap $860 million in domestic sales in 1996. The drug is expected to become even more popular as evidence mounts that estrogen replacement helps prevent heart ailments and possibly Alzheimer's disease.

■ Late in 1996, American Home Products purchased 40 percent of Genetics Institute—the shares that it did not already own. Under the terms of the 1992 agreement under which AHP initially acquired a 60 percent interest in Genetics, the company was granted the option to acquire the remaining equity interest. According to John R. Stafford, CEO of American Home Products, "In 1992, we recognized the potential in Genetics Institute to be a premier biotechnology company and the need to have biotechnology capabilities in order to be a top-tier pharmaceutical company." The purchase of these shares will permit the coordination of the company's Wyeth-Ayerst research efforts with those of Genetics Institute.

Total assets: $20.785 million
Current ratio: 1.81
Common shares outstanding: 638 million
Return on 1996 shareholders' equity: 27%

	1996	1995	1994	1993	1992	1991	1990	1989
Revenues (millions)	14,088	13,376	8,966	8,305	7,874	7,079	6,775	6,747
Net income (millions)	1,883	1,338	1,528	1,469	1,371	1,375	1,160	1,102
Earnings per share	2.96	2.21	2.49	2.37	2.19	2.18	1.85	1.77
Dividends per share	1.57	1.51	1.47	1.43	1.33	1.19	1.08	.98
Price: High	66.5	49.9	33.6	34.5	42.1	43.1	27.6	27.3
Low	47.1	30.9	27.7	27.8	31.6	23.3	21.5	19.9

* Excluding nonrecurring items.

American Water Works Company

1025 Laurel Oak Road, P.O. Box 1770, Voorhees, NJ 08043 ❑ Investor contact: James H. Moran (609) 346-8200 ❑ Dividend reinvestment program available: (800) 736-3001 ❑ Ticker symbol: AWK ❑ S&P rating: A ❑ Value Line financial strength rating: A

In addition to being the most capital-intensive of all utilities, the water business in the United States is highly fragmented. Ninety percent of the country's estimated 60,000 separate water systems serve fewer than 3,000 people each and are finding it increasingly difficult to provide the capital required to remain viable and to provide adequate service. Thus, regional approaches are emerging as the preferred solution to the nation's water service challenges.

American Water Works Company, Inc. is a holding company of water utilities. Together with its twenty-three wholly owned water service companies, it represents the largest regulated water utility business in the United States.

Subsidiaries serve a population exceeding 6 million people in more than 700 communities in 21 states, from Pennsylvania and Tennessee in the East and Southeast to Indiana and California in the Midwest and West.

Each is dedicated to providing safe, reliable water service at the lowest possible price, consistent with a reasonable return to investors and fair compensation for employees.

Although some subsidiaries began operation in the early nineteenth century, American's origin can be traced back to 1886, when American Water Works & Guarantee Company was founded. In 1914, the company changed its name to American Water Works & Electric. In response to the Public Utility Holding Company Act of 1935, the company was reorganized as American Water Works Company, Inc.

The American Water Works Service Co. provides professional and staff services to the water companies, each of which operates independently. These services include accounting, engineering, operations, finance, water quality, information systems, personnel administration and training, purchasing, insurance, safety, and community relations. This arrangement, which provides these services at cost, affords each company a degree of support that would otherwise be difficult to obtain on an economical or timely basis.

Shortcomings to Bear in Mind

- The weather plays an important part in the fortunes of a typical water company. They do best during hot, dry summers, since this stimulates the use of water for showers, lawns, and gardens. However, if the weather is excessively dry, the government may step in and ration the use of water for car washing, gardens, and lawns.

  On the other hand, if the region is deluged with rain, there is far less reason for customers to water their lawns and gardens. They may even take fewer showers if the temperature is cool.

  American Water Works, for its part, is not as seriously hurt by a dry summer in one or two of its territories, assuming the weather is not severe in its other jurisdictions. Smaller water companies, by contrast, usually serve parts of a single state or city and are more vulnerable to droughts or other vagaries in the weather.

- A water utility—like all public utilities—is closely regulated by a state commission. Each state has its own commission, some of which are more politically motivated than others. They tend to settle rate cases by favoring the consumer, rather than the company. In recent years, most state commissions have reduced the amount they will permit the company to earn on common equity. Typical awards are in the 11% or 12% range. If the company disagrees with the decision of the commission, it may go to court, in hopes of overturning a harsh award. More often than not, the courts side with the politicians.

American Water Works has to cope with twenty-one different commissions, since it operates in twenty-one states. This has one disadvantage: It means keeping track of twenty-one commissions and trying to keep from offending them or incurring their wrath.

It has an important benefit, however. The company does not stake its whole livelihood on one commission, which may be unreasonable. What it amounts to is the protection of geographic diversification.

- Public utilities fret about interest rates. There are two reasons: For one thing, they borrow a lot of money, and high interest rates boost their costs. Second, they offer investors a good source of income. However, when interest rates rise, some investors may sell their utility shares and go elsewhere to take advantage of the higher interest rates. When this happens, the shares of the utility decline.

Reasons to Buy

- In January of 1997, the board of directors raised the quarterly dividend 8.6 percent, to 19 cents per share. It was the 22nd consecutive annual dividend increase.
- The water utility industry is extremely fragmented, but it is becoming less so as takeovers reduce their ranks. Even so, there are still more than 60,000 independent water systems. Most are owned by financially constrained local municipalities or private investors. The attraction of many of these smaller utilities to the larger water companies is the risk reduction they can provide through geographic diversification.

The smaller entities have another serious problem: Water utilities have had to spend large sums of money in recent years in order to bring their plant and equipment up to the standards mandated by the Safe Drinking Water Act, the Clean Air Act, and other regulations. In this realm, the larger, investor-owned utilities are much better suited to tap the financial markets in order to raise the needed cash to solve regulatory mandates.

To meet today's standards of quality, reliability, and affordability requires ever-increasing technical expertise, financial resources, and operational efficiencies. In this environment, size and financial strength become essential elements in satisfying the water service needs of customers. Yet 90 percent of the water systems in the nation serve fewer than 3,300 people each, and 97 percent serve fewer than 10,000.

- American Water Works has been active on the acquisition front. The company made over fifty acquisitions in the 1990s alone. Most have been privately owned systems. In 1996, American Water Works purchased the water utility operations of Pennsylvania Gas and Water Company, a subsidiary of Pennsylvania Enterprises. This business provides drinking water to about 400,000 people in sixty-two communities in northeastern Pennsylvania. The $410 million purchase represents the largest acquisition of its kind in the history of the water utility industry.

In 1997, the company acquired the Howell Township water system in New Jersey. It serves a population of 16,000.

- Analysts who follow the water utility industry project strong earnings gains for American Water Works for the following reasons:
  - Rate increases to cover the increasing investment needs to provide quality water utility service.
  - Acquisition of small water systems.
  - The provision of services under contract to smaller suppliers.
- The water utility business is less competitive than other utility businesses. For one thing, it is not threatened by the competitive pressures weighing down the electric and telephone utility businesses. Water is a relatively inexpensive commodity to obtain but a difficult one to transport, which makes competition in the industry less likely. Barriers to entry include the immense cost of infrastructure development and necessary proximity to a water supply.
- One of the key characteristics of the consolidation of the water utility business is the demand for high water quality. Unlike any other utility service, water companies must protect the safety of their product because people drink it. Pollution of water sources, better testing technology, and government regulation are requiring additional water filtration, chemical treatment, and extensive water monitoring.

For many water systems, that means skyrocketing costs and greater technical expertise in the operation and monitoring of water treatment facilities. Assuring water quality today requires an ongoing investment in research, construction, testing, and monitoring.

A leader in the water business, American Water and its subsidiaries have long committed the capital and employee resources needed to maintain a high level of water quality across the twenty-one-state system of water utilities.

Recently, new regulation and public concern have centered on naturally occurring parasite contaminants such as giardia and cryptosporidium. American Water Works has reacted in anticipation of these regulations with the incorporation of particle-count monitoring, improved disinfection, and upgraded filtration. In addition, with regulation targeting more stringent control of by-products from the use of chlorine and other chemicals, process modification and alternative disinfectants are being introduced into existing facilities.

Another potential future treatment requirement is the removal of radon from some well water sources. American Water Works has tested every source of well water in its operations and is prepared to introduce either aeration or granular activated carbon filtration when needed.

- The greater technical complexity of water service today feeds the consolidation of the water business. Water systems across the country are being called on to find and develop additional water sources to support community growth, or to replace unusable or inefficient sources. At the same time, computerized water treatment plants require greater operational expertise and scientists, chemists, microbiologists, and engineers are needed to understand and implement new water quality standards.

The 4,000-person professional and technical work force of American Water Works is balanced and has the expertise and includes some of the best talent in the industry for solving water quality, engineering, and operational problems. The company's research scientists and microbiologists have worldwide acceptance and stature. What's more, the company has often been asked by the U.S. Environmental Protection Agency and state agencies to assist in difficult settings and in research.

Total assets: $1,276 million
Current ratio: .47
Common shares outstanding: 77.9 million
Return on 1996 shareholders' equity: 10%

	1996	1995	1994	1993	1992	1991	1990	1989
Revenues (millions)	895	803	770	718	657	633	571	527
Net income (millions)	102	92	74	79	72	76	57	48
Earnings per share	1.31	1.26	1.17	1.15	1.04	1.14	.93	.78
Dividends per share	.70	.64	.54	.50	.47	.43	.40	.37
Price: High	22.0	19.6	16.1	16.1	14.2	13.4	9.8	10.8
Low	17.8	13.4	12.6	12.3	10.3	7.8	6.3	8.4

GROWTH AND INCOME

Ameritech Corporation

30 South Wacker Drive, 35th Floor, Chicago, Illinois 60606 ◻ Investor contact: Sari L. Macrie (312) 750-5353 ◻ Dividend reinvestment plan available: (800) 233-1342 ◻ Listed: NYSE ◻ Ticker symbol: AIT ◻ S&P rating: A- ◻ Value Line financial strength rating: A+

Ameritech is one of the seven regional Bell operating companies, sometimes referred to as RBOCs. More often, these huge companies are called Baby Bells—a bit of a misnomer, since all have annual revenues in excess of $10 billion.

Up until 1984, these seven regional companies were part of American Telephone & Telegraph Co., which has since shortened its name to AT&T Corporation.

For its part, Ameritech provides local phone service in five midwestern states: Illinois, Michigan, Ohio, Indiana, and Wisconsin.

Shortcomings to Bear in Mind

Competitive Access Providers (CAPs) have been chipping away at the Baby Bells' special access market share for several years. These companies, such as MFS Communications and Teleport, target high-usage business customers to offer connection to long-distance companies— thus bypassing local companies, such as Ameritech. These upstarts, moreover, are able to invade the turf of the regional companies because of their low rates. The reason they can sell for less is because they are not required to contribute to the cost of providing unprofitable service to some residential customers—most of whom live in rural areas, which, by their very nature, are unprofitable. The Baby Bells are required to serve all customers, since their service must be universal.

Reasons to Buy

- According to one analyst, Ameritech is the most efficient of the Baby Bells, with only twenty-eight employees per 10,000 phone lines. The industry average is thirty-four employees per 10,000 lines.

- Ameritech now has price regulation in all five states in which it operates. This is in contrast to rate-of-return regulation, which limits the amount of profit that the company can earn. In effect, price regulation rewards cost-cutting and efficiency, while rate-of-return regulation does not.

- Sales of Ameritech call management services, Caller ID, voice mail, call waiting, call forwarding, and more, increased 24 percent in 1996. Growth was powered by increasing demand for convenience and mobility in communications, the need to juggle work and family, and the push by businesses to become more efficient and competitive.

    To further accelerate this growth, the company markets Ameritech telephones that make calling features easier to use. What's more, the company offers free trials and attractive packages of services.

- Superior service and aggressive marketing have been successful in enhancing growth in cellular. Ameritech gained more than 620,000 new customers in 1996, bringing the total to 2.5 million. The company now offers cellular service in U.S. market areas with a total population of more than 34 million—including all major metropolitan areas where Ameritech provides local phone service—and the company reaches customers through more than 1,000 retail outlets across the Midwest. Importantly, Ameritech's monthly customer loss rate is less than 1 percent, or half the industry average.

    For the second year in a row, J. D. Power and Associates recognized Ameritech as number one in cellular customer satisfaction in Chicago and Detroit, the company's two largest cellular markets.

- Paging is one of Ameritech's fastest-growing services. The company, moreover, is speeding sales by expanding its distribution channels. In 1996, Ameritech began selling paging services through its consumer sales organization, reaching an untapped market. Plus, the company made it easy for consumers to order pagers and to activate service simply by calling an 800 number. As a result, Ameritech's 1996 customer growth rate nearly tripled, compared with 1995, and paging customers now top 1.1 million. Also helping drive sales growth are new features, such as fax notification, voice mail notification, and alphanumeric paging, which displays word and number messages for customers.

- Ameritech is doing well in directory advertising by adding convenience, expanding distribution, and including more local information. In 1996, the company launched Ameritech Internet Yellow Pages. This online version of Ameritech's Pages Plus directories gives the nation's more than 35 million Internet users an easy way to reach local merchants and more than 10 million businesses.

    In the company's printed directories, moreover, it is customizing its products in each local community to meet the needs of its customers—including maps, zip codes, e-mail addresses, and convenient specialty guides to add value and promote usage. More than 40 million customers and 495,000 advertisers will use Ameritech's Pages Plus Yellow Pages in 1997.

- Nor can we forget the company's largest business, local service. Ameritech added 647,000 access lines in 1996, bringing the total to 19.7 million. Call management services increased 24 percent. Fueling this growth are increasingly mobile, communications-intensive lifestyles that trigger dramatic increases in the use of faxes, PCs, and the Internet, both at home and at work.

    Ameritech is a leader in this market. The company is expanding its array of offerings including its new National Directory Assistance, which lets customers obtain a listing for anywhere in the country simply by making a local call. In addition, Ameritech is becoming an aggressive, disciplined full-service marketer at the retail level. Its network, moreover, is state-of-the-art. Fully 83 percent of Ameritech's customers lines are digital, and 95 percent are served with fiber optics.

- Ameritech's local growth strategy also includes successful marketing of the company's services on a wholesale basis, since most of its competitors will resell Ameritech's network services. Three years ago, Ameritech led the industry in building a full-scale wholesale business. Today, Ameritech serves more than 3,000 network and information providers—including cellular, PCS, and other communications companies—who buy the company's services and use them in their product offerings. In 1996, Ameritech reached long-term wholesale agreements with a number of companies planning to provide local service in Ameritech's traditional areas.

- By adding services that are logical extensions of its core business, Ameritech is able to broaden customer relationships, create new revenue streams, and build exciting platforms for future growth. For example, Ameritech is number one in Canada and number two in the United States in security monitoring, a market that's projected to grow 12 percent a year. The company is building cable TV networks in communities across the Midwest, supported by innovative programming developed through a partnership that includes The Walt Disney Company. Ameritech is also developing in promising growth areas, such as Internet access, managed services for large businesses, electronic commerce, support for call centers and more.

- Ameritech is moving forward on all fronts to enter the long distance business in 1997, pending final regulatory approvals. Long distance is a huge growth opportunity for the company. In 1996, Ameritech served more than 3,000 network and information providers, including cellular companies.

- For some years now, the RBOCs have been fighting off CAPs, who are providing low-cost service to large customers. To their credit, however, the regional Bells long ago became aware that these competitors were hurting their business. To blunt this invasion into their territory, Ameritech and the other Bells have been trimming costs and upgrading their networks in order to compete with these smaller, more nimble upstarts. In addition, they have been diversifying their investment portfolios—investing in international telecommunications ventures and in wireless networks in the United States—to offset the potential negative impact of the erosion of their local market monopolies.

- Although the regulated part of the company's business may not seem very exciting, its cellular operation is something else. The U.S. cellular industry first saw the light of day in 1983. At that time, the Federal Communications Commission (FCC) issued cellular licenses to the telephone companies that enabled them to provide wireless telephony in their existing service territories, or LATAs. For the first time, the RBOCs were able to participate in a competitive and largely unregulated industry. While ownership and control of cellular telephone licenses are governed by the FCC, cellular rates are not regulated like the local telephone rates, and profits are not limited by a mandated rate of return.

The Baby Bells represent a large slice of the domestic cellular industry. At the end of 1996, the RBOCs had an aggregate of some 12 million users on their systems. This represented between 70 and 80 percent of the total U. S. POPs, or potential customers. Most analysts are convinced that cellular offers the industry's greatest growth potential.

Over time, the Baby Bells' cellular operations have provided insight into their ability to compete and their relative fitness for an era of deregulation.

Ameritech has operations largely in the Midwest, one of the most stable economic regions in the nation. This has served the company well through management changes and varying market tactics that were responsive rather than active. Recently, Ameritech has taken the offensive and is pursuing

market share through a more aggressive pricing strategy. This strategy resulted in a strong surge in net additions in 1994, from 274,000 to 439,000, or a total penetration rate in excess of 5 percent. However, analysts point out that Ameritech was late in acquiring properties to augment its franchise. On the other hand, the company did participate in the PCS auctions, paying $158 million for Cleveland and Indianapolis, or $20 per POP. Analysts believe that Ameritech generated cellular income of $275 million in 1994, on 32.5 percent margins. Overall, they estimate that Ameritech's cellular operations amount to 3 to 5 percent of total earnings per share.

Total assets: $23,707 million
Current ratio: 0.55
Common shares outstanding: 549 million
Return on 1996 shareholders' equity: 28.7%

		1996	1995	1994	1993	1992	1991	1990	1989
Revenues (millions)		14,917	13,428	12,570	11,865	11,285	10,983	10,773	10,316
Net income (millions)		2,134	1,888	1,688	1,488	1,318	1,233	1,254	1,238
Earnings per share		3.83	3.41	3.07	2.74	2.46	2.32	2.37	2.30
Dividends per share		2.16	2.03	1.94	1.86	1.78	1.72	1.61	1.49
Price:	High	66.9	59.4	43.1	45.6	37.0	34.9	34.9	34.1
	Low	49.6	39.8	36.3	35.1	28.1	27.9	26.3	23.4

GROWTH & INCOME

Amoco Corporation

200 East Randolph Drive, P.O. Box 87703, Chicago, Illinois 60680-0703　□　Investor contact: Charles K. Koepke (312) 856-6431　□　Dividend reinvestment plan available: (800) 446-2617　□　Listed: NYSE　□　Ticker symbol: AN　□　S&P rating: B+　□　Value Line financial strength rating: A+

Amoco, the fifth-largest domestic oil company, is veering away from its wildcatting strategy of the 1980s and concentrating its oil and gas exploration on proven reserves.

Amoco is a parent company to three subsidiaries that form an integrated oil and chemical enterprise. AN (that's its ticker symbol) is North America's largest natural

gas producer and the seventh-largest U.S. crude producer; it has the third-largest number of refinery runs.

Exploration and Production
Business Activity
● Explores for, produces, and markets crude oil and natural gas worldwide.

• Currently exploring for additional resources in about nineteen countries.

• Major producing areas are Argentina, Canada, China, Egypt, the Netherlands, Norway, Sharjah, Trinidad, United Kingdom, and the United States—specifically the Gulf of Mexico, Kansas, Louisiana, New Mexico, Oklahoma, Texas, and Wyoming.

1996 Highlights

• Successfully bid on two exploration areas and made two crude oil discoveries in eastern Venezuela.

• Discovered major natural gas fields in Egypt, Gulf of Mexico, and Trinidad.

• Began construction of LNG (liquefied natural gas) export facility in Trinidad.

• Initiated drilling program in the Caspian Sea.

• Captured winning bid for half ownership and the role of operator in newly privatized Bolivian oil and natural gas company.

Competitive Advantages

• Low-cost operations.

• North American private natural gas reserve leader; number one in production.

• Large Canadian heavy-oil resources.

• Participating in Caspian Basin development.

• Technological leadership position in 3-D seismic imaging, enhanced recovery, and reservoir management.

• Development of natural gas infrastructure in the Middle East and South America.

• Critical natural gas infrastructure position in North Sea with Central Area Transmission System (CATS).

Petroleum Products
Business Activity

• Converts crude oil into high-quality petroleum products at five U.S. refineries located at Texas City, Texas; Whiting, Indiana; York, Virginia; Mandan, North Dakota; and Salt Lake City, Utah.

• Transports, distributes, and supplies crude oil and petroleum products through one of the most extensive pipeline systems in the United States.

• Markets petroleum products to motorists and industrial customers and offers convenience merchandise and related services to motorists.

1996 Highlights

• Expanded cobranded alliance with McDonald's Corporation.

• Terminated programs to establish marketing operations in Central Europe to concentrate on North American opportunities.

• Opened five Oxxo Express stations in Mexico with more planned for 1997.

• Reduced average daily inventory by 5 million barrels.

Competitive Advantages

• Technological leader in processing of lower-cost heavy crude oil.

• Gasoline brand rated number one in quality in consumer survey for marketing area.

• Achieved leading premium gasoline sales ratio in marketing area.

• Innovative brand management strategy.

• Alliance with McDonald's Corporation.

• Leader in U. S. pipeline operations.

• Cost-effective products supplier from purchase point to delivery.

Chemicals
Business Activity

• Produces purified terephthalic acid (PTA).

• Makes olefins, such as ethylene and propylene.

- Manufactures alpha-olefins, used in plastics, detergents, and synthetic lubricants.
- Produces polypropylene, which is used in fibers, packaging, and consumer goods, and converts it into woven carpet-backing and fabrics and yarn for home, automotive, industrial, and medical applications.
- Produces industrial chemicals used to make paint, caulk, resins, coatings, lubricants, and fuel additives.
- Produces carbon fibers (graphite) and high-performance engineering polymers.

1996 Highlights
- Acquired Albemarle Corporation's alpha-olefins and related business.
- Divested foam products and polystyrene businesses.
- Began operating new PTA plant in Malaysia and expanded capacity at Cooper River, South Carolina, and Geel, Belgium, plants.
- Completed PX joint-venture plant in Singapore; expanded capacity at Texas City, Texas, plant.
- Started up new copolymer polypropylene plant at Geel, Belgium.

Competitive Advantages
- Diverse, highly integrated product portfolio in areas such as aromatics/PX/PTA; refinery feed stocks/olefins/alpha-olefins/polymers and industrial chemicals. PX stands for paraxylene, a precursor of purified terephthalic acid (PTA).
- Geographically positioned to serve local markets at competitive costs.
- Proprietary technologies.

Shortcomings to Bear in Mind
- Amoco does not have an impressive record of growth. Earnings per share have not made steady progress. In the past sixteen years, for instance, there

have been five declines. In the 1980–1996 period, earnings per shares advanced only modestly, rising from $3.27 to $5.69, a compound annual growth rate of 2.7 percent. In the same sixteen-year span, moreover, dividends per share advanced from $1 to $2.60, a moderate growth rate of 6.2 percent.

Reasons to Buy
- Over the past decade, Amoco has become a recognized leader in the refining, marketing, and transportation business. The company has been successful in improving asset allocation, controlling costs, upgrading facilities and operations, as well as in segmenting the business with a focus on results.

    What's more, Amoco's domestic refinery utilization has been at record levels—well above industry averages. The company is the market-share leader in most of its thirty-state marketing region; it is also the leading retailer of premium gasolines. Amoco's customers rank the company's gasoline quality as superior to competitors.
- The unprecedented global trend toward open market–based societies suggests more economic growth. In turn, that should lead to robust growth for the oil and chemical industries, the basic underpinnings of the world economy.
- Amoco is the largest producer of natural gas, as well as the largest private holder of natural gas reserves in North America. This predominance in natural gas has not led to riches in recent years, mostly because of a series of mild winters. On the other hand, natural gas is a premier fuel, primarily because it is clean-burning, which cannot be said of coal, oil, or gasoline. If the United States experiences some frigid winters, natural gas prices will pick up, and producers of this premium fuel will prosper.

- In an expansion into new territory, Amoco submitted the winning bid in December 1996 for half ownership and the role of operator in a newly privatized Bolivian oil and natural gas company. The award gives the company a significant stake in Empresa Petrolera Chaco, which has proved hydrocarbon reserves estimated at 1.4 trillion cubic feet of natural gas and 35 million barrels of oil, as well as the potential for discovering new hydrocarbon reserves.
- During 1996, Amoco continued to expand its presence in the Asia/Pacific growth area. The company began operating a new PTA plant in Malaysia. Another new plant is scheduled to begin operations in 1997 in Indonesia. Amoco has an 80 percent interest in a joint-venture PTA plant in China, which will start production later in the decade. In January of 1997, the company started up a joint-venture PX plant in Singapore. These facilities join Amoco's existing PTA joint-venture plants in Taiwan and South Korea. In addition, the company is expanding plants in Cooper River, South Carolina, and Geel, Belgium.
- Amoco is the world's leading manufacturer of purified terephthalic acid (PTA), the preferred raw material for polyester. Fiber from polyester is used for apparel, home textiles, and applications such as tire cord and seat belts.

Solid growth is expected for polyester containers used for soft drinks, food, and household products. Industry demand for PTA is expected to increase by 8 percent annually through the year 2000, with the highest growth in the Asia-Pacific region. Amoco's wholly owned PTA plants in South Carolina, Alabama, and Belgium and joint-venture plants in Taiwan, South Korea, Brazil, and Mexico have a total annual capacity of 4.1 million tons, about 40 percent of the world's capacity.

- In the spring of 1997, Amoco announced that with the coming of competition to the electric utility industry, the company plans to use its marketing experience in the already deregulated natural gas market to begin a similar operation selling retail electricity.

Amoco is also looking forward to electricity deregulation because of its large internal needs. In Illinois, for instance, the company spends about $25 million a year on power consumption. Companywide, these costs amount to hundreds of millions of dollars a year. The savings could approach 25 percent, according to a company official.

Total assets: $32,100 million
Current ratio: 1.16
Common shares outstanding: 497 million
Return on 1996 shareholders' equity: 18.1%

	1996	1995	1994	1993	1992	1991	1990	1989
Revenues (millions)	36,078	31,004	26,048	25,336	25,280	25,325	28,010	23,966
Net income (millions)	2,834	1,862	1,789	1,753	1,440	1,216	1,764	1,610
Earnings per share	5.69	3.76	3.60	3.52	2.91	2.41	3.48	3.12
Dividends per share	2.60	2.40	2.20	2.20	2.20	2.20	2.04	1.90
Price: High	83.5	71.9	64.1	59.3	53.8	55.0	60.4	55.8
Low	65.0	56.4	50.9	48.1	41.8	45.6	49.3	36.8

CONSERVATIVE GROWTH

AMP, Incorporated

Eisenhower Boulevard, Mail Stop 176-43, P.O. Box 3608, Harrisburg, PA 17105-3608 □ Investor contact: William Oakland (717) 592-6371 □ Dividend reinvestment plan available: (717) 780-4869 □ Listed: NYSE □ Ticker symbol: AMP □ S&P rating: B+ □ Value Line financial strength rating: A++

The world leader in electrical/electronic connection devices, AMP has nearly a 17 percent market share in this $27 billion market. AMP employs 45,000 in 244 facilities in fifty countries.

Well over 100,000 types and sizes of terminals, splices, connectors, cables, cable and panel assemblies, printed wiring boards, electro-optic devices, networking units, sensors, switches, touch-screen data entry systems, wireless components and assemblies, and application tooling are supplied to over 200,000 locations of original equipment makers and service organizations who install and maintain equipment.

The company's growth from sales of $32 million in 1956 (when AMP became publicly owned) to $5.47 billion in 1996 (a 13.7 percent compound annual growth rate) has been achieved primarily by serving growth industries, developing new products, and entering new geographic markets. This growth has been directly linked to the growth of the electronics and electrical/transportation equipment industries.

During the 1980s, the growth rate of the connector market began to slow as a result of price erosion, industry corrections, and market/industry recessions. To continue providing shareholders with an annual growth rate nearer the 15 percent the company once enjoyed, AMP began a program of diversification into related components, connector-intensive assemblies, and total interconnection systems. This diversification strategy, implemented by new product development and acquisitions, significantly increased the potential size of markets addressed by AMP.

AMP products are as commonplace as they are ordinary. If you have a personal computer on your desk at home or in the office, chances are that AMP made some of the components, particularly the cords in the back or some of the sockets that hold those famous Intel chips.

Highlights from 1996
- Sales were up 5 percent, to a record $5.47 billion (up 7 percent in local currencies).
- Earnings per share declined from $1.96 in 1995 to $1.31, after $.58 per share, one-time charges ($195 million pretax). Earnings before one-time charges were $1.89 in 1996 and $2.11 in 1995.
- Restructuring actions were taken to eliminate some unprofitable product lines and consolidate some facilities, reducing employment by 1,000.
- Savings from restructuring are expected to reach $50 million annualized when fully implemented.
- Shareholders' equity increased 1 percent to $2.79 billion; ROE declined to 10.3 percent from 16.2 percent.
- RD&E increased to $579 million.
- Dividend increased 4 percent in 1997 to an indicated rate of $1.04 per share. This was the forty-fourth consecutive annual increase.
- Three new international subsidiaries were formed.
- Seven acquisitions: Cablesa, Ferroperm, Fibernet, Georgetown Cable, HTS, Madison Cable, Parm Tool.
- Highest customer rating for the ninth consecutive year.

Shortcomings to Bear in Mind

- AMP's results in 1996 were hurt by two factors: a slowdown in orders, mainly for terminals and connectors; and lower gross margins stemming from reduced selling prices and underutilization of the company's production capacity.

- A possible problem area could be the consumer electronics segment. Recent surveys have noted the emergence of lukewarm consumer sentiment in the U.S. and European markets. The cause of this is the growing uncertainty among individuals about their financial future, reflecting in part continued corporate downsizing; in addition, no major new product category has been created in recent years, and few new "blockbuster" products have emerged. Instead, companies are relying on exposure to fast-growing markets, particularly the Asia-Pacific region, to boost sales growth.

Reasons to Buy

- Analysts are convinced that AMP will remain the leader in the connector industry. As connection systems become more complex, AMP should remain in the forefront in solving customers' problems. What's more, it is expanding its already excellent position with existing customers, and it is becoming more than just a connector supplier.

  In recent years, AMP has broadened its definition of its interconnection market to include cable assemblies, backplanes, and other value-added components and subsystems. In addition, it has established footholds in emerging markets, such as the Smart House, fiber optics, and communications products and systems.

- With an estimated average annual earnings growth rate of 11 or 12 percent, AMP should grow faster than the connector industry as a whole, as customers continue to shrink their preferred supplier lists.

- In recent years, AMP has expanded into new related product and market areas via its Global Interconnect Systems Businesses (GISB) division, through acquisitions, minority interest investments, and strategic alliances.

  The company has entered into or expanded its offerings of sensors, fiber optic components, cable and wiring assemblies, and panel assemblies, which adds tens of billions in dollars of additional served markets.

- The company has created several unique technology-based systems that allow employees to deliver industry-leading service to customers. AMP FAX, a twenty-four-hour-a-day facsimile service, gives buyers immediate access to more than 70,000 AMP drawings, specifications, instruction sheets, and catalog pages. By following recorded instructions on their touch-tone phones, callers (some 28,000 a month) enter part numbers and within minutes find the documents they requested on their own fax machines. At AMP's Product Information Center, specially trained correspondents use computers with four separate screens to check several sources simultaneously; they answer almost 90 percent of the more than 25,000 calls they receive each month without involving an engineer.

- Mass storage/disk array equipment can store large quantities of data to support midrange, mainframe, database, and networking computer systems. AMP developed a comprehensive, high-density, high-performance connector system with direct involvement with industry leaders EMC, Hewlett-Packard, Sun Microsystems, and Seagate for this fast-growing segment of the computer industry. These connectors allow direct attachment of high-performance disk drives in system enclosures without expensive cable assemblers.

- AMP is the top connector supplier to the regional automotive industry. Sales to this market represent over a third of the regional total. Success in the automotive market has been due largely to increased automobile production, increased number and sophistication of electronic systems per car, and the company's ability to support the profitability and competitiveness of its customers. The ability to support customers' goals has also helped AMP become a top supplier to transplanted computer manufacturers in the region, thanks primarily to global account management and global sourcing capabilities.

- Satellite receiver systems for large apartment buildings, apartment complexes, and hotels require a series of amplifier and distribution boxes to transmit signals to various units. Specially designed multiple coaxial connectors are making these systems more cost-effective by integrating four interconnections into one. Installation time and cost is 10 percent of what it would be if four separate connectors were used.

- During 1996, AMP continued to build a foundation for increased growth and profitability. New products, application machines, and processes grow from research, development, and engineering. This spending increased to $579 million from $568 million in 1995. What's more, patent applications reached a new high and focused on the faster-growing industries.

    Acquisitions, an integral part of the company's strategy, continued. AMP added seven companies that expanded its capabilities in cable, cable assemblies, electrical connectors, and networking/premises wiring products and services.

In addition, the company expanded nearly twenty facilities, established three new international subsidiaries, and opened representative offices in four countries.

- AMP is the first U.S. company to receive an Enterprise Wide ISO 9000 certification. It covers forty-eight North American locations. For the ninth consecutive year, AMP was the top-rated supplier in an independent survey of U.S. connector buyers.

- AMP is over three times larger than the next largest connector company and has between 16 and 17 percent of an industry estimated at $27 billion in 1996. With over 1,600 participants, the industry is highly fragmented with many specialized producers. AMP has by far the broadest range of connection products and geographic coverage. Although worldwide connector industry sales were flat in 1996, a 6-to-8 percent annual growth rate is expected for the rest of the decade.

- Spending on research, development, and engineering for the creation and application of new and improved products and processes has been maintained at 11 percent of sales—$579 million in 1996. This has resulted in a very strong patent position. In 1996, the company received 220 U.S. patents, ranking twentieth among all U.S. companies.

    AMP has over 3,700 patents issued or pending in the United States and over 12,000 in other countries. The company's technical spending creates a steady stream of new products. Over 300 new product part numbers are now issued daily.

    Over 20 percent of current sales are products introduced in the last five years. Over 6,000 AMP engineers, scientists, technicians, and support people occupy over 1.3 million square feet—the most extensive interconnection technology facilities in the world.

- In the first quarter of 1997, backlog climbed $38 million, despite $20 million negative currency effect.
- International sales exceeded $3 billion in 1996. In 1996, AMP established subsidiaries in Israel, Chile, and China (Qingdao) and representative offices in Croatia, Egypt, Russia (St. Petersburg), and Vietnam.

During the 1990s, the company added over 3.2 million square feet of floor space for a current total of 6.3 million square feet in 167 international facilities in 49 countries.

AMP sees great potential for continued geographic expansion in its business. Huge markets are emerging, as many more countries develop a middle class with insatiable demands to obtain electrical and electronic products, to build more advanced infrastructure, and to strengthen their manufacturing capabilities.

Total assets: $4,686 million
Current ratio: 1.73
Common shares outstanding: 220 million
Return on 1996 shareholders' equity: 10.3%

	1996	1995	1994	1993	1992	1991	1990	1989
Revenues (millions)	5,468	5,227	4,028	3,451	3,337	3,095	3,044	2,797
Net income (millions)	415	427	369	297	290	260	287	281
Earnings per share	1.89	1.96	1.76	1.42	1.38	1.23	1.35	1.32
Dividends per share	1.00	.92	.84	.80	.76	.72	.68	.60
Price: High	46.1	46.3	39.7	33.6	34.4	30.0	27.6	24.7
Low	32.8	35.1	28.8	27.3	26.3	20.4	18.9	20.0

AGGRESSIVE GROWTH

Applied Industrial Technologies

3950 Euclid Avenue, Cleveland, Ohio 44115 □ **Investor contact: John R. Whitten (216) 881-8900** □
Dividend reinvestment plan available: (800) 542-7792 □ **Fiscal year ends June 30** □ **Listed: NYSE** □
Ticker symbol: APZ □ **S&P rating: B** □ **Value Line financial strength rating: B+**

Applied Industrial Technologies (formerly Bearings, Inc.) is one of the nation's leading independent distributors of replacement bearings, power transmission equipment, fluid power components, industrial rubber products, and related specialty maintenance items. The new name became effective January 1, 1997.

Nearly a third of the company's revenue is derived from sales of mechanical, electrical, and fluid power-transmission components. These lines include components for belt drives and chain drives, clutches, brakes, conveyor belting, gears, speed reducers, electric motors, pumps, cylinders, motors, valves, and hose.

The company serves a broad base of customers in virtually all segments of American industry—more than 125,000 active customer accounts. AIT's products are sold to a broad array of industrial concerns as well as to schools and universities, hospitals, high-technology companies, agricultural enterprises, or any other entity possessing equipment that contains bearings, power-transmission components, or related items.

About 85 percent of sales are to the maintenance, repair, and operations (MRO) market, with the balance to the original equipment (OEM) market.

While no one single customer or industry accounts for a significant portion of sales, the largest concentrations are in pulp and paper, primary metals, food, lumber, mining, textile, air transportation, and agriculture.

In all, the company has access to more than 900,000 line items produced by more than 2,500 manufacturers.

At the end of fiscal 1996 (which ended June 30, 1996), Bearings had 330 branches, 8 distribution centers, and 30 mechanical, fluid power, and industrial rubber service shops in 42 states.

The Recent Past

In the late 1980s, the company embarked on a program of change to reshape itself into a more efficient and responsive company.

By diversifying its product mix and adding value in the selling process, Bearings (as it was then known) could offer its customers solutions to problems rather than just a part to replace a worn-out one.

In fiscal 1990 and 1991, the company broadened its product line and geographic distribution with the acquisition of King Bearing. In addition, considerable resources were spent on the development of OMNEX 2.0, the company's comprehensive online order entry and inventory management system.

This transition accelerated in fiscal 1992, with the installation of a new management team. During the year, APZ also completed the conversion to OMNEX 2.0.

The OMNEX 2.0 system is among the most sophisticated computer systems in use in the industrial distribution business. Every user on the system has access to the company's inventories nationwide. Pricing,

ordering, and other features, such as substitute products and customer order history, are part of this comprehensive and unique system. New features that help improve customer service, response time, and speed are regularly added to the OMNEX 2.0 system.

Developments in 1996

• In February 1996, the company acquired Engineered Sales, Inc., of St. Louis, an applied-technology distributor of world-class hydraulic, pneumatic, and electro-hydraulic components to OEM markets. Engineered serves the highly competitive aeronautical and farm and machine equipment markets with critical fluid power engineered services.

• The company signed a ten-year master marketing and procurement agreement with EDS SupplySource, a procurement outsourcing service. Through this service—designed to streamline procurement processes for large, national organizations—customers of SupplySource are now able to access the full range of APZ's MRO component technologies.

• Construction was completed on a new regional distribution center in Douglas County, Georgia, near the Hartsfield–Atlanta International Airport. The 155,000-square-foot facility is the company's largest distribution center.

Shortcomings to Bear in Mind

■ More than half of current sales come from nonbearings items, including rubber products such as conveyor belts, hoses, valves, and other fluid-power parts, and motors and transmission gears.

But this approach poses different risks. In the past few years, demand has been high for these maintenance and repair items, but if the economy falters, AIT's sales-growth prospects will slacken as customers cut back on purchases.

In addition, profit margins are being squeezed by AIT's inability to pass on some recent price increases.

Reasons to Buy

- Beyond offering products, Applied Technologies takes pride in its value-added services, such as applied technology selling, inventory management and analysis, maintenance training, and availability of trained product specialists, as well as machining and repair shop services.
- Applied Technologies' core business (replacement bearings for industrial applications) generates excess cash that can be used to help make acquisitions, further reduce debt, and to enable the company to increase the dividend.
- Gaining a bigger share of the fluid-power market is an important part of the company's overall strategy. It is of high priority because the market is growing at an annual rate of about 10 percent, as fluid power gradually replaces older technologies. In addition, gross margins are in the low to mid-30s, compared with the low to mid-20s for bearings. The higher gross margin reflects both the technology content of the products and limited distribution authorizations.
- Product diversification has enabled Applied Technologies to offer its customers a more thorough approach to solving maintenance repair and operation challenges. It has also provided significant opportunities for growth in sales and profitability.

As the replacement bearings business has matured, competitive pressures have forced down the profitability of bearing products. New technologies offer not only access to faster growing markets but also product lines that are more profitable. In addition, the markets in which APZ now competes are estimated at over $20 billion, compared with only $1.7 billion for the bearings market alone.

- Since John Dannemiller become CEO of Applied Technologies a few years ago, the company has been on an acquisition spree. In 1990, for instance, the company acquired a West Coast distributor that handled bearings but also such items as rubber conveyor belts and pumps and valves for hydraulic and pneumatic power systems. Next came Mainline Industrial Distributors of Appleton, Wisconsin, distributor of power transmission products, which also expanded AIT's presence in the Midwest. Other acquisitions followed.

Applied Technologies' wagon is now hitched to some very lively horses. The company's new hydraulic equipment business is growing at 35 percent, with 30 percent gross profit margins. Hoses and conveyor belts are galloping at 55 percent a year and earn 27 percent gross margins. Drive systems, such as chains, gears, and controls, are moving at 24 percent a year, with 25 percent gross profit margins.

- But Dannemiller's acquisitions did more than strengthen APZ's margins. They positioned the company beautifully for the industrial restructuring that has been taking place in U.S. industry. Companies are now trying to cut costs by consolidating suppliers and reducing paperwork. Philip Morris, for example, dealt with thousands of suppliers and was spending over $150 to process each purchase order. It decided to pare its suppliers to an elite list of twelve. The old Bearings wouldn't have had a chance. To be sure, it stocked 250,000 items, but they were mostly different types of bearings. The new Applied Technologies distributes 800,000 items, almost everything you need to keep machinery running. The company thereby retained the Philip Morris account. Other customers—industrial giants such as PPG Industries, Motorola, Chrysler, and Milliken—also threw additional business AIT's way.

Another major customer added in early 1996 is Vulcan Materials, the leading stone-crushing company and an industrial chemicals producer. Bearings will be supplying and servicing Vulcan at hundreds of locations around the country, according to Mr. Dannemiller. One obvious result is sharply higher volume per customer.

Total assets: $404,072,000
Current ratio: 2.26
Common shares outstanding: 12.5 million
Return on 1996 shareholders' equity: 12.3%

	1996	1995	1994	1993	1992	1991	1980	1989
Revenues (millions)	1,144	1,055	936	831	818	814	651	630
Net income (millions)	23.3	16.9	12.7	8.9	3.0	4.3	14.5	18.3
Earnings per share	1.90	1.47	1.12	.82	.28	.41	1.35	1.63
Dividends per share	.54	.47	.43	.43	.43	.43	.37	.32
Price: High	33.8	25.3	25.0	20.7	15.5	15.8	19.0	21.9
Low	24.0	18.3	18.5	13.7	11.2	10.5	8.9	16.0

AGGRESSIVE GROWTH

Archer Daniels Midland

Address: P.O. Box 1470, Decatur, Illinois 62525 ◻ Investor contact: (217) 424-2592 Charles P. Archer ◻ Listed: NYSE ◻ Dividend reinvestment plan not available ◻ Ticker symbol: ADM ◻ S&P Rating: A ◻ Value Line financial rating: B+ ◻ Fiscal year ends June 30

Archer Daniels Midland operates world-wide. It buys, transports, stores, processes, and trades agricultural products, including corn, wheat, soybeans, peanuts, cottonseed, sunflower seeds, barley, flaxseed, sugar cane, and rice. Its customers include virtually every major U.S. food company.

ADM's operations break down as follows:

- Oilseed processing, which includes soybean, peanut, canola, flaxseed, and cottonseed operations that provide protein to the consumer food and animal feed industries, as well as vegetable oil to the food industry and industrial markets.
- Corn milling, which includes HFCS, ethanol, traditional syrups, and bioproducts.

- Wheat milling, which includes rice milling, corn dry milling, and sorghum.
- Other products, which include cane sugar, pasta, barley malting, grain merchandising, private-label pet food, and hydroponics businesses.

ADM's wet milling plants turn a typical bushel of corn (dry basis) into the following:

- 31.0 pounds of starch
- 12.3 pounds of 21 percent protein feed
- 2.5 pounds of 60 percent gluten meal
- 1.5 pounds of corn oil

The starch can be converted either to 33 pounds of sweeteners or to 2.5 gallons of ethanol. In addition, 2 pounds of margarine can be made from the corn oil.

The wet milling industry uses nearly 1 billion bushels (about 28 million tons) of corn every year. This makes corn one of America's most important resources.

As recently as 1979, corn sweeteners made up only 28 percent of U.S. per-capita nondiet sweetener consumption. Today that figure is well over 53 percent, with high fructose corn syrup (HFCS) leading the way.

Since coming into its own in the mid-1980s, HFCS has replaced sugar as the main ingredient in every major American soft drink. It's also used in bakery and dairy products, fruits, jams, and jellies, as well as scores of snacks.

During the past ten years, while ADM has gone through a period of rapid growth, the company has made important changes in the way it operates. Today, Archer Daniels has 165 operating plants, 300 grain elevators, 2,000 barges, and 10,000 railroad cars. What's more, the company's plants are serviced by 15,000 trucks every day. And, on any given day, together with affiliates in Europe, Archer Daniels has 100 cargo ships on the high seas.

Since the mid-1980s, per-capita consumption of grain-based foods has risen 19.8 percent. While this may seem impressive, it appears that the best may be yet to come.

Today, the forces that have driven this increased demand are still in place, forces such as:

- Health consciousness
- Convenience
- Variety
- Ethnic foods
- Population growth, which is likely

to become an even greater factor. According to the Hudson Institute, agricultural output must triple over the next forty years in order to accommodate a doubling of the world's population.

Most of the seventy-five products ADM makes from corn and soybeans are price inelastic, meaning changes in the price of the raw materials can be passed through to the finished product without much impact on consumption.

Ethanol, however, must be priced to compete with products from other raw materials. When corn costs rose due to weather, the company estimates that about $100 million of the increased cost could not be passed on in the past year.

Speaking of ethanol, it has often been described as a product with everything going for it. ADM's ethanol is a corn-derived fuel that reduces air pollution, cleans your car's engine, and helps reduce America's dependence on foreign oil. And unlike fossil fuels, the raw material for its production comes back year after year.

While the vast majority of ADM's ethanol production is used for vehicle fuel blends, the company also has plants that produce neutral grain spirits for beverages, as well as industrial alcohol for fragrances, household cleaners, and other applications. The amount of corn dedicated to ethanol production has risen steadily in the past several years and is today about 400 million bushels.

In June of 1995, the Clinton administration said that it was contemplating an expansion of existing tax subsidies for ethanol. This change, which would be part of a Treasury regulation, is being sought by farm interests and by Atlantic Richfield Co., a major producer of an ethanol variant called ethyl tertiary butyl ether, or ETBE. Expanding tax breaks for ethanol would also benefit ADM, the politically active agricultural giant that produces more than half the ethanol in the United States.

The year 1994 marked the twenty-third anniversary of ADM's entry into corn processing. In 1971, the company's single wet milling plant had an annual processing capacity of 104,000 tons. Today, Archer Daniels has three wet mills, three dry mills, and a processing capacity exceeding 14.2 million tons. The initial finishing capacity consisted of basic glucose syrups and starches. Now, the company offers other starch-derived sweeteners along with fuel and beverage ethanol. What's more, Archer Daniels is a major producer of high fructose corn syrup (HFCS) in the United States. Of nearly 50 million tons of product ADM made from agricultural crops, less than 5 percent was ethanol.

Shortcomings to Bear in Mind

- Since mid-1995, Archer Daniels has suffered through the embarrassment of price-fixing. The product in question is ADM's lysine, which, of course, is not a household word. The assumption is that price-fixing harms the public, but this turns out to be a more dubious proposition than generally realized. For starters, no one is forced to buy lysine, and if lysine makers are gouging, new competitors are free to enter the market. Then, too, lysine is not something that is critical to human survival. Pig farmers can get alone fine without Archer Daniel's lysine. They can easily substitute soy meal or another bulking agent. Having said this, it is true that the federal government has laws prohibiting price-fixing, and ADM was forced to pay a fine of $190 million (including the settlement of civil suits). This was not a huge amount for a company the size of Archer Daniels.
- As is true with any agricultural-based company, ADM's earnings are subject to weather conditions that can impact the price of its raw materials and to government programs and regulations in the United States and overseas. Even so, management has an impressive track record of earnings growth, despite those risks.

- Archer Daniels's earnings are difficult to predict with precision. The commodity nature of the company's businesses discourages even ADM itself from establishing annual budgets. Rather, the company merely strives to run each business as best it can, in view of the existing circumstances of any given week or month. Analysts, moreover, face even more difficulties in forecasting earnings. There are simply too many variables that factor into near-term earnings, including volumes, operating efficiency, pricing, weather conditions, export programs, world trade issues, and raw materials costs as locked in by trading operations.

Reasons to Buy

- ADM grows by continuing to expand its basic businesses: crushing and refining, corn milling, wheat milling, malting barley, and their associated businesses in North America and Western Europe, where Archer Daniels has a strong presence. The crushing of oilseeds remains the company's largest dollar-volume business. Oilseeds other than soybeans are called softseeds. In the softseed business, Archer Daniels expanded its plants at Velva, North Dakota, in 1995. It also expanded its facilities at Lloydminster and Windsor, Canada. The company also plans to operate sunflower and crambe seed plants at Enderlin, North Dakota, and Goodland, Kansas. Along with its Red Wing, Minnesota, flax plant, this gives ADM a strong position in canola, flax, sunflower, cottonseed, peanuts, and crambe seed crushing in North America.
- Archer Daniels's strategy is straightforward: to be a major player in all businesses it enters as well as the low-cost producer.
- Fermentation is ADM's largest and newest research area. Its focus on

production and refining techniques enables the company to produce purified products. The fermentation group is responsible for the products in the BioProducts and Food Additives Divisions, including lysine, Tryptosine, threonine, vitamin C, xanthan gum, riboflavin, astaxanthin, biotin, alpha-amylase, glucoamylase, MSG, citric acid, and lactic acid.

- ADM is very successful when it comes to amino acids product research. In fact, data about ADM Tryptosine, a tryptophan lysine blend, was recently published in the prestigious *Journal of Animal Science*. The data showed that Tryptosine not only increased weight gain and feed efficiency in swine and poultry—just as tryptophan and lysine did—but it did so more cost-effectively.

- Soy protein is another fast-growing area for Archer Daniels. The research group develops new proteins and finds applications for those proteins in various food systems. Exploring the use of soy proteins in dairy-type products such as cheese and frozen desserts is becoming a major new research area. Much of the research continues to focus on soy isolates, soy concentrates, and other soy protein products. Currently, the company is again leading the way by building plants in Decatur, Illinois, and Europoort, Holland, to make isolates, which will improve the flavor of finished products.

- The company depends on a diversity of grain products to offset swings in a single commodity, builds value-added product lines that complement its basic processing divisions, acquires assets at a reasonable price, maintains a strong balance sheet, and actively pursues international opportunities.

- Today, much attention is focused on increased efficiency and improved production. Improving technology, upgrading equipment, and selectively expanding capacity are goals that are consistent with ADM's long-term strategies of being the least-cost and most efficient producer of value-added product lines.

For instance, the company's Gooch Foods pasta operation provides an example of a commitment to increased efficiency. A new production line at the Gooch facility in Steger, Illinois, will increase speed and efficiency in the production of long cuts of pasta, while allowing the expansion of sales into the ever-increasing spaghetti and lasagna business.

- Vertical integration has also progressed rapidly, resulting in many value-added products coming out of the company's river of dextrose and the stream of vegetable oils and proteins.

- In an effort to become a low-cost producer, Archer Daniels Midland controls as many elements of its operating environment as possible. For instance, it produces its own electricity, and owns the bulk of the barges, rail cars, and trucks it needs. In addition, it uses products or by-products of one process as low-cost raw materials for other products. Finally, ADM owns its own steel fabrication plant in Decatur, Illinois, which provides materials for its plant expansions.

- Archer Daniels Midland's corporate culture encourages management to take calculated risks, to hold a long-term view, to disdain bureaucracy, and to control costs. The company does not have a large research staff or budget but is quick to spot and purchase the latest and best research for improved processing efficiencies and for new products.

- Archer Daniels Midland is so huge and efficient and its product lines are so diverse that it can benefit from almost any positive trend affecting worldwide agriculture. Analysts expect the next decade to be prosperous for agribusiness companies for the following reasons:

1. Population growth and rising incomes in developing nations bode well for U.S. agricultural trade. The world population is increasing by an estimated 90 million persons each year. U.S. farm exports are believed to be at the start of a steady climb—rising from $45 million in 1995 to $60 billion by the year 2000. Exports were in a slump following 1981's peak of $43.5 billion. The United States is in a particularly advantageous position for growing and exporting more food, given the amount of arable land and our transportation network infrastructure.

2. Trade treaties such as GATT (Global Agreement on Tariffs and Trade) and NAFTA (North American Free Trade Agreement) will assist exports. NAFTA is particularly important to ADM, in view of Mexico's proximity to the United States and the potential for high fructose corn syrup (HFCS) sales there.

3. Growth in value-added products—especially bioproducts, HFCS, and soybean oil—will bolster margins. What's more, the expanding worldwide demand for meat and poultry benefits Archer Daniels because of increased sales of soybean meal and other feed products.

Total assets: $10,450 million
Current ratio: 2.68
Common shares outstanding: 544 million
Return on 1996 shareholders' equity: 11.3%

	1996	1995	1994	1993	1992	1991	1990	1989
Revenues (millions)	13,314	12,672	11,374	9,811	9,232	8,468	7,751	7,929
Net income (millions)	696	796	484	535	504	467	484	425
Earnings per share	1.21	1.40	.85	.90	.84	.78	.81	.72
Dividends per share	.16	.09	.05	.05	.05	.04	.03	.03
Price: High	23.1	19	19.2	15.8	17.1	17.4	12.9	11.1
Low	15.6	13.6	12.9	12.1	12.1	9.6	8.7	6.2

AGGRESSIVE GROWTH

Automatic Data Processing Inc.

Corporate Accounting, One ADP Boulevard, Roseland, NJ 07068 ◻ Investor contact: William M. Rice (201) 535-7512 ◻ Dividend reinvestment plan not available ◻ Fiscal year ends June 30 ◻ Listed: NYSE ◻ Ticker symbol: AUD ◻ S&P rating: A+ ◻ Value Line financial strength rating: A++

Automatic Data Processing is the largest independent computer-services firm in the United States, with over 375,000 corporate clients. The company's clients include nearly every segment of business and industry, as well as state and local governments.

Automatic Data Processing has three major lines of business:

• Employer payroll, payroll tax, and human-resources information management (56 percent of revenues).

• Brokerage industry market data, back-office, and proxy services (20 percent).

• Industry-specific services to auto and truck dealers (15 percent).

Computerized auto repair and replacement estimating for auto insurance companies and body repair shops and other data services account for the balance of revenues.

Employer Service (ES) is ADP's oldest and largest business, representing 56 percent of revenues. ES provides payroll and employment-related services to about 350,000 employers, ranging in size from 5 employees to over 50,000. Services include payroll processing, payroll software, timekeeping systems, payroll direct deposit, payroll tax-filing, unemployment compensation management, human resource information systems, and benefits administration support.

ADP pays more than 18 million U.S. workers and is five times the size of its largest competitor. Despite this leading position, ADP still has exceptional growth opportunities with a U.S. labor market of 110 million employees.

1996 Significant Events
- ADP continued its unequaled growth record by reporting its 140th consecutive quarter of record highs in both revenue and earnings per share.
- Revenue growth by major business unit was as follows:
Employer Services 18 percent
Brokerage Services 20 percent
Dealer Services 26 percent
Claims Services 27 percent
- Employer Services paid over 22 million wage earners worldwide on payday. In addition, 35 million W-2s were issued to U.S. employees.
- Employer Services electronically moved $150 billion from the firm's clients to 2,000 different government agencies, accompanied by 11.5 million employer tax returns.
- Employer Services acquired GSI, a European computer services company based in Paris. GSI is the European leader in payroll and human resource information services.

- Brokerage Services processed 100 million trades, 38 percent more than the prior year.
- Brokerage Services Investor Communications mailed annual reports, proxies, and interim reports to over 235 million shareholders.
- Dealer Services acquired Sandy Corporation, a leading performance-improvement, consulting, training, and communications company for the automotive industry.
- Dealer Services now has over 16,000 clients using on-site systems and communications networks to manage every area of sales and operations.
- Dealer Services installed over 375 of its new paperless office product called Document Storage and Data Archiving (DSDA), and sold its 19,000th LaserStation.
- Claims Services installed its 2,400th Pen Pro laptop, the industry's first pen-based auto estimating system.
- Claims Services signed pilots or roll-outs of its new bodily injury audit service with twelve of the top fifteen auto insurance companies.

Shortcomings to Bear In Mind
- Although Automatic Data Processing is a superb company, it is rarely selling at a rock-bottom price. Quite often, it sells at a price/earnings ratio of 20 or more. In the 1990–1996 period, its average P/E was about 21. Meanwhile, its dividend yield was barely above 1 percent. Such stocks tend to be volatile and subject to occasional sinking spells.

Reasons to Buy
- In fiscal 1996 (ended June 30, 1996), revenues expanded for the 47th consecutive year.
- Automatic Data Processing currently pays 18 million employees each payday, about 15 percent of the U.S. work force.

It has penetrated 25 to 30 percent of its traditional, mainstream market, employers with 50 to 500 employees. The future objective is to reach this level of penetration in the lower-end payroll market. There are only two major competitors, Ceridien and Paychex, and Automatic is more than four times as large as either of these payroll-processing companies. Recently, AUD acquired the Application Group, a $30-million-revenue client/server payroll software implementation/systems integration firm. It has also acquired WTR, a small benefit consulting company that specializes in flexible 401(k) processing systems for medium-sized businesses.

- Revenues and earnings for Automatic Data Processing are accelerating, helped by the growth in the major lines of business. What's more, margins are widening, primarily as a result of continued productivity improvements, aided by automation.
- The company has achieved a thirty-four-year record of consistent, double-digit quarterly earnings gains, which analysts expect to persist, aided by continuing strength in its main lines of business.
- Automatic Data Processing has an enviable record of consistent growth. In the 1986–1996 period, earnings per share rose from $.36 to $1.57, a compound annual growth rate of 15.9 percent. What's more, earnings per share have increased every year since 1962. In the same ten years, dividends per share expanded from $.09 to $.40, a 16.1 percent growth rate. Finally, book value per share in this period climbed from $2.26 to $8.05, a compound growth rate of 13.6 percent. Dividends have been increased for twenty-two consecutive years.

- The company is sound financially. Long-term debt of $403.7 million compares with equity of $2,315.3 million. Coverage of debt interest, moreover, is an exceptional twenty-seven times. The company is rated A++ by Value Line for financial strength, which is the service's best rating.
- The company has expanded its sights internationally, establishing its auto dealer business in Germany and beginning to move it into Mexico.
- Analysts anticipate that Automatic Data Processing will focus more aggressively on acquisitions. AUD should continue to make smaller acquisitions that complement its current portfolio, but AUD is likely to be on the lookout for a large new business to add to its portfolio. The company's recent purchase of National Bio (with annual revenues of $10 million) represents a foray into health care information systems. National Bio's product for insurance companies allows estimation of bodily injury claim costs and the ability to monitor provider overbilling. AUD plans to extend National Bio's property and casualty insurance client base and perhaps expand the service to areas such as workers' compensation and fraud analysis.
- The company's brokerage business and its interest income tend to hedge each other. As interest rates rise, AUD earns a higher return on its $3-billion float from the tax filing business and $1 billion in cash. For every 50 basis points increase in short-term municipal rates, the company adds about $.06 to annual earnings per share as its investments mature. However, as interest rates increase, trading volume may decline. In sum, the businesses hedge one another, with interest income a slightly larger influence. However, about 60 percent

of Automatic Data Processing's portfolio benefits immediately from short-term swings, with the rest invested in staggering three- to five-year instruments, benefiting over time.

- Various macroeconomic trends are likely to be favorable earnings influences in the coming years, including rising employment, higher interest rates, and healthy auto dealer markets.
- AUD is investing considerably in and achieving strong growth from areas such as brokerage quotation terminals, proxy solicitation services, and auto accident damage estimation.
- Finances are strong, with well over $1 billion in corporate cash, the $3 billion in average daily float from the tax-filing service, and cash flow nearly 50 percent above reported earnings level.
- Momentum remains strong in most of ADP's businesses. New-client bookings

in the payroll-processing segment have been climbing by about 15 percent in recent quarters, and client-retention rates have improved.

- The company is also benefiting from higher domestic employment rates, which have boosted the number of paychecks per client that it processes.
- Another important aspect of this business: The company also performs tax-filing as an add-on service, which results in a $3-billion average daily float; those funds are generating larger revenues as a result of higher interest rates.
- Revenues from auto-dealer systems have risen by 25 percent in recent quarters. Automatic Data has recently acquired auto-dealer data-services companies in Taiwan and Belgium, as well as the insurance-claims operations of Autoinfo, Inc.

Total assets: $3,840 million
Current ratio: 1.74
Common shares outstanding: 289 million
Return on 1996 shareholders' equity: 20.3%

	1996	1995	1994	1993	1992	1991	1990	1989
Revenues (millions)	3,567	2,894	2,469	2,223	1,941	1,772	1,714	1,678
Net income (millions)	455	395	334	294	256	228	212	188
Earnings per share	1.57	1.39	1.19	1.04	.92	.82	.72	.63
Dividends per share	.40	.24	.27	.24	.21	.19	.16	.14
Price: High	45.8	66.9	59.6	56.9	55.5	46.4	30.1	25.4
Low	35.6	57.6	47.6	46.9	38.8	25.0	22.6	17.9

CONSERVATIVE GROWTH

Baldor Electric Company

P.O. Box 2400, Fort Smith, Arkansas 72902 ❏ Investor contact: Lloyd G. Davis (501) 646-4711 ❏ Dividend reinvestment plan is available: (800) 633-4236 ❏ Listed: NYSE ❏ Ticker symbol: BEZ ❏ S&P rating: A ❏ Value Line financial strength rating: B++

Baldor Electric designs, manufactures, and markets electric motors and drives. It also has a stake in speed reducers, industrial grinders, buffers, polishing lathes, stampings, and repair parts.

Industrial electric motors account for about 82 percent of BEZ's business. The AC (alternating current) motor product line ranges in size from 1/50 to 600 horsepower. The DC (direct current) motor product line ranges from 1/50 through 700 horsepower.

Industrial control products, which include servo products, brushless DC and SCR controls, and inverter and vector drives, account for 16 percent of BEZ's business.

Marketing is conducted throughout the United States and in more than fifty-five countries. The field sales organization is made up of over fifty independent manufacturers' representative groups, including twenty in the U.S., with the rest in Canada, Europe, Latin America, Australia, and the Far East. Export and international sales account for about 14 percent of revenues.

Highlights of 1996

In 1996, Baldor Electric introduced its smallest ever servo motor and control. At the top end is BEZ's new 800-HP AC motor and control. Here are some other 1996 additions to the company's product line:

- "All-stainless" washdown motors
- Explosion-proof inverter drive motors
- Encoderless vector controls
- Spindle drive motors
- Chemical processing industry motors
- Multi-axis servo and vector controls
- Crane/hoist industry inverter and vector controls
- Larger (125-to-300-HP) explosion-proof motors
- 50 Hertz metric frame motors
- Washdown speed reducers
- Hollow-shaft speed reducers

Shortcomings to Bear in Mind

- In 1996, the company's revenue growth was not impressive. It can be blamed on the delay in the production of one of the company's new products, the SmartMotor. This programmable motor was introduced in 1995. It was supposed to be ready for production at the beginning of 1996. However, it did not come online until about mid-year and thus did not add much to results in 1996.

But the SmartMotor is likely to be important in the years ahead. The company has received thousands of inquiries since announcing the Baldor SmartMotor. Customers don't see it as merely an inverter bolted onto a motor. It's the most closely matched motor and control available today, in one easy-to-use package. Compatibility problems are simply eliminated, and installing it is faster and less expensive than installing separate motors and controls.

In short, the Baldor SmartMotor offers customers another choice from among its wide range of drive products.

Reasons to Buy

- Over the past ten years, Baldor's share of the domestic motor market has nearly doubled, reaching close to 13 percent in 1996. For many years, the company's strength has been in small integral horsepower motors, from 1 to 20 horsepower. Baldor's goal has been to hold on to and expand that strength, while aggressively increasing its market share in both the smaller and larger horsepower ranges.

The company's strategy is to offer its customers more choices. That means more washdown motors, more explosion-proof motors, more Super-E premium-efficient motors, in more sizes—smaller and larger. No other motor manufacturer gives customers as many choices as Baldor.

- BEZ has a solid record of growth. In the 1984–1996 period, earnings per share climbed from $.37 to $1.29, a compound annual growth rate of 11 percent. In the same twelve-year stretch, dividends per share expanded from $.08 to $.38, a growth rate of 13.9 percent. I used this period so as not to distort the growth rate—earnings dipped from $.37 in 1984 to $.26 in 1986.

- In April of 1997, the company announced the acquisition of Optimised Control Ltd. Based in Bristol, England, Optimised Control is a leading designer of motion control products. This move strengthens Baldor's position as a broad-based supplier of industrial motors and drives. Customers worldwide regard the motion control products of Optimised Control as highly flexible and easy to use.

- Baldor Electric is research-oriented and continually develops new products. It invests nearly 5 percent of sales each year in R&D. An example is the 1996 introduction of motors wound with ISR (Interior Spike Resistant) wire. Baldor was the first and is still the only motor maker to offer this new, advanced wire in all its AC motors of one horsepower and up. The readers of *Plant Engineering* magazine voted motors wound with ISR wire the 1996 "Product of the Year."

   ISR magnetic wire helps Baldor motors withstand up to one hundred times more electrical stress from inverters. The result is longer motor life, reduced downtime, and better overall value for BEZ's customers.

   As an example, in British Columbia, Canada, the forest products industry has begun specifying ISR wire in all motors used in their mills. And almost all new office buildings in British Columbia specify ISR wire in HVAC systems.

- Information is an important competitive advantage for Baldor. The company's CD-ROM electronic catalog, first introduced in 1994, is now in its third edition. It is used by over 30,000 customers. BEZ's Internet Web site, moreover, is visited daily by users around the world.

- In 1997, the company introduced the Baldor Matched Performance drives "sizing and selection" software. This tool helps customers match the proper motor and control for their application. In addition to English, this software is available in French, German, Spanish, and Italian.

- The long-awaited move to factory automation is gaining momentum, which is good news for Baldor. Such core industries as pulp and paper, mining, and petrochemical, for instance, are devising new, more efficient methods of operation. These include applications perfect for Baldor's extensive line of high-performance drives, from logging and sawmilling to textiles and plastics.

- Electric motors and drives are used in virtually all industries. Many of Baldor's new products help open opportunities in new products. Take, for example, the high-precision, robotic positioning needs of medical equipment and semiconductor manufacturers. These represent new and fast-growing markets for Baldor servos, especially the company's new palm-size BSM 50 brushless servo motor.

- Baldor engineers have been working for several years on a line of commercial-duty motors. These motors are designed for use in commercial applications such as ventilation blowers used in shopping malls and fast-food restaurants, where industrial motors are "too much" for the job. Baldor has also developed special flange-mount pump commercial motors. The company estimates the domestic market for these commercial motors to be as much as $400 million.

- Baldor has been promoting energy efficiency since the 1920s, long before it was the popular consideration it is today. In recent years, BEZ pioneered new motor technology development through such products as washdown motors, common keypad language drives, the Baldor SmartMotor, and motors wound with ISR magnet wire.

- Today, the industrial drives business is growing much faster than the motor business. In fact, within a couple of years, the company believes it will be as big as the entire industrial motor business. This nearly doubles BEZ's opportunities for growth domestically and abroad.

  Baldor high-performance drives are now being used in applications previously handled by fixed-speed motors. The result is far greater productivity, flexibility, and reduced operating costs.

- For many years, new products (products introduced in the past five years) have represented about 25 percent of Baldor's annual sales. In 1996, that number grew to 30 percent, and management believes it will continue to grow.

- As noted earlier, Baldor likes to give customers a choice. Today, the company offers two basic types of AC drives. The most common is an inverter. The more advanced technology is the vector. Both can control a motor's speed, but only the vector drive can control the motor's torque, independent of speed, in precise, small increments.

  Baldor vector drives also offer "autotuning." This exclusive Baldor feature automatically matches the vector to the motor it's controlling.

  In 1989, BEZ became one of the first companies to offer a general-purpose vector drive. Today, the company's present generation vectors are one of the fastest growing segments of its drives business.

- Officers and directors own 19.4 percent of Baldor stock—usually a sign that they share stockholders' concerns.

Total assets: $325,486
Current ratio: 3.12
Common shares outstanding: 26 million
Return on 1996 shareholders' equity: 17.1%

	1996	1995	1994	1993	1992	1991	1990	1989
Revenues (millions)	503	473	418	357	319	286	294	282
Net income (millions)	35	32	26	19	15	12	14	13
Earnings per share	1.29	1.12	.93	.69	.56	.44	.54	.50
Dividends per share	.38	.34	.28	.22	.18	.18	.18	.16
Price: High	25.0	26.5	18.1	16.4	12.5	9.3	8.1	9.1
Low	18.5	17.3	14.2	10.8	8.2	5.8	6.0	5.7

INCOME

Banc One Corporation

P. O. Box 710251, Columbus, Ohio 43271-0251 ▫ Investor contact: Jay S. Gould (614) 248-0189 ▫
Dividend reinvestment plan available: (800) 753-7107 ▫ Listed: NYSE ▫ Ticker symbol: ONE ▫ S&P
rating: A+ ▫ Value Line financial strength rating: A

Banc One is a bank holding company that provides a full range of consumer and commercial banking and related financial services. At the year end of 1996, the corporation operated 1,502 banking offices in Arizona, Colorado, Illinois, Indiana,

Kentucky, Louisiana, Ohio, Oklahoma, Texas, Utah, West Virginia, and Wisconsin.

Banc One also engages in credit card and merchant processing, consumer and education finance, mortgage banking, insurance, venture capital, investment and merchant banking, trust, brokerage, investment management, equipment leasing, and data processing.

Shortcomings to Bear in Mind

■ Banc One's acquisition of First USA—a credit card issuer with about $22 billion in managed receivables and 16 million cardholder accounts—has some short-term drawbacks. The company paid a steep price, or more than 5.6 times First USA's book value and 20 times estimated 1997 earnings. In 1997, the acquisition could dilute Banc One's earnings by 7 percent. However, in 1998 the acquisition may no longer be dilutive.

On the other hand, this bold move gives Banc One a good shot at revenue growth. First USA is number three among credit card issuers and could add about 2 percent to ONE's annual growth rate. For its part, Banc One has not been a major player in the acquisition game. Going forward, credit cards are likely to account for 40 percent of ONE's earnings, or far above the 15 percent current level.

Reasons to Buy

■ Over the past ten years, Banc One has recorded the highest average return on assets and the fourth-highest return on equity among the twenty-five largest U.S. banking organizations. In 1996, return on equity was 17.11 percent, an increase from 16.77 percent in 1995. Return on assets was 1.48 percent.

■ Over the past decade, Banc One has increased its dividend fifteen times; in

that span, the cash dividend has grown at better than a 13 percent rate. On January 23, 1996, the company paid a 10 percent stock dividend. That represented the fourteenth 10-percent stock dividend paid since 1968. In the 1986–1996 period, dividends climbed from 41 cents a share to $1.36, a compound growth rate of 12.7 percent. In the same ten-year stretch, earnings per share expanded from $1.06 to $3.23, a growth rate of 11.8 percent.

■ Although Banc One has not been a leader in the realm of acquisitions, it appears to be changing its stripes. In 1996, these are the banks that joined the Banc One fold:

● Premier Bancorp, Inc., a one-bank holding company headquartered in Baton Rouge, Louisiana, joined Banc One on January 2, 1996. Under its new name (Banc One Louisiana Corporation) it had assets of about $6.3 billion, as of December 31, 1995. It operated 150 banking offices throughout the state.

● Liberty Bancorp, Inc., headquartered in Oklahoma City, Oklahoma, agreed on December 28, 1996, to join Banc One. Liberty, with assets of about $2.9 billion, operates twenty-nine banking offices in Oklahoma City and Tulsa.

● First USA reached an agreement on January 19, 1997, to join Banc One. First USA, Inc., is a financial services company specializing in the bank credit card business. Over the past decade, specialized issuers and processors have developed great economies of skill and scale, enabling them to offer broader product lines and pricing options that are not economical for other issuers to match. First USA is well known for its low-cost structure, its marketing savvy, and its cutting-edge technology.

What's more, First USA is the leader among the bank card companies in the United States today.

- The Banc One consolidated finance company is the sixth-largest in the United States, based on assets.
- The bank's automobile dealer finance company has relationships with more than 10,000 car dealerships in the country.
- Banc One's national small business banking group is the third-largest lender to small businesses in the country.
- ONE's education financing division is the third-largest in the nation.
- Early in the decade, Banc One operated eighty-eight separately chartered banks. By January 1997, that number had been reduced to forty-two, with nine states operating under single charters. By the end of 1997, Banc One will be operating with single charters in only eleven states.

    As a consequence, ONE has been able to reduce running-rate operating expenses in all states that have been consolidated to single charters. This activity also permits statewide implementation of new products and services (allowing more choices for customers) that require economies of scale to be practical.

- With a continuing move toward more electronic access, the role that traditional banking centers play is certainly maturing. Of the Retail Group's some 2,200 unique point of access, only 1,502 are banking centers. While the inevitable direction indicates a future less dependent on bricks and mortar and more dependent on technology, the transition promises to continue well into the next century. In the meantime, the branch banking office's role will continue to be transformed to meet the changing needs of the bank's customers. That transformation includes increasing ease of access and presenting a more focused product offering.

    Ease of access means closer proximity to the bank's customers and expanded hours of operation. A focused and consistent product offering means that no matter where customers go, they know exactly what to expect at any Banc One banking center.

- As an important part of the Retail Group, Banc One Mortgage Corporation is offering customers more choices. One of the segment's new strategies offers customers loans from a range of mortgage companies in addition to Banc One. Now customers receive the benefits, but not the hassle, of shopping around. They can be assured of receiving the best terms available from many major lenders.

    In addition, the mortgage operation now tracks mortgage rates and terms and alerts customers when the time is right to refinance. Still more choices are coming up. Beginning in 1997, customers are now able to sign up for the Mortgage Corporation's Internet service to check rates from a number of lenders, including Banc One. Customers are now able to go online to prequalify for a mortgage, use a mortgage calculator to determine how much they can afford to borrow, compare products and rates, and ultimately apply for mortgage loans.

- Banc One Investment management had a good year in 1996. Its mutual fund operation, for instance, grew to $15.4 billion in assets managed, an increase of 41 percent over 1995. This outstanding growth was due to a 275 percent increase in sales of The One Group, its retail distribution channel.

    Of the twenty-six mutual funds in The One Group, over half performed in the top third of their Lipper Universe in 1996. Lipper is a leader in mutual fund ranking. What's more, 60 percent of the fixed-income funds were in the Lipper top quartile and The Group One Intermediate Bond Fund placed in the top ten of all funds in its Lipper cate-

gory. Finally, The One Group Ohio Municipal Bond Fund was ranked number one in its Lipper category for 1996.

Total assets: $101,848 million
Return on average assets: 1.48%
Common shares outstanding: 427 million
Return on 1996 shareholders' equity: 17.1%

	1996	1995	1994	1993	1992	1991	1990	1989
Loans (millions)	73,119	64,391	61,096	52,927	37,453	29,659	20,043	17,658
Net income (millions)	1,426	1,278	1,005	1,121	781	530	423	363
Earnings per share	3.23	2.91	2.20	2.66	2.17	1.92	1.66	1.51
Dividends per share	1.36	1.24	1.13	.97	.81	.69	.63	.57
Price: High	47.9	36.5	34.5	40.7	35.4	31.7	19.9	20.2
Low	31.3	22.8	22.0	29.3	27.9	15.0	11.4	12.2

GROWTH & INCOME

The Bank of New York Co., Inc.

48 Wall Street, 16th Floor, New York, New York 10286 ◻ Investor contact: Nicholas C. Silitch (212) 495-1721 ◻ Dividend reinvestment plan available: (800) 524-4458 ◻ Listed: NYSE ◻ Ticker symbol: BK ◻ S&P rating: B+ ◻ Value Line financial strength rating: A

The Bank of New York is the fifteenth largest bank holding company in the United States, with total assets of more than $53 billion at the end of 1996.

The company provides a complete range of banking and other financial services to corporations and individuals worldwide through its core businesses. These services include securities and other processing, credit cards, corporate banking, retail banking, trust, investment management, and private banking and financial market services.

The company's principal subsidiary, the Bank of New York, is one of the largest commercial banks in the United States. It was founded in 1784 by Alexander Hamilton and is the nation's oldest bank operating under its original name.

The bank is an important lender to major U.S. and multinational corporations and to midsize companies nationally. It is the leading retail bank in suburban New

York. The bank is also the largest provider of securities-processing services to the market and a respected trust and investment manager.

The Bank of New York ranks as the ninth-largest commercial bank issuer of credit cards in the country. It also provides cash management services to corporations located primarily in the Mid-Atlantic region.

BNY Financial Corporation is the second-largest factoring operation in the United States and the largest in Canada. (Factoring takes place when a borrower sells his accounts receivable to a lender at some discounted value.) For over fifty years, the company has served the factoring needs of leading designers and manufacturers of apparel, as well as the textile, carpet, service, furniture, electronics, and toy industries, among many others.

The Bank of New York Commercial Corporation specializes in secured lending to a broad spectrum of midsize companies throughout the United States, including retailers, distributors, manufacturers, and service companies. It ranks among the top ten companies engaged in asset-based lending.

The Bank of New York Mortgage Company originates and services single and multifamily mortgages in New York, New Jersey, and Connecticut. Through its nine loan production offices, it offers a broad range of mortgage products and is a leading lender in affordable housing programs.

BNY Associates, Inc., is an investment bank providing a broad range of financial advisory services primarily to middle market companies throughout the United States.

BNY Leasing Corporation is a leading provider of domestic and cross-border leveraged lease products, offering investment capital to major equipment-intensive industries throughout the world. Its Transportation Finance Division originates, invests in, and syndicates an array of asset-backed lending products to the global aviation and rail industries.

Highlights of 1996

Record net income of $1.02 billion exceeded the $914 million earned in 1995 by 12 percent. Record earnings per fully diluted common share also climbed 12 percent to $2.41, from the prior year's $2.15. Return on average assets reached a record 1.90 percent, well ahead of the 1.72 percent reported in 1995. Return on average common equity was also a record 19.98 percent, exceeding the 19.42 percent of 1995.

The company repurchased a total of 48 million shares of its common stock during the year, thereby completing the share buy-back authorizations announced in 1995 and 1996. In December 1996, the company announced an additional share buy-back program of 30 million shares, with plans to complete the repurchase during 1997. Studies show that share repurchases tend to help the stock outperform the general market.

Asset quality improved throughout 1996 as nonperforming assets decreased 14 percent to $254 million. Nonperforming assets have now declined for twenty-two consecutive quarters and represent only 0.7 percent of total loans and other real estate assets. The reserve coverage that the Bank of New York maintained against these assets was a strong 355 percent at the end of 1996.

Shortcomings to Bear in Mind

- BK's loss provision in 1996 shot up to double the prior year's level, due largely to major problems in its credit-card portfolio. However, the Bank of New York has sold its worst-performing block of business. In the future, the bank should be operating with a stronger balance sheet, enabling the loss provision to return to a healthier level.

Reasons to Buy

- The Bank of New York is the number one provider of American Depositary Receipts and corporate trust and government securities clearance services and is a market leader in its remaining businesses, including stock transfer, domestic and international custody, securities lending, unit investment trusts, and mutual funds custody.

  The bank experienced internal growth in 1996 in all of these products, most in excess of 10 percent. High growth rates in these businesses are expected to continue, with American Depositary Receipts, stock transfer, corporate trust, and government securities clearance being particularly strong.

- The Bank of New York is benefiting from acquisitions. In 1996, the bank agreed to acquire the corporate and municipal trust businesses of Riggs Bank and Wells Fargo & Company. BK also successfully completed the conversion process for its acquisitions of the custody businesses of BankAmerica and J. P. Morgan, both announced in 1995.

- American depositary receipts (ADRs) enable U.S. investors to invest in dollar-denominated equity and debt securities of foreign companies and government agencies, and provide the issuers of these securities access to the U.S. capital markets.

Growth in this business has been very strong, driven by the increased globalization of the capital markets. Trading volume for listed ADRs has been growing at a compound annual rate of 22 percent since 1990, and this growth rate reached 24 percent in 1996. Trading volume on U.S. exchanges totaled 10.8 billion depositary receipts in 1996, valued at $341 billion.

Bank of New York continues to lead the industry, establishing 161 sponsored programs for companies in thirty-five countries in 1996 and over 62 percent of all new public sponsored depositary receipt programs. For the last five years, BK's share of all new programs has averaged over 60 percent. The company now issues depositary receipts or more than 1,000 non–U.S. companies in over fifty countries, representing 57 percent of total sponsored programs.

- The bank is a leading supplier of corporate services, handling about 40,000 issues with over $500 billion in principal amount outstanding. The number of issues increased 18 percent in 1996; principal grew 11 percent.
- Growth in the bank's existing book of businesses was strong, with fees up over 20 percent in 1996. Bank of New York achieved a leading position among its competitors, being named trustee on

over 1,600 corporate and municipal issues in 1996, amounting to more than $150 billion.

- As stock transfer agent, Bank of New York provides shareholder record keeping, dividend paying and reinvestment, proxy tabulation, and exchange services to corporate issuers of equity securities.

Demand for individual record keeping services is increasing, with numerous spin-offs creating new public equities. Also, many companies that had performed those services in-house are turning to outsourcing. Add-on services such as stock option plans, dividend reinvestment plans, employee stock purchase plans, odd-lot buybacks, tenders, and exchange offers have expanded and diversified the bank's stream.

During 1996, BK's client base expanded 28 percent in both the number of companies and the number of shareholder accounts. Bank of New York now performs these services for more than 450 companies with over 10 million shareholders. Fees grew 12 percent in 1996, with an expanded customer base providing a solid platform for future growth.

- The Bank of New York is one of the largest custodians for mutual fund management companies, providing domestic and global custody, portfolio accounting, and pricing and fund administration services. In total, the bank acts as custodian for well over 1,000 mutual funds for eighty-three management companies.
- The Bank of New York has consistently invested in the technology necessary to improve its processing efficiency and accommodate incremental volume. As an example, BK designed a personal computer–based information delivery system called *Workstation* that allows

the bank's processing customers to access a range of securities-related data captured by the bank from their own office. Software the bank has developed, moreover, has allowed the bank to adapt this technology for use in virtually all of its securities-processing businesses.

Total assets: $53,649 million
Return on Average Assets: 1.90%
Common shares outstanding: 285 million
Return on 1996 shareholders' equity: 20%

	1996	1995	1994	1993	1992	1991	1990	1989
Loans (millions)	36,229	36,031	32,291	29,600	26,388	26,988	31,972	34,393
Net income (millions)	1,020	914	749	559	369	122	308	51
Earnings per share	2.41	2.15	1.85	1.36	1.06	.32	1.00	.07
Dividends per share	.84	.68	.55	.43	.38	.42	.53	.49
Price: High	36.1	24.5	16.6	15.6	13.7	9.0	10.4	13.8
Low	21.8	14.3	12.5	12.7	7.5	4.1	3.3	9.2

AGGRESSIVE GROWTH

Becton Dickinson and Company

1 Becton Drive, Franklin Lakes, New Jersey 07417-1880 □ Investor contact: Ron Jasper (800) 526-0458 □ Dividend reinvestment plan available: (201) 324-0498 □ Fiscal year ends September 30 □ Ticker symbol: BDX □ S&P rating: A+ □ Value Line financial strength rating: B++

Becton Dickinson is the world's largest manufacturer of syringes, needles, insulin-delivery devices, and blood-collecting devices and a major producer of infectious disease diagnosis systems and high-end cellular analysis instruments.

While Becton is considered a broad-based hospital-supply company, four businesses account for a good 65 percent of total corporate revenues and at least 80 percent of operating profits. These four core operations are the following:
- Diabetes-care products
- Hypodermic needles and syringes
- Blood-collecting devices
- Microbiology products

These products are ubiquitous in almost all healthcare settings. Becton's core business consists of some of the most basic tools used to deliver medical care in the United States (and internationally, to a large extent), so the company carries a high name recognition in the healthcare community.

Reasons to Buy
- Analysts believe that Becton Dickinson can record double-digit earnings gains for at least the next five years. They attribute their optimism to accelerating sales growth overseas, an improving sales mix in the United States, and sharply rising free cash flow, which is being used to make selected acquisitions and in an aggressive share-repurchase program.
- Becton Dickinson has been growing at a solid pace. In the 1986–1996 period, earnings per share climbed from $.66 to $2.11, a compound annual rate of 12.3 percent, nor did earnings dip in any of those years. In the same ten-year span, dividends per share expanded from $.17 to $.46, a growth rate of 10.5 percent.

Finally, book value per share during the 1986–1996 stretch advanced from $4.90 to $10.72, a growth rate of 8.1 percent.

- In 1995, the company launched an automated mycobacteria culturing system, the BACTEC 9000 MB, based on the same fluorescence technology used in the MGIT manual identification system to detect mycobacteria such as tuberculosis. The 9000 MB provides faster time-to-result, with a high degree of safety, quality, and convenience.

- An important element in analysts' more positive view of Becton Dickinson is its accelerating sales overseas, where Becton's major markets tend to be highly fragmented. In addition, the rate of conversion to disposable medical products abroad has been less than half that in the United States.

- Becton Dickinson expects to benefit from increasing demand for its products around the world. Markets such as Latin America, where trade barriers are continuing to fall, and China, which is experiencing strong economic growth, are but two examples of potential growth opportunities for Becton Dickinson.

- After a successful introduction in Europe, Becton Dickinson has received FDA clearance to market the FACSCount system for diagnostic use in the United States. Used in monitoring patients with HIV infections, it is the first clinical system dedicated to obtaining absolute counts of CD4, CD8, and CD3 T lymphocytes. Precise CD4 counts are critical to monitoring the progression of AIDS. As the HIV virus destroys the body's immune system, the number of CD4 cells drops. Because treatments and therapies are prescribed in conjunction with a patient's absolute number of CD4 T lymphocytes, there has been a need for an accurate, precise, consistent, and readily available method of monitoring the number of these cells.

The FACSCount system meets this vital need with a compact, easy-to-use bench top unit that requires minimal setup and training time. The system is designed to reduce the number of steps required to handle samples for testing, thereby decreasing the opportunities for the operator to be exposed to contaminated blood. This FACSCount system is the culmination of years of effort to bring the accuracy and sophistication of the company's cytometry technology to a clinical setting, with a cost-effective system that is now accessible to physicians around the world.

The performance characteristics of the FACSCount system make it the ideal instrument for decentralized testing sites. Among these, the company is aggressively targeting small- to medium-sized hospitals, AIDS treatment groups, small reference laboratories, and public health departments.

- Domestic sales of insulin needles and syringes are expected to increase in the high single digits during the next few years, fueled by the estimated 5 percent annual growth in the number of Americans suffering from diabetes, plus the trend toward multiple insulin injections. Recent scientific studies have shown that the use of multiple daily injections of insulin reduces the severity of the disease's longer-term deleterious effects. Becton Dickinson, which accounts for about 90 percent of the domestic insulin syringe market, has entered into an arrangement with Eli Lilly, the largest domestic producer of insulin products, and Boehringer Mannheim, a major manufacturer of glucose monitoring devices, to provide information to diabetics regarding the best manner in which to control their disease. Over time, this program should accelerate the trend toward multiple daily insulin injections. The company is also reviewing a number of noninvasive techniques to monitor glucose levels in diabetics. This device could reach the market before the end of the decade and further enhance the company's overall position in the diabetic sector.

■ Becton is the leader in flow cytometry, an innovative technology in the area of cellular analysis, enabling healthcare professionals to obtain new information on a wide range of immune system diseases, such as AIDS and cancer.

■ Becton Dickinson's products and instruments for infectious disease diagnosis are used to screen for microbial presence, to grow and identify organisms, and to test for antibiotic susceptibility. Accurate and timely diagnostic information helps target the use of drugs and other therapies, thereby increasing a patient's chances for rapid recovery and reducing total healthcare costs.

■ With a strong base of proprietary technology, Becton Dickinson holds a leading worldwide market position in peripheral vascular access devices for infusion therapy and is an important supplier of components and procedural kits for regional anesthesia.

■ Becton holds a strong market position in hypodermic needles and syringes and pre-fillable systems and offers a wide array of safety products for medication delivery in many areas of the world.

■ As a world leader in evacuated blood collection systems, Becton Dickinson makes products that ensure the safe and accurate collection of blood and other samples to meet the needs of the rapidly changing laboratory environment.

■ Becton's tissue culture business serves research scientists in the academic and biopharmaceutical industries. The company's innovative plasticware and reagents are used to advance the fundamental understanding of diseases and potential therapies.

■ The company's use of computer-aided design and manufacturing technology enables Becton to bring quality products to market faster and at a lower cost. One such technology is stereolithography, which uses a laser system to quickly create a three-dimensional physical object from a computer-aided design model. Engineers can use this extremely accurate model as a prototype, improving both the quality of the product design and the speed of the product development process.

■ Becton Dickinson's new FIRST PICC catheter is a less invasive way to feed fluids, drugs, and blood products into a patient's circulatory system. This type of catheter can stay in the body for a period of weeks, months, or even years, reducing a patient's length of hospitalization and risk of infection.

■ In 1997, the company launched a peripherally inserted central catheter, named FIRST PICC. It is the latest entry by Becton's infusion therapy business, based in Sandy, Utah. The FIRST PICC brand catheter can remain in the body for weeks or months, long after the patient has left the hospital. This makes the catheter an especially attractive choice as customers work to contain healthcare costs by reducing the length of patient stays in the hospital.

■ In 1997, Becton also introduced the BACTEC 9050 instrument, the latest member of the BACTEC 9000 series for continuous monitoring of blood culture vials. Ideally suited for laboratories that process fewer than 150 blood culture sets each month, the BACTEC 9050 system is supported by the same full line of BACTEC media that has made the BACTEC system of auto-

mated blood culturing the system of choice by laboratories for over twenty-five years.

Total assets: $2.890 million
Current ratio: 1.68
Common shares outstanding: 125 million
Return on 1996 shareholders' equity: 20.8%

	1996	1995	1994	1993	1992	1991	1990	1989
Revenues (millions)	2,770	2,712	2,560	2,465	2,365	2,172	2,013	1,812
Net income (millions)	283	252	227	213	201	190	182	158
Earnings per share	2.11	1.80	1.51	1.36	1.29	1.22	1.17	1.00
Dividends per share	.46	.41	.37	.33	.30	.29	.27	.25
Price: High	45.5	38.0	24.9	20.4	21.0	20.4	19.2	15.6
Low	35.4	24.0	17.1	16.3	16.1	14.5	13.9	12.1

INCOME

BellSouth Corporation

1155 Peachtree Street, N. E., Room 14B06, Atlanta, GA 30309-3610 ▫ Investor contact: Nancy Humphries (404) 249-2000 ▫ Listed: NYSE ▫ Dividend reinvestment plan available: (800) 631-6001 ▫ Ticker symbol: BLS ▫ S&P rating: B+ ▫ Value Line Financial Strength A+

BellSouth Corporation, with more than 22 million access lines in nine Southern states, provides local telephone service and long distance access to more customers than any other company in the United States.

BLS markets a full array of telecommunications services to businesses and consumers, including private networks, advanced data services, MemoryCall voice mail, Caller ID, TouchStar services, and other Custom Calling Features.

BellSouth is one of the world's largest wireless communications companies, serving more than 4.8 million cellular customers in major markets throughout the United States and in twelve other countries.

BellSouth leads the industry in Yellow Pages advertising and directory publishing. The largest of the Bell holding companies,

BellSouth had 1996 revenues of more than $19 billion, as well as assets in excess of $32 billion.

Major Accomplishments in 1996

● BellSouth boosted its financial strength in 1996 with record earnings per share of $2.53, before a one-time gain of 35 cents on the sale of paging operations. This was a 12.9 percent increase, compared with earnings of $2.24 in 1995 (before special charges).

● The BellSouth brand stands for convenience, reliability, and value. The company is aggressively communicating that message to customers in the South with a wide variety of innovative advertising campaigns, marketing programs, and sports sponsorships.

● BellSouth continues to hit its two main strategic targets in the international marketplace—expanding its existing operations and expanding into new markets. In 1996, BLS soared past the 1 million mark in cellular customers overseas, inaugurated services in Panama, and increased the company's ownership percentage in Denmark. Already in 1997, BellSouth has acquired majority ownership of Peruvian telecommunications company Tele 2000.

• J. D. Power and Associates' first-ever survey of customer satisfaction in the local telecommunications industry came up with a clear winner in 1996—BellSouth. Then in February 1997, the University of Michigan and the American Society for Quality Control reported that BellSouth topped all others in local telephone services on the American Consumer Satisfaction Index. BellSouth Mobility also won the J. D. Power and Associates Award for the second year in a row.

• BellSouth's new service, BellSouth.net, breaks down the barriers between consumers and the Internet. Within weeks of its launch in August of 1996, BellSouth.net won the loyalty of tens of thousands of Web surfers with its high-quality, reliable connection to the Internet and features such as local home pages that can be customized, Internet tutorials, a Rapid Response Help Desk, and flexible pricing.

• BellSouth fared well on its highly visible commitment to the 1996 Olympic Games. BellSouth's local telecommunications network transmitted all the voice, video, and data during the seventeen-day Olympiad. The company transmitted more than 100,000 cumulative hours of video originating from the International Broadcast Center to television networks around the world without missing a frame. In the Atlanta area alone, the company processed more than 1 billion telephone calls.

Shortcomings to Bear in Mind

■ BellSouth expects to begin broadcasting digital television through wireless cable TV in New Orleans and Atlanta in the fall of 1997 and in other markets in 1998. The advantages of wireless include the potential to broadcast over 100 channels as well as local programming, without installing an expensive network. BellSouth hopes to capitalize on its strong brand name in the Southeast and could eventually give customers one bill for both television and telephone services.

On the other hand, the company is aware that wireless cable TV presents marketing challenges because the service can only be sold to households that are in the line of sight of the broadcasting towers. Homes obscured by tall buildings, high hills, or heavy foliage are ineligible for wireless service. What's more, high humidity has also been a problem with some systems.

One spokesman for BellSouth acknowledged that the company was "making a late entrance into an already competitive market" where it will compete not only with existing cable providers but with digital satellite broadcast companies as well.

Reasons to Buy

■ In 1996, BellSouth became the first telecommunications company to grow by more than 1 million domestic access lines in a single year. The company's wireless operations around the world grew by an unprecedented 1,354,000 customers.

■ BellSouth's first core strategy is to strengthen its position as the South's premier communications company; it accomplished that feat in 1996. For the third year in a row, BellSouth set a record for the number of new access lines, 1,002,000. This expansion is unprecedented in the industry, and the 4.7 percent growth rate is the highest for any calendar year in BellSouth's history.

- In 1996, new retail distribution channels and marketing promotions for Internet access, work-at-home, fax machines, and children's phones spurred record sales of 285,000 additional residential lines. In addition, sales of calling features, such as BellSouth's Caller ID and MemoryCall voice messaging service, continued to grow rapidly. The company, moreover, has activated more than 29 million of these "vertical services" for its customers. Despite this record demand, BellSouth held cash operating expenses in telephone operations to just a 2.7 percent increase, compared to 6.3 percent growth in revenues from network services.

- The company's strategy in the booming domestic marketplace for wireless communications is to continue to expand BellSouth's already strong "footprint" of wireless coverage in the South. In 1996, BLS expanded its domestic cellular operations by 765,000 customers and increased the market penetration rate of its services from 7.1 percent to 8.9 percent. What's more, the company racked up a 24.3 percent gain in net income and achieved operating cash flow of more than $1 billion for the first time, based on its percentage ownership.

- To make it easy for customers to buy its wireless products, BellSouth has always been a leader in distribution. The company is adding to its channels while lowering costs. BLS now has 275 company-owned retail stores. It will provide its customers with bundled wireless and wireline services as regulations permit.

- BellSouth's international strategy is to continue to increase its existing operations and expand into new markets and related network services. The company is taking strengths that are second nature to it in the United States and finding market opportunities abroad that it can leverage these advantages into solid returns for investors.

- BellSouth's share of international cellular revenues topped $971 million in 1996, a 58 percent increase over the prior year. The company's customer base, moreover, nearly doubled, reaching 1,244,000. Even in the face of this explosive demand, growth potential remains strong because overseas markets are in early stages of development, and usage by customers is high. Market penetration by the company's international operations (the percentage of the population that uses wireless phones) is less than one-fourth what it is in BellSouth's domestic markets, and many customers rely on wireless as their primary phone service. For example, the average customer in Latin America spends some 53 percent more per month than the company's typical cellular customer in the United States.

- Long distance is nearly a $7 billion business in BellSouth's territory. The company intends to capture 20 percent market share within five years of entry. In less than a year after the Telecommunications Act of 1996 opened up the marketplace to wireless, BLS earned long-distance business of nearly 1.5 million phone customers. As the law required, the company has opened its networks to competitors, and it will be ready to enter the wireline long-distance market in its region in 1997.

- BellSouth has a disciplined, three-pronged strategy in video services. First, the company is acquiring wireless cable licenses in good markets. BLS has acquired franchises or has talks underway in New Orleans, Atlanta, and Miami. Second, BellSouth will take advantage of the economic growth it has in the booming Sunbelt to selectively build new cable TV systems at the same time it extends its core telecommunications network. Third, the company will compete hard for cable customers where the market potential is clear.

- Investors have been hearing a lot about the new wireless service called Personal Communications Services. BellSouth plans to compete in PCS. Its PCS strategy is simple: Focus on its region and be first to market. What's more, BellSouth was first to market with its 1996 PCS launch in the Carolinas and East Tennessee. The company is marketing under the BellSouth brand and keeping this new digital technology easy for the customer with great features and simple prices. PCS adds 8 million potential customers to the BLS regional wireless footprint. Already in 1997, the company has acquired new licenses that expand its coverage to thirty-seven more markets in six Southern states— cities such as Tampa, Florida, and Savannah, Georgia—and agreed to swap cellular properties in Wisconsin and Illinois for new or increased ownership of twenty-three wireless markets primarily in the South.

- Many investors, of course, are wondering how BellSouth plans to take advantage of the popularity and explosive growth of the Internet. The company's Internet access service, BellSouth.net, is off to an excellent start. BellSouth launched service in eleven markets in 1996, and in just four months the company signed up tens of thousands of customers. The company's CEO, Duane Ackerman, points out that "we are rolling out BellSouth.net service in new markets all the time. Our pricing is competitive and flexible, and our quality and reliability are unmatched. As with any BellSouth service, our customers can get help twenty-four hours a day, seven days a week."

Mr. Ackerman goes on to say that "The World Wide Web is exciting, and the consumer Internet market gets most of the media attention. Just as important, we also have a great suite of Internet/Intranet services called Commerce-Link for our business customers. The history of many huge markets—personal computers are a good example—shows that trend-setting products and applications often establish themselves with customers first at the work place. That's one reason we're extremely attentive to the electronic commerce needs of our large and small business customers."

Total assets: $32,568 million
Current ratio: 0.97
Return on 1996 equity: 22.4%
Common shares outstanding: 993 million

	1996	1995	1994	1993	1992	1991	1990	1989
Revenues (millions)	19,040	17,886	16,845	15,880	15,202	14,446	14,345	13,996
Net income (millions)	2,863	(1,232)	2,160	1,880	1,618	1,507	1,632	1,642
Earnings per share	2.88	(1.24)	2.11	1.79	1.69	1.56	1.69	1.74
Dividends per share	1.45	1.41	1.38	1.38	1.38	1.38	1.34	1.26
Price: High	45.9	43.9	31.8	31.9	27.7	27.5	29.6	29.1
Low	35.3	26.9	25.3	25.2	21.7	22.7	24.5	19.5

GROWTH AND INCOME

Bristol-Myers Squibb Company

345 Park Avenue, New York, N. Y. 10022 ◻ Listed: NYSE ◻ Investor contact: Ms. Sarah E. G. Smith (212) 546-3775 ◻ Dividend reinvestment plan available: (800) 356-2026 ◻ Ticker symbol: BMY ◻ S&P rating: A ◻ Value Line financial strength rating: A++

Bristol-Myers Squibb is a leading, diversified health-care and personal-care company. Its list of products includes ethical (prescription) drugs, over-the-counter preparations, diagnostics, infant formulas, orthopedic implants, as well as health-and-beauty aids.

BMY's product portfolio is deep. The company has sixty pharmaceutical products with more than $50 million in annual sales and thirty-five with more than $100 million. This diversification helped to offset the loss of revenue and profit from Capoten, the ACE inhibitor that is now off patent protection in the United States. Sales of Capoten in 1996 were down 29 percent, to $1.1 billion.

BMY's pharmaceutical categories consist of cardiovascular preparations (19 percent 1996 revenues) such as Capoten, Capozide, Corgard, Corzide, Pravachol, and Monopril. Drugs to treat infections (12 percent of sales) include Duricef, Cefzil, Maxipime, and Videx. Anticancer drugs (13 percent) include Taxol, Paraplatin, and VePesid. Drugs for the treatment of central nervous system disorders (5 percent of revenues) include Serzone and Buspar. Other drugs (9 percent of revenues) include Glucophage for the treatment of diabetes and Estrace, an estrogen replacement preparation.

In the medical devices sphere (12 percent of 1996 sales), the company's Zimmer operation produces hip and knee implants and powered orthopedic surgical instruments.

Bristol-Myers Squibb, like most ethical drug companies, also has a stake in nonprescription health products, such Enfamil infant formulas and analgesics such as Bufferin, Excedrin, and Nuprin.

Finally, among its toiletries and beauty aids (12 percent of 1996 sales), the company is well known for its Clairol preparations, Matrix Essentials and Clairesse hair colorings. It also makes Vitalis, Ban, and other products.

Highlights of 1996

• Maxipime (cefepime), a broad-spectrum cephalosporin antibiotic, received clearance from the U.S. Food and Drug Administration (FDA).

• The FDA granted Pravachol (pravastatin), Bristol-Myers Squibb's widely prescribed cholesterol-lowering drug, an expanded indication for use in patients with elevated cholesterol and heart disease as a means to slow the progression of plaque buildup in the arteries and reduce the risk of heart attack.

• The landmark Cholesterol and Recurrent Events trial (CARE) found that Pravachol reduces risk of recurrent heart attack and death by 24 percent in patients with normal cholesterol who have had a previous heart attack—the largest group of heart attack survivors.

• Zimmer launched Osteobond Copolymer Bone Cement, the first truly new bone cement product in nearly 20 years.

• Zimmer acquired Seabrook Medical Systems Inc., a Cincinnati, Ohio-based manufacturer of heat- and cold-inducing therapeutic products used in the treatment of hypothermia, hyperthermia, arthritis, and sports injuries.

• Bristol-Myers Squibb received 123 product or product line registrations for a variety of pharmaceuticals, medical devices, nutritional products, and consumer products in Central and Eastern Europe, including for Pravachol in Romania, the LCO Logica Hip System in the Czech Republic, and Enfamil in Russia.

• Bristol-Myers Squibb (Guangzhou) Ltd., the company's fourth joint venture in China, was formed to house Bristol-Myers Squibb's personal care business in China.

• Clairol launched the Herbal Essences line of shampoos and conditioners in China.

Shortcomings to Bear in Mind

■ In Bristol-Myers Squibb's medical devices businesses, overall performance was flat, reflecting an increasingly competitive marketplace, more government regulation, and a transition to innovative products that are just entering the market. The company expects that 1997 will see growth of advanced hip and knee prosthetic systems at Zimmer and new ostomy, wound, and skin care systems at ConvaTec.

■ There is also the matter of Capoten, an exceptional drug with low side effects that is used to treat high blood pressure (which physicians refer to as hypertension). Capoten was a pioneer among the so-called ACE inhibitors, but now there are a number of strong competitors. Merck, for instance, has a solid share of the market.

But the real problem with Capoten is the patent expiration, which took place in February of 1996. At that time, generic firms introduced lower-priced versions of Capoten, available under its generic name of captopril. Five companies, including Mylan, Novopharm, and Royce Laboratories, have received FDA approval for the sale of captopril. In addition, Bristol's own

generic subsidiary, Apothecon, has FDA approval to market a generic version of Capoten.

Reasons to Buy

■ BMY's position within prescription drugs, orthopedic implants, over-the-counter medicines, and consumer products provides the company with a solid strategic positioning.

■ The company has four strong businesses, pharmaceutical, nutritionals, consumer products, and medical devices, each of which fields a broad line of high-quality products. These products are first or second in sales in ten of its fifteen largest product lines.

■ During the past two decades, the business environment in which Bristol-Myers Squibb operates has become increasingly complex. The company has responded in a number of ways. It has entered new therapeutic areas, made major commitments to R&D, expanded marketing, and added or divested businesses as needed, culminating in one of the largest events in the history of corporate America, the merger of Bristol-Myers and Squibb in 1989.

■ Bristol's nonpharmaceutical businesses, which include medical devices, nonprescription health products, and consumer products, should outpace the substantially larger pharmaceutical business, in terms of sales and earnings growth, over the next few years.

■ The market for generic drugs is growing rapidly worldwide, and BMY is pursuing a long-term strategy to capitalize on it. In the United States, Bristol-Myers's Apothecon division is a leading generics marketer and has introduced the heart drug nadolol (Corgard is the trade name product) as a generic. In Europe, meanwhile, where growing numbers of prescriptions now are filled with generics, the Pharmaceutical

Group bought an equity stake in Azupharma GmbH, one of Germany's leading generics companies.

- Bristol-Myers Squibb has paid a dividend to its shareholders for an unbroken sixty-four years since becoming a public company in 1933. What's more, the company has increased the dividend each year since 1972.

- Estrace is now the third-best-selling estrogen replacement therapy in the U.S. market, due, in part to the fact that it has the lowest oral dose indicated for preventing osteoporosis.

- Glucophage is a novel antidiabetic agent indicated for first-line or combination treatment of type II diabetes. Type II diabetes is the most prevalent form. It affects over 13 million of the 14 million who suffer from diabetes. Glucophage is believed to work by increasing peripheral utilization of glucose (sugar), increasing the production of insulin, decreasing hepatic glucose production, and altering intestinal absorption of glucose. The advantage of Glucophage over standard diabetic therapy is its action outside the liver. Conventional antidiabetic agents work solely by increasing insulin production. They sometimes lead to excessive insulin levels and associated low blood glucose levels (hypoglycemia), a complication that Glucophage avoids.

- Longer term, Bristol-Myers Squibb may have a big winner in cancer therapy with the monoclonal antibody-doxorubicin combination product, which has shown good efficacy in solid tumors in animals.

- The company's pharmaceutical business, exclusive of Capoten, grew a remarkable 21 percent in 1996, a rate that matches many of BMY's best competitors. What's more, Pravachol reached over $1 billion in sales and continued to increase market share. At the same time, TAXOL (paclitaxel), Glucophage, Monopril, BuSpar, and many other new pharmaceutical products exhibited double-digit growth in 1996. In fact, several of the company's key products grew 30 or 40 percent.

- Sustagen, a nutritious flavored milk-substitute for preschool and school-age children and pregnant or lactating mothers, is particularly popular in Latin America and Asia. As Mead Johnson seeks to standardize the product's formulation, Sustagen has become a cornerstone of the division's efforts to globalize its business.

- In 1996, BMY's Clairol hair coloring business began to retake market share from the competition and is the leading hair coloring company in the United States. What's more, with the great success of Herbal Essences, Clairol also is the fastest-growing hair care company in the nation. Herbal Essences is a line of shampoos and conditioners made from 99 percent natural and plant-derived ingredients. A year earlier, Bristol-Myers Squibb introduced Natural Instincts, the first hair coloring to contain natural ingredients, such as ginseng, aloe, and chamomile.

Total assets: $14,685 million
Current ratio: 1.44
Return on 1996 equity: 46.0%
Common shares outstanding: 501.6 million

	1996	1995	1994	1993	1992	1991	1990	1989
Revenues (millions)	15,065	13,767	11,984	11,413	11,156	11,159	10,300	9,189
Net income (millions)	2,850	2,600	2,331	2,269	2,108	2,056	1,748	1,440
Earnings per share	2.84	2.57	2.29	2.20	2.04	1.98	1.67	1.38
Dividends per share	1.50	1.48	1.46	1.44	1.38	1.20	1.06	1.00
Price: High	58.2	43.6	30.5	33.6	45.1	44.7	34.0	29.0
Low	39.0	28.9	25.1	25.4	30.1	30.6	25.3	22.0

Campbell Soup Company

Campbell Place, Camden, New Jersey 08103-1799 □ Investor contact: Leonard F. Griehs (609) 342-6428 □ Dividend reinvestment plan available: (201) 324-0498 □ Listed: NYSE □ Fiscal year ends about July 31 □ Ticker symbol: CPB □ S&P rating: B+ □ Value Line financial strength rating: A+

Campbell Soup Company originated in Camden, New Jersey, in 1869 as a canned-food processor. The business formed by Abram Anderson and Joseph Campbell, known as the Joseph A. Campbell Preserve Company, canned tomatoes, vegetables, jellies, soups, condiments, and mincemeat.

In 1897, Dr. John T. Dorrance joined his uncle's business and quickly made his mark on history with the development of condensed soup. By eliminating the water in canned soup, he lowered the costs for packaging, shipping, and storage. The company was able to offer a 10 1/2-ounce can of Campbell's Condensed Soup for a dime, compared with more than 30 cents for a typical 32-ounce can of soup.

The product became so popular with Americans that in 1922, the company formally included "Soup" as its middle name and incorporated in New Jersey as Campbell Soup Company.

In 1994, Campbell Soup Company celebrated 125 years of satisfying American appetites. Some of the most popular varieties enjoyed by generations still hold a warm spot with soup lovers today: Tomato Soup, introduced in 1897, is the third most popular soup; Chicken Noodle and Cream of Mushroom, both introduced in 1934, hold first and second positions in popularity, respectively, and are among the six best-selling grocery items in the country. Combined, Americans consume about 2.5 billion bowls of these three soups alone each year.

The idea to use condensed soups in recipes originated in a cookbook entitled *Helps for The Hostess* published in 1916. Recipes developed after World War II,

such as "Green Bean Bake" and "Glorified Chicken," fed scores of baby boomers and have become classic dishes that live on today.

Cooking with soup remains so popular that Americans use more than 440 million cans each year in a variety of recipes. Moreover, soup ranks behind only meat/poultry, pasta, and seasonings/spices as the ingredient most often used to prepare dinner.

The three major operating components of Campbell Soup are:

● U.S. Operations, which includes U.S. Soup, Frozen Foods, Meal Enhancement Group, and Global Foodservice

● International Grocery Division, which includes Global Soup, Swift-Armour, as well as operations in a host of countries

● Bakery and Confectionery, which includes Pepperidge Farm, Arnotts, Godiva Chocolatier, and Continental Sweets.

Frozen Foods Group

In 1955, the company acquired the Omaha-based C. A. Swanson and Sons, the creators of TV dinners, known nationwide for its first frozen dinner that consisted of sliced turkey and gravy on cornbread dressing with buttered peas and whipped sweet potatoes. Sales took off, and 7 million dinners were sold.

In addition to the original line of Swanson frozen dinners and pot pies, the company's frozen brands grew to include Great Starts breakfasts, Fun Feasts kids' dinners, and Hungry Man dinners.

In 1982, Campbell Soup Company added Mrs. Paul's frozen seafood and specialty vegetable products to its mix. Mrs. Paul's Kitchens, Inc., was the brainchild of a Philadelphia entrepreneur, Edward Piszek. Freezing food was a new concept in the late 1930s and early 1940s, but Piszek saw the potential for frozen foods when industry production doubled after World War II. By the early 1980s, with Americans becoming more aware of diet and the health benefits to be gained from fish, Piszek saw that Mrs. Paul's Kitchens needed fresh support to sustain growth. Campbell's Soup acquisition of Mrs. Paul's Kitchens, Inc., enabled Mrs. Paul's to become one of the top brands in the frozen food category.

Meal Enhancement Group

Vlasic Foods, Inc., began in 1916 as a family-owned business, started by an immigrant cheesemaker from Austria. Long recognized for their authentic Eastern European flavor, Vlasic pickles received national attention in the 1970s with the appearance of its successful television ad campaign that introduced the Vlasic Stork, the still recognizable and popular advertising character with the Groucho Marx voice.

Campbell Soup bought Vlasic Foods, Inc., in 1978, and the product line continues to grow with a variety of pickles, relishes, peppers, and sauerkraut. A further extension into the condiment realm also includes Early California brand assortment of olives. Vlasic recently introduced a new product concept, Sandwich Stackers. Sliced long and flat, Sandwich Stackers fit neatly inside sandwiches and provide a crunch in every bite. Today, Vlasic is the number one brand of shelf-stable pickles and olives in the United States.

Another popular Campbell brand is Open Pit Barbecue Sauce. Acquired in 1988, Open Pit includes two lines of authentic barbecue sauces: Traditional Blue Label and Thick & Tangy. Four new varieties were introduced in 1994 to take advantage of continued growth in barbecue-style cooking.

V8 100 percent Vegetable Juice, acquired in 1948, has grown to become one of Campbell's most successful and recognized labels. The recent, upbeat Drink Your Vegetables advertising campaign positions V8 as a delicious beverage, satisfying to a variety of consumers.

Campbell's Pork and Beans has been a part of the product line since the early 1900s, when Dr. Dorrance observed that Monday was a lost production day while workers waited for meats to simmer to the soup stock stage. Pork and beans was added to the production line and canned on Mondays so the plant and the workers would be fully utilized. With about 16 percent of the market, today's varieties include Homestyle Pork and Beans, Old Fashioned Beans in Molasses, and Hot Chili Beans, among others.

Global Foodservice

Campbell's Global Foodservice serves a growing and expanding market for Campbell Soup Company as the away-from-home markets set the stage for global expansion in a variety of venues. Besides the traditional restaurant and institutional markets for mass feedings such as hospitals and schools, the growth of internationally known, popular fast-food restaurants requiring new and creative menu options have expanded this segment for Campbell.

Campbell's global presence in the rapidly growing food service segment is not limited to soups and entrées, but also includes Pepperidge Farm baked goods, snack items, and biscuits. Fresh Start Bakeries supplies the quick-service restaurant market with sandwich buns and English muffins. The Sona and Rowats brands offer canned baked beans, vegetables and fruit products, and pickle products in the United Kingdom. Vlasic pickles and condiments can also be found in the internationally expanding, fast-growing, fast-food market. V8 juice and a line of sauces and gravies complete the picture.

Shortcomings to Bear in Mind

One brokerage house has a negative view of Campbell Soup. It views CPB as in a far less dynamic near-term situation than it was during the major 1990–1994 restructuring period. Unlike companies such as Wrigley, Kellogg, and CPC, whose international positions are already established, Campbell has yet to build foreign infrastructure, which can be time-consuming and expensive.

Reasons to Buy

- Campbell Soup again set new records in fiscal 1996:
  - Sales rose 6 percent to a record $7.68 billion.
  - Net earnings surged 15 percent to a record $802 million.
  - Earnings per share expanded 15 percent to $1.61.
  - Cash from operations climbed to a new peak of $1.21 billion.
- In North America, Campbell Soup has leadership in the condensed, ready-to-serve, and broth categories of soup. Other leaders are V8 vegetable juice, Vlasic pickles, Pace Mexican sauces, Swanson canned poultry, Franco-American gravy, Pepperidge Farm premium biscuits and crackers, and Godiva super premium chocolates. Outside the United States, brand leadership is best exemplified by Arnott's biscuits (Australia), Homepride sauces (UK), Swift pâtés (Argentina), and Campbell's condensed soup (Mexico).
- In net earnings growth, Campbell is the only company to rank in the top quartile of its industry for six years in a row.

- The first strategy of Campbell's business is product innovation and leveraging brand power. Campbell's Chicken Noodle Soup, with 33 percent more meat, is just such an example. So, too, are Vlasic Sandwich Stackers pickles. National advertising for Pepperidge Farm Goldfish crackers drove a 25 percent sales increase in fiscal 1996. New advertising—Live Life on all Eight Cylinders—is driving V8 vegetable juice sales. Innovative marketing has made Food Service the company's fastest-growing division. Campbell's cream soups, like mushroom, broccoli, and celery, now have "all the taste and are 98 percent fat-free."
- A major acquisition was completed in early 1995. Campbell paid just over $1 billion for Pace Foods, the leading domestic producer of Mexican sauces in the United States, with annual sales of $220 million. Pace Foods, the San Antonio–based market leader in Mexican sauces, expanded its presence dramatically in its first full year since becoming the largest acquisition in Campbell's history. From its home in the heart of salsa country, Pace made inroads into new markets by using advertising and sampling to dramatize the authentic taste of fat-free and virtually calorie-free Pace Thick and Chunky salsa. These initiatives boosted sales 36 percent in the U.S. Northeast, where synergies with Campbell's existing sales force had major impact. Celebrating its fiftieth anniversary in 1997, Pace is building ever more loyalty in the Southwest through sponsorship links to the Dallas Cowboys.
- From the days when ads featuring the famous Campbell Kids proudly boasted "21 kinds of soup...10 cents a can," the company has grown to become the market leader in soup, with 80 percent of the wet soup market.

- The familiar red and white label can be found in contemporary versions of soup as ready-to-serve, dry, microwavable, and ramen noodle soups. Other Campbell's soups brands include ready-to-serve Home Cookin, Chunky, and Healthy Request, a specially formulated line that is low in sodium, fat, cholesterol, and contains no MSG. Further components of the soup business also include Swanson canned chicken, beef, and vegetable broths.
- An important element of the total prepared soup market includes the many diverse forms of packaging, such as dehydrated soups in pouches, single-serve cups, and block forms.
- Each year, nearly 99 percent of American households purchase Campbell soups. On average, consumers stock six cans of Campbell's in the pantry at all times.
- Campbell expands its traditional base by keeping track of trends and changing tastes not only in American cuisine but in consumer preferences worldwide.
- With the implementation of ECR (efficient consumer response) initiatives, particularly CPR (continuous product replenishment), Campbell has gained a leading-edge position. Sales are measured and matched against inventory on a daily basis to ensure an unbroken chain of supply from manufacturing plant to store shelf and to avoid a buildup of surplus warehouse inventories. It is the company's form of "just in time" and creates a competitive advantage for Campbell and its customers.

Total assets: $6,632 million
Current ratio: 0.73
Common shares outstanding: 247 million
Return on 1996 shareholders' equity: 30.8%

	1996	1995	1994	1993	1992	1991	1990	1989
Revenues (millions)	7,678	7,278	6,690	6,586	6,263	6,204	6,206	5,672
Net income (millions)	802	698	630	557	491	402	306	13
Earnings per share	1.61	1.40	1.26	1.11	.98	.79	.59	.03
Dividends per share	.67	.61	.55	.46	.36	.28	.25	.23
Price: High	42.1	30.6	23.0	22.7	22.6	21.9	15.5	15.2
Low	28.0	20.5	17.1	17.6	15.8	13.5	10.9	7.6

AGGRESSIVE GROWTH

Caterpillar Inc.

100 N. E. Adams Street, Peoria, Illinois 61629-5310 ◻ Investor contact: James F. Masterson (309) 675-4549 ◻ Dividend reinvestment plan available: (309) 675-4619 ◻ Listed: NYSE ◻ Ticker symbol: CAT ◻ S&P rating: B ◻ Value Line financial strength rating: A

Caterpillar is the world's largest manufacturer of earthmoving machinery and equipment, which generally accounts for over three-quarters of sales and earnings. The company is also a major producer of diesel and natural gas engines and electric power stand-by generation systems.

CAT products include tractors, scrapers, graders, compactors, loaders, off-highway trucks, and pipelayers.

Caterpillar supplies equipment to a number of markets, such as transportation, energy, housing and forest products, commercial and industrial construction, and food and water.

The company is by far the worldwide leader in earthmoving construction equipment and a leader in diesel engines and power-generation systems. Analysts believe that CAT's share is as high as 75 to 80 percent in large bulldozers and loaders. The company's field population may be five or six times larger than that of its largest competitor, which provides a continuous demand for its highly profitable replacement parts.

A Review of 1996

It was the third successive year of record-setting sales and profits. Sales and revenues reached a record $16.5 billion, a 3 percent increase over 1995. Profits reached $1.36 billion, a 20 percent increase over the prior year. Exports from the United States set a record, at $5.5 billion, up 7 percent over 1995.

Sales inside the United States were $7.7 billion in 1996, a gain over 1995 of 3 percent. Higher machinery sales offset a decline in engine sales. Contrary to early projections, the U.S. economy registered moderate growth and, combined with higher construction and mining activity, kept industry demand for machines near 1995's outstanding level.

Turbine sales were up in 1996, primarily in oil and gas applications. Sales of engines to truck and bus manufacturers fell as demand for heavy trucks declined significantly. However, diesel and gas engine sales remained near 1995 levels in other applications.

Sales outside the United States were $8.14 billion, a 1 percent increase over 1995. They represented 51 percent of worldwide sales, down a percentage point from 1995. Sales gained in the Asia/Pacific, Africa/Middle East, and Latin American regions, but were down in Europe/CIS and Canada.

Shortcomings to Bear in Mind

- Caterpillar's balance sheet is somewhat leveraged, since its debt exceeds its common equity. In 1996, these two sectors were about equal in size, which accounts for the financial strength rating given this stock by both Standard & Poor's and Value Line. The reason for this weakness dates back to 1991 and 1992, when the company lost money. Thus, the equity dropped from (millions) $4,540 in 1990 to $1,575 in 1992 but has since rebounded to $4,155 in 1996.

- Among the major machinery producers, Caterpillar derives the highest proportion of its global sales—about 23 percent, excluding Russia and China—from developing markets. Therefore, it has the greatest exposure to any slowing in growth rates for Latin America and the Asia-Pacific region.

- Caterpillar faces formidable global competition from Japan's Komatsu Ltd. On the other hand, CAT's strong performance in 1996 came despite the roughly 40 percent runup in the value of the dollar vs. the yen during a recent 18-month span, a shift that made Komatsu's products more competitive internationally.

- The company has been waging a five-year war with the United Auto Workers over wages and benefits. This tussle remains unresolved. Management says it is committed to this strategy, despite the union's woes. Although the union returned to work in December of 1996, its members refused to ratify the no-frills contract offered by the company. They are working without one.

Despite the uneasy standoff, the union's return has helped Caterpillar meet surging demand. And so far, the company has been able to play hardball with the union and win nearly every inning.

Reasons to Buy

- Not all investors are convinced that Caterpillar can continue to perform well, as they look back to the 1980s when the domestic economy was in low gear, causing CAT's earnings to plummet. Analysts, however, believe that this analogy is flawed. They contend that the operating and competitive environments of the two periods are vastly different. In the 1980s, companies like Caterpillar were selling into markets that were in secular decline. In addition, the currency in the 1980s was overvalued. What's more, Caterpillar during those years was opposed by aggressive, market-share-oriented foreign competitors whose costs were lower than CAT's.

   By contrast, in the 1990s, as a result of restructuring, CAT (with a significantly more profit-oriented corporate structure) is now the world's low-cost producer. Finally, Caterpillar is now selling an almost totally new product line against higher-cost competitors.

- Working faster and smarter than its competitors. That's always been the company's goal. What's more, Caterpillar has accelerated its efforts to achieve it as it approaches the twenty-first century.

   Caterpillar has streamlined the process to introduce new products, reducing it from more than six years to three or less. In 1996, the company introduced forty-eight new or improved products, such as the D11R Carrydozer, the C-10 and C-12 truck engines, and the 793C off-highway truck. Moreover, Caterpillar has introduced a total of 244 new or improved products since 1992.

- A $1.8 billion investment has made the company's factories the industry's most modern, hastening changes to both products and processes. On the other hand, it takes more than manufacturing prowess. A global leader must marshal the forces of new technologies. As a consequence, Caterpillar is working to make things like virtual reality standard weapons in the company's design arsenal. It is now linked electronically with many suppliers, moving designs, releases, and shipping schedules at the speed of light.

   By leveraging technology, coupled with hard work and understanding the customer's needs, Caterpillar is taking distribution and customer support to the next level. Computer-processed orders speed both the manufacture and delivery of products and parts. Satellite-fed information helps technicians provide quick diagnosis and service to products at the work site.

- In the next decade, global competitiveness will separate the leading companies from all the rest. That's why Caterpillar is a leader in the industrial countries. It's why the company has increased its investment in China, the CIS (the Commonwealth of Independent States), and the developing countries of the world—areas that are expected to grow by a least double the rate of industrial countries. The greatest needs—for roads, dams, bridges, and electric power generation (EPG)—are needs best met by the machines and engines of Caterpillar.

   The developing world now accounts for 23 percent of CAT sales. These include Caterpillar Xuzhou, which manufactures excavators in China, and Caterpillar Poland Ltd., which will produce heavy fabrications in Poland. Then, too, there are new dealers such as Wagner International in Mongolia and Jardine Machinery China Limited in China.

- Caterpillar is also expanding its product line, staying close to its core strengths, for example, in agricultural products, where sales have grown fivefold since 1996. Another expanding product line is power generation systems, where business could triple by 2001 and where the company added MaK Motoren GmbH, a world leader in state-of-the-art large diesel engines. In paving products Caterpillar now offers more models than any other manufacturer. Still other areas where the company is doing well include compact machines, where the company is poised to capitalize on its strengths in a fast-growing business. Finally, in industrial gas turbines, sales could double in the next five years.

■ The countries of the world will always be creating new infrastructures or repairing the old, like a new north–south expressway near Kuala Lumpur, Malaysia, or a massive water

reservoir to serve Los Angeles, California. New runways are needed at the airport in Stuttgart, Germany, and new office buildings in Johannesburg, South Africa. Human needs and desires will always require mineral exploration to satisfy the needs of progress in places like the Alumbrera copper mine in Argentina, or the An Tai Bao coal mine in China.

What's more, the world will always need new sources of energy, such as a utility grade powerhouse that uses Caterpillar Electrical Power Generation components to provide prime power to one of Guatemala's newest steel mills. Barge-mounted generators supply the only power to numerous communities in the Philippines. In short, there are endless needs for Caterpillar machines, engines, and services.

Total assets: $18.728 million
Current ratio: 1.68
Common shares outstanding: 386 million
Return on 1996 shareholders' equity: 36.3%

	1996	1995	1994	1993	1992	1991	1990	1989
Revenues (millions)	16,522	16,072	14,328	11,615	10,194	10,182	11,436	11,126
Net income (millions)	1,361	1,136	955	681	(218)	(135)	210	497
Earnings per share	3.54	2.86	2.35	1.68	(.54)	(.34)	.52	1.22
Dividends per share	.75	.60	.22	.15	.15	.26	.30	.30
Price: High	40.5	37.6	30.4	23.3	15.6	14.4	17.2	17.2
Low	27.0	24.2	22.2	13.4	10.3	9.4	9.6	13.2

INCOME

Cedar Fair, L. P.

P. O. Box 5006, Sandusky, Ohio 44871-5006 ◻ Investor contact: Brain C. Witherow (419) 627-2233 ◻
Dividend reinvestment plan available: (800) 756-3353 ◻ Listed: NYSE ◻ Ticker symbol: FUN ◻ S&P
rating: Not rated ◻ Value Line financial strength rating: B+

Cedar Fair, L. P. owns and operates four seasonal amusement parks. The parks are family-oriented, providing clean and attractive environments with exciting rides and entertainment. The operating season is generally from May through September.

The parks charge a basic daily admission price that provides unlimited use of virtually all rides and attractions. Admissions account for about 52 percent of revenues, with food, merchandise, and games contributing 42 percent and accommodations the other 6 percent.

Going into the 1987 season, when the Partnership was created, Cedar Fair was made up of only two parks with combined attendance of 4.1 million and net revenues of $96 million. Going into the 1997 season, Cedar Fair had expanded to four parks with a combined attendance of 6.9 million and net revenues of $251 million.

During that ten-year stretch, cash distributions per unit grew from a $1.05 annual rate in 1987 to $2.50 in 1996, an increase of 138 percent, for a 10.2 percent compound annual rate of growth. Cedar Fair units opened for trading at $10 on April 29, 1987. On December 31, 1996, they closed at $36.88.

The Four Parks That Make Up Cedar Fair

Cedar Point, which is on Lake Erie between Cleveland and Toledo, is one of the largest seasonal amusement parts in the United States. It serves a market area of 22 million people.

Valleyfair, situated near Minneapolis/St. Paul, is the largest amusement part in Minnesota. It draws on a population of 8 million people in a multi-state market area.

Dorney Park & Wildwater Kingdom is near Allentown, Pennsylvania. It is one of the largest amusement parks in the Northeast, serving a total market area of 35 million people.

Worlds of Fun/Oceans of Fun in Kansas City, Missouri, is one of the largest amusement parks in the Midwest and serves a total market area of 7 million people.

Highlights of 1996

In 1996, Cedar Fair enjoyed its best year ever. Attendance at the four parks was up 10 percent from the prior year, with Worlds of Fun's full-year contribution accounting for most of the increase.

At Cedar Point, the introduction of Mantis, the park's fourth world-class coaster, created significant interest. Mantis is the highest, steepest, and fastest stand-up roller coaster in the world. Mantis provided over 1.8 million rides in its debut year and joins a team of three other world-class coasters: Magnum, Mean Streak, and Raptor.

Combined guest per capita spending showed a healthy increase in 1996, rising 5 percent to a record $31.75 from $30.29 in 1995.

Financially, results were impressive for the thirteenth consecutive year. Net revenues increased to $251 million, a 15 percent increase over the prior year. Operating income was up 11 percent to $81 million, and net income increased to $74 million or $3.18 per share.

Tax Considerations

Cedar Fair is a publicly traded master limited partnership (MLP). The MLP structure is an attractive business form because it allows the partnership to pay out the majority of its earnings to its owners without first paying significant federal and state income taxes at the entity level, avoiding what is known as the corporate form as double taxation of earnings. The benefit extends through 1997 under present law.

Ownership of Cedar Fair, L. P. units is different from an investment in corporate stock. Cash distributions made by the partnership are treated as a reduction of basis and are generally not taxable. Instead, unitholders must pay tax only on their pro rata share of the Partnership's taxable income, which is generally lower. The Partnership provides the tax information necessary for filing each unitholder's federal, state, and local tax returns on IRS Schedule K-1 in late February each year.

The tax consequences to a particular unitholder will depend on the circumstances of that unitholder; however, income from the partnership may not be offset by passive tax losses from other investments. Prospective unitholders should consult their tax or financial advisors to determine the federal, state, and local tax consequences of ownership of these limited partnership units.

Ownership of limited partnership units may not be advisable for IRAs, pension and profit-sharing plans, and other tax-exempt organizations; nonresident aliens, foreign corporations, and other foreign persons; and regulated investment companies.

Shortcomings to Bear in Mind

- Weather can have an important impact on the attendance at an amusement park. If it's cold and rainy, attendance will suffer. In 1996, Dorney Park & Wildwater Kingdom ran into this problem. A very promising season was impacted severely by a cool, wet summer, particularly in July and August, reducing attendance at water parks and most other outdoor attractions in the East.

  Worlds of Fun also experienced poor weather in 1996, particularly in the early season. As a positive factor at this park, 1996 was the debut of an exciting new ride, Detonator. Thrill riders loved shooting straight up a 200-foot tower, from 0 to 45 mph in one second, then dropping back to earth at free-fall speeds. Detonator was the first major new ride at Worlds of Fun in several years.

- Some investors are concerned that the tax status of Cedar Fair will change at the end of 1997. Since it is no secret, I doubt that the stock is in for a shock. Actually, when Cedar Fair converts to a corporation, it will then be attractive to mutual funds and other institutions who are reluctant to buy in its present configuration.

  During the early part of 1997, a bipartisan group of fifteen Ways and Means Committee members introduced legislation that would permit Master Limited Partnerships whose partnership tax status expires at year end 1997 to preserve their tax status. If this bill makes it through Congress, these stocks, according to analysts, would react quite positively.

Reasons to Buy

- Although the Cedar Fair Partnership is relatively young (it was created in April of 1987), it owns four amusement parks with considerable longevity. In 1995, Cedar Point, the flagship park, celebrated its 125th anniversary. That same year, Valleyfair celebrated its 20th season. Dorney Park opened its 114th season in 1997. Finally, Worlds of Fun first opened in 1973 and celebrated its 25th summer in 1997.

- Not content to rest on their laurels, these amusement parts are upgraded every year. They represent an investment of more than $160 million over the past ten seasons, establishing Cedar Point as the roller coaster capital of the world and a major Midwest vacation destination and transforming ValleyFair into a premier regional amusement park.

  In addition, the acquisition of Dorney Park & Wildwater Kingdom in 1992 and Worlds of Fun/Oceans of Fun in 1995 has added significantly to Cedar Fair's revenues, profits, and long-term growth opportunities.

- During this ten-year period, the company has invested more than $100 million in capital improvements at Cedar Point, building seven major rides, including four world-class coasters, a major water park, a new hotel, and a major renovation and expansion of another hotel property.

- At Valleyfair, FUN added a mega-coaster, a number of smaller rides, and a family entertainment center. In the five seasons that the company has operated Dorney Park, it has added two major rides, a themed children's attraction, several food facilities, and a new main entrance. At Worlds of Fun, the company added a major thrill ride and other park improvements in its first year of ownership.

Why all this investment? The key to Cedar Fair's success, both short- and long-term, is continuous reinvestment in its parks to make them better every season. It is management's core belief that it should provide guests a better product year after year.

- Cedar Point received a singular honor in November of 1996 at the International Association of Amusement Parks and Attractions annual trade show and convention in New Orleans. Cedar Point won the industry's most prestigious award. The Applause Award is presented by *Amusement Business*, the trade publication for the industry, and Liseberg Amusement Park in Sweden. The award is given to only one amusement or theme park in the world every two years "whose management, operations, and creative accomplishments have inspired the industry with foresight, originality, and sound business development."

- Steel Force, a gigantic megacoaster in the tradition of Magnum and Wild Thing, came to Dorney Park in 1997. Steel Force's giant frame climbs 200 feet in the air and is the tallest roller coaster on the eastern seaboard. It plunges 205 feet into a dark underground tunnel, taking thirty-six passengers on a three-minute journey over a mile of track at speeds topping 75 mph.

The coaster features several unique design elements, including two coaster tracks running through the underground tunnel in opposite directions, passenger trains shooting three times through the coaster's steel support structure at high speed, and two points during the ride where passengers will feel the weightless effect of near-zero gravity.

Total assets: $304,104
Current ratio: 0.60
Common shares outstanding: 23 million
Return on 1996 shareholders' equity: 38%

	1996	1995	1994	1993	1992	1991	1990	1989
Revenues (millions)	250	218	198	179	153	128	122	120
Net income (millions)	74	66	61	50	43	36	33	32
Earnings per share	3.18	2.90	2.73	2.26	1.96	1.68	1.55	1.48
Dividends per share	2.40	2.28	2.13	1.89	1.73	1.53	1.35	1.18
Price: High	39.0	37.1	36.6	36.6	29.9	19.0	13.8	13.9
Low	32.3	28.1	26.8	27.0	17.8	12.5	10.4	9.5

Chevron Corporation

225 Bush Street, Room 864, San Francisco, CA 94104-4289 ◻ Investor contact: Meeks Vaughan (415) 894-5690 ◻ Dividend reinvestment plan available: (800) 547-9794 ◻ Listed: NYSE ◻ Ticker symbol: CHV ◻ S&P rating: B ◻ Value Line financial strength rating: A+

Chevron is a worldwide petroleum company with important interests in chemicals and minerals. It is a leading domestic producer of crude oil and natural gas and a marketer of refined products. Chevron is active in foreign exploration and production and overseas refining and marketing.

Supply and Demand

The prices of oil stocks tend to be a reflection of crude oil prices, which are a function of worldwide supply and demand.

Demand is determined primarily by weather and economic conditions. Supply, on the other hand, is influenced by inventories and production levels.

In recent years, OPEC (the Organization of Petroleum Exporting Countries) has been able to control production, at least to some extent, by setting quotas that keep crude prices high enough to benefit them, but low enough to keep non–OPEC producers from getting too competitive with their exploration and drilling or consumers from finding something else to burn.

A Breakdown of Chevron's Operations

Exploration and Production

Chevron explores for and produces crude oil and natural gas in the United States and twenty other countries. The company is the second-largest domestic natural gas producer. In 1996, worldwide net production was almost 1.5 million barrels a day of oil and equivalent gas.

Major producing regions include the Gulf of Mexico, California, the Rocky Mountains, Texas, Canada, the North Sea, Australia, Indonesia, Angola, Nigeria, and Kazakhstan. Exploration areas include the above, as well as frontiers such as Bolivia, Colombia, the Congo, Trinidad, and Tobago.

Refining

CHV converts crude oil into a variety of refined products including motor gasoline, diesel and aviation fuels, lubricants, asphalt, chemicals, and other products. Chevron is one of the largest refiners in the United States.

The company's principal U.S. locations are El Segundo and Richmond, California; Pascagoula, Mississippi; Salt Lake City, Utah; El Paso, Texas; and Honolulu, Hawaii. The company also refines in Canada, Wales, and (through its Caltex affiliate) Asia, Africa, the Middle East, Australia, and New Zealand.

Marketing

Chevron is the leading U.S. marketer of refined products including motor gasoline, diesel and aviation fuels, lubricants, and other products. Retail outlets number 7,750 in the United States, 200 in Canada, and more than 450 in the United Kingdom; Caltex supplies about 7,900 retail outlets worldwide.

Supply and Distribution

The company purchases, sells, trades, and transports (by pipeline, tanker, and barge) crude oil, natural gas liquids (such as propane and butane), chemicals, and refined products.

Chevron has trading offices in Houston, Walnut Creek (California),

London, Abidjan, Ivory Coast, Singapore, Mexico City, and Moscow. What's more, the company has interests in pipelines throughout the United States and in Africa, Australia, Indonesia, Papua New Guinea, Europe, and the Middle East.

Chemicals

The company's main products are benzene, styrene, polystyrene, paraxylene, ethylene, polyethylene, and normal alpha olefins.

Chevron operates plants in ten states and in France, Brazil, and Japan. Through affiliates and subsidiaries, the company operates or markets in more than eighty countries.

Coal and Land

Chevron has a stake in coal. It mines and markets coal, ranking among the top twenty coal producers in the United States.

The company invests in and develops properties, primarily surplus land from other Chevron businesses.

It operates coal mines in New Mexico, Wyoming, Colorado, and Kentucky and has partnership interests in Illinois and Indiana.

Finally, the company has projects in California, with emphasis on the Los Angeles Basin, San Diego, and the San Francisco Bay Area.

Highlights of 1996

• After months of difficult negotiations, the company signed an agreement to build a pipeline linking the super-giant Tengiz oil field in Kazakstan to the Black Sea and the world oil markets beyond.

• The Tengizchevroil joint venture ingeniously developed alternate markets and nearly doubled oil production to a daily average of 112,000 barrels. By year-end, production had reached 160,000 barrels a day.

• Chevron took over as operator of Venezuela's Boscan Field under a fee agreement and started boosting production.

• The merger of the company's Warren Petroleum Company and its natural gas business unit with NGC Corporation was completed, forming one of the largest natural gas and gas liquids marketers in North America.

• Chevron announced the planned merger of its United Kingdom refining and marketing operations with those of Elf Oil and Murphy Petroleum. The new, larger company will be better able to compete in the tough U.K. market.

• Chevron successfully introduced the California-mandated reformulated gasolines. The company is the largest producer of these cleaner-burning fuels, which are improving the state's air quality.

• The company's chemicals operation launched several domestic and international expansion projects and new plants. These are expected to improve Chevron's competitive position when the traditionally cyclic chemicals industry begins its upswing.

Shortcomings to Bear in Mind

▪ One reason why this stock is classified as Growth & Income is because its record of growth is not impressive. In the 1985–1996 period, earnings per share advanced modestly, from $2.10 to $3.99, a compound annual growth of only 6 percent. In the last 10 years, moreover, dividends inched ahead from $1.20 to $2.08, a growth rate of 5.7 percent.

▪ Margins in Chevron's chemical business have narrowed of late, as the high point in the cycle has clearly passed.

▪ Chevron's refining and marketing business has been taking its lumps, since the firm is unable to pass along the higher cost of crude to customers, because of intense retail competition.

Reasons to Buy

- In 1950, world crude oil reserves were estimated at 76 billion barrels, which was about a twenty-year supply at the rate of consumption at that time. In the forty-five years since, the world has used 600 billion barrels, and there's an estimated 1 trillion barrels in proved reserves. The world's oil supply now is greater than it has ever been; if Chevron didn't find another drop of oil, it would still have a fifty-year supply left. For its part, Chevron, in 1996, replaced 112 percent of its worldwide oil and gas production with new reserves.

- There is the perception that the world is turning away from oil. The actual situation is just the opposite. Demand is growing worldwide—as much as 6 to 8 percent a year in parts of the Asia-Pacific region. The experience, technology, and capital of U.S. oil companies are in demand around the globe. When you read about Chevron's new opportunities, you'll be taking an armchair global tour of the Gulf of Mexico, Australia, West Africa, Indonesia, Kazakhstan, China, Papua New Guinea, Canada, and the North Sea.

- Development of Britannia, the largest undeveloped natural gas field in the United Kingdom section of the North Sea, has been given the green light by the U.K. government. Production is scheduled to start late in 1998 at minimum rates of 740 million cubic feet of natural gas and up to 70,000 barrels of condensate a day. Chevron holds a 30 percent interest in the field, which has estimated recoverable reserves of about 2.5 trillion cubic feet of natural gas and 140 million barrels of condensate and natural gas liquids.

  Britannia underlies the Alba oil field, which began producing in January 1994. In August, the first phase of the Alba development produced oil in excess of its design capacity of 75,000 barrels a day. Chevron holds a 33 percent interest in the field, which has estimated reserves of 400 million barrels of oil.

- In many areas of the world, Chevron's long-standing projects keep getting better, benefiting from advances in technology. As the company expands activity offshore Angola, for example, oil production is expected to increase 50 percent over the next five years, from the current level of 400,000 barrels a day (Chevron's share is 39.2 percent).

  In Australia, Chevron and partners are negotiating a $5 billion expansion of the huge Northwest Shelf liquefied natural gas project.

  In Indonesia, Chevron's Caltex affiliate continues to expand oil recovery projects using steam and water injection, as well as new technology, in the Duri and Minas oil fields.

- Chevron is moving into a new U.S. frontier: water depths of more than half a mile in the Gulf of Mexico. Improved technology and a growing infrastructure make deep-water drilling economically attractive and the Genesis project a harbinger of the future. With an estimated 160 million barrels of recoverable oil and oil equivalent gas, Genesis is the first of several planned deep-water projects.

- Chevron Chemical Company plans to increase its international business. New plants are under way in Saudi Arabia, Singapore, and China, and the company's access to superior technology in making benzene and paraxylene is expected to promote further expansion.

Total assets: 34,854 million
Current ratio: 0.89
Common shares outstanding: 652 million
Return on 1996 shareholders' equity: 17.4%

	1996	1995	1994	1993	1992	1991	1990	1989
Revenues (millions)	43,893	37,082	30,340	32,123	37,464	36,461	38,607	29,433
Net income (millions)	2,607	1,962	1,693	1,819	1,593	1,293	2,129	1,461
Earnings per share	3.99	3.01	2.60	2.80	2.35	1.85	3.01	2.08
Dividends per share	2.08	1.93	1.85	1.75	1.65	1.63	1.48	1.40
Price: High	68.4	53.6	47.3	49.4	37.7	40.1	40.8	36.8
Low	51.0	43.4	39.9	33.8	30.1	31.8	31.6	22.7

AGGRESSIVE GROWTH

Cincinnati Financial Corporation

P. O. Box 145496, Cincinnati, Ohio 45250-5496 ◻ Investor contact: T. F. Elchynski (513) 870-2625 ◻ Dividend reinvestment plan available: (513) 870-2000 ◻ Listed: NASDAQ ◻ Ticker Symbol: CINF ◻ S&P rating: A ◻ Value Line financial strength rating: B++

Cincinnati Financial is a regional property-casualty insurer, with about 70 percent of property-casualty premiums produced by small- to medium-sized commercial accounts.

The company now has over $1 billion in premium volume from 1,000 independent agents in twenty-six states. However, about half of the company's business comes from Ohio, Indiana, and Illinois. CINF has historically generated above-average property-casualty operating results.

Founded in 1950 by a group of independent insurance agents who believed that a company operated by agents would prosper, Cincinnati Financial has consistently outperformed its peers.

Cincinnati Financial Corporation is the fourteenth most profitable property and casualty company among publicly traded U.S. stock insurers, based on an average five-year return on equity of 11.3 percent. The company's twelve-month profit margin (net income divided by sales) of 11.9 percent is third among the top twenty-eight ranked insurers.

Based on revenues, Cincinnati Financial Corporation ranks as the twenty-first largest U.S. publicly traded property and casualty insurer or reinsurer. CINF's 14 percent ratio of profits to revenues is the highest of any company ranked in this category.

CINF's strong financial position helps offset catastrophic losses, and the employees' large vested interest in the stock's performance means underwriting is always tight.

Shortcomings to Bear in Mind

- Cincinnati Financial holds large positions in several common stocks. If the prices of these stocks fall at a time when the company needs to raise cash, its cash flow could be hurt.
- All insurance companies have to worry about extraordinary claims, such as fires, earthquakes, floods, and tornadoes. In 1996, the industry had some bad luck. A relentless string of hurricanes (including Bertha and Fran) resulted in catastrophic losses totaling $64.7 million, compared with a more normal $27.1 million in 1995. The after-tax penalty was 73 cents a share in 1996, compared with only 31 cents the prior year.

- Like all financial stocks, CINF is vulnerable to changes in interest rates.

Reasons to Buy

- The best-known independent insurance rating agency is A. M. Best Company, which has been evaluating insurers since 1899. Its ratings are based on a wide range of criteria, from profitability and liquidity to adequacy of reserves, capital, and surplus. Assigned annually and reviewed quarterly, Best's ratings focus on the present and future claims-paying ability of the insurance company.

  The Cincinnati Insurance Companies' property casualty group, and each company in it, have an A++ Best rating. Just 7 percent of companies and 3 percent of ratings units received this top rating in 1996.

- Are the most profitable companies for shareholders always the safest ones for policyholders? Ward Financial Group looks at this question each year. They crunch numbers for 3,000 property and casualty insurers and 1,750 life/health insurers to find just fifty that perform strongly while excelling in all measures of safety and consistency over a five-year period.

  The Cincinnati Insurance Companies have qualified for the Ward's 50 property and casualty benchmark list every year since the study began. And CINF is one of just a few companies with affiliates on both Ward's 50 lists: The Cincinnati Life Insurance Company qualified for the Ward's 50 life/health list.

- Considering that CINF operates in one of the most volatile of specialties, regional property/casualty insurance, the company has, nonetheless, carved out an impressive record. In only four instances since 1979 have earnings per share fallen below the prior year's level.

- The independent agents who do business with Cincinnati Financial often give the company the bulk of their business. In fact, the company ranks as either the number one or number two underwriter for over 75 percent of the independent agents it serves.

  Those close relationships result in the company's ability to retain agents' business during downturns in the underwriting cycle and consistently operate at combined ratios well below the industry average. The combined ratio before policyholder dividends was below 100 percent in six of the last ten years, averaging 99.6 percent over this span. The combined ratio is the sum of the expense ratio (as determined by SAP and GAAP), the loss ratio, and the LAE ratio.

- Over 50 percent of the independent agents personally own stock in the company, and seven of the seventeen members of the board of directors are independent agents. Officers and directors of CINF own 17.3 percent of company stock—a strong indication that they will act in the shareholders' interest.

- Cincinnati Financial has a solid record of growth. In the 1986–1996 period, for instance, earnings per share climbed from $1.56 to $3.92, a compound annual growth rate of 9.6 percent. In the same ten-year span, dividends per share expanded from $.38 to $1.46, a compound growth rate of 14.4 percent.

- Cincinnati Financial, unlike most other casualty companies, seeks out quality agents. Typically, casualty companies work with 10,000 independent agents. By contrast, CINF deals with fewer than 1,000 agents. When the company enters a new market, it tends to deal with a select group of high-quality agents in that area. In most instances, those agents use Cincinnati Financial as their number one underwriter within a short period of time.

Management's strategy is to build long-term relationships with agents by offering consistent pricing, as well as competitive, flexible products tailored for each account. National surveys of independent agents consistently report that CINF receives high rankings with regard to fairness and efficiency in claims and flexibility. In 1994, Cincinnati Financial was ranked as the number one choice among commercial and multiperil carriers. In addition, the company was chosen as the number one or number two underwriter of choice among 80 percent of the independent agents.

- Because underwriting results are consistently favorable and leverage ratios are conservative, management has adopted a somewhat aggressive approach on the investment side by overweighting equities. Unrealized appreciation in a sizable concentrated equity portfolio has contributed to exceptional growth in book value over time.
- Cincinnati Financial has consistently increased dividends by 10 to 15 percent a year. What's more, the dividend has been increased for thirty-six consecutive years.
- Many industry observers are concerned about the increasing frequency and severity of natural catastrophes. While most of the hurricanes and earthquakes in recent years have not occurred where CINF operates, it has considered the possibility of major catastrophes and has prepared to soften the financial impact.

The company purchased reinsurance to cover high catastrophe losses. This means the company is insured for those losses up to $175 million. Per these contracts, Cincinnati Financial would pay the first $25 million of a catastrophe loss, then 5 percent of the next $150 million and any amounts above $175 million. Reinsurance companies would pay $142.5 million of a $175 million catastrophe.

As it turns out, $175 million is well above the largest single catastrophe loss in the company's history. In 1989, Hurricane Hugo caused $45.3 million in losses to CINF policyholders. Reinsurance agreements then in force recovered $31.5 million of this amount.

Cincinnati Financial is careful about marketing in areas prone to catastrophe losses that could approach or deplete its reinsurance. California is not in the company's marketing territory. CINF studies its earthquake, hurricane, and tornado exposure whenever it enters a new territory or appoints additional agencies.

Cincinnati Financial closely underwrites its earthquake and wind exposure so that the company can obtain the proper premium for the risk. In the past, some companies have overlooked this basic principle of insurance and priced their policies too low. When disaster struck and they could not pay policyholder claims, the public's respect for the insurance industry diminished, and some people called for government-run disaster insurance programs. Cincinnati Financial believes it is in the best interest of policyholders to find ways for responsible private insurers, not taxpayers, to provide this insurance.

- Cincinnati Financial invests for the long term, targeting common stocks with records of dividend growth and potential for capital appreciation. This buy-and-hold strategy brings the company a steady stream of income that compounds over the years.
- Management's goal is to provide quality coverage to small- and medium-sized accounts in the Midwest. Cincinnati Financial's strategy is to focus on

modestly rising prices on a selective basis. Many companies focus on cash flow underwriting, whereby planned insurance losses are absorbed by strong growth in investment income. Cincinnati Financial has never embraced this concept. Rather, its goal has been to seek out above-average accounts that meet strict underwriting standards and price them aggressively at inception and renewal.

The company generally offers a three-year rate guarantee on many of its coverages. About 60 percent of its commercial policies are written with the three-year guarantee. Beside providing the customer with stable pricing, CINF benefits from reduced expenses, because of the decline in the amount of renewal paperwork.

Cincinnati Financial has always been guided by a policy of neither raising nor lowering prices excessively but rather selectively raising rates where and when needed. This pricing strategy has helped to build and improve loyalty among the independent agents and to build polity count.

Total assets: $7,046 million
Common shares outstanding: 56 million
Return on 1996 shareholders' equity: 7.7 percent

	1996	1995	1994	1993	1992	1991	1990	1989
Premiums earned	1,365	1,245	1,171	1,092	992	891	828	783
Net income (millions)	224	227	201	202	171	146	129	115
Earnings per share	3.92	3.99	3.55	3.57	3.07	2.66	2.37	2.12
Dividends per share	1.45	1.28	1.16	1.02	.93	.80	.74	.65
Price:　High	65.0	63.6	52.8	60.5	56.9	37.1	27.1	25.0
Low	53.3	46.0	41.7	45.4	32.4	23.5	19.5	15.9

GROWTH & INCOME

The Clorox Company

1221 Broadway, Oakland, California 94612 ◻ Investor contact: Karen M. Rose (510) 271-7385 ◻ Dividend reinvestment plan available: (201) 324-0498 ◻ Listed: NYSE ◻ Ticker symbol: CLX ◻ S&P rating: A ◻ Value Line financial strength rating: A+

In 1913, a group of Oakland businessmen founded the Electro-Alkaline Company, a forerunner of the Clorox Company. The company originally produced an industrial-strength liquid bleach sold in 5-gallon crockery jugs to industrial customers in the San Francisco Bay area.

A household version of Clorox liquid bleach was developed in 1916 and subsequently was distributed in sample pint bottles. Demand for the product grew, and its distribution was gradually expanded nationally until it became the country's best-selling liquid bleach.

Clorox was a one-product company for its first fifty-six years, including the eleven years from 1957 through 1968, when it operated as a division of Procter & Gamble Co. Following its divestiture by Procter & Gamble in 1969, the company has broadened and diversified its product line and expanded geographically. Today, Clorox manufactures a wide range of products that are marketed to consumers in the

United States and internationally. It is also a supplier of products to food service and institutional customers and the janitorial trades.

Although the company's growth in the first few years after divestiture came largely through the acquisition of other companies and products, strong emphasis is now being given to the internal development of new products.

The company's line of domestic retail products includes many of the country's best-known brands of laundry additives, home cleaning products, cat litters, insecticides, charcoal briquettes, salad dressings, sauces, and water filtration systems. The great majority of the company's brands are either number one or number two in their categories.

Included in Clorox products are such well-known names as Formula 409, Liquid-Plumr, Pine-Sol, Soft Scrub, S.O.S, Tilex, Armor All, Kingsford charcoal, Match Light, Black Flag insecticides, Fresh Step cat litter, Hidden Valley salad dressing, and Kitchen Bouquet.

Clorox's Professional Products unit is focused on extending many of the company's successful retail equities in cleaning and food products to new channels of distribution such as institutional and professional markets and the food-service industry.

Internationally, Clorox markets laundry additives, home cleaning products, and insecticides, primarily in developing countries. What's more, Clorox is investing heavily to expand this part of its business. Overall, Clorox products are sold in more than seventy countries and are manufactured in thirty-five plants at locations in the United States, Puerto Rico, and abroad.

Highlights of Fiscal 1996
• Case volume, a reliable measure of growth, was up a healthy 10 percent.

• Net sales grew 12 percent and crossed over the $2 billion mark for the first time.

• Full-year net earnings increased 11 percent.

• Earnings per share were up 13 percent.

• Free cash flow of $130 million was driven by a record $406 million of cash from operations.

• The company's return on equity increased from 22 percent to 24 percent.

• Dividends per share were $2.12, a 10.4 percent increase over the prior year. In July, the company increased the dividend by 9.4 percent to an annual rate of $2.32.

• The Clorox Value Measure (CVM) grew by 20 percent in 1996, or well above the goal of 12 percent.

In fiscal 1993, Clorox adopted an economic value measure called the Clorox Value Measure. CVM is an internal performance tool that guides the company's decisions in a way that increases stockholder value over the long term. It recognizes not only the importance of the profits generated by the business but also the investment required to produce those profits. Finally, management's internal goals are focused against the key drivers of CVM: Operating Profit Margin, Asset Turnover, and Volume Growth.

Since implementing CVM as the company's internal performance measure, it has increased at an annual compound rate of 21 percent. During the same period, total stockholder return increased at an annual compound rate of 22 percent, while the Standard & Poor's 500 increased at an annual compound rate of only 14 percent.

Shortcomings to Bear in Mind
■ Volumes for the company's two largest food brands, Hidden Valley bottled salad dressing and K. C. Masterpiece

barbecue sauce, were hurt in fiscal 1996 by the effects of bad weather. Shipments of bottled salad dressing, moreover, reflected continued category softness, a hangover from the storms of 1995 that drove up lettuce prices and forced consumers to find less expensive alternatives to salads. The same bad weather that rained on the company's charcoal business in the spring of 1996 also impacted shipments of barbecue sauce.

Reasons to Buy

- Despite unrelenting competitive activity, the company's Household Products Division achieved record results in 1996. Total shipments of laundry and home cleaning products reached a fiscal year record, driven in part by the success of two new scented products: Floral Fresh Clorox liquid bleach and Lemon Fresh Pine-Sol cleaner.

    Introduced in the fall of 1995, Floral Fresh Clorox was 20 percent ahead of objective by year-end, had become the second largest Clorox scented bleach, and helped the eighty-year-old brand achieve a remarkable fifty-two-week market share of 65.9 percent.

    The company's expertise in fragrance technology also made possible the development of Lemon Fresh Pine-Sol, which was introduced in 1995. Volumes for the total Pine-Sol franchise surged, and the brand ended the year with record shipments and share. The original Pine-Sol was introduced in 1949 and acquired by Clorox in 1990. By combining meaningful product improvements with aggressive marketing, the company has virtually doubled volumes for this popular cleaner during Clorox's six years of ownership.

- In home cleaning, where Clorox has been the leading manufacturer for five years, new product activity aimed at extending successful franchises and adding incremental volume continued at a high level in 1996. Lemon Fresh Pine-Sol was joined by Professional Strength Pine-Sol, which contains 60 percent more pine oil and 40 percent more cleaners than regular Pine-Sol.

    Still more new product introductions included Soft Scrub gel cleanser, Formula 409 Fresh Scent glass & surface cleaner, and S.O.S scrubber sponges.

- Meanwhile, business abroad has been brisk. In fiscal 1996, shipments were up sharply. They included gains in every region in which the company operates and were balanced between Clorox's base business and acquisitions.

    What's more, the overseas business grew rapidly and was profitable despite substantial investment spending. Growth continued to be fueled by twenty new product introductions and by acquisitions.

- Two strategic acquisitions in Latin America contributed to building what is now an important presence in this major market. Here's a summary. In Argentina The Poett San Juan line of aerosol insecticides, all-purpose cleaners, a toilet disinfectant, and an air freshener were major additions to Clorox Argentina's portfolio of bleaches and cleaners.

    In Chile the company's Clorox brand, the leading bleach, was joined by the Clorinda line of bleaches, making Clorox clearly the leading producer of bleach in that country.

    Additionally, the company acquired the Lestoil brand, which, while distributed regionally in the United States, is the leading line of household and bathroom cleaners in Puerto Rico.

By the end of 1996, Clorox had become the leading or second-largest marketer of liquid bleach in twenty countries outside the United States.

- The company is benefiting from its improved focus. Since 1992, Clorox has been more effective at channeling capital away from marginal units (many of which have been divested) toward areas in which the company has been able to achieve market leadership. The flagship bleach business is one example. It's difficult for competitors to make inroads here because of CLX's formidable infra-

structure. The company has further enhanced its position by focusing on specialized needs (such as cleaning color fabrics) and tastes (various scents). And tuning into specialized needs has been a major strength in the company's household cleanser business. Efforts to persuade consumers to adopt different cleansers for different sorts of needs (stains, grease, dirt, and so forth) on varying surfaces (glass, walls, porcelain, for instance) are helping the company outperform this seemingly mature category.

Total assets: $2,179 million
Current ratio: .91
Common shares outstanding: 51.6 million
Return on 1996 shareholders' equity: 23.8%

	1996	1995	1994	1993	1992	1991	1990	1989
Revenues (millions)	2,218	1,984	1,837	1,634	1,717	1,646	1,484	1,356
Net income (millions)	222	201	180	168	144	131	154	146
Earnings per share	4.28	3.78	3.35	3.07	2.65	2.43	2.80	2.63
Dividends per share	2.12	1.92	1.86	1.71	1.59	1.47	1.29	1.09
Price: High	110.3	79.3	59.5	55.4	52.0	42.4	45.4	44.5
Low	70.0	55.3	47.0	44.0	39.5	35.0	32.1	30.1

AGGRESSIVE GROWTH

The Coca-Cola Company

One Coca-Cola Plaza, N. W., Atlanta, Georgia 30313 ◻ Investor contact: Gavin A. Bell (404) 676-2121 ◻ Dividend reinvestment plan available: (404) 676-2777 ◻ Listed: NYSE ◻ Ticker symbol: KO ◻ S&P rating: A+ ◻ Value Line financial strength rating: A++

Coca-Cola is the world's largest soft drink company. Its brands include Coca-Cola, Sprite, Fanta, Tab, diet Coke, caffeine-free Coca-Cola, diet Cherry Coke, diet Sprite, Mr. PiBB, Mello Yello, Fresca, and PowerAde. Foreign operations account for 71 percent of sales and 82 percent of profits.

Coca-Cola's Food Division is the world's largest distributor of juice products such as Minute Maid, Bright and Early, Bacardi, Five Alive, and Hi-C. The company owns a 45 percent interest in Coca-Cola Enterprises, its largest bottler.

The Beverage Division primarily manufactures soft drink and noncarbonated beverage concentrates and syrups. These are sold to independent (and company-owned) bottling/canning operations and fountain wholesalers.

The Company's Bottlers

Coca-Cola has business relationships with three types of bottlers: independently owned bottlers, bottlers in which the company has a noncontrolling ownership interest, and bottlers in which it has a controlling ownership interest. Independently owned bottlers are bottlers in which the company has no ownership interest.

These bottlers produced and distributed about 40 percent of Coca-Cola's 1996 worldwide unit case volume. The other bottlers represent businesses in which Coca-Cola has invested. In 1996, bottlers in which the company owns a noncontrolling ownership interest produced and distributed an additional 45 percent of the company's total worldwide unit case volume.

Controlled and consolidated bottling and fountain operations produced and distributed about 15 percent of total worldwide unit case volume for the company's products.

Coca-Cola invests heavily in certain bottling operations to maximize the strength and efficiency of its production, distribution, and marketing systems around the world. These investments often result in increases in unit case volume, net revenues, and profits at the bottler level, which, in turn, generates increased gallon shipments for the company's concentrate business. As a result, both the company and the bottlers benefit from long-term growth in volume, cash flows, and shareowner value.

Shortcomings to Bear in Mind

- Coca-Cola has been a stellar performer in recent years. The stock has been one of the best components of the Dow Jones Industrial Average. As a consequence, its P/E ratio is extremely high. Those who prefer low-P/E stocks may choose to select stocks with lower multiples.

Reasons to Buy

- This is a classic growth stock. In the 1986–1996 period, earnings per share climbed from $.26 to $1.40, for a compound annual growth rate of 18.3 percent. What's more, the stock was split four times during this period. Dividends also performed well, advancing from $.13 to $.50, a growth rate of 14.4 percent.

- The stock is extremely high quality. Standard & Poor's gives the company its highest rating (A+), as does Value Line (A++).

- Coca-Cola posted another year of record volume in 1996. Worldwide unit case volume was up 8 percent, following equally strong growth in 1995. Around the world, the company sold 13.7 billion units cases of its beverages in 1996. Sales of its flagship brand, Coca-Cola, climbed nearly 450 million unit cases in 1996, a 6 percent increase over the prior year; Sprite grew by more than 138 million unit cases, up 13 percent, marking its third consecutive year of double-digit growth.

- In 1996, Coca-Cola took a number of steps to further strengthen its worldwide bottling system, including creation of its newest anchor bottler, Coca-Cola Erfrischungsgetranke AG, in Germany.

- The company began construction of its twenty-third bottling plant in China in 1996. What's more, it passed—by a wide margin—the 200-million-case mark in annual unit case sales in that country. Coca-Cola is convinced that those twenty-three plants give the company an enviable ability to drive sales in the market of 1.2 billion people. In addition, CEO Roberto C. Goizueta believes that its China story "is just beginning, as we continue to invest aggressively in the world's most populous nation."

- In the United States, where Coca-Cola's soft-drink business continues to grow well ahead of the industry and its major competitors, confounding the critics who assume that the company must be nearing the crest of its success, the company expanded its lead in 1996, with more than a 43-percent share of sales. Coca-Cola increased unit sales by more than 1 billion unit cases for the second straight year. Sales of Coca-Cola Classic grew by almost 60 million unit cases, an increase of more than 3 percent on top of its already huge volume base, while unit case sales of Sprite increased 18 percent, making it the fastest-growing major soft-drink brand in the United States for the second consecutive year.

- Coca-Cola was honored again in a 1997 issue of *Fortune*. The company was proclaimed "America's Most Admired Company" for the second year in a row.

- Coca-Cola has been making a concerted effort to differentiate its entire line of packaging, so that all of its beverages are marketed in packages as easily recognizable as its contour bottle. The company updated the look of its cans for Coca-Cola and diet Coke, and it's exploring a contour can for Coca-Cola, as well. What's more, Coca-Cola has extended the reach of its popular plastic "dimple" bottle for Sprite, with launches in several nations around the world, including Argentina, Russia, and Great Britain.

- While furthering the distinctive appeal of its global brands, including Coca-Cola, Sprite, diet Coke (also known as Coca-Cola light) and Fanta, the company also continues to develop new products to satisfy different tastes. In 1996, the company launched more than twenty-five new brands around the world, including Urge, a citrus-flavored brand, in Norway. Norwegian retailers named Urge that country's most successful product launch in 1996, and already it is a favorite with its teenage target market.

- As Coca-Cola continues sharpening its bottling and customer networks, it is applying the same intensity and focus to the logistical and technical support it provides that system. For instance, to boost the system's procurement capabilities, it reorganized its Global and Trading group and brought in new talent to extend the company's expertise in that function. What's more, to strengthen Coca-Cola's distribution and customer service systems, it formed two aligned groups within its Marketing and Technical Operations divisions, one focused on the execution of sales and merchandising programs, the other on logistics, warehousing, and delivery.

- In 1996, the company developed new portable backpacks to deliver refreshment to fans at sports venues and other special events, such as Sprite NBA-themed play areas to entertain young people at schools and state fairs, and customized themed vending machines to engage amusement park visitors.

- The company's sponsorship of the Centennial Olympic Games gave Coca-Cola ample opportunities to create unique and memorable experiences for fans around the world. But it didn't stop there. Through its support of nearly seventy sports worldwide, Coca-Cola brought life to events like the 1996 World Cup Cricket and the African Cup of Nations football tournament. Finally, the company is already applying what it learned from those activities to its sponsorship of upcoming sporting events such as the World Championships in Athletics and the Tour de France in 1997, and the Olympic Winter Games and the World Cup in 1998.

- One simple statistic tells the company that its opportunities for continued growth are vast. In 1996, Coca-Cola sold 13.7 billion unit cases of its products, a billion more than the year before. But that total, when measured against the world's population, still represents less than 2 of the approximately 64 ounces of fluid human beings need every day.

Another statistic reinforces its conviction even further: If every person in the world drank one more serving of Coca-Cola products every day, its unit case volume would increase more than 600 percent.

- In 1996, Coca-Cola created a new anchor bottler on the European continent, Coca-Cola Erfrischungsgetranke AG (CCEAG), serving 40 percent of the important German business.

The company's largest anchor bottler, Coca-Cola Enterprises, now serves three more European countries after acquiring its wholly owned operations in France and Belgium.

Coca-Cola completed the acquisition of ten Coca-Cola bottlers in northern Italy, now consolidated into one bottler with greater opportunities for efficiency and growth.

- In Venezuela, the company acquired the Cisneros Group in 1996. That veteran bottler's alignment with the Coca-Cola system is a dramatic leap forward for Coca-Cola's business in a very promising region. Elsewhere in Latin America, the company also acquired equity stakes in two Chile-based bottlers, Embotelladora Andina and Embotelladoras Polar, in both cases building stronger ties in the markets they serve.

- Currently, 55 percent of the world's population lives in markets where the average person consumes fewer than ten servings of the company's beverages per year, offering high potential growth opportunities for Coca-Cola and its bottlers. In fact, the emerging markets of China, India, Indonesia, and Russia combined represent about 44 percent of the world's population, but, on a combined basis, the average per-capita consumption of the company's products in these markets is about 1 percent of the level in the United States.

- In a brassy grab for market share, Coca-Cola over the past year has embarked on a special drive to occupy almost every nook and cranny in the United States: schools, churches, nail salons, karate studios, rehabilitation clinics, and softball fields, anywhere a person might even think about having a soft drink.

If that sounds like overkill, well, that is precisely the point.

Total assets: $16,161 million
Current ratio: .89
Common shares outstanding: 2,488 million
Return on 1996 shareholders' equity: 60.5%

	1996	1995	1994	1993	1992	1991	1990	1989
Revenues (millions)	18,546	18,018	16,172	13,967	13,074	11,572	10,236	8,966
Net income (millions)	3,492	2,986	2,554	2,188	1,884	1,618	1,382	1,193
Earnings per share	1.40	1.19	.99	.84	.72	.61	.51	.42
Dividends per share	.50	.44	.39	.34	.28	.24	.20	.17
Price: High	54.3	40.2	26.7	22.5	22.7	20.4	12.3	10.1
Low	36.1	24.4	19.4	18.8	17.8	10.7	8.2	5.4

Colgate-Palmolive Company

300 Park Avenue, New York, New York 10022-7499 ▫ Listed: NYSE ▫ Investor contact: Craig Jones (212) 310-2575 ▫ Dividend reinvestment plan available: (212) 310-2575 ▫ Ticker symbol: CL ▫ S&P rating: B+ ▫ Value Line financial strength rating: A

Colgate-Palmolive is a leading global consumer products company, marketing its products in more than 200 countries and territories under such internationally recognized brand names as Colgate, Palmolive, Mennen, Ajax, Axion, Protex, Kolynos, Fab, Fabuloso, Soupline, Suavitel, and Hill's Science Diet. More than 70 percent of its sales come from international operations.

Colgate's growth strategy is tightly focused on five core categories that account for 96 percent of sales: Oral Care, Personal Care, Household Surface Care, Fabric Care, and Pet Nutrition.

With 72 percent of its sales and earnings coming from abroad, Colgate is making its greatest gains in overseas markets, including emerging markets in Asia and Latin America.

Travelers, for instance, can find Colgate brands in a host of countries:

• They'll find Total toothpaste with a proprietary antibacterial formula that fights plaque, tartar, and cavities, in more than seventy countries.

• The Care brand of baby products is popular in Asia.

• Colgate Plax makes Colgate number one in mouth rinse outside the United States.

• The Colgate Zig Zag toothbrush, popular in all major world regions outside the United States, helps make Colgate the number one toothbrush company in the world.

• Axion is an economical dishwashing paste popular in Asia, Africa, and Latin America.

Oral Care

Colgate is the global leader in oral care, and number one worldwide in toothpaste and toothbrushes. Colgate's Oral Care products include toothbrushes, toothpaste, mouth rinses, and dental floss, as well as pharmaceutical products for dentists and other oral health professionals.

Success in the realm of Oral Care is due in large measure to Colgate's 200 Oral Care scientists and dentists. Recognized worldwide for leadership in their field, these professionals enable Colgate to provide consumers with advanced oral care technologies and products—from patented plaque-fighting toothpaste and mouth rinse formulas to toothbrushes that provide precise cleaning action.

Personal Care

Colgate leads many segments of the personal care market, including some of the fastest growing. For instance, Colgate is the number one market leader in liquid soaps in the United States and globally. It is number two in baby care products and under-arm protection worldwide.

Strong brands include:

1. Irish Spring
2. Softsoap
3. Palmolive—one of the world's most popular personal care names, available as a soap and, in many countries, as shampoo and conditioner.
4. Colgate also manufactures Mennen deodorants, baby care products, and men's toiletries.

Strong research and development capabilities enable Colgate to support these and other brands with technologically sophisticated products for consumers' personal care needs.

Household and Fabric Care

Ajax, Palmolive, and Murphy's Oil Soap are three of the household names through which Colgate markets its wide variety of household cleaning and laundry products. These products include powder and liquid soaps for use in the sink and dishwasher; powder and liquid laundry detergents, including convenient super-concentrates and refills and the highly regarded Murphy's Oil Soap, North America's leading wood cleaner.

Pet Nutrition

Colgate, through its Hills Pet Nutrition subsidiary, is the world's leader in specialty pet food. Hills markets its pet foods primarily under two well-established brands:

1.   Science Diet, which is sold by authorized pet supply retailers, breeders, and veterinary hospitals, enables pet owners to provide their dog or cat a nutritionally balanced diet every day.

2.   Prescription Diet, available only through veterinarians, is specially formulated for dogs and cats with disease conditions.

A Review of 1996

• Net income rose 17 percent to a record $635 million, and earnings per share climbed to $2.10, compared with $1.79, excluding a restructuring provision in 1995.

• Gross profit margin improved by 120 basis points to 49.1 percent, with every geographic region participating. The company is becoming steadily more profitable by introducing new value-added products in Oral Care and Personal Care, Colgate's fastest-growing and most profitable categories, and by realizing efficiencies in its worldwide operations.

• Operating cash flow reached a record $917 million, up 13 percent, providing funds for growth investments, debt reduction, and dividends to shareholders.

• A record 602 new products were introduced worldwide, lifting market shares and contributing to the 27 percent of the company's 1996 sales from products introduced in the last five years.

In the United States, Colgate introduced eighteen new products and gained market share in many categories, including dishwashing liquid, toothpaste, and deodorants. In Europe, the company doubled its new product activity and holds leadership positions in toothpaste, fabric softeners, household cleaners, and bleach.

• Hill's Pet Nutrition continues to lead the specialty pet food segment in the U.S. and globally, increasing sales 10 percent, adding six new countries, and beginning European manufacturing in 1996.

• A restructuring begun in late 1995 is progressing on target to save the company $50 million in 1997 and $100 million annually by 1998. To date, fourteen factories have been closed or reconfigured.

• In Brazil, the CADE antitrust agency approved Colgate's acquisition of Kolynos Oral Care. A growing business in nineteen countries, Kolynos achieved excellent sales and profits in 1996 and introduced new toothpaste, toothbrush, and mouth rinse products.

Shortcomings to Bear in Mind

■ Colgate's balance sheet is leveraged, with long-term debt exceeding shareholders' equity. Coverage of debt interest is less than impressive, at 5.2 times.

Reasons to Buy

■ Colgate-Palmolive's strategy for achieving strong sales growth and increased profitability takes different paths in the industrial world, as contrasted with the less-developed regions. New products, highly creative advertising, and consumer research are important everywhere.

In high-growth, emerging markets, Colgate is building consumption and sales by launching affordable formulas and sizes, while in industrial nations, the emphasis is on innovative high-margin new entities.

Colgate is also standardizing product formulas and sizes and taking advantage of regional economies of scale around the world, with special emphasis in the industrialized world on reducing operating costs.

- Today, more than 60 percent of the world's people who earn the equivalent of more than $5,000 and therefore can afford to buy all Colgate products live in developing countries. By the year 2005, this percentage is expected to increase to 70 percent. Colgate is investing to increase consumption and market penetration in emerging markets, especially in the largest ones such as China, Brazil, India, Mexico, and Russia. With 24,000 employees in 171 high-growth markets, Colgate has the well-established infrastructure, leading market shares, and excellent community ties to achieve strong growth in these regions.
- Globally, Colgate is reducing the cost of ingredients by purchasing from fewer suppliers. In fragrances, for instance, the company has reduced its suppliers from more than twenty-five to only a handful that are capable of supplying Colgate's needs.

The money the company saves increases its profitability and enables it to invest more aggressively in brand-building advertising. Direct, effective advertising of superior global brands like Colgate, Palmolive, Mennen, Ajax, and Protex is why the company's products lead the market in so many coun-

tries. Finally, total advertising increased significantly in 1996.

- Colgate continues to invest in its future by focusing 60 percent of its capital spending on savings-oriented projects that improve margins and increase operating profit quickly.
- Colgate has generated gross profit margin improvements for a decade. Using various strategies, the company has been improving the gross profit margin by one-half to a full percentage point a year. It has done this with a three-pronged, margin-improvement strategy that is expected to continue the trend. Here is why:
1. Technology is the starting point. Global formulas enable Colgate to efficiently manufacture and market high-technology, premium products worldwide, while proprietary engineering systems and vertical integration reduce the company's raw material and packaging costs.
2. Second, Colgate increasingly is shifting its business mix to focus on its most profitable product forms and categories.
3. Finally, the company is taking full advantage of its worldwide presence and critical mass to capture manufacturing and purchasing efficiencies through a focused program of capital spending on rapid-payback, high-return cost savings projects.
- Colgate's global reach lets the company conduct consumer research in countries with diverse economies and cultures to create product ideas with global appeal. The new product development process begins with the company's Global Technology and Business Development groups analyzing consumer insights from various countries to create products that can be sold in the greatest possible number of countries. Creating "universal" products saves time and

money by maximizing the return on R&D, manufacturing, and purchasing. To ensure the widest possible global appeal, potential new products are test-marketed in lead countries that represent both developing and mature economies.

- While other blue chip companies talk about efforts to become global, Colgate-Palmolive is already there. About two-thirds of the company's profits come from abroad (compared with about 50 percent for Procter & Gamble). Colgate is especially strong in the less-developed world, where per-capita use of basic household products (which aren't nearly as well established as here at home) is still expanding at a vigorous pace.

Total assets: $7,902 million
Current ratio: 1.25
Common shares outstanding: 294million
Return on 1996 shareholders' equity: 31.2%

	1996	1995	1994	1993	1992	1991	1990	1989
Revenues (millions)	8,749	8,358	7,588	7,141	7,007	6,060	5,691	5,039
Net income (millions)	635	541	580	548	477	368	321	280
Earnings per share	2.10	1.79	1.91	1.69	1.46	1.29	1.14	.99
Dividends per share	.94	.88	.77	.67	.58	.51	.45	.39
Price: High	48.3	38.7	32.7	33.6	30.3	24.6	18.9	16.2
Low	34.4	29.0	24.8	23.4	22.6	16.8	13.2	11.0

AGGRESSIVE GROWTH

Compaq Computer Corporation

P. O. Box 692000, Houston, Texas 77269-2000 ◻ Investor contact: Daryl J. White (800) 433-2391 ◻ Dividend reinvestment plan not available ◻ Listed: NYSE ◻ Ticker symbol: CPQ ◻ S&P rating: B ◻ Value Line financial strength rating: A+

Compaq Computer Corporation, a *Fortune* 500 company, is the fifth-largest computer company in the world and the largest global supplier of personal computers. As the leader in distributed enterprise solutions, Compaq has shipped over a million servers. In 1996, the company reported worldwide sales of $18.1 billion. Compaq products are sold and supported in more than 100 countries through a network of more than 38,000 organizations, including authorized retailers, distributors, and third-party maintainers.

CPQ is the number one PC maker and is now trying to move into the top three position among all computer makers. This may not be that difficult, considering that Compaq is already in the number three position among domestic providers.

Financial strength for the company is top-notch, and earnings momentum is also impressive.

Compaq sometimes works in conjunction with other firms in the development and marketing of its products. For instance, in early 1997, Compaq entered into a strategic relationship with Mitsubishi Electric and its subsidiary, Advanced Display, to develop flat-panel monitors. In December of 1996, the company and VideoServer agreed to develop audiographics collaboration and videoconferencing solutions for Internet-enabled desktop users.

Analysts look favorably on Compaq, viewing the company's completely refreshed product line that should bolster revenue growth. They point out that corporate America is replacing older desktop products. Compaq is also experiencing strong gross profit margins, a level that looks sustainable in light of the new products and efforts to cut manufacturing and logistical costs.

What's more, analysts are encouraged by Compaq's vigorous efforts to reposition itself as a systems company, a push that should lead to more profitable server and networking equipment opportunities.

Shortcomings to Bear in Mind

- In one sense, the fundamentals in the computer industry remain strong, mainly due to a growing global appetite for technology products that increase productivity. On the other hand, the industry is still dominated by intense competition that can quickly turn today's leaders into tomorrow's losers. That's because buyers are rarely content to use outdated models. They demand that vendors constantly introduce new, more powerful, and cheaper versions of successful products, while keeping a tight rein on operating expenses.
- Some investors are concerned about disappointing sales reports by consumer-electronic stores. The cachet of the Compaq brand, combined with competitive pricing (partly permitted by tighter inventory control), suggest that the company's PCs may have held their own. Looking ahead, the jury is out as to whether Compaq's and rivals' new Pentium/MMX PCs, with better multimedia capabilities than older Pentium models, will lead to a pickup

in consumer demand. Most domestic households that want Pentium PCs probably have them already and may not see the need to upgrade at present. However, the consumer market accounts for only about 20 percent of the company's business, limiting its impact on profits.
- Compaq's role in the Japanese economy, specifically in the personal-computer market, the world's second-largest, has been shrinking. Compaq's market share in Japan has fallen for two straight years, slipping to 3.4 percent in 1966 from 3.9 percent in 1994, according to the market-research firm International Data Corporation.

Compaq's once-commanding lead in the market for high-end "servers"—the muscular PCs at the heart of corporate PC networks—has vanished, taken by competitors NEC Corp. and Fujitsu Ltd.

Reasons to Buy

- Revenues are expected to expand as Compaq benefits from pent-up corporate desktop demand, coupled with a completely revamped product line and growing revenue contributions from new workstation and networking products. Server demand is likely to remain robust, as corporations continue to off-load data and applications from larger systems. Gross margins, moreover, which trended higher in 1996, are expected to improve further. This reflects the strength of new products, lower manufacturing costs, and a greater mix of more profitable workstation and networking products.
- In the fall of 1996, CPQ entered the workstation market with its Professional Workstation line. This product family features Intel's Pentium processor, Window NT operating system, and hundreds of specialized applications. Prices range from $4,300 to $10,000.

- A profitable trend in the computer industry is the continued movement toward client-server computing. This model promotes the use of networks of cheap, yet powerful, PCs and servers, in contrast to the larger, more expensive, and proprietary mainframe computers.
- Another key trend is the growing implementation of corporate "intranets," which are internal corporate networks based on existing Internet technologies. These intranets require high-powered servers that are fueling a new product class for many hardware companies. Fundamentals in the PC industry will remain challenging to all participants, according to analysts, as new competitors and price pressures challenge profitability. Even so, analysts expect that strong international growth and a strong upgrade cycle will boost prospects. They view Compaq as an attractive investment as these developments unfold.
- Up until recently, Compaq concentrated its efforts on business and high-end consumer systems. Now, it is offering a product designed from the case up for first-time, low-budget buyers. The Presario 2100 retailed for just under $1,000 when it hit stores in March of 1997. The matching V400 monitor adds an additional $300 or so.

  To be sure, keeping the price low required compromises, but Compaq chose carefully and in ways that were designed to make the 2100 easier to use. For example, the computer case is sealed, simplifying the design and eliminating the need for expansion slots and bays. Market research indicated to the company that most buyers never open the case. As a consequence, Compaq built in everything it felt budget shoppers would want. Preloaded software is basic: Windows 95 and the all-purpose Microsoft Works, among others. Compaq has done more than build a cheap computer. The company has redesigned the entry-level PC for both low cost and unprecedented simplicity.
- Compaq's management views the future with great optimism. According to the firm's CEO, Eckhard Pfeiffer, "Compaq is in a position to gain market share and increase profits. We enter 1997 with the strongest, broadest Internet-enabled and cost-effective product line in history. We're clearly focused on the high-growth segments of the information technology industry with products like our new industry-standard, NT-based professional workstations—a market segment that's forecast to grow more than 40 percent a year out to 2000."
- Compaq has always been interested in extending the PC-centered digital revolution to every age group. And that includes preschoolers. In 1996, for instance, Compaq teamed up with Fisher-Price and announced a line of intuitive, highly interactive, computing products that enable children to steer, honk, joystick, and throttle their way through animated educational worlds. These aptly named "Wonder Tools" merge the best of computers and toys. They're opening a new chapter in interactive education and play as well as a new chapter in consumer electronics for the home.
- One key to the success of Compaq is its president, Eckhard Pfeiffer. Since 1991, when he took over a company destined for a bleak future, he has exploited one industry trend after another to transform Compaq into an $18 billion supplier of everything from laptops, to mainframe servers, to high-speed networking gear. In nearly every business, Compaq is growing faster than the market and is on a tear to hit sales of

$40 billion by the year 2000, a goal that the 51-year-old Pfeiffer set in mid-1996.

Pfeiffer wants Compaq to be the king of convergence. He's planning to vault ahead of such industry leaders as IBM, Hewlett-Packard, and Sony to stake out new markets in the home, the office, and in digital communications.

- Some analysts believe that the crown jewel of Compaq is its Systems Business. The company is the world's leading supplier of servers and super-servers in a market that's undergoing dramatic growth. According to market research from IDC, Compaq supplies 36 percent of the worldwide market for servers, or 2.5 times that of its nearest competitor, IBM.

  In fact, Compaq's servers are the reference platform for Microsoft, Oracle, Novell, SAP, and many other leading software developers. More and more global customers are standardizing on the company's servers to run their businesses.

- Compaq is in the process of planning an array of specialized, low-cost Internet appliances for consumer and commercial customers. Some will appeal to consumers who are interested chiefly in surfing the Web, sending E-mail, and conducting electronic commerce. Other versions will appeal to commercial customers who run specialized applications that do not require the rich function-ality of a high-end PC.

  Without question, the Web is becoming the customer connection tool par excellence. Thus, Compaq has resolved to make its Web site a world-class electronic medium that will serve as a highly personalized, low-cost, intuitive channel for recurring interactions with customers.

- In the spring of 1997, Compaq told customers that it would build business computers when they are ordered, rather than basing production on market forecasts. At the same time, Compaq moved to reduce its reliance on its dealer network for deliveries by shipping some models to customers straight from the factory.

  In making this announcement, Compaq took aim at the lean operations and low prices of two rivals: Dell Computer and Gateway 2000. Both sell directly to customers. This shift is part of a trend among large PC makers that traditionally have sold computers through wholesalers and firms known as resellers or integrators, which add software and accessories to machines. Companies such as Compaq, IBM, and Hewlett-Packard too often haven't had the right machines ready for customers at the right time and have been hurt when new chips and other parts have made current models outdated.

Total assets: $10,526 million
Current ratio: 2.44
Common shares outstanding: 271 million
Return on 1996 shareholders' equity: 21.5%

	1996	1995	1994	1993	1992	1991	1990	1989
Revenues (millions)	18,109	14,755	10,866	7,191	4,100	3,271	3,599	2,876
Net income (millions)	1,313	1,030	867	470	248	230	432	319
Earnings per share	4.66	3.75	3.21	1.81	.98	.87	1.62	1.24
Dividends per share	nil	nil	nil	nil	nil	nil	nil	nil
Price: High	87.1	56.8	42.1	25.3	16.6	24.8	22.6	18.8
Low	35.9	31.1	24.2	13.9	7.4	7.4	11.8	9.9

ConAgra, Inc.

Corporate Communications, One ConAgra Drive, Omaha, NE 68102-5001 □ Investor contact: Walter H. Casey (402) 595-4154 □ Dividend reinvestment plan available: (800) 840-3404 □ Ticker symbol: CAG □ S&P rating: A+ □ Value Line financial strength rating: A □ Fiscal year ends last Sunday in May

ConAgra is a diversified international food company. It operates across the food chain around the world. CAG's products range from convenient prepared foods for today's busy consumers to supplies farmers need to grow their crops.

ConAgra has operations in thirty-two countries and has a stake in a vast array of food and food-related sectors. Its business segments include the following:

Grocery/Diversified Products

This segment accounted for 21 percent of sales in fiscal 1996 and 50 percent of profits. The Grocery/Diversified Products segment consists of those companies that produce branded shelf-stable and frozen food products.

Major shelf-stable grocery brands include Hunt's and Healthy Choice tomato products, Wesson oils, Healthy Choice soups, Orville Redenbacher's and Act II popcorn, Peter Pan peanut butter, and Van Camp's canned beans.

Major frozen grocery brands include Healthy Choice, Banquet, Marie Callender's, Kid Cuisine, Morton, Chun King, and La Choy.

Diversified products companies include Lamb-Weston (frozen potatoes); Arrow Industries (maker of private-label products); and business interests in seafood, pet products, and frozen microwave products in the United Kingdom.

Refrigerated Foods

This segment was responsible for 52 percent of sales in fiscal 1996 and 27 percent of profits. Refrigerated Foods consists of beef, pork, and lamb products (Monfort and Armour); branded processed meats (Armour, Swift Premium, Eckrich, and Healthy Choice); poultry (Butterball and Country Pride); cheeses (County Line); and refrigerated dessert toppings (Reddi Wip).

Food Inputs and Ingredients

In fiscal 1996, this part of ConAgra accounted for 27 percent of sales and 23 percent of profits. Food Inputs and Ingredients businesses include crop protection chemicals and fertilizers; grain processing (flour, oat, and dry corn milling; barley processing); and worldwide commodity trading (grains, oilseeds, edible beans, and peas, as well as other commodities).

Shortcomings to Bear in Mind

■ Fiscal 1996 was a difficult year for the flour milling industry. Wheat prices were at record highs, and supplies were tight. For the second consecutive year, flour exports from the United States were very low, freeing up domestic capacity and intensifying competition. New entrants in the industry added more capacity, and the per-capita consumption of flour declined slightly for the first time in a decade.

In this environment, compounded by poor results in Canada, ConAgra's Flour Milling's earnings declined in fiscal 1996. In addition to beginning the process of selling the Canadian business, ConAgra Flour Milling is restructuring the U.S. flour milling business to improve efficiency, quality, and profitability. What's more, the company got out of the bulk durum flour business in 1996 and closed two bulk durum mills.

Reasons to Buy

- Golden Valley Microwave Foods is a leader in the development of foods exclusively for preparation for microwave ovens. Formerly part of ConAgra Diversified Products Companies, Golden Valley became part of ConAgra Grocery Products Companies early in fiscal 1996. The resulting closer association with the Orville Redenbacher's business will allow the company to take better advantage of synergies between the firm's two popcorn businesses.

- ConAgra Diversified Products Companies include Lamb-Weston, Arrow Industries, the company's seafood business, a pet products business, and a frozen microwave food business in the United Kingdom.

  Lamb-Weston is a leading processor of frozen potato products, primarily french fries for food service markets. Lamb-Weston supplies most of the leading restaurant chains and food service distributors in the United States, as well as in Europe and Asia.

- Arrow Industries, Inc., is a leading manufacturer and national distributor of private-label consumer products for the grocery trade, principally supermarket retailers and wholesalers. Products include dried beans, rice, popcorn, pepper and spices, aluminum foil, plastic bags and wraps, flexible packaging, paper plates and bags, vegetable oil, charcoal, and lighter fluid.

- ConAgra Agri-Products Companies' major businesses provide inputs that farmers need to grow their crops: crop protection, chemicals, fertilizers, and seeds.

  United Agri Products (UAP) is the leading distributor of crop protection chemicals to North American markets and a major marketer of fertilizers. UAP serves customers in most major agricultural regions of the United States and Canada. UAP distributes a broad line of pesticides and fertilizers manufactured by major chemical and fertilizer companies. It also formulates and distributes its own products under the Clean Crop label. What's more, it operates Cropmate retail outlets in the Midwest and Louisiana. Finally, it markets animal healthcare products.

- ConAgra's grain processing businesses include flour milling in the United States, Canada, and Puerto Rico; oat milling in the United States, Canada, and the United Kingdom; dry corn milling in the United States and Germany; tortilla manufacturing in the United States; barley malting in Australia, China, Denmark, and the United Kingdom; specialty food ingredient manufacturing and marketing in the United States; feed ingredient merchandising in the United States, Canada, and Mexico; and animal feed production and marketing in the United States, Puerto Rico, Spain, and Portugal.

  ConAgra Flour Milling is a leader in the U.S. flour milling industry, with twenty-seven mills in fourteen states and seven jointly owned mills, three in the United States and four in Canada.

- The packaged food industry's ability to meet evolving consumer lifestyles and tastes should enable companies such as ConAgra to sustain their long, successful record of higher sales and profits. In addition, rising domestic and world standards of living, increasing world trade liberalization, and the significant adoption of progressive economic policies throughout the world should provide U.S. food packagers adequate opportunities for long-term growth.

■ ConAgra is a large participant in the soybean industry, involved at the beginning and end of the soybean supply chain. The company sources, stores, merchandises, and transports millions of bushels of soybeans annually. ConAgra refines and packages soybean oil, such as Wesson oil, for retail and food service markets. The company uses soybean oil to manufacture branded products and soybean meal for animal feeds.

However, Soybean crushing has been the missing link for ConAgra in the United States soybean industry. ConAgra Trading and Processing Companies will build a soybean crushing, refining, and packaging complex in Mt. Vernon, Indiana, along the Ohio River. The complex will support ConAgra businesses and capitalize on many synergies.

● The plant will be fully integrated; soybeans will be received, processed, refined, and packaged at one location.

● The soybean crushing facility will be one of the largest in the United States, processing 5,600 tons of soybeans daily.

● The complex will also include an oil refinery, a packaging/bottling plant, grain elevators, and a barge facility.

● Investment in the facility will be $170 million. The complex is scheduled to be completed in 1998.

■ During fiscal 1996, ConAgra Grocery Products Companies completed building a new sales organization. The Grocery Products sales and in-store merchandising force was expanded from 350 to 800 people supporting ConAgra Frozen Foods products and Hunt-Wesson products.

In addition, ConAgra Frozen Foods replaced broker representation with a new 180-person direct sales force. This new sales model improves ConAgra Grocery Products' ability to deliver consumer value, improve customer service, increase sales, and maintain industry leadership.

■ United Agri Products (UAP) is the leading distributor of crop protection chemicals to North American markets and a major marketer of fertilizers. This core inputs business serves customers in most major agricultural areas of the United States and Canada. UAP distributes a broad line of branded pesticides, fertilizers, and seeds; formulates and distributes its own products under the Clean Crop label; and operates Cropmate retail outlets in the Midwest and Louisiana. Annual sales are about $2.5 million.

Total assets: $11,197 million
Current ratio: 1.04
Common shares outstanding: 226 million
Return on 1996 shareholders' equity: 24.3%

	1996	1995	1994	1993	1992	1991	1990	1989
Revenues (millions)	24,822	24,109	23,512	21,519	21,219	19,505	15,501	11,340
Net income (millions)	545	496	437	392	372	311	232	198
Earnings per share	2.34	2.06	1.81	1.58	1.50	1.42	1.25	1.09
Dividends per share	.95	.80	.70	.60	.52	.45	.39	.33
Price: High	54.8	34.5	29.4	34.3	36.2	32.5	21.2	15.9
Low	37.6	28.2	23.0	22.8	24.5	19.7	14.1	12.0

CPC International, Inc.

International Plaza, P. O. Box 8000, Englewood Cliffs, NJ 07632-9976 ◻ Investor contact: John W. Scott (201) 894-2837 ◻ Dividend reinvestment plan available: (201) 324-0498 ◻ Listed: NYSE ◻ Ticker symbol: CPC ◻ S&P rating: A+ ◻ Value Line financial strength rating: A+

CPC is an international food company that focuses on three worldwide businesses: soups, sauces, bouillons, and related products. Among the company's well-known consumer brands are such items as Hellmann's Mayonnaise, Knorr soups and sauces, Mazola corn oil, Skippy peanut butter, Argo corn starch, Karo corn syrup, and Mueller's pasta.

CPC also focuses regionally on several selected consumer foods businesses and a corn-refining business that supplies the food industry and other manufacturers.

CPC's consumer foods business, accounting for 70 percent of the company's worldwide sales, consists of several regional businesses and three worldwide businesses: Knorr soups, sauces, bouillons, and related products; Dressings; and Food Service.

Worldwide sales of Knorr soups, sauces, bouillons, and related products were $3.1 billion in 1996, 7.9 percent higher than 1995. Knorr and other related products are marketed by CPC in fifty-nine countries.

Worldwide sales of mayonnaise, other dressing, and corn oil were $1.9 billion in 1996, up 6.4 percent. CPC's dressings business comprises mayonnaise and other ready-to-use dressings that enhance and add flavor to foods. Marketed by CPC in forty-five countries, chiefly under the Hellmann's brand, this range of value-added products is based upon superior dressings-related technologies and consumer-driven innovation.

Food Service

CPC's food service business (known as Caterplan in most markets outside the United States) supports the operators of restaurants, cafeterias, and other places where food is served. CPC's largest food service operation is in Europe. It is increasingly focused on faster leveraging of pan-European products, such as the Knorr ready-to-use liquid gourmet sauces introduced in 1996 in eight countries.

CPC's food service business in North America introduced thirteen varieties of pourable salad dressings, Hellmann's and Best Foods Deli Blend spoonable dressing, and a line of Knorr instant gravies. It also added Knorr Primerba herbs in oil, a product developed by CPC in Europe.

Restructuring

CPC is in the midst of a major restructuring. In early 1997, the company announced that it intended to spin off its corn refining business to shareholders. It will become an independent, publicly owned company.

Management is convinced that this move will strongly benefit both of the resulting companies: CPC International, a global packaging food company that comprises its existing grocery products, baking, and food service operations; and the new corn refining company. The separation is to be accomplished by the end of 1997.

1996 Achievements

• Earnings per share rose 7.1 percent, to $3.93. Net income was up 5.9 percent, to $580 million, on strongly growing sales and volumes. The consumer foods and baking businesses, which accounted for more than 90 percent of the company's earnings in 1996, increased their net income, on an estimated pro forma basis, by more than 20 percent. This more than offset the decline of more than 80 percent in the company's corn refining earnings, calculated on the same basis.

• The company increased the dividend 7.9 percent in September of 1996.

• Total return to shareholders (dividends plus appreciation in the price of the stock) was 15.4 percent. Over the last five years, cumulative return to CPC shareholders is 95 percent, compared with 55 percent on average for CPC's food company peer group, as well as the S&P Foods Index.

Shortcomings to Bear in Mind

* Until the spinoff of the corn refining company, CPC International looks for the industry-related problems to have a dampening effect on the total company performance. The extraordinarily volatile commodities market of 1996 and its extremely high corn costs, however, are a thing of the past. On the other hand, the recovery of this business from 1996's severely depressed profit levels is likely to be gradual, as overcapacity in the high fructose corn syrup sector of the industry puts strong competitive pressure on HFCS pricing.

Reasons to Buy

■ Strategic acquisitions are a key element in CPC's strategy for growth. All three of the important acquisitions the company made in 1995 are meeting management's expectations. In fact, the Pot Noodle hot snacks business, acquired in the United Kingdom, has outstripped its most optimistic projections for volume and profit growth. In baking, CPC successfully merged the acquired business with its existing baking operations and achieved the synergies and added earnings that were projected. In addition,

the company introduced more than one hundred new products to drive volume and profit growth. In France, CPC has made significant progress in revitalizing the Lesieur dressings business, acquired during 1995.

■ Among top strategic priorities is a vigorous step-up in CPC's new product innovations rate throughout the company. CPC Germany, its most powerful new-product generator, forecasts that more than 20 percent of its 1997 sales of retail products will come from products new in the last three years.

In 1996, the company made a major move toward this goal with the launch of new Hellmann's and Best Foods pourable salad dressings in the United States; this was quickly followed by a launch of the same products in Latin America. In the first few months of 1997, the company extended its presence in the category, adding a line of fat-free pourable dressings under the same brands in the United States.

In the Knorr product family, innovation went beyond unique new products to the way in which the company launches them: more rapidly than ever before and often simultaneously in multiple countries, thus maximizing the power of its resources and speeding the addition of new profits.

■ Without abandoning CPC's traditional commitment to appropriate adaptation for local tastes, the company recognized the convergence across borders of many consumer preferences, as well as the imperative to maximize efficiency.

Knorr Spaghetteria pasta dishes and Knorr culinary cubes have been quickly and successfully introduced across Europe over the past two years. In Latin America, the company's joint venture with General Mills's International Dessert Partners launched a new line of dessert products under the combined Betty Crocker and Maizena brands in five Latin American countries simultaneously.

- While many U.S. food companies are just beginning to venture into international markets, CPC has operated internationally for ninety years. Its established presence and experience on five continents give the company a critical edge, positioning it to establish its brands quickly and powerfully.

    For example, geographic expansion is paying off handsomely in Central Europe, where the company's earnings increased 50 percent in 1996. In Asia, the company's expansion in China continues with the opening of a plant in Beijing and the establishment of a joint venture in Shanghai.

- Throughout the company, CPC is realizing the benefits of the restructuring programs that it executed over the past several years. In the last two years, for instance, CPC has shut down thirteen plants worldwide and consolidated production in more efficient and strategically located facilities. What's more, the company has dramatically reduced the number of product ingredients and packaging elements it uses. It has also implemented a new program of global and regional purchasing.

    The savings CPC achieved through restructuring and an unrelenting search for cost-saving opportunities are enabling the company to increase substantially its marketing investments to drive volume growth.

- In the 1986–1996 period, earnings per share climbed from $1.15 to $3.93 with no dips along the way—a compound annual growth rate of 13.1 percent. In the same ten-year span, dividends advanced from $.57 to $1.58, a growth rate of 10.7 percent.

- In October of 1995, CPC acquired the baking business of Philip Morris's Kraft food unit for $865 million in cash. The transaction created a $1.7 billion basket of such well-known brands as CPC's Thomas' English muffins, Arnold breads, Kraft's Entenmann's cookies and cakes, Freihofer's and Oroweat breads, and Boboli pizza crusts.

- Knorr products were first introduced in Germany in 1838 and today are sold in twenty-two European markets, most recently in Russia, where a CPC team began selling imported Knorr products at the start of 1994.

    Across Europe, the Knorr brand is a market leader: number one in soups and bouillons; number two in sauces, and a strong performer in other categories.

- Knorr bouillon is number one in Latin America. New Knorr products include a stir-fry bouillon cube for preparing a variety of dishes and new extensions of the Knorr Sopao soup line in Brazil. In Mexico new products include new rice dishes, bean dishes, and soups in cups.

Total assets: $7,875 million
Current ratio: 0.84
Common shares outstanding: 145 million
Return on 1996 shareholders' equity: 27.8%

	1996	1995	1994	1993	1992	1991	1990	1989
Revenues (millions)	9,344	8,432	7,425	6,738	6,599	6,189	5,781	5,103
Net income (millions)	580	548	482	455	431	404	374	328
Earnings per share	3.93	3.67	3.17	2.95	2.78	2.61	2.42	2.11
Dividends per share	1.58	1.48	1.38	1.28	1.20	1.10	1.00	.88
Price: High	84.2	74.5	55.6	51.1	51.5	46.8	42.4	36.9
Low	64.9	51.6	44.3	39.9	39.8	36.0	31.0	24.7

Deere & Company

John Deere Road, Moline, Illinois 61265-8098 □ Investor contact: Marie Ziegler (309) 765-4491 □
Dividend reinvestment plan available: (309) 765-4539 □ Fiscal year ends October 31 □ Listed: NYSE □
Ticker symbol: DE □ S&P rating: B+ □ Value Line financial strength rating: A+

Deere & Company and its subsidiaries manufacture, distribute, and finance a full line of agricultural equipment; a broad range of industrial equipment for construction, forestry, and public works; and a variety of commercial and consumer equipment. The company also provides credit, managed healthcare plans, and insurance products for business and the general public.

In fiscal 1996 (ended October 31, 1996), the company's businesses broke down as follows:

	Revenues	Profits
Farm equipment	54%	58%
Industrial equipment	17	13
Lawn and grounds care	15	8
Credit	14	16
Insurance, health care, and other	8	5

Agricultural Equipment

John Deere is the world's leading producer of agricultural equipment. The company offers full lines of tractors, combine harvesters, tillage tools, seeding equipment, hay equipment, cotton pickers and strippers, cultivators, and other equipment.

John Deere agricultural products are manufactured in the United States, Canada, Germany, France, South Africa, Mexico, Argentina, and Brazil, and sold in more than 160 countries.

The company's objective is to increase its competitive advantage; not only to introduce important technology advances, but also to develop products that strategically address a spectrum of customer needs, new geographic markets, and new niche markets.

In August 1996, forty-two new or updated agricultural products were introduced. Many were new and updated tractors, including the 7000 TEN-series row-crop tractor update, the 8000T-series track versions of the renowned 8000-series row-crop tractor line, and the new 9000-series four-wheel-drive tractors that leveraged the 8000 series design concepts for comfort and visibility. Other new products like commercial sprayers and commercial hay balers were targeted at markets where the company had not been competing.

The Agricultural Equipment Division's growth plans include expanding its geographic presence. The Mercosul trade agreement facilitated the company's 1996 entry into the tractor market in Brazil, Latin America's largest agricultural equipment market.

A sale of 1,049 combines, over two years, was made to the Ukraine and a $114 million sale of combines and cotton pickers to Kazakhstan was recently announced for 1997.

The company continues to move toward a joint venture in China to produce small combines.

Power Systems Group

John Deere is a major producer of heavy-duty industrial engines for off-highway vehicles and stationary power applications, and other power train components, including transmissions from its Funk Manufacturing subsidiary.

In the segment of the off-highway diesel engine market where it has chosen to participate, the 50- to 500-horsepower class, John Deere ranks second in the world and has the largest internal volume base of all competitors.

Overall sales were up 15 percent in 1996. Gains were driven by two major factors: sales of John Deere agricultural and industrial equipment that use Deere-made engines, and growing demand from original equipment manufacturers (OEM). Outside engine sales represent about 37 percent of Deere's engine volume. External markets range from construction and forestry to irrigation, generator sets, airline ground-support equipment, marine applications, and specialized agricultural equipment.

PowerTech engines were in full production in 1996. The new 425-horsepower, 12.5-liter engine powers the John Deere 9400 four-wheel-drive agricultural tractor that was introduced in August 1996. The new engines are more fuel-efficient, quieter in operation, and easier to service. One key feature is that the new engines are capable of meeting stringent off-highway air-emissions standards being phased in through January 1998.

Power Systems growth hinges on developing new products, such as the clean-burning natural-gas engines. Natural-gas engines were installed in Blue Bird buses on a limited basis in 1996.

The engine group is looking for international expansion, too. Sales outside of North America increased again in 1996, partly due to engine sales made to a Deere-Renault tractor venture. Also, the company's existing engine factory in Argentina was expanded and is providing engines for tractors being assembled in Brazil.

Commercial and Consumer Equipment
The company is the world's largest manufacturer in the premium outdoor power equipment industry. John Deere produces and markets a broad line of lawn and garden tractors, mowers, and other outdoor power products for commercial uses, including golf and turf care professionals, and homeowners worldwide.

Deere's position overseas continues to strengthen. The company holds a majority interest in SABO Maschinenfabrik GmbH, which produces high-quality walk-behind mowers for homeowners and also an important line of commercial rotary and reel mowers for European markets. SABO provides an excellent base for further expansion in Europe.

Shortcomings to Bear in Mind
- In the second quarter of fiscal 1997 (which ended April 30, 1997) commercial and consumer equipment, which includes lawn and garden, experienced lower earnings than the other divisions. Operating profit fell 28 percent to $58 million from $81 million in the same period of 1996. Deere said the decline was because of costs associated with discontinuing a lawn trimmer during the quarter.

Reasons to Buy
- A strong agricultural economy helped lead to record results in 1996 for the Worldwide Agricultural Equipment Division, John Deere's largest business. Worldwide sales rose 16 percent, to $6.1 billion. Operating income was $821 million, up 28 percent. Overseas sales were a highlight, posting an increase of 31 percent. The overseas improvement was broad-based, but sales gains were particularly impressive in Europe, as well as Argentina and Australia.

   In rising 8 percent, North American agricultural equipment sales reached $3.8 billion in 1996. Sales volumes were higher for most product categories, with tractors and seeding equipment showing the biggest increases. North American sales benefited from improved farm incomes as a result of higher crop prices, more acreage under cultivation, and above-average yields.

- As one of John Deere's flagship products, the all-new 9000-series tractors are a good example of how the company's businesses work together to produce and market new products and lend service support. For starters, the 9000-series tractors, which muster up to 425 horsepower, are equipped with PowerTech engines from Deere's own engine works in Waterloo, Iowa. The standard axles and transmissions, too, are made by Deere in Waterloo. Hydraulic cylinders, responsible for the machines' capacity to do heavy lifting, are produced at Deere facilities in Moline, Illinois.

On the customer side, purchasers of 9000-series models are likely to receive financing or leasing assistance from John Deere Credit. Many dealers are protected against property and casualty loss by Deere's own insurance organization. Should the tractors require parts, an extensive parts and aftermarket operation is standing by to deliver, often overnight.

- Global demand for American grains is strong and seems likely to remain so. Increasing affluence in many nations around the world is raising the quality of diets, and increasing the per-capita consumption of meat. This requires up to 7 pounds of grain per pound fit for consumption. Meanwhile, both China and Japan report that their arable land is declining 1.5 percent a year, reflecting population pressures and other uses. These factors have created a much sounder base of overseas demand than fifteen or twenty years ago, when export demand largely depended on the vagaries of the Soviet Union's requirements.

- Deere & Company, riding a wave of strong demand for agricultural equipment, reported a 17 percent jump in fiscal second quarter of 1997 earnings.

In that period, the company earned $319.5 million, or $1.25 per share, compared with $272.7 million in the second quarter of 1996, when it earned $1.04. Revenues increased 14 percent, to $3.52 billion, from $3.09 billion in the comparable period of the prior year.

The company said it expects sales for the full year to exceed the prior year's by 8 percent. Hans Becherer, Deere's chief executive, said, "The remainder of 1997 should benefit from a growing global economy, healthy agricultural markets, and generally high levels of farm confidence."

Mr. Becherer commented that Deere has posted strong results for the past two years, as farmers, cash rich from high commodity prices, have replaced their aging equipment by snapping up the company's green machines. Tractors and combines, two of the most expensive farm machines Deere makes, were among the most critical in boosting the recent earnings.

Total assets: $14,653 million
Current ratio: 2.20
Common shares outstanding: 255 million
Return on 1996 shareholders' equity: 26.5%

	1996	1995	1994	1993	1992	1991	1990	1989
Revenues (millions)	9,640	8,830	7,663	6,479	5,723	5,848	6,779	6,234
Net income (millions)	817	706	604	168	37	15	411	380
Earnings per share	3.14	2.71	2.34	.73	.16	.06	1.81	1.69
Dividends per share	.80	.75	.68	.67	.67	.67	.67	.43
Price: High	47.1	36.0	30.3	26.1	18.0	19.1	26.1	21.4
Low	33.0	21.7	20.4	14.1	12.3	13.3	12.5	14.7

Diebold, Incorporated

P. O. Box 3077, North Canton, Ohio 44720-8077 ◻ Investor contact: Donald E. Eagon, Jr. (330) 490-3770 ◻ Dividend reinvestment plan available: (800) 766-5859 ◻ Listed: NYSE ◻ Ticker symbol: DBD ◻ S&P rating: A ◻ Value Line financial strength rating: A+

Founded in 1859 as a manufacturer of safes and bank vaults, Diebold today is a world leader in providing card-based transaction systems and security and service solutions to the financial, education, and healthcare industries.

The company manufactures and services automated teller machines (ATMs), electronic and physical security systems, electronic-payment systems, and software for global financial and commercial markets.

Headquartered in North Canton, Ohio (southeast of Cleveland), Diebold has international offices in Canada, Mexico, the United Kingdom, Germany, Venezuela, Hong Kong, and China. It has manufacturing facilities in Ohio, Virginia, South Carolina, Germany, and China.

Diebold is at the forefront in systems integration, specializing in self-service and security applications and software. While the financial industry has long been Diebold's core market, the company is also expanding into other spheres, including healthcare, education, retail, government services, and the international marketplace.

Internationally, Diebold has been advancing into developing markets in regions that are experiencing unprecedented economic growth, such as China, Latin America, and Eastern Europe, while strengthening its competitive position in mature markets, such as Western Europe and Canada.

Diebold also supplies POS and EFT systems in the United States through an exclusive agreement with Schlumberger Limited.

Diebold's MedSelect System products are targeted to the medical supply inventory control and dispensing markets. Diebold's MedSelect product line includes a state-of-the-art automated medication dispensing system that enables healthcare institutions to manage supplies more cost-effectively while ensuring quick and accurate response to patient needs. The system features open-platform software and interconnectivity to most existing hospital systems to enhance administrative efficiency.

In addition, Diebold is evolving into a complete systems solution provider with innovative software that ties multiple networks, hosts, servers, and databases together with a broad spectrum of multinational systems. The Integrated Campus Access Management (ICAM) system is gaining popularity with educational and medical institutions by tying together self-service and security systems and administrative functions.

Customers

Diebold's primary customer is the financial industry. However, a growing portion of revenues derive from nonfinancial customers, including universities, colleges, corporate campuses, hospitals, and retail businesses.

The largest ATM deployers in the United States are Bank of America, Electronic Data Systems Corp., and Affiliated Computer Services, Inc. The first two of these are InterBold product customers. InterBold is the ATM joint venture between Diebold and International Business Machines Corporation (IBM).

The latter two have large off-premises networks in places such as retail stores and hotels, rather than in bank branches. This is indicative of a trend for a growing portion of ATMs to be installed in off-premises locations.

About forty college and university campuses now have ICAM systems. The list includes universities such as Texas A&M, Michigan, Illinois, Texas, Florida, New York, Missouri, and Memphis; state universities in Oklahoma, South Carolina, Florida, Montana, California, and Michigan; colleges such as Williams, Wellesley, and Boston; and Rensselaer Polytechnic Institute.

Competition

Diebold is the only company with ATMs accounting for such a major portion of its revenues.

ATMs

InterBold is the leading provider of ATMs in the United States and the second-largest in the world, as measured by shipments of new units. AT&T, through its subsidiary AT&T Global Information Solutions, is InterBold's largest competitor in the ATM market. Fujitsu is the only other supplier with a two-digit percentage share of the global market. Several other companies, notably Omron, Oki, Hitachi, Siemens Nixdorf, and Olivetti, are international competitors.

Advanced Card Systems

VeriFone of Redwood City, California, is currently the leading U.S. supplier of electronic payment systems (EPS).

Medical Automated Dispensing Products

Pyxis is the leader in this new market.

Security Products

Diebold is a leading provider of security equipment to U.S. financial institu-tions. Major global competitors include Mosler of Hamilton, Ohio; LeFebure Corp. of Cedar Rapids, Iowa, a division of U.K.–based De La Rue, Inc.; Fichet-Bauche, a division of Fichet of France; Racal-Chubb Ltd. of the U.K.; Honeywell, a U.S. company; and ADT Ltd., with headquarters in the United Kingdom. In addition, there are about one hundred smaller equipment companies that share this worldwide market.

Service

Diebold holds the leading position in the customer service business for financial institutions in the United States. AT&T Global Information Solutions is the leading domestic competitor for ATM maintenance contracts. Regional and local third-party providers account for a growing share of the worldwide service market. Diebold's service capabilities are proving attractive to nonfinancial security system owners, who often need to improve repair and maintenance programs.

Shortcomings to Bear in Mind

- Diebold does not have an impressive record of growth to support its high P/E ratio. In the 1986–1996 period, earnings per share advanced from $.53 to $1.42, a compound annual growth rate 10.4 percent. In the same ten-year stretch, dividends per share expanded from $.22 to $.45, a growth rate of 7.4 percent.

Reasons to Buy

- The U.S. financial industry has been important to Diebold's performance for 138 years. The major consolidation occurring in the banking and thrift industries is benefiting Diebold as financial institutions merge and cen-tralize operations, accompanied by replacement or upgrading of ATMs, integration of differing electronic secu-rity systems, and remodeling of branches.

Financial institutions are also developing fee-based products and services as additional income sources. ATMs and service contracts enable financial institutions to control personnel costs.

- The strong performance of financial institutions in recent years has permitted them to invest in systems that streamline operations and enhance productivity. Financial institutions have been adding ATMs at a rapid pace, and branch operating costs have fallen as a result. Increased ATM usage frees bank personnel to meet new customers, handle questions, and sell new products.
- Since the beginning of this decade, Diebold has been pursuing a strategy of market diversification. By adapting its products and services for universities, hospitals, office complexes, and airports, Diebold is successfully penetrating nonfinancial markets.
- Institutions around the world are enhancing security systems in the face of increasing crime and terrorism. Diebold's leading expertise in electronic security and self-service technology for the financial industry has positioned the company to take advantage of opportunities outside its traditional markets.
- Government programs are turning to card-activated electronic benefits transfer systems as a better way to distribute and control benefits. Diebold is currently developing a system for Mississippi and has proposals out for several other state contracts.
- Emerging economies and established markets offer significant potential for Diebold's continued strategic growth outside the United States. The competitive advantages Diebold products have demonstrated in the United States are proving equally compelling for international customers.

- Diebold, through its InterBold joint venture with IBM, is pursuing international ATM markets.
- Technological advances by InterBold may also lead to increased market share. The joint venture with IBM provides technological access that is accelerating the evolution of ATM technology, which includes LAN connectivity, biometric processing, and interactive video terminals.
- Adding features to ATMs will increase applications and should increase sales. Full-feature InterBold ATMs can handle a wide range of transactions, such as dispensing stamps, issuing transit and theater tickets, check-imaging, and coin dispensing. The ATMs can also deliver marketing messages while customers are waiting for transactions to be processed.
- Diebold's systems integration software business is growing rapidly, reflecting a move from selling hardware to selling solutions. Diebold's 1/Link software enables a financial institution to combine a variety of functions, such as ATMs and EPS, under one network.
- The popularity of smart cards and other card systems is rising around the globe. Diebold is a U.S. leader in smart card software development. Smart cards are being used in an increasing number of applications such as healthcare, campus systems, and stadium card systems.

For smart cards and other types of systems, Diebold software is key to the total solutions the company provides. Designed to be flexible, upgradable, and powerful, Diebold software enables customers to integrate their existing systems with new applications to improve performance and efficiency.

Total assets: $859 million
Current ratio: 2.10
Common shares outstanding: 69 million
Return on 1996 shareholders' equity: 18.0%

	1996	1995	1994	1993	1992	1991	1990	1989
Revenues (millions)	1,030	863	760	623	544	506	476	469
Net income (millions)	97	76	64	48	41	36	32	36
Earnings per share	1.42	1.11	.93	.71	.61	.53	.47	.54
Dividends per share	.45	.43	.39	.36	.33	.32	.30	.28
Price: High	42.3	27.6	20.8	18.3	12.2	10.5	9.3	9.4
Low	22.4	14.7	15.1	11.6	9.3	6.5	5.9	7.2

AGGRESSIVE GROWTH

Dover Corporation

280 Park Avenue, New York, N. Y. 10017-1292 ◻ **Investor contact: John F. McNiff (212) 922-1640** ◻
Dividend reinvestment plan not available ◻ **Listed: NYSE** ◻ **Ticker symbol: DOV** ◻ **S&P rating: A** ◻
Value Line financial strength rating: A+

Dover's businesses are divided into five segments:

• Dover Resources manufactures products primarily for the automotive, fluid handling, petroleum, and chemical industries. In 1996, Dover Resources represented 15.9 percent of sales and 18.8 percent of profits.

• Dover Industries (20.8 percent of sales and 20.6 percent of profits) makes products for use in waste handling, bulk transport, automotive service, commercial food service, and machine tool industries.

• Dover Technologies (24.3 percent of sales and 26 percent of profits) builds primarily sophisticated automated assembly equipment for the electronics industry, industrial printers for coding and marking, and, to a lesser degree, specialized electronic components.

• Dover Diversified (17.9 percent of sales and 19 percent of profits) builds sophisticated assembly and production machines, heat transfer equipment, and specialized compressors, as well as sophisticated products and control systems for use in the defense, aerospace, and commercial building industries.

• Dover Elevator International, Inc. (21.1 percent of sales and 15.6 percent of profits) manufactures, installs, and services elevators, primarily in North America.

Acquisitions

The company emphasizes growth and strong international cash flow. It has a long-standing and successful acquisition program. In the 1991–1995 period, for instance, Dover made forty-seven acquisitions at a total acquisition cost of $962 million. These acquisitions have had a substantial impact on the company's increase in sales and earnings since 1991.

The company's acquisition program traditionally focused on acquiring new or stand-alone businesses. However, since 1993, increased emphasis has been placed on acquiring businesses that can be added on to existing operations. The company aims to be in businesses marked by growth, innovation, and higher-than-average profit margins. It seeks to have each of its businesses be a leader in its market as measured by market share, innovation, profitability, and return on assets.

Highlights from 1996

• Profit improvement at Dover Elevator International was noteworthy, up 179 percent from 1995, a year that was burdened by write-offs. Even so, on an operating basis, profits climbed 39 percent for the elevator segment.

• Imaje, acquired in 1995, had a superb year; sales improved, with margins in excess of 30 percent. Imaje earned more than $50 million in 1996.

• Belvac achieved another earnings record with profits more than triple the level recorded in 1993. Belvac has benefited from the surge in demand for its beverage can necking machines.

• A-C Compressor made a turnaround in 1996. It was helped by a renewed focus on its strengths in selected niches in the huge, worldwide compressor market, which stimulated significant profit improvement, with the possibility of more to come in 1997.

• The successful design and launch of a new product (Universal GSM-2) allowed Universal to remain "best in class" in the market for flexible, fine-pitch electronic component placement. This helped Universal achieve its second-best earnings level within an overall market that was down sharply from 1995.

• Dover sold Dieterich Standard and Measurement Systems in 1996. While it is not Dover's normal practice to sell businesses that are performing well, in this instance the company responded to its perception, born of experience, that these businesses had limited growth potential. In addition, the sale was made on an attractive basis by synergistic buyers. Most of the net proceeds were used to repurchase Dover common stock.

• Dover invested $282 million in making acquisitions, repurchased $63 million of its own stock, and spent $125 million on capital expenditures, for a combined record investment of $470 million.

Shortcomings to Bear in Mind

▪ The new elevator market in North America (where most of the company's elevator business is done) remains depressed and highly competitive but with some renewed growth in the hydraulic segment. Dover Elevator International's new regional field operations structure, combined with an increase in the new elevator sales force and a focused effort on the Oildraulic product line, resulted in record bookings of these low-rise elevators. While the domestic market for traction elevators remains depressed, particularly in the high-rise commercial market, Dover Elevator was able to take advantage of selective growth in the hotel and resort industry. Overall, bookings rose 6 percent in 1996, with new elevator backlogs increasing 9 percent during the year.

▪ Hill Phoenix (part of Dover Diversified) continued to struggle in 1996 with its plan for a significant earnings turnaround, as profits improved only slightly and sales declined. Hill Phoenix produces electrical distribution systems. Manufacturing problems were greatly reduced, however, improving the company's quality and on-time performance. This should lead to a modest increase in shipments and a much better profit in 1997.

▪ Pathway Bellows (another operating under Dover Diversified), which now includes Thermal Equipment product lines, also had a disappointing financial year in 1996, with unexpected expenditures to correct field problems on several previously installed pieces of equipment. These two operations produce a line of metal and fabric expansion joints, autoclaves, as well as industrial cleaning equipment.

Reasons to Buy

- Dover has an exceptional record of earnings increases, with only one dip in the past ten years (in 1991, EPS dropped to $1.05 from $1.28). In the 1986–1996 period, earnings climbed from $.61 to $3.01, a compound annual growth rate of 17.3 percent. In the same span, dividends expanded from 23 cents to 64 cents, a growth rate of 10.8 percent.

- Late in 1996, Dover Technologies completed the second-largest acquisition in Dover's history—Everett Charles Technologies of Pomona, California. This company has established a leadership position in each of three niches within the electronic test market. It is the leading producer of machines for the testing of circuitry on printed circuit boards before these boards are populated with components—that is, bare board testing. It is also the leader in design and manufacture of test fixtures for populated boards, operating seven facilities around the world. What's more, Everett Charles is the largest producer of spring-loaded test probes, which are used in both bare-board and populated-board testing. As printed circuit board design becomes increasingly complex, the need for sophisticated testing will increase. Dover views Everett Charles as a platform for further growth, both internally and through acquisitions.

- Also in the fourth quarter of 1996, Dover Resources completed another stand-alone acquisition, Tulsa Winch, a long-established producer of winches and speed reducers. Tulsa serves many industrial markets and has achieved a solid record of growth and profitability.

- During 1996, Dover made eight more add-on acquisitions, involving the investment of $91 million. These eight businesses will extend the geographic markets for existing Dover companies. The companies acquired in 1996 had a (pro forma) full-year sales volume of about $175 million, only a portion of which has been included in the company's 1996 financial results. Because most of these acquisition investments came late in the year and the level of full first-year acquisition premium write-offs will be high, these businesses will contribute only a few cents per share to Dover's earnings in 1997—but significantly more in future years.

- Sargent Controls and Aerospace (which is part of Dover Diversified) improved its profits significantly in 1996 on a sales gain of more than 20 percent. Strong shipments of hydraulic controls for aircraft and increased billings on submarine projects fueled the gain. Work on the navy's new SSN23 submarine has proceeded much more smoothly than on its two predecessors. This contract was appropriately priced, especially when compared to the original two shipsets of this class, when development time and costs were underestimated and a 30- to 40-ship building program was expected. Sargent Controls expects to continue its current levels of profitability for the next several years, but growth beyond this will depend on product diversification and government decisions about future upgrading of the submarine fleet.

- Rotary Lift (which is part of Dover Industries) again achieved record profits in 1996, with an increase of more than 30 percent, as the company continued to expand its market-leading position in the North American automotive lift market. Rotary made further manufacturing improvements to reduce costs and expand capacity. Its strategy has been to invest heavily in manufacturing equipment and systems and then to use its low-cost producer position and high levels of quality and service to increase unit volume. This strategy has proven extremely successful, with profits doubling in the past three years on a 50 percent sales increase. A strong effort has been launched to expand Rotary's North American success to Europe through focused export programs and acquisitions.

Total assets: $2,993 million
Current ratio: 1.49
Common shares outstanding: 112 million
Return on 1996 shareholders' equity: 28.7%

	1996	1995	1994	1993	1992	1991	1990	1989
Revenues (millions)	4,076	3,746	3,085	2,484	2,272	2,196	2,210	2,120
Net income (millions)	340	278	202	158	129	125	156	144
Earnings per share	3.01	2.45	1.77	1.39	1.12	1.05	1.28	1.14
Dividends per share	.64	.56	.49	.45	.43	.41	.38	.35
Price: High	55.1	41.7	33.4	30.9	23.8	21.9	20.6	19.8
Low	36.6	25.8	24.9	22.5	19.1	17.3	13.8	13.6

INCOME

Duke Energy

422 South Church Street, Charlotte, North Carolina 28242-0001 ◻ Listed: NYSE ◻ Investor contact: Allen J. Stewart (704) 382-5087 ◻ Dividend reinvestment plan available: (800) 488-3853 ◻ Ticker symbol: DUK ◻ S&P rating: A- ◻ Value Line financial strength rating: A+

Duke Power Company was founded in 1905 and is one of the nation's largest investor-owned electric utilities. Duke Power and its subsidiary, Nantahala Power and Light Company, operate three nuclear generating stations, eight coal-fired stations, and thirty-eight hydroelectric stations.

The company consists of ten business units that, except for electric service provided within Duke Power's service area, are part of Associated Enterprises Group.

The company is looking increasingly to its subsidiaries and diversified activities as sources of additional growth. Duke Energy seeks to capitalize on opportunities to enhance value by leveraging existing expertise and other resources. During 1994, the company reorganized, placing all subsidiaries and diversified activities into the Associated Enterprises Group (AEG).

AEG includes Church Street Capital Corp.; Crescent Resources, Inc.; Duke Energy Group, Inc.; Duke Engineering & Services, Inc.; Duke/Fluor Daniel; Duke Merchandising; DukeNet Communications, Inc.; Duke Water Operations; and Nantahala Power and Light Company.

The company's objective is to significantly increase AEG's contribution to Duke Energy's total net income.

The company provides electric power to 1.7 million customers in the Piedmont section of North and South Carolina, which has a population of 4.8 million. The breakdown of revenues is 32 percent residential, 24 percent commercial, and 29 percent industrial, with the other 15 percent classified as "other." The company's generating capacity includes coal, 43 percent; nuclear, 39 percent; and other fuels, 18 percent.

Shortcomings to Bear in Mind

- Although Duke Energy may be termed one of the premium electric utilities—an aristocrat, if you will—it nonetheless lacks any evidence of solid growth. In the 1986–1996 period, earnings per share increased from $2.02 to $3.37, a compound annual growth rate of 5.3 percent. In the same ten-year stretch, dividends per share advanced from $1.32 to $2.08, a growth rate of 4.7 percent. However, during those years, the dividend payout held steady, declining slightly, from 65.3 percent to 64.0 percent. This 64 percent payout ratio, however, is far better than most electric utilities. Clearly, these are not impressive growth rates, but they are distinctly better than those for many other electric utilities. If you feel inclined to own an electric utility, Duke Energy serves very well for an investor seeking liberal income, with modest growth potential.

- The electric utility industry is transforming from a group of franchised monopolies to a more competitive industry. The Energy Policy Act of 1992 and a number of initiatives by the Federal Energy Regulatory Commission have introduced active competition on a wholesale level.

  On the retail side, industrial customers, eager to pare operating costs wherever possible, are seeking concessions and evaluating other supply options. Low-cost utilities with excess capacity are eyeing new markets outside their traditional franchises. Power marketers are eager to enter the business. Although retail competition is not currently allowed in North Carolina and South Carolina, regulators in some forty states have at least begun to study the issues surrounding retail competition. As a result, competitive pressures are growing in all segments of the business.

  On the other hand, these questions have been priorities for Duke Energy for some time. As a result, the company continues to focus on success in a competitive marketplace and the long-term creation of value for Duke shareholders. For its part, Duke intends to accomplish the following:

  - Achieve returns in the top quartile of the Standard & Poor's electric utilities index;
  - Significantly increase earnings of the company's diversified businesses;
  - Maintain a strong credit rating;
  - Achieve a high level of customer satisfaction.

Reasons to Buy

- In many ways, Duke is already realizing success in achieving the objectives it has set for itself. The company is a low-cost supplier of energy. Duke Energy's average price per kilowatt-hour is competitive on a local, regional, and national basis. Duke's coal-fired plants have led the nation in efficiency for more than two decades. The Lincoln Combustion Turbine facility was completed in 1996 under budget and ahead of schedule.

- Duke Energy is uniquely positioned to capitalize on its expertise in designing, building, and operating generating facilities. Duke is one of only a few domestic utilities that has historically designed, built, and operated its own power plants. The expertise Duke gained in those areas over the years has been retained through Duke Engineering & Services, Inc. and Duke/Fluor Daniel (DE&S), both business units with the Associated Enterprises Group (AEG).

  AEG also enables Duke Energy to take greater advantage of new business opportunities both in the United States and offshore. Much of Duke Energy Group's international business involves power projects in South America, while

DE&S has projects throughout the world. Through Duke Energy's partnership with Louis Dreyfus Electric Power, one of the largest power marketers in the United States, Duke Energy is positioning itself to become a major participant in the new power marketing business.

- Duke Energy is merging with PanEnergy in a deal valued at more than $7.5 billion. PanEnergy is one of the top energy services firms in the United States. It distributes over 15 percent of the natural gas consumed domestically. Under the terms of the agreement, each PanEnergy share was converted into 1.0444 shares of Duke. The combined entity has a market capitalization of $23 billion.

- The dividend of Duke Energy has been increased for twenty consecutive years.

- Most analysts agree that Duke is among the nation's premier electric utilities. Studies show that high-quality utilities outperform the average and lower-quality utilities over longer periods. In fact, says one analyst, over the last one-, three-, and five-year periods, the higher-quality names have been significant outperformers.

- While Duke's industrial rates are considered competitive, the company has established a number of innovative rates designed to provide more value to existing customers and to attract new customers to the service area. For instance, Duke offers an economic development rate that allows qualifying customers to take advantage of a declining credit on new or incremental load, based on the customer's standard rate schedule, over a four-year period. Participating customers receive a 20 percent credit on the new load the first year, declining by 5 percent each year. To qualify, customers must meet minimum load and other requirements, including consideration of employment and investment impacts.

What's more, Duke is currently piloting an hourly pricing rate for general service and industrial customers. Qualifying customers can buy electricity above a baseline level at marginal hourly prices. Prices vary based on conditions affecting the Duke system, such as weather and plant availability, and are provided to customers a day in advance.

Another rate, designed to help attract new industry, is available only in South Carolina. To qualify, a company must manufacture products that are distinctly different from those of existing businesses. The primary goal of this rate is to offer attractive rates to manufacturers who can help diversify the region's economic base. The company believes that economic diversity in its sales base is an important factor in maintaining industrial revenue growth. Moreover, a more diverse industrial base ultimately benefits not only Duke Energy but also the people who live in the service territory.

- Duke Energy meets its customers' needs for electricity primarily through a combination of nuclear-fueled, fossil-fueled, and hydroelectric generating stations.

Over the past twenty years, Duke's fossil-fueled generating system has consistently been cited by *Electric Light & Power* magazine as the country's most efficient fossil system, as measured by heat rate. Heat rate is a measure of efficiency in converting the energy contained in a fossil fuel such as oil, natural gas, or coal into electricity. A low heat rate means Duke burns less coal to generate a given quantity of electricity, lowering operating costs and helping keep rates competitive.

- Duke Energy Corp. will participate in an international consortium to build and own Nueva Renca, a 370-megawatt, gas-fired combined-cycle plant to be situated adjacent to the existing Renca power generating facility in Santiago, Chile. The new facility will cost about $230 million. The partners in the consortium are Duke Energy, Chilgener S.A. of Chile, Nova Corporation of Canada, and Compania General de Electricidad S.A. (CGE) of Chile.

The companies have formed Sociedad Electrica Santiago, S.A. (ESSA) to own the facility. Duke Energy's equity interest in ESSA is 24 percent or about $22 million. Construction began in 1995 with operation scheduled for 1997.

- Duke Energy offers attractive incentive rates for businesses to relocate and expand within its service territory. Duke's Economic Development Rate awards an initial 20 percent discount during the first year for industrial customers who expand their electricity consumption by one megawatt and either hire a minimum of seventy-five new employees or invest at least $400,000 in capital upgrades. Several dozen companies have qualified for the program.

Total assets: $ 13,470 million
Current ratio: 1.53
Return on 1996 equity: 14.2%
Common shares outstanding: 204.8 million

	1996	1995	1994	1993	1992	1991	1990	1989
Elec Revenues (millions)	4,758	4,677	4,279	4,282	3,962	3,817	3,705	3,693
Net income (millions)	730	715	639	626	508	584	538	572
Earnings per share	3.37	3.25	2.88	2.80	2.21	2.60	2.40	2.56
Dividends per share	2.08	2.00	1.92	1.84	1.76	1.68	1.60	1.52
Price: High	53.0	47.9	43.0	44.9	37.5	35.0	32.4	28.3
Low	43.4	37.4	32.9	35.4	31.4	26.8	25.5	21.4

GROWTH AND INCOME

E. I. DuPont de Nemours & Company

1007 Market Street, Wilmington, DE 19898 ▫ Investor contact: John W. Himes (302) 774-4994 ▫ Dividend reinvestment plan available: (800) 953-2498 ▫ Listed: NYSE ▫ Ticker symbol: DD ▫ S&P rating: B+ ▫ Value Line financial strength rating: A+

Although DuPont is the largest domestic chemical company, it is much more. With annual revenues of about $44 billion, DuPont links its fortunes to a host of business sectors including oil, natural gas, gasoline, agricultural chemicals, industrial and specialty chemicals, titanium dioxide, fluorocarbons, nylon, polyester, aramid and other fibers, polymer intermediates, films, resins, adhesives, electronic products, automotive paints, coatings, and pharmaceuticals.

The company operates 200 manufacturing and processing facilities in 40 countries. Exports from the United States totaled $3.8 billion in 1996, making DuPont one of the largest U.S. exporters. Foreign operations accounted for 48 percent of sales and 33 percent of net income in 1996. The fastest growth is coming from

Asia/Pacific and South America. Contributions by industry segment in 1996 were:

	Sales	Net Income
Chemicals	9%	14%
Fibers	16	20
Polymers	15	22
Life sciences	6	17
Diversified businesses	7	5
Petroleum exploration and pro.	10	16
Petroleum ref. mkt. and trans.	36	6

In its fibers segment, DuPont has a diversified mix of specialty fibers produced to serve end uses such as high-strength composites in aerospace, active sportswear, and packaging.

Polymers consists of engineering polymers, elastomers, and fluoropolymers.

DuPont's diversified businesses include agricultural products, coal, electronics, films, and imaging systems.

In its chemical operations, DD is primarily focused on brand-name downstream materials rather than commodity items. They include Stainmaster carpet; Lycra, Spandex, and Dacron polyester fiber; Teflon and Silverstone nonstick systems; as well as DuPont automotive paints.

DuPont is also the largest agrochemical producer in the United States and Asia.

The company is highly integrated vertically, including Conoco's oil, gas, refining, and marketing operations.

Shortcomings to Bear in Mind

- DuPont produces basic chemicals used in the automobile and housing industries, both of which are subject to the vagaries of the economy. In short, DuPont is currently enjoying robust earnings, but it could suffer, along with other cyclical stocks, if another recession is lurking around the corner. On a more positive note, DuPont is much less cyclical than chemical companies that rely on basic chemicals with no brand identity.
- Although DuPont has a solid growth rate, its earnings have not marched ahead every year. In the past ten years, earnings per share dipped from the prior year 4 times.

Reasons to Buy

- Achieving sustained, profitable growth in today's global marketplace requires clear competitive advantage. DuPont defines that advantage as being number one or two in both market position and technology in its chemicals and specialty businesses that are global in scope. About two-thirds of the company's businesses are already positioned as global leaders by this measure. Among them are Lycra, titanium dioxide, agricultural products, fluoroproducts, nonwovens, aramids, and photopolymers.
- Research and development is essential to DuPont's growth strategy, and the company continues to use its technological strength to add superior competitiveness. DD expects R&D to revolutionize the productivity of its manufacturing assets. A third of DuPont's revenue growth is targeted to come from new products. Research programs balance near- and long-term opportunities. The company's agricultural products pipeline includes fourteen new crop protection chemicals. In pharmaceuticals, Cozaar is the fastest-growing antihypertensive drug introduced in the last decade. Two other promising drugs are in the DuPont Merck research pipeline. Other development programs are focusing on the commercialization of new products and

processes from a radical new catalyst system for polyolefins and a series of new technologies for polyester. Both polyesters and polyolefins are large markets that are growing rapidly and represent potential for DuPont, based on new technologies.

- During the 1986–1996 period, DuPont's earnings per share climbed from $1.06 to $3.24, a compound annual growth rate of 11.8 percent. During that same ten-year span, dividends per share expanded from $.51 to $1.12, a growth rate of 8.2 percent. What's more, the payout ratio is low enough to permit the company to continue investing aggressively in its future.

- In March of 1997, Cytogen Corporation (CYTO) and DuPont Merck Pharmaceutical Company reported that the Food & Drug Administration granted marketing clearance for Quadramet, to treat severe pain associated with cancers that have spread to bone. Quadramet became commercially available in 1997. Quadramet was developed by CYTO under a license from Dow Chemical. The product will be made and marketed by the Radiopharmaceuticals Division of DuPont Merck Pharmaceutical, which is a partnership between DuPont and Merck.

- Fluorine chemistry is a core DuPont technology. The company buys flurospar, a naturally occurring mineral, and converts it into fluorochemicals, which can also be further upgraded into fluoropolymers. Fluoroproducts are particularly valuable because of their unique inertness, lubricity, and heat-transfer properties.

 The largest and fastest-growing segment is Teflon wire and cable jacketing polymers. They provide flame- and smoke-resistance that allows low-cost plenum installations for the rapidly growing LAN (local area network) market. Teflon, however, is more expensive than polyvinylidine polymers. On the other hand, Teflon can be high-speed-melt extruded as a coating. This eliminates the need for an overlay wrap.

- DuPont has paid dividends annually since 1904.

- The company's polymers unit has been thriving due to sales of engineering plastics to the auto industry.

- DuPont's big fibers division produces nylon, polyester, Spandex, aramids, and a host of other synthetic fibers.

- A new generation of herbicides is contributing to increased earnings at DuPont's agricultural chemicals division.

- DuPont is the world market-share leader in most of its businesses, including nylon, polyester, specialty fibers, titanium dioxide (which makes certain substances opaque, such as paint, paper, and plastic), thermoplastics, and other products.

- DuPont operates in about seventy countries worldwide, with about 180 manufacturing and processing facilities that include 150 chemicals and specialties plants, 5 petroleum refineries, and 24 natural gas processing plants.

- The company has more than forty research and development and customer service labs in the United States and more than thirty-five labs in eleven other countries.

- Conoco, DuPont's petroleum subsidiary, explores for crude oil and natural gas or produces crude oil, natural gas, or natural gas liquids in sixteen countries. Conoco markets gasoline and other refined petroleum products in the United States and twenty other countries.

- Productivity gains have enabled the company to gain new business and thus improve earnings without raising prices.

- DuPont is different from most other chemical companies in two ways: its strong brand franchises (such as Stainmaster, Lycra, and Teflon) and its ownership of Conoco, which is 40 percent of overall sales. Thus, DuPont can differentiate itself from the commodity-type chemical companies, since most of the company's chemical products are downstream specialties, with 50 percent of sales abroad.

  In addition, the company's business mix has only a tiny portion that can be deemed primary ethylene derivatives, and only about 16 percent of total sales are to construction and automotive markets, with only about half of that being in the more cyclical United States.

What's more, even within the automotive segment, the largest business is refinish paint, which is fairly insensitive to the OEM auto cycle. In elastomers, DuPont expects 20 percent growth over the next five years from its new joint venture with Dow Chemical. And, within the construction market, analysts believe market share gains are being made by the new Stainmaster carpet products, as well as by Corian and Tyvek. DuPont has number one or two positions in virtually every business it is in.

Finally, 40 percent of sales emanate from Conoco, which trends with the petroleum industry, rather than with the U.S. chemical cycle.

Total assets: $37,987 million
Current ratio: 1.01
Common shares outstanding: 1,158 million
Return on 1996 shareholders' equity: 19.9%

	1996	1995	1994	1993	1992	1991	1990	1989
Revenues (millions)	43,810	42,163	39,333	37,098	37,799	38,695	40,047	35,534
Net income (millions)	3,636	3,293	2,777	1,667	1,697	1,732	2,310	2,480
Earnings per share	3.24	2.91	2.04	1.23	1.25	1.29	1.70	1.77
Dividends per share	1.12	1.02	.91	.88	.87	.84	.81	.73
Price: High	49.7	36.5	31.2	26.9	27.4	25.0	21.2	21.1
Low	34.8	26.3	24.1	22.3	21.8	16.4	15.7	14.4

CONSERVATIVE GROWTH

A. G. Edwards Inc.

One North Jefferson Avenue, St. Louis, Missouri 63103 ◻ **Investor contact: David W. Mesker (314) 955-3510** ◻ **Dividend reinvestment plan not available** ◻ **Fiscal year ends February 28** ◻ **Listed: NYSE** ◻ **Ticker symbol: AGE** ◻ **S&P rating: A** ◻ **Value Line financial strength rating: B+**

A. G. Edwards, Inc., is a holding company whose subsidiaries provide securities and commodities brokerage, investment banking, trust, asset management, and insurance services.

Its principal subsidiary, A. G. Edwards & Sons, Inc., is a financial services company with more than 560 locations in forty-eight states and the District of Columbia.

A. G. Edwards & Sons provides a full range of financial products to individual and institutional investors and offers investment banking services to corporate, governmental, and municipal clients.

A. G. Edwards continued to expand both the number of its registered investment professionals and its nationwide branch office network in fiscal 1997 (ended February 31, 1997), further strengthening its securities distribution capability.

In the past year, the number of A. G. Edwards registered representatives surpassed the 6,000 mark, closing the year at 6,070, an increase of 5 percent. Based on the number of registered representatives, A. G. Edwards is the sixth-largest brokerage firm in the nation.

The firm added 33 locations to its branch office network (the most since 1991), bringing the total number of branches to 569 by fiscal year-end.

Shortcomings to Bear in Mind

- Rising interest rates or a falling stock market would have an adverse impact on investors. Since A. G. Edwards is heavily dependent on commission business, its revenues would be hurt by such developments.
- Without a doubt, the brokerage business is more competitive today than ever before. Full-service firms are expanding. Banks are offering brokerage services. Discount brokers are thriving. Mutual funds are marketing directly to investors. And "do-it-yourselfers" are benefiting from the longest bull market in recent history. Despite all these negatives, A. G. Edwards has continued to grow, as you will see below.

Reasons to Buy

- In my opinion, A. G. Edwards is a breed apart when it comes to brokerage houses. I think this statement by the firm's President and CEO, Benjamin E. Edward III, from the 1995 annual report, aptly expresses why the St. Louis–based firm is exceptional.

Our industry's problems and scandals over the past three decades (the "tax-sheltered" limited partnerships of the '70s, the leveraged buyouts and junk bonds of the '80s, and the derivatives of the '90s) can all be laid at the feet of management; they were all poor management calls. Yet our regulators seem to think they can prevent future scandals by beating up on the investment broker, or the almost nonexistent "rogue broker." I maintain that 95 percent of all member-firm brokers would take excellent care of their clients (it's in their self-interest to do so) if only management wouldn't interfere by pressuring them into meeting sales goals or selling proprietary products or the "product of the month." Under the commission system, which has worked successfully for 150 years, brokers are paid by the clients they work for. They work for the client at a brokerage firm. We should not change the system. We want investment brokers doing the bidding of their clients, not that of "management."

Corporate America is in excellent shape, and I look for improved earnings and employment. Owning stocks is still the best way to build an estate and meet long-term financial goals. Our system is a good one; let's not mess with it. Abusers should be punished, not the system changed.

- As a result of stock splits and stock dividends, an investment of 100 shares of A. G. Edwards stocks at the time of the firm's initial public offering in calendar 1971 has grown to 2,418 shares today.
- A steadily increasing dividend has reflected A. G. Edwards' continued revenue and earnings growth. Over the past ten years, the dividend has grown from $.24 per share to $.64, an average 10.3 percent growth per year. In the same ten-year span, earnings per share climbed from $1.00 to $3.36, a

compound annual growth rate of 12.9 percent.

- A. G. Edwards is well prepared to ride out a market correction. The company has one of strongest balance sheets in the industry and no long-term debt. What's more, with the majority of its costs variable in nature (mostly commissions paid to brokers), the brokerage house can easily ride out the vagaries of a cyclical industry with only moderate impact on margins.

- A. G. Edwards's commitment to its clients' interests is the basis for management's decision to refrain from developing its own investment products, such as in-house mutual funds, where suitable products are readily available in the marketplace. The firm is convinced that offering in-house products could impede its investment brokers' freedom to objectively assist clients in judging the best and most appropriate investment opportunities.

- The practice at A. G. Edwards is to manage its bond inventory for the primary purpose of meeting client demand for products, rather than to generate profits for the firm's account. Management believes that committing capital to pursue trading profits as an important source of revenue would expose the firm to excessive risk and compromise its commitment to putting its clients' needs ahead of those of the firm.

- Alex Bigelow, A. G. Edwards Vice President and Branch Manager, West Palm Beach, Florida, states his belief in the philosophy espoused by the firm:

    What I enjoy most about working for A. G. Edwards is that the culture here allows me to concentrate on being the best branch manager I can be. There are no "products of the month" or monthly sales goals for my branch to contend with. There's much more of an emphasis on people, with the belief that if you hire the right people, the business will naturally follow. A. G. Edwards doesn't offer up-front money to attract new brokers.

    When I recruit new investment brokers, I look for people with character who have a drive to succeed but aren't looking for the shortest route to success. For investment brokers to succeed at A. G. Edwards, they have to care about what they do and care about what's best for the client.

- A. G. Edwards is one of the lowest-risk firms in the volatile brokerage industry because of its extremely strong capital position, solid earnings record, and above-average dividend yield. AGE has avoided the troubles currently afflicting other brokers because investment banking and trading comprise a much smaller part of its total business.

- The Edwards Information Network (EIN) presents live broadcasts of world, market, and A. G. Edwards news throughout the day to each investment broker. The network programming was expanded in 1993 and improved to include more timely and useful information, including hourly updates with late-breaking news. EIN operates with a full-time staff of broadcasting professionals that gathers and reports news from the major services, including Dow Jones, Reuters, Bloomberg, and CNN. The network broadcasts twelve hours of news and informational programming every business day to the firm's investment brokers throughout the country.

- In the unlikely event that you are not convinced that this is a superior firm, here are some remarks by Louis Harvey, President of DALBAR, Inc., Boston, Massachusetts:

    For the last 20 years, my company has conducted nationwide market research on the financial services industry through customer and employee satisfaction surveys and other means. Today, it appears financial services firms are genuinely trying to change to be more customer-driven, rather than product- or profit-driven. The customer orientation is nothing new to A. G. Edwards, which has historically had a client focus and often receives high marks from both clients and its own brokers in DALBAR surveys. In my opinion, one of the things that distinguishes A. G. Edwards is that it doesn't build its own products. If you have your own products, there are pressures to sell your products. Not having them allows A. G. Edwards brokers to focus on clients without the burden of responsibility for products.

Total assets: $4.244 million
Current ratio: 1.42
Common shares outstanding: 64 million
Return on 1996 shareholders' equity: 18.6%

	1996	1995	1994	1993	1992	1991	1990	1989
Revenues (millions)	1,696	1,454	1,178	1,279	1,074	939	675	607
Net income (millions)	219	171	124	155	119	106	59	59
Earnings per share	3.36	2.65	2.00	2.57	2.06	1.88	1.10	1.09
Dividends per share	.64	.60	.56	.46	.40	.37	.29	.29
Price: High	35.0	27.0	24.4	25.4	25.7	24.6	11.7	12.1
Low	22.5	17.5	16.5	18.0	13.8	8.3	6.5	7.3

CONSERVATIVE GROWTH

Emerson Electric Company

P. O. Box 4100, St. Louis, Missouri 63136 ◻ Listed: NYSE ◻ Investor contact: Craig Ashmore (314) 553-1705 ◻ Dividend reinvestment plan available: (314) 553-2197 ◻ Ticker symbol: EMR ◻ Fiscal year ends September 30 ◻ S&P rating: A+ ◻ Value Line financial strength rating: A++

Emerson Electric is a leading manufacturer of a broad list of intermediate products such as electrical motors and drives, appliance components, and process-control devices. The company also produces hand and power tools, as well as accessories.

Founded some 105 years ago, Emerson is not a typical high-tech capital goods producer. Rather, the company makes such prosaic things as refrigerator compressors, pressure gauges, and In-Sink Erator garbage disposals—basic products that are essential to industry.

Without question, Emerson Electric is one of the nation's finest companies and should be a core holding in any portfolio devoted to growth of capital.

Emerson Electric's extraordinary record of thirty-nine consecutive years of increased earnings per share and forty straight years of higher dividends indicates a winning strategy that would be a laurel to rest on for many companies.

Instead, the company seems almost uneasy with its illustrious past and is determined to carve out a future with a somewhat different strategy. But before we delve deeper into the inner workings of EMR, let's glance at its eight segments:

Process Control
Emerson is the worldwide leader in measurement and analytical instrumentation, valves, regulators, distributed control

systems, and automation software for process and industrial markets. This business is leading the nation's change from centralized control to field-centered solutions that incorporate digital technologies, standard communication protocols, and software advances in diagnostic and predictive maintenance capabilities.

Fractional Horsepower Motors

Emerson is the world's largest manufacturer of motors for appliances; heating, ventilating, and air conditioning (HVAC); refrigeration equipment; and specialty applications. This business continues to build strong global relationships with appliance and HVAC customers and is a recognized technology leader, as evidenced by the state-of-the-art Motor Technology Center and the 1994 acquisition of Switched Reluctance Drives Ltd.

Heating, Ventilating, and Air Conditioning Components

Emerson is the global leader in compressors, hermetic terminals, thermostats and valves for heating, ventilating, air conditioning (HVAC), and refrigeration markets. As the technological leader, this business is leading the industry's transition from reciprocating to scroll compressors. Copeland Compliant Scroll technology is being expanded into a full product offering for air conditioning and refrigeration applications worldwide.

Tools

Emerson is a major producer of power tools and accessories, plumbing tools, hand tools, ladders, fans, and disposers for consumer and professional markets.

This business is well positioned to serve fast-growing home improvement centers in North America and Europe. The company's joint ventures with Robert Bosch GmbH continue to provide a significant source of value creation.

Industrial Components and Equipment

Emerson is the leading supplier of ultrasonic and vibration welding, ultrasonic cleaning, materials testing, industrial electric heating, fluid control, emergency power control, index drives, fine particle separation, electrical enclosures, and lighting equipment for industrial markets.

This business serves the capital goods equipment needs of the world's emerging economies and continues to strengthen its North American, European, and Asia Pacific positions with innovative new products.

Appliance Components

Emerson is the leading producer of controls, thermal-protection devices, sensors, and electric heating elements for major appliance manufacturers worldwide. This business benefits from the continuing globalization of appliance manufacturers and their incorporation of electronic appliance controls.

Industrial Motors and Drives

Emerson is the global leader in industrial motors, variable-speed drives, mechanical power transmission equipment, bearings, and diesel generator sets for industrial applications.

The acquisition of Leroy-Somer, F. G. Wilson, and Control Techniques expanded the Industrial Motors and Drives' global market and technology leadership positions. They also provided Emerson with the capability to engineer application-specific industrial motor and variable-speed drive solutions.

Electronics

Emerson is a leading producer of Uninterruptible Power Supplies (UPS), power conditioning equipment, environmental control systems, site monitoring systems, power conversion equipment, and electronic components for the world's computer, telecommunications, and industrial markets. This business continues to penetrate the Micro-UPS market, expand its European and Asia Pacific presence, and strengthen its telecommunications and industrial market positions.

Shortcomings to Bear in Mind

- Emerson is establishing a manufacturing base in low-wage Eastern Europe and continues to set up plants and sales offices in Asia, many via joint ventures. This new strategic direction comes with certain costs, however, including those for opening new plants and sales offices.

Reasons to Buy

- Emerson's strategic partnerships and acquisitions enhance customer relationships by broadening product lines, offering additional technological capabilities, and increasing geographic presence. Among these joint ventures is one formed with Caterpillar in 1996 for standby power applications. This partnership combines the complementary strengths of F. G. Wilson's best cost manufacturing position and Leroy-Somer's leadership in alternators with Caterpillar's strengths in diesel engines and its extensive global dealer network. Customer demand in standby power generation is high in developing countries, where power sources may be insufficient or unreliable.
- Earnings have advanced with monotonous regularity for thirty-nine consecutive years. What's more, dividends have been boosted for forty straight years. To my knowledge, this is the longest period of sustained growth in both earnings and dividends of any publicly traded, U.S.-based manufacturer of industrial products. This earnings and dividend consistency can be attributed to a management process that emphasizes tight

cost controls, growth in niche markets, and intelligent acquisitions. In the past ten years (1986–1996), for instance, EPS climbed from $.94 to $2.27, a compound annual growth rate of 9.3 percent. In the same span, dividends advanced from $.46 to $.98, a growth rate of 7.9 percent.

- Analysts regard Emerson as being extremely well positioned over the next several years. Its industrial end-market orientation, focus on manufacturing, global presence in its core activities, and superior financial attributes should serve it in good stead. What's more, analysts are particularly impressed with the concentration on products that allow end users to lower their production costs while paying heed to environmental concerns.
- Copeland is the world's largest manufacturer of air conditioning and refrigeration compressors. In the 1980s, the company began product development incorporating a revolutionary Compliant Scroll technology for use in compressor applications. Scroll technology, when compared with traditional reciprocating compressors, has operating characteristics that offer higher efficiency, lower noise, and enhanced reliability.

  In 1987, Copeland launched its first Scroll product, the Aspen. This compressor was the first high-efficiency, high-volume Scroll compressor engineered for domestic air conditioning applications.
- As it tries to expand its leadership position in a more diversified global marketplace, Emerson will work to maintain its low-cost advantage. The developing markets afford significant potential demand. However, they also create the potential for increased competition. As a consequence, Emerson's new strategy includes using the cash flow that its

strong market positions provide for activities designed to increase its usefulness to its customers and to differentiate itself from its competitors. Those activities include the following:

- Developing improved new products that expand and redefine the market, rather than merely respond to it;
- Improving technologies that could warrant higher prices for Emerson and its customers;
- Providing systems solutions for its customers' problems.

■ A strong global presence gives Emerson the ability to meet the local needs of customers worldwide. In fiscal 1996, international sales represented nearly 44 percent of the company's total sales. In Europe, sales totaled $2.9 billion. The company is strategically positioned to continue to grow in Western Europe, to participate in the emerging economies of Eastern Europe, and to serve export markets of the Middle East and Africa.

The region with the greatest growth potential is Asia Pacific. In fiscal 1996, consolidated sales into this region reached $1.2 billion. Emerson is expanding its presence in this region through investments in sales, service, and manufacturing locations and by forming joint ventures with local partners.

Total assets: $10,481 million
Current ratio: 1.39
Common shares outstanding: 224 million
Return on 1996 shareholders' equity: 19.9%

	1996	1995	1994	1993	1992	1991	1990	1989
Revenues (millions)	11,150	10,013	8,607	8,174	7,706	7,427	7,573	7,071
Net income (millions)	1,018	908	789	708	667	632	613	588
Earnings per share	2.28	2.03	1.76	1.58	1.49	1.42	1.37	1.32
Dividends per share	.98	.89	.78	.72	.69	.66	.63	.56
Price: High	51.8	40.8	33.0	31.2	29.0	27.5	22.2	20.0
Low	38.8	30.8	28.2	52.8	23.4	18.4	15.4	14.8

INCOME

Energen Corporation

2101 Sixth Avenue North, Birmingham, AL 35203-2784 ▢ Investor contact: Julie Spafford Ryland (800) 654-3206 ▢ Dividend reinvestment plan available: (800) 654-3206 ▢ Listed: NYSE ▢ Ticker symbol: EGN ▢ Fiscal year ends September 30 ▢ S&P rating: A ▢ Value Line financial strength rating: B++

Energen Corporation is a diversified energy company involved in natural gas distribution (its principal endeavor), as well as oil and gas exploration and production.

Energen's natural gas utility (Alagasco) distributes clean-burning, energy-efficient natural gas to about 460,000 customers across central and northern Alabama.

Energen's earnings rose to $1.95 per share in fiscal 1996, from $1.77 the prior year. The 10 percent increase was due to the following:

- Good results from Alagasco, the company's gas distribution subsidiary, which was helped by higher gas deliveries
- Solid earnings from Taurus Exploration, primarily because of increased

production resulting from a greater level of spending and higher prices.

Oil and Gas Exploration

Energen's oil and gas exploration and production company focuses on conventional oil and gas activities, including offshore Gulf of Mexico exploration and development.

Taurus Exploration, Energen's oil and gas exploration and production subsidiary, focuses on building reserves and production by acquiring producing properties with development potential and supplementing returns with Gulf of Mexico exploration and development.

In 1996, Taurus invested $108 million in producing properties with development potential and $18 million in offshore exploration and development. Among the company's acquisitions was the purchase of $105 billion cubic feet (Bcf) of coalbed methane reserves for $61 million.

Between acquisitions and twelve successful offshore exploratory and development wells, Taurus added net reserves of 172 Bcf equivalent (Bcfe). Reserves remaining to be produced at year-end increased 164 percent to a record 251 Bcfe, while production increased 60 percent to a record 16 Bcfe.

By the end of the century, Energen expects Taurus and Alagasco to be contributing about equally to consolidated earnings. What's more, the company is targeting consolidated ROE to exceed the utility's return. Finally, management envisions Energen as a much larger company by the year 2000, having a market capitalization of more than $500 million.

Shortcomings to Bear in Mind

- Value Line gives Energen an average rating for financial strength, B++. However, Standard & Poor's accords the utility a very solid A rating.

- Natural gas utilities are hostage to the weather. If the winter is mild, utilities sell less gas. The summer weather, on the other hand, is not very important, since only a small amount of gas is used in air conditioning, though that sector holds considerable promise for the future. An electric utility, in contrast, can be hurt by a mild summer, since air conditioning can generate huge revenues during a torrid June, July, and August.

- Public utilities are subject to the vagaries of interest rates. There are two reasons: Investors are often on the lookout for a better return. If interest rates rise, income-oriented investors may be tempted to sell their utility shares and invest elsewhere, which depresses the price of utility shares.

  The second reason: Utilities tend to be major borrowers, since they have to invest in new distribution facilities. By the same token, when interest rates fall, it augurs well for public utilities.

Reasons to Buy

- Record earnings were achieved by Alagasco in fiscal 1996 for the sixth consecutive year. The company's earnings climbed to $35.3 million, compared with $32.5 million in 1995. The 8.6 percent increase resulted from Alagasco earning its allowed rate return on equity. Alagasco earned 13.2 percent in 1996, up from 12.9 percent the prior year.

- Although Alagasco's customer growth rate may not be as strong as some other southern utilities, the company maintains a solid penetration rate in the new housing market. Natural gas is installed in 84 percent of the new single-family homes and 64 percent of the multifamily homes constructed in the utility's service territory. Its overall market saturation is above 70 percent.

- Energen's gas distribution utility has expanded its customer base through the acquisition of municipally owned gas distribution systems in Alabama. Since 1985, twenty-two municipal systems have been acquired. These have added 44,000 customers to Alagasco's system.
- After several years of lackluster results from its exploration and production operations, Energen's management realized that if it were to expand the company, significant investments would be required. In fiscal 1996, a five-year growth plan to invest about $500 million in exploration and production activities was implemented.

    Energen has begun its transformation from a natural gas distributor with a modest investment in exploration and production, to an energy company with half of its earnings to be derived from exploration and production by the year 2000. Through its Taurus Exploration subsidiary, Energen expects to spend more than $400 million to acquire producing properties with development potential, plus an additional $100 million for offshore exploration and development.

    Taurus spent $126 million in 1996. So far, the company has been successful. Operating earnings jumped to $4.5 million in fiscal 1996 from $483,000 in the prior year, reflecting a 60 percent rise in oil and gas production and a 164 percent increase in reserves.
- Compared with many public utilities, Energen has an impressive record of growth. In the 1986–1996 period, earnings per share advanced from $.81 to $1.95, a compound annual growth rate of 9.2 percent. In the same ten-year period, dividends per share expanded from $.70 to $1.17, a growth rate of 5.3 percent. Equally important, the dividend was not increased at the expense of the payout ratio. Based on 1996's earnings and dividend, the payout ratio was only 60 percent—a far cry from many utilities that pay out in excess of 80 percent of earnings. Finally, the book value per share advanced from $9.30 to $16.88, a growth rate of 6.1 percent.
- Natural gas utilities have some advantages over electric utilities. For one thing, they are not as concerned about competition. Natural gas is a preferred fuel, compared with coal, oil, and electricity. It is plentiful and clean-burning. Thus, it is not a target of anti-pollution activists. It can be burned in vehicles instead of gasoline and has some advantages. It is less expensive than gasoline and does less harm to the engine. Of course, it is unlikely to dislodge gasoline anytime soon, except as a fuel for urban vehicles such as buses, delivery vans, and taxis.
- In April of 1997, Mike Warren, CEO of the company, said, "Our emphasis for the remainder of the year will be on exploration." Mr. Warren went on to say, "Beginning in May, we plan to drill approximately six to eight exploratory wells in the Gulf of Mexico with partner United Meridian Corporation (UMC). We also have increased our working interest position with UMC from 12.5 percent to 20 percent."
- Many natural gas utilities are entirely dependent on their revenues from their utility function. This has some disadvantages. For one thing, utilities are regulated and are unlikely to experience high growth. If the state regulators are tough to deal with—and most state regulators are consumer-oriented—the utility may languish.

    On the other hand, when the company is active in exploration, there is the opportunity to increase earnings without the fear of regulation. For its part, Energen derives a hefty portion of its earnings from its oil and gas exploration—30 percent. What's more, exploration is not tied to weather or season. On the other hand, if natural gas prices are weak, this segment of the company will be hurt.

- In the spring of 1997, Energen's oil and gas exploration and production subsidiary, Taurus Exploration, completed the purchase of San Juan Basin properties. Proved reserves in the acquired properties total about 225 billion cubic feet equivalent, of which some 95 percent are high–BTU content natural gas; about 80 percent of the long-lived reserves are developed and producing. The acquisition includes some 1,750 producing wells, with Taurus operating about half of them.

- Analysts view Energen as one of the financially strongest gas utilities, based on the company's strong balance sheet, ample cash flow, and high debt coverage ratio. Common equity represents 61 percent of total capitalization, compared with an industry average of 52 percent. A strong cash flow stream, moreover, will typically fund 100 percent of the company's capital expenditures. Finally, Energen's debt obligations are small and easily covered by operating earnings. Senior debt is rated "A" by Standard & Poor's.

- Alagasco was voted one of the 100 Best Companies to Work for in America. According to the survey's authors, Energen was included because of its management's willingness to listen to employee suggestions and its infatuation with stamping out "dinosaur thinking."

Total assets: $570,971,000
Current ratio: 0.66
Common shares outstanding: 11.2 million
Return on 1996 shareholders' equity: 11.6%

	1996	1995	1994	1993	1992	1991	1990	1989
Revenues (millions)	399.4	321.2	377.1	357.1	332.0	325.6	324.9	308.6
Net income (millions)	21.5	19.3	21.8	18.2	15.8	14.2	13.3	11.2
Earnings per share	1.95	1.77	2.01	1.77	1.54	1.42	1.35	1.19
Dividends per share	1.17	1.13	1.09	1.05	1.01	.96	.91	.84
Price: High	31.2	25.1	23.9	26.8	19.3	18.9	20.5	24.4
Low	21.8	20.1	19.3	18.1	15.0	16.0	16.0	15.4

GROWTH & INCOME

Enron Corp.

P. O. Box 1188, Houston, TX 77251-1188 □ Investor contact: Mark E. Koenig (713) 853-5981 □ Dividend reinvestment plan available: (713) 853-6315 □ Listed: NYSE □ Ticker symbol: ENE □ S&P rating: A- □ Value Line financial strength rating: B++

The outlook for natural gas is bright, both in the United States and around the world. As the world's first natural gas major, Enron's ability to solve complex energy problems with innovative, reliable, and unique energy solutions is consistent with that outlook.

Enron is unique in that it possesses expertise in all aspects of the natural gas business, from production at the wellhead to electricity generation at the power grid.

In 1996, 40 percent of Enron's net income was derived from new businesses that didn't exist ten years ago. These are businesses created by Enron, such as specialized energy financing, wholesale electricity marketing, natural gas risk management, and international infrastructure development.

Enron has a stake in all sectors of the natural gas sphere, through its business units:

Enron Gas Pipeline Group/Enron Ventures Corporation

Enron Gas Pipeline Group (GPG) is pursuing market expansion in both new and mature service territories through projects that deliver reliable energy supplies. GPG operates Enron's North American interstate and intrastate natural gas pipelines, which, combined with Enron's international pipelines, comprise one of the world's largest natural gas transmission systems, totaling more than 36,000 miles.

Enron Ventures Corporation (EVC) provides worldwide engineering and construction services to both Enron and third parties and is poised for future growth. EVC engineered and constructed the 1,875-megawatt gas-fired cogeneration plant at Teesside, United Kingdom, the largest of its kind in the world, and currently is manager of over $3 billion of engineering and construction projects on three continents. EVC also manages Enron's investments in clean fuels activities and in EOTT Energy Partners, L.P.

Enron Capital & Trade Resources/ Enron Energy Services

Enron Capital & Trade Resources (ECT) is the largest purchaser and marketer of natural gas and the largest nonregulated wholesale marketer of electricity in North America. ECT markets natural gas liquids worldwide and manages the world's largest portfolio of fixed-price natural gas risk management contracts. The company offers physical and financial energy prod-

ucts and services in the United States, the United Kingdom, the Nordic countries, and other European markets and is a leader in arranging new capital for the North American energy industry.

Enron Energy Services (EES) was recently established to pursue significant opportunities in the deregulating natural gas and electricity markets. As industrial, commercial, and residential consumers across the country are able to choose their supplier of natural gas and electricity, EES will offer Enron's innovative products and services to these new customers.

Enron International

Enron International (EI) provides a broad range of services for Enron's international activities, including project development, fuel supply, and financing. It manages Enron's interests in Enron Global Power & Pipelines L.L.C., which owns and manages operating projects in developing markets. EI's integrated infrastructure portfolio includes power plants, pipelines, liquefied natural gas and gas liquids facilities, and its portfolio of development projects is valued at $20 billion. The company is significantly expanding its traditional international asset infrastructure development business by also offering merchant and risk management services in emerging markets.

Exploration & Production/Enron Oil & Gas Company

Enron's exploration and production (E&P) operations are conducted by Enron Oil & Gas Company (EOG), one of the leading low-cost, fast-track, independent E&P companies in the United States with a growing presence in international markets. EOG, which is majority owned by Enron, has captured new opportunities by transferring its broad technical and management expertise to untapped exploitation projects around the world. In 1996,

EOG increased its worldwide production by 12 percent to 353 billion cubic feet of natural gas equivalents and replaced 201 percent of production on an "all sources" basis, including 164 percent through drilling additions. The company's proved reserves total more than 4 trillion cubic feet of natural gas equivalents.

Enron Renewable Energy Corporation

Enron Renewable Energy Corporation (EREC) was recently established to further position Enron as a world leader in the renewable energy market. EREC's activities include the development of solar and wind energy power plants and the manufacture and sale of solar and wind generation equipment. The company focuses on building relationships with host countries that give priority to clean energy projects for long-term infrastructure solutions. EREC has solar and wind energy development projects underway worldwide.

Shortcomings to Bear in Mind

- The ups and downs of the weather can have a great impact on the sale of natural gas. This is because natural gas depends heavily on the product's use in space heating. This use, moreover, is growing, since natural gas is clean-burning, unlike coal and oil. To a lesser extent, the vagaries of the weather can also affect revenues of electric utilities, particularly during the summer, when air conditioning sales are important.
- In 1993, Enron signed a contract to buy gas produced from two North Sea fields, called the J-block, operated by Phillips Petroleum. The contract is "take-or-pay," meaning that even if Enron doesn't take physical possession of the gas, it has to pay $3.25 per thousand cubic feet (mcf) and take delivery sometime later. Enron thought it could sell the gas to new British electric power plants, but the plants were never built.

Meanwhile, the price of gas in Britain has plunged to $1.45 per mcf, less than half what Enron is obligated to pay now.

Reasons to Buy

- In the industrialized nations, Enron continues to seize opportunities. A few years ago, for instance, the company completed the first independent power plant in the United Kingdom. At present, it provides about 4 percent of all electricity used in that country.

  Enron is the first non-Nordic company to go into Norway and market electricity in that newly deregulated market, which represents about 12 percent of all the electricity supplies of continental Europe.

  In both instances, Enron was in early because the company pushed for change before it was a reality; and when it came, Enron was there. Enron is also working as part of a consortium to construct a large, clean-power project in Italy. What's more, the company is the turnkey construction contractor and 50-percent owner of a power project in Turkey.
- In India, Enron has gone forward with the first major, private-foreign-investment energy project in that country's history. The $1 billion Phase One power project in Dabhol, just south of Mumbai (formerly Bombay), will provide electricity for the entire state of Maharashtra, the most industrialized state in India. Phase Two will provide even more electricity and the first liquefied natural gas (LNG) receiving facility in the country. This will be one of the largest natural gas power plants in the world.
- In Argentina, Enron is an owner and the operator of the largest natural gas pipeline in South America, which the company has expanded about 26

percent since the pipeline was sold to Enron in 1992. Enron also has operating pipelines in Colombia and Bolivia and is developing a very large pipeline and power plant projects to serve the enormous Brazilian market.

- During 1996, the company completed and put into operation the first Western-developed independent power project in China.
- In 1997, *Fortune* magazine called Enron the most innovative company in America, for the second time in a row, and the most admired company in its industry for the fourth year in a row.
- In the spring of 1997, Enron's infrastructure business had three large power projects valued at $3 billion. Three more projects, targeted to start in 1997, are valued at over $1 billion. These projects are part of a backlog of more than $20 billion.
- Enron Gas Pipeline Group (GPG)/Enron Ventures Corporation (EVC) achieved strong financial operating results in 1996 and made significant progress on future growth strategies. The companies reported earnings before interest and taxes in 1996 of $570 million, compared with $442 million in 1995, excluding $83 million in nonrecurring 1995 fourth-quarter charges. GPG's interstate natural gas pipelines increased total throughput volumes to 9 billion cubic feet per day and embarked on significant expansion programs.
- Enron Capital & Trading Resources (ECT) recently created Enron Energy Services (EES) to serve the $300-billion retail natural gas and electricity markets. EES will leverage ECT's strong base as the nation's leading wholesale marketer of natural gas and electricity by customizing innovative energy products and services to meet the needs of retail customers.

As states across the nation begin to deregulate their natural gas and electricity markets and as those markets continue to converge, EES looks forward to providing end-users with a broad range of energy choices at more competitive prices. EES's goals include having the systems and sales force capacity to handle up to 1 million customers by year-end 1997 and ultimately to position Enron as the leader in retail marketing.

EES has been very successful in selected natural gas and electric retail marketing pilots, including a statewide electricity pilot in New Hampshire, where individual customers are free to select the power provider of their choice.

- The timing of Enron's decision to compete in the world renewable energy market couldn't be better. Recent studies by the Department of Energy project a 50 percent increase in world energy demand over the next twenty years, putting significant pressure on conventional energy supplies and elevating environmental concerns. But with improved technology, development expertise, and unique economies of scale, Enron Renewable Energy Corporation (EREC) is developing clean, low-cost products that should capture a growing percentage of that demand and meet the needs of a burgeoning new customer base.

Total assets: $16,137 million
Current ratio: 1.07
Common shares outstanding: 255 million
Return on 1996 shareholders' equity: 17%

	1996	1995	1994	1993	1992	1991	1990	1989
Revenues (millions)	13,289	9,189	8,984	7,986	6,415	5,698	5,460	4,631
Net income (millions)	505	465	453	386	329	232	202	226
Earnings per share	1.86	1.73	1.70	1.46	1.21	.98	.86	.97
Dividends per share	.86	.81	.76	.71	.67	.63	.62	.62
Price: High	47.5	39.4	34.6	37.0	25.1	19.2	15.7	15.3
Low	34.6	28.1	26.8	22.2	15.3	12.4	12.6	8.9

GROWTH AND INCOME

Exxon Corporation

P. O. Box 140369, Irving, Texas 75014-03699 □ Investor contact: Mr. Peter Townsend, V.P. (214) 444-1900
□ Dividend reinvestment program available: (800) 252-1800 □ Listed: NYSE □ Ticker symbol: XON □
S&P rating: A- □ Value Line financial strength rating: A++

Exxon, one of the two largest oil companies in the world (the other is Royal Dutch Petroleum), has a stake in every facet of the industry, including exploration for and production of crude oil, refining, natural gas, petrochemicals, and metals.

Exxon benefits from wide light/heavy crude oil price differentials because of the complexity of the company's refineries, which are geared to the processing of heavy crude oils.

In the Far East, Exxon is expanding its business in both refining and in marketing.

In Europe, where Exxon has a competitive refining network and a critical mass in marketing, it should benefit significantly from an improvement in the European refining business. Exxon, in fact, is among the most leveraged, major international oil companies in European refining.

1996 Highlights
• Record earnings for the second year in a row. Net income rose 16 percent to $7.5 billion.
• A 26 percent return to shareholders (dividends plus capital gains).

• Dividend increased for the fourteenth consecutive year.
• Record exploration and production earnings, a 23 percent return on capital employed.
• Resource additions were the highest in thirty years. The company again replaced more than 100 percent of its oil and gas production.
• In refining and marketing, operating performance was strong, and worldwide petroleum product sales and refinery throughputs were the highest in a decade and a half. Mitigating this was a combination of higher raw material costs caused by increased crude prices and an increasingly competitive marketplace.
• The highest gas sales in fifteen years.
• The highest petroleum product sales in seventeen years.
• Record chemical sales volumes. The company's chemicals business posted record sales volumes and achieved solid returns during a more typical year for petrochemical industry margins, which were down from their record levels of 1995. As in the refining and marketing

business, higher costs for raw materials had an impact on results.

- Record electric power earnings.

Shortcomings to Bear in Mind

■ More than thirty years after it first invested in a little electricity-generating business in Hong Kong, Exxon is making the great leap into power generation on the Chinese mainland. One analyst commented, "What China represents for Exxon is one of the world's last regulated investment opportunities in energy, and the hottest market for power. The question is: What took them so long?" Sure and steady Exxon isn't known for daring moves. Utilities, not multinational oil companies, have led the race to satisfy Asia's exploding hunger for power.

Reasons to Buy

■ In 1996, Exxon had record earnings and significant additions to its resource base. Here are some of the company's accomplishments in 1996:

- Exxon's exploration and production business realized substantial improvements in profitability while making major additions to its resource base that further strengthened its prospects for growth.
- Earnings were the highest ever, up 48 percent from 1995. Return on capital employed was the highest since 1985. These improvements resulted from higher crude and natural gas prices coupled with more efficient operations and Exxon's diverse, balanced portfolio of high-quality oil and gas holdings.
- Total oil-equivalent liquids and gas production remained essentially flat from 1995, but it is forecast to grow in 1997.
- Unit operating costs have fallen about 11 percent since 1992, which

will help sustain profitability over a range of oil and gas prices.

- Exxon's total oil and gas resource base consists of proved reserves and all other discovered resources expected to ultimately become commercial. It has grown by 14 percent over the past decade, to 40 billion oil-equivalent barrels today.
- New field resources, totaling almost 2.2 billion oil-equivalent barrels in 1996, were the largest additions to the resource base in nearly three decades. These additions were more than double the amount of oil and gas produced. Finding costs of 50 cents a barrel were the lowest in twenty years.
- Also, for the third year in a row, and on average for the past ten years, additions to the proved oil and gas reserves category exceeded production. Proved reserve additions were 1.1 billion oil-equivalent barrels, which replaced 108 percent of production, excluding property sales.
- Exxon is the nation's largest producer and proved reserves holder.
- 1996 gas production available for sale was 2.1 billion cubic feet per day—the highest since 1984.

■ Three deep-water developments (greater than 1,350 feet) with estimated total resources of more than one billion oil-equivalent barrels are under way in the Gulf of Mexico. The Ram-Powell project (Exxon interest is 31 percent) is scheduled to start up in 1997 in 3,200 feet of water, followed in 1999 by Genesis and Ursa (Exxon interests are 38 percent and 16 percent, respectively).

■ In Europe, gas production for sale reached 3.4 billion cubic feet per day, the highest since 1979, and accounted for 13 percent of West European industry production.

■ Technology for finding and producing oil and gas is evolving rapidly. For example, recent advances in deep-water production capabilities, horizontal drilling, and 3-D seismic processing have helped to add reserves and decrease finding and production costs.

Exxon holds a leadership position in exploration and production technology and is committed to maintaining that position.

Key to Exxon's strategy for technical leadership is an active research program. Exxon Production Research Company is a premier technical organization that invests more than $100 million annually to develop new technology for a wide spectrum of operational challenges. The following are some examples of recent research accomplishments:

● Advanced Exxon technology for geochemical analysis can differentiate the molecular components of very small hydrocarbon samples. The new techniques, using only a drop of oil, provide a better understanding of the origins of oil and gas, which leads to improved predictions of where new fields may be found.

● 3-D seismic analysis and geological mapping have been integrated with computer-driven visualization to fundamentally improve the speed and accuracy of subsurface geological interpretations. These improved interpretations reduce the risk associated with wildcat and appraisal wells.

● Hydrates (icelike, crystalline mixtures of light hydrocarbons and water) can plug an oil or natural gas flowline. The problem is particularly severe where discoveries are in deeper, colder water and at greater distances from processing facilities. Exxon has established an advanced test facility to develop improved techniques for controlling hydrates. This research will reduce the cost of field developments, especially gas fields in frontier regions.

■ Exxon's refining and marketing business builds upon a long-standing presence in the large, mature markets of North America and Western Europe, where extensive efficiency and rationalization programs have greatly improved the company's position as a leading competitor.

Exxon's well-placed network of refining and distribution facilities in West European markets has provided a competitive advantage for the company's expansion into East European countries.

■ In the Asia-Pacific region, Exxon's one hundred years of operating experience in Thailand, Malaysia, Singapore, and Hong Kong have enabled the company to participate in those places' growth and provide a springboard for establishing a significant presence in newly merging markets, particularly China. About one-third of Exxon's current downstream capital spending is in Asia-Pacific.

■ In 1996, Exxon's refining operations increased production of higher-value products and improved efficiency.

Refineries implemented Exxon Research and Engineering technology to increase yields of high-value products, including chemical feed stocks, from fluid catalytic cracking units.

■ In 1996, Exxon advanced cogeneration projects at refineries and chemical facilities in the United States and England. Cogeneration, the process of making steam and electricity simultaneously, is about 30 percent more efficient than making them separately. General Sekiyu K.K. (Exxon interest, 49 percent) signed a twenty-year agreement to supply 545 megawatts of electric power to Tokyo Electric Power Company by burning heavy oil, a low-value product.

- The Exxon refinery in Karlsruhe, Germany, will merge with the adjacent Oberrheinische Mineraloelwerke GmbH refinery. The combined facility will be one of the most competitive in Europe.
- In China, Exxon is a leading international supplier of fuels, lubricants, and asphalt. In 1996, the company expanded in the world's most populous nation. Retail sales grew by about 60 percent; lubricant sales rose 16 percent. Exxon moved ahead with its first lube oil

blending plant in the nation at Tianjin and acquired a majority interest in a project that includes an import depot and lube oil blending plant in Zhejiang Province.

- In 1996, Exxon Chemical announced plans to form a 50–50 joint venture with Union Carbide Corporation to research, develop, market, and license leading-edge technologies to manufacture polyethylene. The venture will capitalize on Exxon Chemical's leading position in metallocene catalysts, which produce polyethylene of outstanding quality.

Total assets: $95,527 million
Current ratio: .94
Common shares outstanding: 2,484 million
Return on 1996 shareholders' equity: 16.5%

	1996	1995	1994	1993	1992	1991	1990	1989
Revenues	134,249	123,081	101,459	99,504	103,160	102,847	105,519	86,656
Net income (millions)	7,510	6,470	5,100	5,280	4,810	5,600	5,010	4,655
Earnings per share	2.80	2.55	1.84	2.11	1.91	2.23	1.98	1.83
Dividends per share	1.56	1.50	1.46	1.44	1.42	1.34	1.24	1.15
Price: High	50.6	43.0	33.6	34.5	32.8	30.9	27.6	25.8
Low	38.8	30.1	28.1	28.9	26.9	24.8	22.4	20.8

AGGRESSIVE GROWTH

Federal Signal Corporation

1415 West 22nd Street, Oak Brook, Illinois 60521-9945 ◻ Investor contact: Henry L. Dykema (630) 954-2020 ◻ Dividend reinvestment plan available: (630) 954-2000 ◻ Listed: NYSE ◻ Ticker symbol: FSS ◻ S&P rating: A+ ◻ Value Line financial strength rating: A

Federal Signal, founded in 1901, is an acquisition-oriented manufacturer and worldwide supplier of safety, signaling, and communications equipment.

The company also has a stake in the manufacture of fire trucks, ambulances, street sweeping and vacuum loader vehicles, parking-control equipment, custom on-premise signage, carbide cutting tools, precision punches, as well as related die components.

The company has achieved twenty-nine consecutive years of record sales. It

has also scored record earnings in all but one of the last twenty-one years, including each of the last ten years.

Federal Signal is managed on a decentralized basis and is comprised of four major operating groups:

- Safety Products
- Sign
- Tool
- Vehicle

The Safety Products Group includes the Signal Products Division, Aplicaciones Tecnologicas VAMA S.L., Justrite

Manufacturing, and Federal APD. These divisions primarily serve public and industrial safety, parking-control, and security markets. The Signal Products Division consists of Emergency Products, Electrical Products, Federal Warning Systems, and Commercial Products.

The Tool Group consists of Dayton Progress, Bassett Rotary Tool, Manchester Tool, and Dico. A broad range of consumable tools for metal stamping and metal cutting applications is manufactured for more than 14,000 industrial customers around the world.

The Sign Group manufactures on-premise identification signs and visual communications displays throughout the continental United States from twenty-three manufacturing and sales facilities.

The Vehicle Group includes Emergency One, Superior Emergency Vehicles, Elgin Sweeper, Guzzler Manufacturing, Vactor Manufacturing, and Ravo International. These companies are world leaders in the fire/emergency apparatus, street sweeping, industrial vacuum, and municipal combination catch basin/sewer cleaning equipment markets as a result of strong distribution channels and continuing product innovations.

Highlights of 1996
• For the fourth year in a row, each of the company's four operating groups experienced increased sales and earnings. Net income per share was $1.35 in 1996, up 19 percent from the $1.13 reported in 1995. Excluding unusual items, 1996 earnings were $1.29, up 6 percent over the $1.22 earned the prior year. Return on equity was a lofty 23.8 percent in 1996, up from 22 percent in 1995.

Shortcomings to Bear in Mind
▪ Sales in 1996 increased 10 percent, to $896 million. While net income was up 20 percent, operating income was up only 7 percent. Several problems, each manageable by itself, combined with significant investments in new product development and process changes adversely impacted sales and reduced operating margins by 0.3 percent. The key issues were the following:
• Federal Signal's fire access platform operation in Finland (Bronto) was reorganized to eliminate its low-end non–fire-related access platform line. This was successfully completed shortly after midyear, and the business achieved good operating margins in the second half and modest operating earnings for the year.

Reasons to Buy
▪ Analysts believe that Federal Signal will continue to benefit from strong municipal demand for its increasingly diverse line of emergency/maintenance vehicles and safety products (municipal revenue streams typically lag behind the cycle), a strengthening presence in international markets, operating improvements and synergies generated at recently acquired companies, an ongoing, focused acquisition strategy, and a probable escalation in investor interest in companies with proven resistance to economic downturns.
▪ Federal Signal has a consistent record of growth. In the 1986–1996 period, earnings per share climbed from $.25 to $1.35, a compound annual growth rate of 18.4 percent. In the same ten-year stretch, dividends per share advanced from $.15 to $.58, a growth rate of 14.5 percent.
▪ The company is conservatively capitalized, with 89 percent of the balance sheet made up of shareholders' equity.
▪ The cornerstone of Federal's growth over the last two decades has been acquisitions. These acquisitions have either taken the form of stand-alone

companies that maintain their own unique identities or add-on acquisitions of businesses or product lines that are usually fully integrated into an existing Federal Signal business. The common thread between stand-alone and add-on acquisitions is that they are all related in important ways to the company's existing businesses.

Federal Signal's acquisition strategy is focused on expansion of the company's current lines of business. In addition, they must exhibit these characteristics:

- Operate in attractive industries;
- Offer leadership positions in niche markets;
- Have good prospects for growth;
- Would either benefit significantly from synergies with the company's existing strengths in marketing and manufacturing or would expand its markets geographically, especially internationally.

A critical part of the acquisition process is the valuation of each acquisition candidate. Federal's valuation methodology is based on its expectation of the future cash flows of the candidate and an estimate of its future business value.

■ Each of Federal Signal's operating units has defined its own specific critical success factors that are the most important variables for growth and profitability. These factors are targeted for improvement each year and are monitored appropriately. For example, in 1996, Dayton Progress planned and achieved a 3 percent increase in manufacturing labor productivity. Other success factors cover areas such as customer satisfaction, speed of new product development, and supplier relationships. To be sure, the largest improvements most often occur in the company's newly acquired businesses. Even so, Federal Signal is making steady progress in long-held businesses as well.

■ All of the company's domestic sales are from businesses that have the leading position in their main markets. Certain of Federal Signal's businesses have a leading position in individual foreign countries, but it has many foreign markets where the company can expect to substantially improve share.

For example, substantial share improvements can be expected in markets such as Europe's emergency signaling markets; here Signal Products has the innovative products to break down competitive barriers. The best example of their use of innovative products in 1996 was the major sale of customized policy car equipment to be used by Italy's Polizia di Stato.

■ Most of Federal Signal's targeted growth will come from its current businesses. Yet, the company needs to acquire businesses that fit well with its current groups in order to achieve its long-term growth goal. Focused on expansion within the company's current line of business, Federal targets companies that:

- Operate in attractive industries.
- Offer leadership positions in niche markets.
- Have good prospects for growth.
- Would either benefit significantly from synergies with the company's existing strengths in marketing and manufacturing or would expand the company's markets geographically, especially internationally.

■ Diversity of markets is a key reason why Federal Signal has consistently improved performance over the years. Sales have increased in each of the last thirty-one years, and earnings have increased in twenty-two of the last twenty-three years.

Total assets: $704 million
Current ratio: 0.71
Common shares outstanding: 45 million
Return on 1996 shareholders' equity: 23.8%

	1996	1995	1994	1993	1992	1991	1990	1989
Revenues (millions)	896	816	677	565	518	467	439	414
Net income (millions)	62	52	47	40	34	31	28	23
Earnings per share	1.35	1.13	1.02	.86	.75	.68	.61	.50
Dividends per share	.58	.50	.42	.36	.31	.27	.22	.19
Price: High	28.3	25.9	21.4	21.0	17.6	15.2	10.8	7.1
Low	20.9	19.6	17.0	15.7	12.4	9.3	6.2	4.2

GROWTH & INCOME

Fifth Third Bancorp

38 Fountain Square Plaza, Cincinnati, Ohio 45263 □ Investor contact: Neal E. Arnold (513) 579-4356 □ Dividend reinvestment program is available: (513) 744-8677 □ Traded: NASDAQ □ Ticker symbol: FITB □ S&P rating: A+ □ Value Line financial strength rating: A

Fifth Third Bancorp is a $20.5 billion, regional bank holding company that provides commercial banking, retail banking, trust and investment, and third-party data processing services to customers primarily located in the tristate region of Ohio, Indiana, and Kentucky, through some 414 full-service branch offices.

The company has a disciplined sales and cost culture that has resulted in an annual revenue growth rate of 19 percent over the past fourteen years, compared with 8 percent for its peers. What's more, FITB has an expense-to-revenue ratio of 45 percent, which is much better than the low-60 percent ratio for most banks. Fifth Third has established the most consistent, fastest-growing earnings record in the business. It has a fifteen-year EPS growth rate of 14 percent over the past fifteen years.

Fifth Third Bank traces its origins to the Bank of the Ohio Valley, which opened its doors in Cincinnati in 1858. In 1871, the bank was purchased by the Third National Bank. With the turn of the century came the union of the Third National Bank and the Fifth National Bank, eventually to become known as Fifth Third Bank.

Fifth Third focuses on the consumer and small and medium-sized businesses within its marketplace and on electronic processing businesses on a national basis.

Since 1979, the company's return on assets has been at least 1.60 percent (on an originally reported basis), and equity usually is 10 percent of average assets. The business focus tends to be on developing the deposit and fee side of a relationship first.

The company's financial condition is excellent, and the operation is the most efficient of the top fifty bank holding companies in the nation.

Fifth Third Bancorp is an anomaly in the banking industry. Its financial strength is unquestioned, with a common equity ratio of 9.8 percent. Yet despite its significant equity position, the company has no problem sustaining its +17 percent return on common equity. This revolves around a number of factors.

• First and foremost, a superior use of technology has enabled the company to operate more efficiently, as exemplified by its exceptional overhead ratio. At 43.5 percent in 1996, its overhead ratio was the best of the top fifty banking companies in the country.

• Second, the company has an aggressive marketing (an incentive) culture that penetrates all employee levels.

• Third, the company is small enough to go into other geographical markets and to underprice business initially until a critical mass has been developed. This tactic is currently being deployed successfully in Cleveland, Toledo, and Indianapolis.

• Fourth, the company has one of the best credit cultures in the business, with consistently low net charge-off ratios and a reserve-to-loan ratio that never varies outside of a range of 1.50 to 1.80 percent.

• Finally, a well-balanced approach to its four main business lines virtually ensures consistently superior financial results.

Shortcomings to Bear in Mind

■ There is no question that Fifth Third is a superior bank. However, it is not cheap—in fact, it is rarely cheap. Its P/E multiple is typically two or three points higher than most other regional banks. Although this bank is not too large to be a possible target of an acquisition, its high P/E ratio might be somewhat of a deterrent.

■ Its dividend yield in also below average. On the other hand, the dividend has been increased in each of the past twenty-one years. The rate of growth, moreover, is 15.8 percent per year, a truly impressive performance.

Reasons to Buy

■ Looking at the results for 1996, revenue growth exceeded the level of 1995 by 22 percent. Although acquisitions in the fourth quarter of 1995 and the first quarter of 1996 helped, most of the revenue growth was internally generated

through a focus on new products, fee initiatives, new campaigns and promotions, and, of course, aggressive selling.

For example, trust and data processing revenue increased 20 percent and 17 percent, respectively, through new customer sales and referrals. International and letter of credit fee income grew 10 percent, as the bank helped its commercial customers conduct their businesses abroad. Other examples include 41 percent growth in mortgage loan fee income, driven by strong origination in all of the bank's markets, as well as significantly higher ATM revenues as more ATMs were deployed to enhance customer convenience.

■ Fifth Third's balance sheet is as strong as ever. The bank's capital ratios and leverage are at the top of the industry, a fact continuously recognized by rating agencies, analysts, investors, and regulators.

■ At .49 percent, Fifth Third's current ratio of net charge-offs to average loans and leases is about the same as its historical average. What's more, the bank's reserve for credit losses is more than five times nonperforming assets. FITB's loan losses are lower than average for other banks, and its level of underperforming assets is among the best.

■ In 1996, Salomon Brothers ranked Fifth Third as the number one U.S. bank in overall profitability, capital, productivity, and credit quality.

■ Acquisitions have played a prominent role in the growth of FITB. Deposit acquisitions, in particular, provide an increasingly effective way to employ surplus capital and acquire liquidity. For example, during 1996, the company completed four acquisitions totaling about $2.3 billion in assets and deposits. Fifth Third has proven adept at assimilating acquisitions with minimal dilution, with both dollar net income and EPS growing at virtually the same rate.

Not only do acquisitions provide benefits with respect to funding, they also provide an opportunity to elevate profitability through enhanced sales efforts. The company, moreover, has been extremely adept in penetrating the customer base and selling additional products and services that may not have been marketed by the original institution. Consequently, Fifth Third has been able to augment earnings potential of underperforming institutions. What's more, the company is able to increase return on assets on many of its acquisitions by as much as 50 basis points over the course of three to five years.

- Management normally increases its dividend about every nine months. For instance, in September of 1996, the company increased its dividend by an impressive 24 percent. During the past eighteen years, this unique growth company has boosted the dividend twenty-five times, resulting in an average growth rate of 15 percent. Moody's has suggested this company is in an elite class among all publicly held corporations, firmly ranked in the top 1 percent for its ten-year growth of dividends.

- The Fifth Third culture promotes a hard-work ethic, aggressive selling skills, and quality earnings growth. Fifth Third bankers take a disciplined approach to lending, and frugality is an ingrained part of the employees' mode of operation. Emphasis is on profitability and profitable growth. The consistency of the bank's operating philosophy and a well-integrated incentive program reinforce the Fifth Third culture. In addition to incentive programs,

all employees participate in the bank's profit-sharing plan, which has contributed, on average, 13 percent to 14 percent of their total compensation.

- Consumer demand for retirement planning products, information, and services is at an all-time high. A recent issue of *Pensions & Benefits Week* magazine states that 56 percent of employers with 500 to 1,000 employees currently offer a retirement savings plan, and that this number is expected to grow by 66 percent by the year 1998.

The Fountain Square 401(k) Advantage was designed by Fifth Third to provide companies with the tools to chart the right course for their employees' retirement.

- Fifth Third Bancorp was recently ranked number one in overall capitalization, profitability, and credit quality among the nation's one hundred largest banking companies by the *United States Banker* for the second time in three years.

- A unique facet of the FITB story is its fast-growing data-processing subsidiary, Midwest Payment Systems (MPS). This operation has grown at a rate faster than the core banking operation and the market, in turn, has begun to factor the growth of this earnings stream into the company's valuation. Over the course of the last seven years, revenues have expanded at a compound annual rate of 17 percent.

MPS is among the major players in the electronic funds transfer industry. Each year, it processes more than 1.7 billion automated teller machine (ATM) and point-of-sale transactions for more than 1,100 financial institutions and 18,000 merchants throughout the world.

Total assets: $20,549 million
Common shares outstanding: 106 million
Return on 1996 assets: 1.78%
Return on 1996 shareholders' equity: 17.8%

	1996	1995	1994	1993	1992	1991	1990	1989
Loans (millions)	12,514	11,513	10,286	8,811	7,475	5,807	5,497	5,164
Net income (millions)	335	288	244	196	164	138	120	108
Earnings per share	3.22	2.91	2.53	2.19	1.83	1.56	1.36	1.24
Dividends per share	.10	.96	.80	.68	.60	.52	.45	.40
Price: High	74.3	51.0	36.7	39.3	36.0	30.3	16.4	17.7
Low	43.5	31.3	30.0	33.0	26.5	13.1	10.3	13.2

GROWTH AND INCOME

Fleetwood Enterprises, Inc.

P. O. Box 7638, Riverside, CA 92513-7638 ◻ Investor contact: Paul M. Bingham (909) 351-3504 ◻ Dividend reinvestment plan not available ◻ Fiscal years end last Sunday in April ◻ Listed: NYSE ◻ Ticker symbol: FLE ◻ S&P rating: B+ ◻ Value Line financial strength rating: A

Fleetwood Enterprises, Inc., a *Fortune* 500 company, is the nation's leading producer of manufactured housing and recreational vehicles. The company operates plants in eighteen states and in Canada.

Fleetwood's manufactured housing group has become the largest domestic home builder by producing quality factory-built homes at affordable prices.

Recreational vehicles built by Fleetwood include motor homes, travel trailers, folding trailers, and slide-in truck campers, all of which are designed to make vacation travel, outdoor recreation, and other leisure activities more enjoyable.

Fleetwood's supply operations provide fiberglass components and lumber products to the company's core businesses and also manufacture a diverse array of products for outside customers.

Industry Overview

The manufactured housing industry continued to prosper in fiscal 1996 (which ended the last Sunday in April 1996), extending the current growth cycle that began in fiscal 1992. With the benefit of a healthy economy and growing demand for affordable housing, the industry produced nearly 340,000 homes in calendar 1995, a 12 percent gain over the prior year.

The strength of consumer demand for manufactured homes during the latest up-cycle is evidenced by the doubling of industry volume in four years. Encouragingly, the industry continues to gain market share from site-built housing, with manufactured housing now representing 24 percent of all new single-family homes sold in the United States.

Affordability continues to be the key factor driving industry growth. Even so, improved construction quality, innovative design, and financing availability have also been instrumental in moving the industry to higher levels.

Another Solid Year for Fleetwood in 1996

Fleetwood's Housing Group continued its growth pattern in 1996, achieving record sales for the sixth consecutive year. Healthy demand for Fleetwood-manufactured homes drove revenues to a new high of $1.44 billion, 5 percent ahead of the prior year's $1.37 billion.

The company produced 68,990 homes in 1996, making Fleetwood America's largest homebuilder by a substantial margin. In the manufactured housing industry, Fleetwood maintained its leading position with a 20.1 percent market share, almost as much as the next three competitors combined.

In the three years leading up to 1996, the firm's housing group was involved in an ambitious expansion effort, adding roughly 75 percent to its production capacity. By contrast, 1996 was somewhat quieter, with the addition of one new plant in Texas. Current plans are to bring seven new manufacturing plants onstream in fiscal 1997. This move alleviates capacity constraints and allows the company to resume its market-share growth.

Recreational Vehicle Industry Trends

The health of the recreational vehicle business in fiscal 1996 was largely influenced by the slow-growth economy. A sluggish sales pattern for manufacturers was established early in the year. RV dealers reduced their inventory exposure, causing manufacturers' shipments to fall behind the level of retail activity.

For calendar 1995, total RV industry deliveries to retailers were down 8.4 percent from a record 1994, while retail demand for the industry inched ahead a modest 2.4 percent. In the early months of 1996, inclement weather in many regions of the country had a dampening effect on the RV business.

Company Background

Fleetwood's motor homes, which are self-propelled vehicles used primarily for vacations, camping, and other leisure activities, are sold under the American Eagle, Bounder, Flair, Jamboree, Pace Arrow, Southwind, Tioga, American Dream, and other names.

Conventional motor homes made by Fleetwood are fully self-contained, sleep four to eight people, and range in length from 22 feet to 40 feet. The company also sells compact motor homes ranging from 19 feet to 31 feet.

Fleetwood's travel trailers are designed to be towed by pickup trucks, vans, or other vehicles and are similar in use and features to motor homes.

Fleetwood also produces slide-in truck campers that fit in the bed of pickup trucks. The company also makes folding trailers.

Manufactured houses are factory-built homes that are transported to home sites in one or more sections and installed, using their own chassis on either temporary or permanent foundations. Fleetwood's homes range from 650 to 2,560 square feet and are priced from $11,000 to $120,000, with most selling for less than $25,000.

Operations are benefiting from strong demand for manufactured housing. In addition, prospects are enhanced by continued market share growth and the company's solid financial position.

Fleetwood's housing business is driven by affordability, and the company is the low-cost producer. This is partly because Fleetwood buys $200 million in lumber a year, directly from the mills, and 70,000 appliance units. The discounts on those volumes give the company a major pricing advantage over most competitors. The average Fleetwood unit price is about $20,000 (at wholesale), and there are double and triple units as well. Most Fleetwood homes are sold to people in rural and semirural areas, where land is less expensive.

Shortcomings to Bear in Mind

■ Despite the favorable long-term characteristics of Fleetwood's businesses, it would be naive for an investor to think that its future growth path will continue upward without interruption. The fact is, Fleetwood is in economically sensitive businesses that expand and contract with such factors as employment growth, interest rates, availability of financing, consumer confidence, and economic conditions in general.

Reasons to Buy

- Looking out several years, Fleetwood's management believes the business prospects are bright for all of its businesses. For one thing, demographic factors seem to favor both of its core businesses well into the next century. Over the next fifteen years, the fastest-growing segment of the population will be people in the 45–65 age group—the prime buyers of recreational vehicles.

    With so many people reaching retirement age, it is also likely that many will want affordable housing in temperate climates that are well suited for retirement living. Manufactured housing, at half the cost per square foot of site-built homes, can satisfy that demand and also the needs of young couples trying to escape apartment living.
- Directors and officers control about 21 percent of the outstanding common stock.
- The company has no long-term debt related to manufacturing operations.
- To a large degree, Fleetwood's success can be attributed to its regional focus, which facilitates the development of innovative floor plans and attractive decor that appeal to a broad segment of each distinct market. Design groups stay close to the market by interacting with plant management teams, Fleetwood retailers, and focus groups comprised of retail customers. This process gives designers the opportunity to develop and refine design concepts and monitor industry trends and consumer preferences as they affect specific Fleetwood product lines. The result of this product design leadership is evident in Fleetwood's consistent market share growth.

- The company's supply subsidiaries, which have a stake in the supply of fiberglass components and lumber product to affiliated companies, have aggressively set their sights on growth through external sales. Recent results demonstrate that their strategies are effective.
- The company's fiberglass manufacturing operations in California and Indiana, long established producers of quality open-fold fiberglass parts, continue to broaden their product offerings. New process capabilities include closed-mold fiberglass operations and expanded use of rotational molding and thermo-forming methods that produce a wide array of specialty products from composite plastics.

    Overall, these operations supply high-quality parts for such diverse applications as recreational vehicles, medium- and heavy-duty trucks, manufactured housing, medical and dental equipment, personal watercraft, entertainment devices, food-service displays, pools and spas, golf equipment, and many others.

Total assets: $1,109 million
Current ratio: 1.02
Common shares outstanding: 38 million
Return on 1996 shareholders' equity: 12.7%

	1996	1995	1994	1993	1992	1991	1990	1989
Revenues (millions)	2,809	2,856	2,369	1,942	1,589	1,401	1,549	1,619
Net income (millions)	79.6	84.6	67.4	56.6	40.2	30.4	55.0	70.5
Earnings per share	1.71	1.82	1.46	1.23	.89	.69	1.21	1.53
Dividends per share	.60	.55	.50	.47	.43	.41	.38	.32
Price: High	37.2	27.3	26.9	24.6	18.4	14.6	15.3	13.3
Low	23.1	17.9	16.5	12.7	10.3	7.9	11.0	8.5

FPL Group, Inc.

700 Universe Boulevard, P. O. Box 14000, Juno Beach, Florida 33408-0420 □ Investor contact: Scott W. Dudley, Jr. (561) 694-4697 □ Dividend reinvestment plan available: (800) 736-3001 □ Listed: NYSE □ Ticker symbol: FPL □ S&P rating: B □ Value Line financial strength rating: A

FPL Group, Inc., is the parent of Florida Power & Light Company, one of the largest investor-owned electric utilities in the nation.

FPL serves 7 million people, or about half of the population of Florida, in an area covering almost the entire eastern seaboard of Florida and the southern third of the state. Cities served by Florida Power & Light include St. Augustine, Daytona Beach, Melbourne, Stuart, West Palm Beach, Fort Lauderdale, Miami, Bradenton, Sarasota, Fort Myers, and Naples.

The region continues to experience vibrant growth, driven by Florida's attractive climate, natural beauty, and exceptional quality of life.

FPL Group's other operations include ESI Energy, a major participant in the growing independent power business, and Turner Foods Corporation, one of the largest citrus producers in Florida.

In 1996, FPL Group's net income reached a record level, $579 million, and earnings per share increased 5.4 percent, to $3.33. The company achieved positive cash flow for the third consecutive year, enabling FPL to further improve its balance sheet. Since 1993, the company has generated almost $1.7 billion in free cash, compared to the prior four years when it needed external financing of more than $2 billion.

What's more, during 1996 FPL Group retired more than $500 million of debt and preferred stock and repurchased about two million shares of common stock. Over the past three years, the company has reduced its debt ratio (as a percent of total capital) from 48 percent to 40 percent.

Although electric utility stocks did not fare well in 1996 compared with the overall stock market, FPL Group continued to perform substantially better than the industry as a whole. Since FPL's restructuring in 1990, the company's annualized total return of 15 percent is considerably greater than the 10 percent total return of the Dow Jones Electric Utilities Index. Total return includes dividends plus stock price appreciation.

Shortcomings to Bear in Mind

- One area in which Florida Power & Light fell short during 1996 was its performance at the St. Lucie nuclear plant. This was reflected in the plant's ratings from the Nuclear Regulatory Commission, which slipped from superior to average.

  What's more, the utility was fined $100,000 by the Nuclear Regulatory Commission for two separate incidents at this nuclear complex. The penalty was for lax security and failure to install a satisfactory emergency preparedness program at St. Lucie. A third violation, concerning questionable modifications to nuclear equipment, was not subject to a fine.

  For its part, FPL's management states that restoring St. Lucie's performance to its previous levels is a top priority. FPL has installed a new management team at St. Lucie, but the solution to the problem may take some time.

Reasons to Buy

- In 1996, operating and maintenance expenses per kilowatt-hour fell for the sixth year in a row. Since 1990, FPL has lowered these costs almost 29 percent. This, along with a substantial decline in interest expense, has enabled the company to keep the price of its electricity about 13 percent lower than the national average. FPL's prices are actually lower today than they were in 1995.

- Florida Power & Light's fossil and nuclear plants established company records for their availability, i.e., the amount of time they were available for service in 1996. They performed well above the industry averages. Nuclear availability increased for the fifth straight year, to 87 percent, compared to the industry average of 77 percent. Fossil availability, moreover, climbed to 92 percent, or well above the industry average of 84 percent. This kind of superior plant performance is especially important in today's increasingly competitive environment; it allows the company to avoid the costs of additional electric capacity and to hold down the price of electricity to customers.

- FPL Group continues to be favorably perceived by the business and investment communities. In *Fortune* magazine's recent survey of America's most admired companies, FPL Group was the second-highest-rated utility in the nation. In the investment community, more analysts recommended FPL Group in 1996 than any other utility by a wide margin.

- FPL Group is continuing to pursue domestic energy investments outside Florida through ESI Energy, the company's independent power producer. ESI has built a successful business concentrating on projects that use environmentally favored technologies such as natural gas, geothermal, and wind.

ESI recently increased its role to become owner/operator of the 663-megawatt Dosell power plant in Virginia, the largest independent combined-cycle gas plant in the United States. The company also began construction of a gas-fired plant in South Carolina and is acquiring a large geothermal plant in California.

- In 1996, FPL Group established a new subsidiary, FPL Group International, to seek investment opportunities overseas, where many countries are experiencing greater growth in electric usage than the United States. These foreign power projects offer new opportunities to satisfy electricity needs, building directly on the company's existing skills. FPL Group International currently has investments in Colombia, Indonesia, and the United Kingdom.

- In 1996, a new program to repurchase up to 10 million shares of FPL's common stock was authorized.

- Until recent years, electric utilities were not unduly concerned with competition. In particular, there was little concern over competition from other electric utilities. By their very nature, they were natural monopolies, with each utility serving exclusively its own area, such as a city or part of a state. In fact, since there was no competition, it was necessary to regulate electric companies. Without regulation, it was feared that power companies would charge whatever the traffic would bear.

That era may be passing. There seems to be a groundswell in favor of letting large users buy their power from the company with the lowest rates, regardless of whether it is ten miles away or 1,000 miles away. At present, this is not feasible at the retail level (although it can be done on a wholesale level), since it requires the permission of the local utility to permit "wheeling."

In other words, an out-of-state utility is normally forbidden permission to wheel its power over another company's lines, unless that company gives it permission to do so and unless it is willing to pay the wheeling cost.

So far, wheeling for retail customers has not been sanctioned. But legislators and regulators are discussing the concept, and it is feared that some may bow to public pressure.

For its part, FPL Group is well aware of what is transpiring and has been since 1990, when it initiated a comprehensive strategy to strengthen the company and enhance shareholder value.

In 1991, moreover, FPL restructured its organization to make it leaner, flatter, and less bureaucratic. Two years later, the company implemented a major program to further reduce its costs of operation. Most recently, FPL instituted a new financial policy to increase its financial strength and flexibility.

As a consequence, FPL's aggressive cost-reduction programs have broken the trend of rising costs. On an inflation-adjusted basis, operating and maintenance expenses per kilowatt-hour are now lower than in 1980, despite greater governmental burdens. What's more, cost-control efforts are continuing.

FPL also enjoys a good location, and unlike many other utilities, is not surrounded by other states. Since it operates on a peninsula, there are competitors only on its northern border. This reduces the number of competitors who might seek to invade its domain.

Also of great importance is the nature of the company's customers. Most of them are residential or commercial. Only a tiny percentage of revenues come from industrial customers:

4 percent. By contrast, a typical utility might obtain one-fourth of its revenues from the industrial sector. It is these large customers who are the most likely to seek lower rates.

- FPL has substantially completed a cost-effective program to expand its generating system. This expansion enables FPL to keep pace with the increasing power needs of its thriving service area. FPL serves several of the fastest-growing cities in the country. With its improving economy, attractive climate, and favorable geographic location, Florida has been referred to as the "center of the Americas." Miami, moreover, is increasingly recognized as a major hub for trade with Latin America.

- Because fuel represents the largest cost component of FPL's operations, the company has implemented several aggressive fuel-cost reduction strategies as part of its cost-control program.

One key strategy is maintaining a diverse energy mix to generate electricity. This offers FPL increased flexibility to take advantage of price and supply changes in individual fuels.

FPL's energy mix in 1996 consisted of 25 percent nuclear, 31 percent natural gas, 19 percent oil, 7 percent coal, and 18 percent purchased power, which is primarily from coal-fired plants.

- FPL Group has been benefiting from a rapidly growing customer base. Despite mild weather conditions, the utility still managed to increase share net by solid earnings gains in 1996. What's more, analysts look for healthy earnings gains in 1997 and 1998. Customer growth rose by an impressive 1.8 percent in 1996, significantly higher than the rate of most other utilities. Moreover, the utility should manage to maintain this rate, helped by the heavy migration of people and businesses into FPL's service territory. The Sunshine State's booming economy created about 100,000 service jobs in 1996. Florida's warm climate and low taxes have proven to be a strong lure for nearly every demographic group, particularly retirees, immigrants, and entrepreneurs.

Total assets: $12,219 million
Current ratio: .92
Common shares outstanding: 173 million
Return on 1996 shareholders' equity: 13%

	1996	1995	1994	1993	1992	1991	1990	1989
Revenues (millions)	6,037	5,593	5,423	5,316	5,193	5,249	6,289	6,180
Net income (millions)	603	553	557	556	511	473	406	454
Earnings per share	3.33	3.16	2.91	2.75	2.65	2.65	2.65	3.12
Dividends per share	1.84	1.76	1.88	2.47	2.43	2.39	2.34	2.26
Price: High	48.1	46.5	39.1	41.0	38.4	37.3	36.5	36.8
Low	41.5	34.1	27.4	35.5	32.0	28.1	26.1	29.0

CONSERVATIVE GROWTH

Gannett Company, Inc.

1100 Wilson Boulevard, Arlington, VA 22234 ◻ **Investor contact: Gracia Martore (703) 284-6918** ◻ **Dividend reinvestment plan is available: (703) 284-6960** ◻ **Listed: NYSE** ◻ **Ticker symbol: GCI** ◻ **S&P rating: A** ◻ **Value Line financial strength rating: A++**

Gannett Company, Inc., is a diversified news and information company that publishes newspapers and operates broadcasting stations and cable television systems. It is also engaged in marketing, commercial printing, a newswire service, data services, news programming, and alarm security services.

The company operates in forty-four states, the District of Columbia, Guam, and the U.S. Virgin Islands.

Gannett is the largest U.S. newspaper group in terms of circulation, with ninety-one daily newspapers, including *USA TODAY*, a variety of nondaily publications, and *USA WEEKEND*, a weekly newspaper magazine. Total average paid daily circulation of Gannett's daily newspapers is about 6.5 million.

Gannett owns and operates sixteen television stations and three FM and two AM radio stations in major markets.

Gannett's cable division serves 465,000 subscribers in five states.

A Review of 1996

The stage was set for a good year in the last month of 1995, when Gannett completed the acquisition of Multimedia. When the deal was announced in the summer of 1995, management thought the company would face a 10-cents-per-share earnings dilution in 1996. As the year unfolded, however, Gannett knew this new business could contribute to earnings right away.

On a negative note, federal regulations prevented the company from keeping a television station in Cincinnati that had been a Multimedia property and a TV station in Oklahoma City that had been in the Gannett family for seventeen years. But Gannett was able to trade those early in 1997 for the NBC affiliate in Buffalo and the ABC affiliate in Grand Rapids.

Separately, Gannett traded six radio stations that the company owned in Los Angeles, San Diego, and Tampa for the CBS television affiliate serving Tampa and St. Petersburg. Prospective purchasers of radio stations the last couple of years were making attractive offers, and Gannett believes that the swap offered was too good to turn down.

The company also closed the Gannett books on its Outdoor Division, selling it to Outdoor Systems, and on Multimedia Entertainment, selling it to MCA. Outdoor had not performed at a level consistent with the company's other properties, and management deemed the talk shows that comprised the Entertainment Division as being mired in a stagnant and crowded field.

However, two other elements of Multimedia that were new to Gannett, cable and alarm security, performed well in 1996.

Gannett's television stations collectively had an exceptional year. Election-year politics and the Olympic Games were major contributors to strong performances at the company's nine NBC stations, but the results went well beyond those two events. Strong sales at those and other Gannett stations helped. Broadcast President Cecil L. Walter is confident operating results at the stations will continue to grow in 1997.

Shortcomings to Bear in Mind

- The newspaper strike that began on July 13, 1995, in Detroit has ended. However, the unions that struck do not yet have contracts and have stated that an advertiser and subscriber boycott will continue. Detroit Newspapers, the agency that prints the Gannett-owned *News* and the Knight-Ridder–owned *Free Press*, continues to publish without interruption. The unions refuse to recognize that their demands remain unre-

alistic, particularly in light of the agency's ability to operate with a reduced work force.

- Gannett's growth record is above average but far from impressive. In the 1986–1996 period, earnings per share advanced from $1.71 to $3.77, a compound annual growth rate of 8.2 percent. In the same ten-year span, dividends expanded from $.86 to $1.42, a growth rate of 5.1 percent, which was well ahead of the pace of inflation.

Reasons to Buy

- Studies show that newspaper readership correlates strongly with higher incomes, professional stature, and community involvement, making Gannett subscribers the readers advertisers covet most. As a newspaper's penetration of high-profile audiences increases, it becomes indispensable to advertisers.
- Gannett's managers are rewarded based on their ability to maximize profitability over the long term. The company encourages them to take risks that enhance the value of the local franchise. Occasionally, they will sacrifice short-term performance for higher future returns.
- The majority of Gannett's newspapers tend to be in smaller cities and are less dependent on classified advertising. Analysts contend that this will be a benefit if the economy softens, compared to newspaper groups that are more cyclical.
- Gannett had eighteen newspapers, including USA TODAY, online by early 1997. The motivation for going online at least initially was not profits, though that certainly is the company's longer-term goal. The company is convinced that it is also a way to protect and perhaps extend Gannett's classified revenue base.

- Newspapers have great opportunities to leverage their leadership positions in local markets. Newspapers already have the information gathering/processing infrastructure in place with strong ties to the local community. Newspapers, which have established for years that they are the repository of local news, will not be pushed aside so long as they continue to do their jobs well. That job includes providing the depth of information that competitors probably won't have and combining it with the visual appeal and easy access that newspapers will need to match their competitors. A number of newspaper sites have done a nice job of making themselves user-friendly and visually attractive and have been appropriately designed for online. *USA TODAY* is one of the best.

- Buoyed by the Summer Olympics, national election, and unprecedented gains in advertising, *USA TODAY* posted its best financial performance ever in 1996, with a significant improvement in revenues and profits.

  The Atlanta Games and presidential race alone added about 5 percent to advertising revenues, which grew a total of 30 percent in 1996, while ad pages rose 30 percent as well. Growth occurred in all categories except automotive.

  The dramatic advertising success of 1996 followed years of steady increases since 1990. Between 1991 and 1995, *USA TODAY* led most major print media in ad page growth, with a 16 percent gain. Advertisers reached an audience that grew by 11 percent over the same period.

  In 1996, circulation grew by 4 percent, to 2,163,940. On Fridays during the fall, the peak circulation season, *USA TODAY* sold nearly 2.8 million copies, about a million more than the *Wall Street Journal*.

- The company's nine NBC affiliates, representing 10 percent of the U.S. television market, led Gannett Television to its best year ever in 1996, with total revenues up 13 percent. The nine stations, including WXIA-TV in Atlanta, controlled the significant share of TV advertising dollars in their markets during the Summer Olympic Games, broadcast by NBC July 19 through August 4.

- Comprehensive Olympics coverage and a strong prime-time line-up translated into heightened viewership for the company's NBC affiliates. KSDK-TV in St. Louis, KARE-TV in Minneapolis-St. Paul, and KUSA-TV in Denver were ranked first, second, and third, respectively, among the top fifty U.S. stations in late evening news ratings during 1996.

- In early 1997, Gannett completed a transaction to acquire WZZM-TV at Grand Rapids/Kalamazoo/Battle Creek, Michigan, and WGRZ-TV at Buffalo, New York, plus other considerations, in exchange for WLWT-TV at Cincinnati and KOCO-TV at Oklahoma City.

- The company's alarm security service increased its revenues by 37 percent and its customer count by 10 percent in 1996. The division ended the year with 111,000 accounts.

  Multimedia Security, headquartered in Wichita, Kansas, distinguishes itself through outstanding customer service. Its central station performance tops the industry, with an average response time of less than 15 seconds, and often less than 10 seconds. Extended service hours (Monday through Saturday, 8 A.M. to 9 P.M., while most competitors work the weekday 8 A.M. to 5 P.M. shift) are part of the company's extra effort.

- Gannett's cable unit serves about 465,000 subscribers in five states.

About 76 percent of its coaxial cable systems have been upgraded with optical fiber.

Why fiber? It has an extraordinary capacity for delivering a flood of voice, video, and data. Gannett engineers put it this way: If coaxial cable were a drinking straw, fiber would be a four-lane tunnel.

With the installation of fiber, Multimedia can provide more services and products. Many franchises have more than doubled the number of cable channels they offer and have positioned themselves to offer hundreds more. Fiber also gives viewers sharper, clearer images.

Total assets: $6,350 million
Current ratio: 0.85
Common shares outstanding: 141 million
Return on 1996 shareholders' equity: 18.5%

	1996	1995	1994	1993	1992	1991	1990	1989
Revenues (millions)	4,421	4,007	3,824	3,642	3,469	3,382	3,442	3,518
Net income (millions)	531	477	465	398	346	302	377	398
Earnings per share	3.77	3.41	3.23	2.72	2.40	2.00	2.36	2.47
Dividends per share	1.42	1.36	1.34	1.30	1.26	1.24	1.22	1.11
Price: High	78.8	64.9	59.0	58.3	54.0	47.0	44.5	49.9
Low	59.0	49.5	46.1	46.8	41.3	35.1	29.5	34.5

CONSERVATIVE GROWTH

General Electric Company

3135 Easton Turnpike, Fairfield, CT 06431 ◻ Investor contact: Mark Begor (203) 373-2816 ◻ Dividend reinvestment plan available: (800) 786-2543 ◻ Ticker symbol: GE ◻ S&P rating: A+ ◻ Value Line financial strength rating: A++

General Electric, a widely diversified company, is the largest electrical equipment manufacturer. Its major businesses include jet engines, industrial products, appliances, materials, NBC Broadcasting, power systems, as well as technical products and services. International sales account for 39 percent of the total. Financial services contribute about 25 percent of operating profits.

General Electric is the sixth-largest domestic corporation, with 1996 revenues of $79.2 billion. Although GE can trace its origins back to Thomas Edison, who invented the light bulb in 1879, the company was actually founded in 1892.

Aircraft Engines

Aircraft engines and related replacement parts are produced for military and commercial aircraft, for naval ships and propulsion, and as industrial power sources.

Appliances

Appliances include refrigerators, ranges, microwave ovens, freezers, dishwashers, clothes washers and dryers, and room air conditioners.

Broadcasting

Broadcasting consists primarily of the National Broadcasting Company (NBC).

Industrial

Industrial encompasses lighting products, electrical distribution and control equipment for industrial and commercial construction, transportation systems, motors, industrial automation products, and GE Supply.

Materials

Materials include high-performance engineered plastics, silicones, super-abrasives, and laminates.

Financial Services

Financial services primarily consist of GE Capital Services (including General Electric Credit Corp. and Employers Reinsurance Corp.).

A Review of 1996

GE had an exceptional year in 1996.

- Revenues increased to a record $79.2 billion, up 13 percent.
- Global revenues increased 18 percent, to $33 billion.
- Earnings were $7.3 billion, up 11 percent.
- Earnings per share of $2.20 were up 13 percent.
- Operating cash flow rose to $9.1 billion, or $3 billion ahead of the previous high.
- The quarterly dividend was increased 13 percent—the twenty-first consecutive year of dividend increases.
- GE repurchased $3 billion of its stock, increased its buy-back program from $9 billion to $13 billion, and extended it through 1998.
- Total return to shareowners in 1996 was 40 percent, after a 45 percent return in 1996.

Shortcomings to Bear in Mind

- With CEO John R. Welch set to retire in four years, there are few more tantalizing questions in corporate America than who will replace the legendary executive. Neither Welch nor the company will discuss succession, and no obvious heir-apparent has surfaced.

  That doesn't mean the race to succeed Jack Welch is not well under way. He has a stable of seasoned lieutenants vying for the job. Over the past year, Welch has given new tasks to a younger crop of possible heirs and fast-trackers in their forties. His two-pronged strategy is to test the front-runners while also developing GE's farm team.

  It's a delicate balancing act. If Welch anoints an heir, he could face a brain drain of GE's most seasoned players. With the race still open, however, headhunters say it has been remarkably difficult to lure would-be CEOs away from the giant conglomerate.

Reasons to Buy

- GE is strong financially, with 94 percent of its capitalization made up of shareholders' equity. Coverage of bond interest, moreover, is a hefty 17.2 times.
- Despite its huge size, the company continues to demonstrate growth. In the 1986–1996 period, earnings per share climbed from $.68 to $2.20, a compound annual growth rate of 12.4 percent. (The company, moreover, has had twenty-one consecutive annual earnings increases.) In the same ten-year span, dividend advanced from $.30 a share to $.95, a growth rate of 12.0 percent.
- Scientists from GE Plastics and Corporate R&D have developed a new process to improve quality and reduce cycle times in manufacturing Lexan polycarbonate for compact disks.
- NBC has a strong position in sports programming, with NFL and college football, tennis, golf, and the splashy and preemptive move to buy the 2000 Summer Olympics in Sydney and the

2002 Olympics in Salt Lake City for $1.2 billion. In 1996, NBC covered the Atlanta Summer Olympics.

- NBC has moved aggressively to expand into cable television. The network has stakes in seventeen cable networks, including CNBC, Court TV, and the History Channel. NBC has also moved swiftly in recent years to introduce new entertainment and new channels in Europe, Asia, and Latin America.

- A new CleanSensor dishwasher from GE Appliances has a revolutionary sensor that measures the soil level of the dish load and automatically adjusts water usage and cycle length—saving consumers time, energy, and money.

- GE Aircraft Engines had impressive results in 1996. The company continued its worldwide leadership as GE and CFM International, its joint company with Snecma of France, again won the majority of commercial engine orders. Major wins were secured with American Airlines, Philippine Airlines, Air France, Northwest Airlines, International Lease Finance Corporation, and Kuwait Airways.

- CFM International's new CFM56-7, which was certified late in 1996, is commercial aviation's fastest-selling engine. With almost 1,000 engines already on order, the CFM56-7 will power the next-generation Boeing 737 series, which began passenger service with Southwest Airlines in 1997. The CFM56-7, which sharply reduces fuel consumption, entered service in 1996 on Swissair's Airbus Industrie A319 aircraft.

- The company had another record year at GE Appliances, as revenues increased 7 percent, to $6.4 billion, driven by U.S. market share gains and record global sales. What's more, GE's profitability significantly outperformed the industry.

Capitalizing on the GE brand's reputation and responding to consumer demand for cleaner, softer water, the company introduced residential water treatment products in 1997. SmartWater by GE is the first full line of water softeners and filtration systems from a major appliance manufacturer.

- The acquisition of 73 percent of DAKO S.A., Brazil's leading gas range manufacturer, was a major 1996 milestone. Based on the GE brand strength in Brazil and expansion of the company's product offerings, GE looks for significant growth in Latin America.

- The company's European appliance operations experienced 18 percent revenue growth in 1996 through the introduction of products built by European suppliers and designed especially for GE, including the GE Profile line of built-in cooking products.

- In Asia, the company's 23 percent revenue growth was driven by creative approaches to new markets. In India, for instance, the company is offering a full line of refrigerators and laundry products with its partner, Godrej. In China, GE's joint venture with Shanghai Communication and Electrical Appliances Commercial Group sells locally produced GE brand products for distribution throughout the country.

- In 1996, GE had its most profitable year in the seventy-year history of the National Broadcasting Company and the fourth consecutive year of double-digit earnings increases. In 1996, NBC dominated the prime-time ratings, launched a new venture with Microsoft, and expanded services around the world.

In entertainment, NBC became the number one American broadcaster, winning all of the year's prime-time ratings "sweeps" and finishing the

1995–1996 season as the most-watched network.

- GE Medical Systems achieved record revenues and earnings in 1996, despite vigorous price competition and a continuing slowdown in the worldwide market for diagnostic imaging equipment. Healthy increases in U.S. and Asian orders helped the company enhance its leading market share positions in the United States and worldwide.

- GE Lighting introduced its new line of ConstantColor Ceramic Metal Halide lamps in 1996. Manufactured in Hungary, the United Kingdom, Canada, and the United States, the ConstantColor lamps blend two technologies—high-pressure sodium, which uses a ceramic arc tube, and metal halide—to generate stable, uniform white light perfect for commercial lighting displays.

Total assets: $272,402 million
Current ratio: 0.87
Common shares outstanding: 3,289 million
Return on 1996 shareholders' equity: 23.5%

		1996	1995	1994	1993	1992	1991	1990	1989
Revenues (millions)		46,119	43,013	60,109	55,701	53,051	51,293	49,696	54,574
Net income (millions)		7,280	6,573	5,915	4,184	4,137	3,943	3,920	3,939
Earnings per share		2.20	1.95	1.73	1.52	1.26	1.28	1.21	1.09
Dividends/share		.95	.85	.75	.65	.58	.52	.48	.43
Price:	High	53.1	36.6	27.4	26.8	21.9	19.5	18.9	16.2
	Low	34.9	24.9	22.5	20.2	18.2	13.3	12.5	10.9

CONSERVATIVE GROWTH

Genuine Parts Company

2999 Circle 75 Parkway, Atlanta, GA 30339 ◻ **Investor contact: Jerry Nix (770) 953-1700** ◻ **Dividend reinvestment plan available: (770) 953-1700** ◻ **Ticker symbol: GPC** ◻ **S&P rating: A+** ◻ **Value Line financial strength rating: A++**

Genuine Parts Company, founded in 1928, is a service organization engaged in the distribution of a wide range of products.

The company's largest division is its Automotive Parts Group, which distributes automotive replacement parts and accessory items. This group operates sixty-three distribution centers, serves some 5,800 NAPA Auto Parts stores, and stocks over 150,000 part numbers.

The Automotive Parts Group operates six remanufacturing plants that distribute products under the name Rayloc. Also in this Group is Balkamp, Inc., a majority-owned subsidiary that purchases packages and distributes service and supply items under the trade name Balkamp to NAPA Distribution Centers.

The NAPA program strives to improve market penetration, reduce costs, and focus on specific customer needs. The great success of the NAPA program has enabled Genuine Parts to become the leading independent distributor of automotive replacement parts and to expand in sales and earnings at a faster rate than the industry.

Industrial Parts Group
The Industrial Parts Group distributes replacement parts and related supplies.

This group distributes over 200,000 items from more than 330 operations located in thirty-eight states. In addition, this Group serves more than 150,000 customers in all types of industries.

Motion Industries, headquartered in Birmingham, Alabama, serves the industrial market from four distribution centers.

Berry Bearing Company, headquartered in Chicago, distributes industrial replacement parts in the Midwest.

Oliver Industrial Supply, headquartered in Lethbridge, Alberta, supplies industrial parts to the Canadian industrial market.

Office Products Group

The Office Products Group distributes a broad line of office products, ranging from furniture and desk accessories to business electronics and computer supplies. This group, operating under the name of S. P. Richards Company, distributes over 18,000 items, from forty-one distribution centers located in twenty-eight states. These distribution centers serve over 7,000 office supply dealers.

Since its beginnings as a modest retailer in 1848, S. P. Richards has evolved into one of the largest office products wholesalers in the nation.

The Lesker Division distributes an extensive office furniture selection to ten states throughout the Mid-Atlantic and Midwest regions from four distribution centers.

Shortcomings to Bear in Mind

- Do-it-yourselfers and professional customers alike have more options than ever when they choose where to buy parts. All of the company's wholesale customers, repair shops, service stations, body shops, and national accounts are also facing more challenges

in pleasing their customers. Nor is it merely the do-it-yourself customers who are increasing their demands for quality products and service at a competitive price. The automotive aftermarket is becoming increasingly crowded with retailers who know how to please the retail trade and are now seeking to acquire wholesale customers as well. NAPA has designed programs to improve its penetration of each of these markets with the goal to continue to gain market share each year.

Reasons to Buy

- In 1996, total sales reached $5.7 billion, a gain of 9 percent, producing Genuine Parts' forty-seventh consecutive year of increased sales. Net income was $330 million, an increase of 7 percent and the thirty-sixth year of profit improvement for the company. On a per-share basis, this was $2.73, an increase of 8 percent over the $2.52 produced in 1995.

- The company's success in 1996 was supported by gains in each of its three industry segments that substantially outpaced industry growth in each group. The NAPA Automotive Parts Group posted an increase of 7 percent, and Office Products was up 9 percent. The leader was the company's Industrial Group, with a gain of 11 percent. Most of this growth reflected unit gains, as price increases continued to be modest in 1996, at less than 2 percent for the total company.

- Genuine Parts is exceptionally strong and is rated A++ for financial strength by Value Line, as well as A+ by the Standard & Poor's Stock Guide. It's easy to see why. The company has virtually no debt, and its ratio of current assets to current liabilities is a solid 3.8

times. Most companies, by contrast, have current ratios below 2.0. Management contends that future expansion will be financed with internally generated funds.

- Growth, although not spectacular, has been well above average and consistent. In the 1986–1996 period, earnings per share climbed from $.68 to $1.82, a compound annual growth rate of 10.4 percent. Similarly, dividends per share expanded from $.37 in 1986 to $.88 in 1995, a compound growth rate of 9.1 percent. Not content to rest on its laurels, the company again boosted its dividend in February of 1997, to an annualized rate of $.96. It was the forty-first consecutive dividend increase.

- The automotive aftermarket has experienced an upturn, beginning in 1993, that is expected to continue. There are several factors contributing to this growth:

    1. The average age of cars and trucks is increasing. Currently, the average age of the vehicle fleet is over eight years; it is expected to surpass nine years by the year 2000.
    2. Vehicle usage is up. Miles driven by personal and commercial drivers are increasing at a 3 percent annual pace.
    3. The vehicle population is climbing steadily, at an average annual rate of 2.6 percent since 1970.
    4. There appears to be significant pent-up demand in discretionary repairs to add potential sales growth. It is estimated that unperformed maintenance approaches $50 million at retail levels.
    5. Government regulations will be one of the key drivers in the future growth of the automotive aftermarket. The most widely known initiative has been the IM240 testing programs mandated by the Clean Air Act of 1990. More stringent emissions programs have always benefited the repair business and created additional parts sales. It is believed that government agencies will continue to tighten emissions regulations in the future and will provide solid support for aftermarket growth.

- The Industrial Parts Group supplies plant surveys, inventory management programs, national supply agreements, and technical instruction.

    The implementation of programs such as Extra Value Service Process (XVS), Electronic Data Interchange (EDI), and Continuous Service Improvement (CSI) helps to secure the extended quality service that customers expect.

    With the advent of an electronic catalog system (ECAT), Motion Industries leads the industry in electronic data retrieval. The electronic catalog provides branches and customers with immediate access to manufacturers' technical and parts information. The group's state-of-the-art computer system, representing the first VSAT satellite system in the industry, gives the Industrial Parts Group the edge on technological advancement.

- Service excellence has always been a focus point for S. P. Richards, which is part of the Office Products Group. By continually monitoring its distribution centers to improve quality control, S. P. Richards reinforced its strong industry reputation in 1996 as a company that will do whatever it takes to satisfy its customers. With thirty-eight full-line distribution centers nationwide, S. P. Richards covers the entire country with overnight inventory, supported by

20,000 products. A full inventory offering, including furniture, desk accessories, business electronics, and computer supplies is stocked in each distribution center, allowing for immediate availability to its customers. This dependable delivery system allows dealers to reduce their investment in inventory.

- While consolidation continues throughout all aspects of the office products industry, dealers have increased their efforts to reduce investment and expense by stocking fewer products. S. P. Richards is well positioned to be the source for those products. Moreover, the company has concentrated its merchandising efforts on bringing new products to market quickly and capitalizing on new growth market opportunities. Its product offering has been broadened with expansion into the fast-growing computer and imaging supply area, janitorial and break-room supplies, and furniture. Further, the company's private label offerings include additional products distributed under the following brand names: "Sparco," "Nature Saver," and "CompuCessory."

- The Lesker Furniture Division, acquired by S. P. Richards in 1993, distributes office furniture from five facilities. Lesker purchases furniture from thirty-six vendors and distributes its products to furniture dealers, interior design dealers, and other furniture resellers located in ten states throughout the Northeast and Midwest regions.

- Horizon USA Data Supplies, a computer supplies reseller located in Reno, Nevada, became an S. P. Richards subsidiary in 1995. Horizon, through three facilities, sells to computer and information processing supplies specialists outside the traditional office products industry. Through Horizon, S. P. Richards has been able to significantly expand its customer base.

Total assets: $2,522 million
Current ratio: 3.41
Common shares outstanding: 182 million
Return on 1996 shareholders' equity: 20.0%

	1996	1995	1994	1993	1992	1991	1990	1989
Revenues (millions)	5,720	5,262	4,858	4,384	4,017	3,764	3,660	3,485
Net income (millions)	330	309	289	258	237	224	224	215
Earnings per share	1.82	1.68	1.55	1.39	1.28	1.21	1.19	1.15
Dividends per share	.88	.84	.77	.70	.67	.64	.60	.53
Price: High	31.7	28.0	26.3	26.0	23.2	21.9	19.0	19.3
Low	26.7	23.7	22.4	21.9	19.3	15.5	14.7	15.5

Goodyear Tire & Rubber Company

1144 East Market Street, Akron, Ohio 44316-0001 ▢ Investor contact: Dianne C. Davis (330) 796-3751 ▢
Dividend reinvestment plan available: (330) 796-3751 ▢ Listed: NYSE ▢ Ticker symbol: GT ▢ S&P
rating: B ▢ Value Line financial strength rating: B++

Goodyear, together with its U.S. and international subsidiaries, manufactures and markets tires for most applications.

The company also manufactures and sells several lines of belts, hoses, and other rubber products for the transportation industry and various industrial and consumer markets. GT also has a stake in rubber-related chemicals for various applications. Finally, the company provides auto repair and other services at retail and commercial outlets.

Goodyear operates plants in the United States and in twenty-seven other countries. The Celeron subsidiaries operate a crude oil pipeline system, which extends 1,225 miles from the California coast to central Texas.

A Review of 1996
- Net income from operations improved for the sixth consecutive year, before one-time charges, reaching an all-time high 10 percent ahead of 1995.
- Shareholders received a 12 percent dividend increase, raising the average annual dividend to $1.12, the highest in company history.
- Worldwide unit sales increased 5.4 percent, and every region captured market share gains.
- One negative note: Dollar sales were less than 1 percent below record sales in 1995, primarily due to pricing pressures and the impact of foreign exchange translations.
- Four major acquisitions with annual sales totaling $770 million were announced or completed—an activity unprecedented in Goodyear's history.

- These acquisitions, when added to the company's capital expenditures, bring Goodyear's total capital investments in 1996 to just under $1 billion. Significantly, they were financed entirely with free cash flow.
- The ratio of debt to debt plus equity was reduced to 29.6 percent, the lowest level since 1985, which meets the company's target range of under 30 percent two years ahead of schedule.
- A company stock buy-back plan was approved in the first quarter of 1997 for up to $600 million. Studies show that stock buy-back plans often help stock prices to outperform the market.
- The book value of the All American Pipeline was written down, and a fourth-quarter charge of $756 million was taken without materially affecting critical balance sheet ratios.
- An offtake agreement will allow Goodyear to produce tires for two Sumitomo Rubber Industries Ltd. subsidiaries in the United States in exchange for production of Goodyear tires in Japan. The reciprocal arrangement facilitates use of existing assets and reduces exposure to economic cycles for both companies.
- A one-time charge of $148 million was recorded in 1996 for streamlining and consolidating operations globally.

Shortcomings to Bear in Mind
- Tire manufacturing is a mature industry in the United States, and it is highly competitive. For that reason, Goodyear, along with other tire makers, is targeting international markets for expansion.

- Earnings in 1997 could be hurt by a stronger U.S. dollar. On the other hand, Goodyear could benefit from the lower cost of raw materials.

Reasons to Buy

- In North America, Goodyear expanded distribution across all channels by 1,500 outlets in 1996 or more than 10 percent. In Europe, Asia, and Latin America, moreover, distribution grew at a similar clip in 1996.
- The company made four key acquisitions in 1996:
  - Debica in Poland gives Goodyear instant market share in Eastern Europe. It is a low-cost facility ideal for growth as a private-label tire supplier to Western Europe, and it was a major contributing factor to Europe's performance in 1996.
  - In the Philippines, Goodyear acquired the tire assets of Sime Darby, the country's leading tire producers, to complement the company's existing plant. This new plant gives GT a cost-competitive base for production of the company's first private-label tires in Asia. The plant will be used for export in the AFTA trading markets and will significantly strengthen Goodyear's position in the region.
  - Engineered Products (a GT Division) purchased Belt Concepts of America, the market leader in quality lightweight conveyor belts. It establishes the company in a growing market segment and strengthens the company's distributors' product lines.
  - Goodyear re-entered South Africa with the purchase of Contred, a much larger and more profitable tire and engineered products company than when GT sold it in 1989. In the interim, Contred has updated its factory; it owns a chain of retail tire stores; and it is the nation's largest retreader. Goodyear's objective is to expand this business with new export sales and to develop world-class tires and conveyor belting for the mining industry.
- Goodyear's start-up acquisitions in China are moving forward, with the company's Dalian Tire plant undergoing expansion and the Qingdao Engineered Products plant now supplying automotive hose to the region. The company's tire joint venture with Ceat in India will be operating at capacity in 1997.
- At the other extreme, Goodyear is eliminating ventures that are not contributing to profits. For instance, the company closed a plant in Greece, sold a property in Singapore, discontinued its PVC operations in Niagara Falls, New York, and disposed of more than one hundred retail stores in the United States and Canada.
- In 1997, tire demand has been steady, and raw material costs have continued to fall.
- Goodyear's operating margins improved to 10.2 percent in 1996, the highest level in its history. This resulted from the company's focus on becoming the industry's low-cost producer.
- The company's principal business is the manufacture of new tires. About 77 percent of total sales are tires. However, the volume of replacement tires is significantly higher than sales to the original equipment market. Replacement tires are the less cyclical part of the business.
- Goodyear is not shy about advertising its wares. Its advertising has been described as "superior and innovative." In North America, the company outspent its major competitors in 1996 and increased advertising in Europe and Latin America by 15 percent over the prior year.

In April of 1997, Bridgestone, the owner of the Firestone brand, unveiled a domestic advertising campaign blitz, contending that its patented technology can stop a car faster on slick roads than Goodyear's hugely successful Aquatred II. Studies have shown that what buyers really care about in a tire is how it handles during wet weather. Goodyear had responded to this need and launched its Aquatred in 1991. For its part, Goodyear says, "We have spent a lot of money on wet traction, and we continue to spend a lot of money on it. Since the fall of 1991, we spent on average eight times as much on advertising than they have spent on their entire marketing campaigns."

- The company sharpens its image by the excitement Goodyear generates on the racetracks of the world with its Eagles. No competitor can claim to prove its tire technology at more of the world's most demanding racing series than Goodyear, or to have earned the dominating record of race wins.

  From above, Goodyear's blimps uniquely build brand equity with millions of consumers through their public service support and television appearances, such as the 1996 Atlanta Summer Olympic Games.

- Starting with raw materials, Goodyear has made substantial improvements in its ability to substitute synthetic rubber for natural rubber. The company is positioning its Chemical Division as an even better supplier of synthetic rubber, and Goodyear is leveraging its capability to acquire materials globally from the most attractive supply sources.

- The Eagle F1 GS is the latest addition to Goodyear's global family of Eagle F1 ultra performance designs; it was conceived in the company's Grand Prix racing success. The newest Eagles have increased handling and wet traction capabilities over preceding designs.

- The ever-expanding light truck and sports utility vehicle market inspired Goodyear's newest version of on-/off-road tires—the Wrangler AT/S. The state-of-the art design, introduced to dealers in early 1997, combines exceptional off-road traction in mud and snow with a quiet ride for highway driving.

- Goodyear led the industry in introducing the Infinitred passenger tire, which offers a lifetime tread life limited warranty for as long as customers own their cars. Infinitred also delivers outstanding wet traction and ride comfort.

- Goodyear remains the number one tire maker in Latin America. With a total tire market approaching $4 billion and one car for every thirteen people, there are expanded opportunities for Goodyear, both in the original equipment and replacement tire markets.

- Despite economic volatility in Venezuela and disappointing growth in Brazil and Argentina, Latin American operations increased income in 1996 and contributed to keeping Goodyear the undisputed market leader in sales of replacement, original equipment, and export tires.

  There are encouraging signs of recovery in Mexico, and internal efforts have realigned the organization to capitalize on the new regional trade agreements: NAFTA, the Andean Pact, and Mercosur. As a result, Goodyear introduced a record number of new products in the region in 1996.

Total assets: $9,672 million
Current ratio: 1.46
Common shares outstanding: 155 million
Return on 1996 shareholders' equity: 20.6%

	1996	1995	1994	1993	1992	1991	1990	1989
Revenues (millions)	13,113	13,166	12,288	11,643	11,785	10,907	11,273	10,869
Net income (millions)	675	611	567	474	367	31	d	295
Earnings per share	4.35	4.02	3.75	3.23	2.57	.26	d	2.56
Dividends per share	1.03	.95	.75	.58	.28	.20	.90	.95
Price: High	53.0	45.4	49.3	47.3	38.0	27.1	23.2	29.9
Low	41.5	33.0	31.6	32.6	26.1	8.4	6.4	21.1

CONSERVATIVE GROWTH

W. W. Grainger, Inc.

455 Knightsbridge Parkway, Lincolnshire, IL 60069-3620 ◻ Investor contact: Robert D. Pappano (847) 793-9030 ◻ Dividend reinvestment plan not available ◻ Listed: NYSE ◻ Ticker symbol: GWW ◻ S&P rating: A ◻ Value Line financial strength rating: A++

W. W. Grainger is a leader in the distribution of maintenance, repair, and operating supplies and related information to the commercial, industrial, contractor, and institutional markets in North America. W. W. Grainger regards itself as a service business.

The company does not engage in basic or substantive product research and development activities. New items are added regularly to its product line on the basis of market information as well as on recommendations of its employees, customers, and suppliers, coupled with other factors.

The company distributes motors, HVAC equipment, lighting, hand and power tools, pumps, and electrical equipment, along with many other items.

In another sphere, W. W. Grainger provides support functions and coordination in benefits, data systems, and data processing, employee development, finance, government regulations, human resources, industrial relations, insurance and risk management, internal audit, legal, planning, real estate, and construction services, security and safety, and taxes and treasury services.

Grainger sells primarily to contractors, service shops, industrial and commercial maintenance departments, manufacturers and hotels, and healthcare and educational facilities. Sales transactions during 1996 averaged $137 and were made to more than 1,300,000 customers.

The company purchases from more than 1,000 suppliers for its General Catalog, most of whom are manufacturers and numerous other suppliers in support of Grainger Integrated Supply Operations (GISCO). The largest supplier in 1996, a diversified manufacturer through twenty-two of its divisions, accounted for 11.2 percent of purchases.

Grainger offers its line of products at competitive prices through a network of stores in the United States and Mexico (349 at December 31, 1996). An average store has fifteen employees and handles about 260 transactions per day. During 1996, an average of 93,300 sales transactions were completed daily. Each store tailors its inventory to local customer preferences and actual product demand.

In 1996, Grainger invested more than $31 million in the continuation of its facilities optimization program, which consisted of new stores, relocated stores, and additions to stores. The company enhanced its marketing capabilities in Mexico by opening its first foreign-based store in Monterrey.

1996 Highlights
- Net sales of $3.5 billion, up 7.9 percent.
- Net earnings of $208.5 million, or $4.04 per share, up 11.7 percent.
- Paid a dividend of $.98 per share, up 10.1 percent.
- Acquired the industrial distribution business of Acklands Limited, with operations throughout Canada and sales of over $300 million for the fiscal year ending January 31, 1996.
- Expanded the company's overall product offering to include 700,000 quality items and access to over 3 million products and numerous services through Grainger Integrated Supply Operations.
- Operated a combined network of 527 stores in all fifty states, Canada, Puerto Rico, and Mexico.
- Opened the company's first non–U.S.-based facility in Monterrey, Nuevo León, Mexico.
- Announced integrated supply agreements with American Airlines, Emerson Electric Company, Lockheed Martin Corporation, and Procter & Gamble.
- Introduced the online version of the General Catalog to Grainger's World Wide Web site.
- Added online ordering capability to Grainger's Web site.
- Formed an Electronic Commerce organization to expand Grainger's presence on the Internet.
- Enhanced the online version of the General Catalog with MotorMatch, a guided interactive search engine.

- Parts Company of America enhanced its capabilities through an alliance with Edward Don & Company, the nation's largest food service equipment and supply distributor.
- Lab Safety Supply launched its entry into the material handling market with the introduction of its 300-page Material Handling Direct Catalog.

Shortcomings to Bear in Mind

■ During 1996, a number of insiders (such as officers and board members) were selling their holdings in Grainger. Although there were some purchases, the number of sales was predominant.

Reasons to Buy

■ Grainger offers to customers services that reduce the hidden costs of MRO (maintenance, repair, and operating) supplies. In many cases, these costs can exceed the cost of the product itself. They include the customer's procurement process, the costs associated with possessing and maintaining inventory, the interface with multiple suppliers, and the use of MRO supplies.

■ Grainger's MRO business is broad-based, serving over 1.3 million businesses and completing over 93,000 transactions each day. Grainger serves customers across all sizes and types.

■ Small businesses represent over 1.1 million of Grainger's customers. Strong relationships with these customers are best achieved using direct marketing methods. Many customers cite a preference for this form of contact. With relatively simple operations and little MRO inventory, small businesses can reduce their total cost of MRO supplies with easy-to-use product information and selection assistance, one-stop service, and inventory nearby. The company's industry-leading General Catalog, broad product line, and network of local stores offer a good solution for these customers.

- Large businesses represent about 200,000 of Grainger's customers, but constitute over two-thirds of the revenues. The Grainger direct sales force is the key relationship builder with this customer group. Customers served by the direct sales force range from medium-sized manufacturing plants to *Fortune* 500 companies. The common thread for these customers is their desire to reduce the total cost of MRO supplies.

  Larger businesses generally have more sophisticated purchasing processes, more MRO suppliers, and more inventory. While product price is always important, the keys to reducing total MRO costs are improving the purchasing process, reducing the interface with multiple suppliers, and applying better inventory management methods. The company's network of leading manufacturers, product availability, order processing systems, and customer inventory management tools form a powerful solution.

- The company increased its 1996 dividend for the twenty-fifth consecutive year. Over the past ten years, the dividend climbed from $.36 to $.98, a compound annual growth rate of 10.5 percent. In the same 1986–1996 span, earnings per share advanced from $1.29 to $4.04, a growth rate of 12.1 percent. What's more, there were no dips along the way.

- Late in 1996, the company announced its intention to reactivate its share-repurchase program. During 1996, the company purchased 409,600 shares, leaving 3.2 million shares available under a 1992 authorization to repurchase up to 5 million shares.

- Grainger made several important improvements to its infrastructure in 1996. The company continued to upgrade its information system within the store and logistics environment. Every store contains a powerful minicomputer and a network of intelligent workstations. To manage this network, Grainger added state-of-the-art monitoring systems in 1996 that manage data traffic across the entire network. As a result, information is available on a more timely basis, and new software is distributed across the network with greater efficiency.

- Lab Safety Supply, a leading direct marketer of safety and related industrial products, serves businesses nationwide from its operations in Janesville, Wisconsin. The Lab Safety Supply General Catalog expanded 20 percent in 1996, offering more than 36,000 items. This operation focused on material handling and maintenance products, items customers often buy in conjunction with safety supplies.

  Building on the early successes, Lab Safety Supply entered the material handling market more definitively with its Material Handling Direct Catalog. This 300-page targeted catalog was a successful market initiative.

  Customer service was raised to new levels in 1996 through the introduction of one-call service. With changes to its internal structure and phone service, Lab Safety Supply now handles order processing, return processing, catalog requests, and other customer services through one call and one agent. This change has significantly reduced telephone hold times and transfers.

Total assets: $2,119 million
Current ratio: 2.72
Common shares outstanding: 51 million
Return on 1996 shareholders' equity: 15.8%

	1996	1995	1994	1993	1992	1991	1990	1989
Revenues (millions)	3,537	3,277	3,023	2,628	2,364	2,077	1,935	1,728
Net income (millions)	209	187	178	149	137	128	127	120
Earnings per share	4.04	3.64	3.47	2.88	2.58	2.37	2.31	2.20
Dividends per share	.98	.89	.78	.71	.65	.61	.57	.50
Price: High	81.5	67.6	69.1	66.8	61.0	55.5	39.2	33.1
Low	62.6	55.5	51.5	51.6	39.0	30.3	27.2	26.3

CONSERVATIVE GROWTH

Hannaford Brothers Company

P. O. Box 1000, Portland, Maine 04104 ◻ Investor contact: Charles H. Crockett (847) 793-9030 ◻
Dividend reinvestment plan is available: (207) 883-2911 ◻ Listed: NYSE ◻ Ticker symbol: HRD ◻ S&P
rating: A+ ◻ Value Line financial strength rating: B+

Hannaford Brothers is a multiregional food retailer. At the end of 1996, Hannaford operated 139 retail food stores, 46 of which are situated in Maine, 19 in New Hampshire, 8 in Vermont, 6 in Massachusetts, 21 in New York, 27 in North Carolina, 2 in South Carolina, and 10 in Virginia.

The 100 stores in the Northeast operate under the names Shop'n Save or Hannaford, while the 39 stores in the Southeast use the names Hannaford, Wilson's, or The Grocery Store.

Of the 139 stores, 102 are large combination stores that offer a wide array of food and nonfood merchandise; 37 are conventional supermarkets. Pharmacy departments are located in 83 of the 139 stores.

Highlights of 1996

Sales and other revenues for 1996 were just shy of $3 billion, an increase of 15.2 percent over 1995. Same-store sales were up 3.2 percent in 1996, compared to 2.5 percent in 1995.

Sales from retail food stores, representing 96.5 percent of total sales, were $2.853 billion, an increase of 15 percent over the prior year. Additional revenues came from wholesale sales to independent customers (2.2 percent) and other sources, such as real estate and trucking (1.3 percent).

In 1996, Hannaford spent $230.6 million on its capital investment program. This included the continued expansion of the company's store base in the Southeast, as well as new stores and improvements in the Northeast.

In addition, a new 465,000-square-foot distribution center was built in Butner, North Carolina, to serve the company's Southeast market.

During 1996, Hannaford's retail selling area increased 7.8 percent, to a total of 4.5 million square feet. In 1997, the company expects to spend $180 million on new, expanded, and relocated facilities in both the Northeast and Southeast. Current plans call for an increase of 11.5 percent in retail sales area.

Shortcomings to Bear in Mind

■ Some analysts believe that the outlook for retail supermarket chains remains neutral. They point out that consumer spending for food is expected to continue to show only modest gains. They concede, however, that "operators are developing new merchandising techniques and controlling expenses to improve overall profitability."

■ By the end of 1997, about one-third of Hannaford's store base will be located in the Southeast, a region the company entered as recently as 1994. These operations are not likely to be profitable for another year or two. On the other hand, opening of additional supermarkets should lead to better penetration of these markets. What's more, increased penetration should result in more efficient use of advertising dollars.

■ There is always the specter of competition. On the other hand, the consolidation in the warehouse club industry has slowed the building of clubs. Although supermarkets have not yet been declared the victors in their struggle to maintain market share against warehouse clubs and discounters, they are increasingly holding their own. But competition will remain vigorous.

What's more, there is a new threat on the horizon—supercenters that sell food and general merchandise are being rolled out by Wal-Mart and Kmart. Over time, these powerhouse retailers could pose the next threat to traditional grocery stores.

Reasons to Buy

■ Creating a business in a new territory requires front-end-loaded investment. In 1995, Hannaford spent $162.3 million and in 1996 an additional $230.6 million, more than half of it in the Southeast.

The company invested $43 million in a new $465,000-square-foot distribution center in Butner, North Carolina, which opened in November of 1996. It now supplies all Hannaford stores in the Southeast. This state-of-the-art distribution center will improve the company's cost of goods, quality of perishables, delivery costs, and in-store stock conditions. Despite these considerable expansion costs, however, Hannaford's earnings expanded by 7.1 percent in 1996.

The company will continue to expand in 1997, with nearly $180 million expected in capital spending that will result in ten new stores, three relocations, and two expansions in the Southeast; as well as one new store, two relocations, and one expansion in the Northeast, coupled with significant improvements in existing stores and technology.

■ In today's busy world, many people want quick, easy meals that require little or no home preparation. Hannaford is satisfying this need by offering more prepared foods in its meal centers. In the company's newest stores, moreover, the meal centers offer and assemble complete meals, in addition to providing a selection of foods that are separately prepared and packaged.

This selection also includes fresh vegetables that are cut and packaged in serving-size containers. Hannaford's meal centers also provide a range of special services, including menu planning, nutrition consulting, party planning, special order assistance, and demonstrations of food preparation techniques.

■ Hannaford's HomeRun began delivering groceries to residents of Brookline, Massachusetts, in February of 1996. During 1997, management plans to evaluate the future of home delivery and the possibility for expansion. Under the HomeRun program, consumers shop from a catalog, placing their order via phone, fax, or the

Internet. Orders are delivered the next day, within a two-hour window selected by the customer. Prices are competitive with those in local supermarkets, and there is no delivery charge on orders over $60.

- The company's new, full-line, Southeast distribution center is situated in Butner, North Carolina, about 15 miles north of Raleigh and near major transportation routes that can get product to Hannaford's stores with a minimum of traffic.

The main distribution building contains 431,000 square feet, and there are 112 truck doors to handle both incoming and outgoing product. In addition to the main distribution building, the center also includes a truck-maintenance facility and a product-recovery center.

The center was built in less than one year at a cost of $43 million and started shipping product to the company's stores in November of 1996.

The Butner distribution center supplies Hannaford stores in the Southeast with dry groceries, frozen foods, and perishables. The building was specifically designed for newer, more efficient forms of materials handling. The freezer, for instance, is situated near the grocery area to more easily combine loads for shipping. A mezzanine level turns overhead storage space into ergonomically enhanced selecting slots.

- Although much of Hannaford's expansion has occurred in the Southeast, the company has not neglected its core markets. During 1996, the company opened three new stores in the Northeast and expanded or relocated three others.

HRD opened a new 45,000-square-foot store in Brattleboro, Vermont, and another, slightly larger store in Williston, Vermont. In Niskayuna, New York, the company added a new 64,000-square-foot store, further enhancing Hannaford's presence in the greater Albany market.

The company moved its first Vermont location in South Burlington, which opened in 1969, to a new, 45,000-square-foot store next door, nearly doubling the sales area.

Hannaford also relocated an older store in Waterville, Maine, to a new 45,000-square-foot facility that had been vacated by a competitor.

In 1997, the company intends to open a 46,000-square-foot store in Guilderland, New York, and will relocate its Rutland, Vermont, store to a new facility that will nearly double its current size.

- Richmond, Virginia, is a good example of how Hannaford builds market presence. From a single site in 1994, the company presence in Richmond has grown to eight stores, with a ninth under construction. This expansion resulted from new construction, as well as from store acquisitions that the company remodeled or relocated to meet Hannaford's standards for layout and customer service. This process will be repeated in the company's other Southeast markets, mainly through new construction.

- Hannaford has demonstrated consistent growth in earnings per share. In the 1986–1996 period, earnings per share climbed from $.51 to $1.78, a compound annual growth rate of 13.3 percent. In the same span, dividends expanded from $.13 to $.48, a growth rate of 14 percent. Equally important, the company pays out a low percentage of its earnings, giving it more capital to invest in its future. In 1996, its $.48 dividend represented only 27 percent of earnings.

Total assets: $1,184 million
Current ratio: 1.11
Common shares outstanding: 42 million
Return on 1996 shareholders' equity: 13.8%

	1996	1995	1994	1993	1992	1991	1990	1989
Revenues (millions)	2,958	2,568	2,292	2,055	2,066	2,008	1,688	1,521
Net income (millions)	75	70	62	55	49	43	42	37
Earnings per share	1.78	1.67	1.50	1.33	1.21	1.08	1.07	.96
Dividends per share	.48	.42	.38	.34	.30	.26	.22	.18
Price: High	34.3	29.0	26.6	25.0	28.5	22.8	20.3	20.4
Low	23.0	23.9	19.8	20.0	16.0	16.4	14.9	10.6

AGGRESSIVE GROWTH

Hewlett-Packard Company

3000 Hanover Street, Palo Alto, CA 94304 ◻ Investor contact: Steve Beitler (415) 857-2387 ◻ Dividend reinvestment plan not available ◻ Fiscal year ends October 31 ◻ Ticker symbol: HWP ◻ S&P rating: A ◻ Value Line financial strength rating: A++

Hewlett-Packard Company designs, manufactures, and services electronic products and systems for measurement, computing, and communication.

Hewlett-Packard's products are used by people in industry, business, engineering, science, medicine, and education.

The company's more than 23,000 products include computers and peripheral products, electronic test and measurement instruments and systems, networking products, medical electronic equipment, instruments and systems for chemical analysis, hand-held calculators, and electronic components.

HWP is one of the nineteen largest industrial companies in the United States and one of the world's largest computer companies. The company had revenues of $38.4 billion in its fiscal 1996 year (ended October 31, 1996).

Nearly 60 percent of Hewlett-Packard's business is generated abroad; two-thirds of that is in Europe. Other principal markets include Japan, Canada, Australia, the Far East, and Latin America. HWP is one of the top eight U.S. exporters.

Hewlett-Packard's domestic manufacturing plants are situated in twenty-eight cities, mostly in California, Colorado, the Northeast, and the Pacific Northwest. The company also has research and manufacturing plants in Europe, Asia-Pacific, Latin America, and Canada.

HWP sells its products and services through some 600 sales and support offices and distributorships in more than 120 countries.

Most of the company's revenue comes from a broad range of computer products and services, including workstations, personal computers, and peripherals—such as tape, disk, and optical storage devices, plotters, and printers.

HWP is the world's number two supplier of powerful desktop workstations for engineering, business, and multimedia applications. HWP also is one of the fastest-growing personal computer companies in the world.

Hewlett-Packard's PC products include the checkbook-size 200LX palmtop PC with built-in Pocket Quicken, and the HP OmniBook family of notebook PCs for mobile professionals.

A Look at the Past

Hewlett-Packard was founded in 1939 by William Hewlett and David Packard. The company's first product, built in a Palo Alto garage, was an electronic test instrument known as an audio oscillator. It improved upon existing audio oscillators in size, price, and performance. One of the infant company's first customers was Walt Disney Studios, which purchased eight oscillators to develop and test an innovative sound system for the classic movie *Fantasia*.

In the ensuing years, the company grew into the world's leading manufacturer of electronic test and measurement instruments for engineers and scientists. Those instruments, systems, and related services are used today to design, manufacture, operate, and repair electronic equipment, including emerging global information networks.

Besides the electronics industry, the principal markets for Hewlett-Packard instruments and systems are the communications, aerospace/defense, automotive, consumer electronics, computer, semiconductor, and components industries, as well as scientific research programs.

In the early 1960s, HWP extended its electronics technology to the fields of medicine and analytical chemistry. Today, the company's medical equipment, including cardiac ultrasound imaging and patient monitoring systems, is used in hospitals and clinics around the world. And HP's computer systems are used in both clinical and administrative areas.

HWP introduced its first computer in 1966 to gather and analyze data produced by HWP electronic instruments. When HWP branched into business computing in the 1970s with the HP 3000 midrange computer, the company launched a new era of distributed data processing, taking computing power out of computer rooms and making it accessible to people throughout an organization.

HWP's midrange computers today offer the performance of mainframe computers at much lower cost. With more than 65,000 in use worldwide, the HP 3000 is one of the most widely installed general-purpose business computers.

Shortcomings to Bear in Mind

- Hewlett-Packard's operating results may be adversely affected if the company is unable to continue to rapidly develop, manufacture, and market innovative products and services that meet customer requirements. The process of developing new high-technology products and solutions is inherently complex and uncertain. It requires accurate anticipation of customers' changing needs and emerging technological trends. The company then must make long-term investments and commit significant resources before knowing whether its predictions will eventually result in products that achieve market acceptance. After a product is developed, the company must quickly ramp manufacturing in sufficient volumes at acceptable costs.

This is a process that requires accurate forecasting of volumes, mix of products, and configurations. Moreover, the supply and timing of a new product or service must match the customers' demand and timing for those particular products or services. In view of the wide variety of systems, products, and services the company offers, the process of planning production and managing inventory levels becomes increasingly difficult.

Reasons to Buy

- In April of 1997, Hewlett-Packard, trying to forge ahead of computer rivals in the nascent market for electronic commerce, agreed to buy VeriFone, for $1.18 billion in stock. VeriFone is best known for the small, gray terminals used to approve credit-card purchases in stores. The company has 5 million of the units installed, controlling three-fourths of the world market for credit-card verification products.

- The merging of measurement, computation, and communication technologies is revolutionizing the way people gather and share information. Emerging global networks and specialized "information appliances" will enable people to share information easily, whether it's text, graphics, audio, or video.

  Hewlett-Packard's expertise is helping create and manage these data highways and provide products that let people plug into the networks. The company's capabilities in measurement, computation, and communication set HWP apart from most other companies that provide either computers or instruments, but not both.

- Analysts believe that Hewlett-Packard's move into the personal computer market will meet with a large measure of success, based on the company's well-known brand name, not to mention its exceptional reputation for a quality product.

- Hewlett-Packard is a dynamic growth stock. Its strong earnings record attests to this. EPS climbed from $.51 in 1986 to $2.54 in 1996, which amounts to an annual compound growth rate of 17.4 percent. In the same ten-year span, dividends, which won't do much to pay the rent, have climbed from $.06 to $.42 in the past ten years, a growth rate of 21.5 percent. In the same 1986–1996 period, book value per share advanced from $4.27 to $13.20, a growth rate of 11.9 percent.

- Hewlett-Packard has become one of the world's top computer service-and-support companies. The company's thirty-five response centers and support offices in 110 countries give customers 24-hour-a-day access to Hewlett-Packard anywhere in the world. HWP also offers a broad range of consulting, management, and financing services to give customers cost-effective, timely, and easy access to information.

- The company's balance sheet is blue chip, with most of the firms's assets in shareholders' equity. Value Line awards the company an A++ for financial strength.

- HWP is the world's leading supplier of printers for individuals, small businesses, and large organization. It has shipped more than 30 million laser and inkjet printers.

- HWP introduced the world's first scientific hand-held calculator, the HP-35, in 1972, and it quickly made the engineer's slide rule obsolete. Today, HWP makes some of the world's most sophisticated and compact business and scientific calculators.

- Hewlett-Packard was among the pioneers in the move to reduced instruction set computing (RISC), a technology that speeds up data processing. The move paid off, as customers snapped up HWP's RISC-based workstations and servers. Most other major manufacturers now have access to RISC technology, but Hewlett, in tandem with semiconductor giant Intel, is developing a next-generation processor that should keep HWP's products competitive.

- Moving to strike early in what is expected to be a multibillion-dollar market, Hewlett-Packard introduced a family of digital photography products in the spring of 1997. It unveiled a $399 digital camera, a $499 printer, and a $499 scanner. The new product is part of Hewlett-Packard's "PhotoSmart" family of digital-photography products.

  Digital photography uses personal computer technology to take, store, and print pictures. Because it is considered a long-term threat to traditional film-based photography, the race to create digital-photography products is expected to be one of the great consumer-product battles of coming years.

- HWP is extending the frontiers of fiber optics, wireless, and visual communications through its more than 9,000 component products that help people communicate quickly, reliably, and cost effectively.

- The company's entrepreneurial flexibility is fostered by a decentralized organization that gives business units considerable decision-making authority.

- HWP's continuing growth is based on a strong commitment to research and development. Each year, the company invests about 8 percent of its net revenue in R&D. This heavy investment—coupled with an ability to manufacture and market leading-edge technology quickly—let HWP provide a steady flow of new and useful products.

Total assets: $27,699 million
Current ratio: 1.69
Common shares outstanding: 1,017 million
Return on 1996 shareholders' equity: 20.3%

	1996	1995	1994	1993	1992	1991	1990	1989
Revenues (millions)	38,420	31,519	24,991	20,317	16,410	14,494	13,233	11,899
Net income (millions)	2,675	2,433	1,599	1,177	881	755	739	829
Earnings per share	2.54	2.32	1.54	1.16	.87	.76	.77	.88
Dividends per share	.42	.35	.26	.23	.18	.12	.11	.09
Price: High	57.7	48.3	25.6	22.3	21.3	14.3	12.6	15.4
Low	36.8	24.5	18.0	16.1	12.6	7.5	6.2	10.1

GROWTH & INCOME

Hubbell Incorporated

P.O. Box 549, Orange, CT 06477-4024 □ Investor contact: Thomas R. Conlin (203) 799-4293 □ Dividend reinvestment plan available: (203) 799-4100 □ Listed: NYSE □ Ticker symbol: HUB.B □ S&P rating: A □ Value Line financial strength rating: A+

Hubbell is a leading manufacturer of electrical connectors and components. In the low-voltage sector (600 volts or less), Hubbell's wiring devices are the premier in plugs and receptacles for industry and specialty markets, such as hospitals. This segment, analysts believe, is the single largest profit contributor to Hubbell. The company is also a leading maker of lighting fixtures for commercial and industrial applications. Industrial controls round out the low-voltage sector.

In the high-voltage sector (more than 600 volts), Hubbell manufactures specialty wire and cable through its Kerite unit, and insulators for electric utilities. In addition, Hubbell's Raco unit manufactures fittings and closures; Kellems is the number one maker of flexible holding devices; and Pulsecom produces data transmission and telecommunications equipment.

In recent years, HUB.B has enhanced its electric utility offering through the acquisitions of A. B. Chance and Anderson Products.

In brief, Hubbell stands out from the crowd in several ways:

• The company generates substantial free cash flow, giving it the funds to pursue acquisitions that enhance revenues and profits.

• HUB.B is still small enough that even a $30 million acquisition can contribute to results.

• Hubbell has the opportunity to boost its core growth rate with the help of new products in divisions such as Pulsecom (which had exceptional growth in 1996).

• The company's operating/pretax profits continue to climb at a better pace than sales—largely because of its improving cost and logistical structures.

• Despite delivering the highest margins and yield in the electrical equipment industry, coupled with 15 percent growth in 1995 and 1996, the stock often trades at no more than a market multiple.

Shortcomings to Bear in Mind

■ The dividend payout ratio is 48.6 percent (based on earnings and dividends in 1996), a little too high for a growth company, but perhaps acceptable for a growth-and-income stock.

■ Some analysts look upon Hubbell as being too conservative. For instance, they point out that the company has too little debt; only 14 percent of its capitalization is in the form of long-term debt. In its defense, management insists that it prefers to maintain a low level of debt so that it has the ability to make acquisitions.

■ Analysts don't expect the company will change its stripes, since the Hubbell family and other insiders own 40 percent of the voting stock—the Class A shares. Although the families' shares are held in trust, the trustees who vote these shares are board members,

including G. Jackson Ratcliffe, the CEO.

Reasons to Buy

■ Pulsecom has been experiencing strong demand for its digital transmission products, as consumers and businesses add more electronics to their homes and offices (such as PCs and fax machines) that require additional telephone connections. In 1996, Pulsecom's profits were up 60 percent on a sales gain of 30 percent.

■ One of the keys to Hubbell's high level of profitability and consistency in its distribution franchise for its traditional electrical products. Hubbell receives a premium price for these products because of its quality and reliability as a supplier.

In addition, Hubbell does not compete with its suppliers, whereas some of its competitors do.

These factors enable Hubbell to maintain solid relationships with its network of independent suppliers. What's more, the company's strong distribution network also facilitates acquisitions, since Hubbell can generally reduce administrative costs of acquired companies by incorporating the new products into its existing structure.

■ According to analysts, a major contribution to 1997's results will be improved margins in the distributor side of Hubbell's business, where warehouse consolidation should result in lower costs. This program is designed to reduce the number of warehouses at its four major locations. The two dozen warehouses the company owned at the beginning of 1997 were an outgrowth of the acquisitions that Hubbell has made over the years, since each acquisition brought along its own warehouse network. The savings from consolidating these warehouses to four units should be substantial.

- In 1996, Hubbell had an active year, making several acquisitions:
  - Adams Ltd., which has a stake in power poles.
  - Cable Dynamics, Inc., which manufactures cable fault detection systems and several electrical metering instrument lines.
  - Anderson Electrical Products, which manufactures components for electric utility and industrial applications, including connectors, transmission line hardware, and substation components.
  - Gleason Reel Corporation, with its leading brand name in reels, cable hardware and handling systems, and ergonomic workstation positioning products.
  - In 1997, the company acquired Fargo Manufacturing Company, which makes distribution and transmission products, principally for the electric utility industry. Fargo, a private company, generates gross margins in excess of 30 percent, operating margins of 13 percent, and it has a considerable amount of free cash. What's more, Fargo has a debt-free balance sheet, with nearly 40 percent of its assets in cash.
- Even though Hubbell has made a number of key acquisitions in recent years, there are still more opportunities to explore. For example, the 250 largest electrical distributors in the United States have aggregate sales of $25 billion. To be sure, HUB.B does not serve the entire market. Even so, Hubbell has total distribution of sales on the order of $700 million. Analysts believe that the industry is destined for further consolidation.
- Hubbell has been known for its excellence in manufacturing and for continuous cost-reduction efforts. As a result, it has one of the highest productivity levels and after-tax margins in the electrical component/connector industry.
- Hubbell's growth has been consistent, although not spectacular. Its exceptional record of consistency is all the more impressive when you take into account that it operates in a cyclical industry. It has only one year in which earnings fell below the prior year. In 1993, EPS fell to $2 from $2.83 (largely because of a $97.3 million restructuring charge, which cut $.93 from 1993 earnings). Over the 1986–1996 period, earnings advanced from $.83 to $2.10, a compound annual growth rate of 9.7 percent. In the same ten-year span, dividends per share climbed from $.32 to $1.02, a 12.3 percent growth rate.
- In most years, Hubbell has a solid return on equity, typically 17 percent or 18 percent.
- Hubbell is completing its third year of a four-year restructuring program that includes consolidation of plants, labor force reduction, the reorganization of certain operations' management and structure, and a realignment of warehousing and product distribution capabilities. This has been the primary driver of the company's operating profit margin improvement. When the program got under way, the profit margin was below 14 percent. It is now over 15 percent and could reach 17 percent in the near future.
- In addition to its restructuring program, Hubbell has the ability to improve margins of acquired companies through cost savings and improved management. For example, one of Hubbell's key strengths is its distribution network, and any new acquisition brought into its Distribution or Power Systems area benefits directly from this. Separate from its restructuring program, Hubbell has made a

major investment of about $5 million over the last few years in its systems, which can also be leveraged to help reduce costs in acquired companies.

■ Hubbell's businesses have a late-cycle orientation and are primarily related to maintenance and repair activities. This high maintenance-and-repair component lends stability to demand. In addition, Hubbell has very low exposure to the sluggish automotive, appliance, and residential sectors.

■ Late in 1996, Hubbell's Pulsecom division announced a partnership with 3Com Corporation. The two companies will develop asymmetric digital subscriber line hardware/software solutions for network service providers. This joint venture combines Pulsecom's strength in manufacturing digital transmission equipment with 3Com's strength in networking.

Total assets: $1,185 million
Current ratio: 2.34
Common shares outstanding: 66 million
Return on 1996 shareholders' equity: 20.1%

	1996	1995	1994	1993	1992	1991	1990	1989
Revenues (millions)	1,297	1,143	1,014	832	786	756	720	669
Net income (millions)	142	122	106	66	94	91	86	79
Earnings per share	2.10	1.83	1.60	1.00	1.41	1.37	1.31	1.20
Dividends per share	1.02	.92	.81	.78	.76	.69	.63	.54
Price: High	43.9	33.1	29.9	28.0	28.6	25.7	21.5	19.9
Low	31.8	24.8	25.0	24.2	21.5	19.1	15.2	13.7

AGGRESSIVE GROWTH

Illinois Tool Works Inc.

3600 West Lake Avenue, Glenview, Illinois 60025 ❑ Investor contact: Linda Williams (708) 657-4104 ❑
Dividend reinvestment plan available: (800) 800-8220 ❑ Listed: NYSE ❑ Ticker symbol: ITW ❑ S&P
rating: A+ ❑ Value Line financial strength rating: A

Illinois Tool Works is a multinational manufacturer of highly engineered fasteners, components, assemblies, and systems. ITW's businesses are small and focused, so they can work more effectively in a decentralized structure to add value to customers' products.

About 250 ITW operating units are divided into two business segments: Engineered Components and Industrial Systems and Consumables. The Engineered Components operating units produce short-lead-time plastic and metal components and assemblies; adhesives and industrial fluids, plastic and metal fas-

teners and fastening tools. Businesses in the Industrial Systems and Consumables segment produce longer-lead-time systems and related consumables for consumer and industrial packaging, inspection, and quality assurance.

The company has subsidiaries and affiliates in thirty-three countries on six continents. Foreign sales, moreover, account for 38 percent of sales and 29 percent of profits.

Although Illinois Tool Works is not a household name, since it does not produce a product that is familiar to the average investor, such as Coca-Cola, Rubbermaid,

Goodyear Tires, or Hewlett-Packard calculators, ITW is, nonetheless, a classic growth stock with a long history of increasing earnings and dividends. What's more, it is still small enough (only $5 billion in sales), so that it should continue to expand for many years to come—often enhanced by acquisitions. By contrast, all of the "household names" named above are vastly larger.

ITW has an interesting history: Founded in 1912, Illinois Tool Works' earliest products included milling cutters and hobs used to cut gears. Today ITW is a multinational manufacturer of highly engineered components and systems.

In 1923, the company developed the Shakeproof fastener, a patented twisted tooth lock washer. This product's success enabled ITW to become the leader in a new industry segment: engineered metal fasteners.

Illinois Tool soon expanded the Shakeproof line to include thread-cutting screws, preassembled screws, and other metal fasteners. By the late 1940s, the line grew to include plastic and metal/plastic combination fasteners. Today, ITW units produce fasteners for appliance, automotive, construction, general industrial, and other applications.

After World War II, the company also expanded into electrical controls and instruments, culminating in the formation of the Licon Division in the late 1950s. Today, ITW units provide a wide range of switch components and panel assemblies used in appliance, electronic, and industrial markets.

In the early 1960s, the newly formed Hi-Cone operating unit developed the plastic multipack carrier that revolutionized the packaging industry. Hi-Cone multipacks today are used to package beverage and food products as well as a variety of other products.

Also in the 1960s, the company formed Buildex to market existing Shakeproof fasteners as well as a line of masonry fasteners to the construction industry. Buildex today manufactures fasteners for drywall, general construction, and roofing applications.

In the mid-1980s, ITW acquired Ramset, Phillips Drill (Red Head), and SPIT, manufacturers of concrete anchoring, epoxy anchoring, and powder actuated systems; and Paslode, maker of pneumatic and cordless nailers, staplers, and systems for wood construction applications. Today, the construction industry is the largest market served by Illinois Tool Works.

In the 1970s, ITW purchased Devcon Corporation, a producer of adhesives, sealants, and related specialty chemicals. Today the company's engineered polymers businesses offer a variety of products with home, construction, and industrial applications.

In 1986, Illinois Tool acquired Signode Packaging Systems, a multinational manufacturer of metal and plastic strapping stretch film, industrial tape, application equipment, and related products. Today, ITW offers a wide range of industrial packaging systems, including Dynatec hot-melt adhesive application equipment.

In 1989, Illinois Tool Works acquired Ransburg Corporation, a leading producer of finishing equipment.

ITW expanded its capabilities in industrial finishing with the purchase of DeVilbiss Industrial/Commercial Division in 1990. Today, DeVilbiss and Ransburg manufacture conventional and liquid electrostatic equipment, while Gema Volstatic (acquired with the Ransburg and DeVilbiss purchases) produces electrostatic powder coating systems.

The company acquired the Miller Group in 1993. Miller is a leading manufacturer of arc welding equipment and related systems. Miller's emphasis on new product development and innovative design fits well with ITW's engineering and manufacturing strategies.

Illinois Tool Works continually strives to expand its capabilities and enhance the competitiveness of its core businesses through new product and market development; niche market penetration; joint venture and licensing arrangements; and acquisitions. These strategies ensure that every ITW business creates value and improves operating efficiencies for every customer.

Shortcomings to Bear in Mind

- In 1996, substantially all of the revenue and operating income increase was due to acquisitions, primarily in the European automotive and appliance industries. Weak European construction markets caused revenues and operating income to decline in the construction businesses, which moderated the revenue and operating income from acquisitions and from the core automotive businesses.

    What's more, margins were down because of the decline in revenues from construction operations, as well as the lower prices and unit volume in the French automotive markets and the weak European appliance market. Foreign currency fluctuations in 1996, compared with 1996, however, had only a minimal effect on revenue and earnings. Seventy-six percent of international revenues are from European operations.

- During most of 1996, insiders (such as officers and board members) were steadily selling their shares of Illinois Tool Works. Presumably, they considered the stock fully valued.

Reasons to Buy

- Illinois Tool Works has an exceptional record of growth. In the 1986–1996 period, earnings per share climbed from $.32 to $1.97, an annual compound growth rate of 19.7 percent. In the same ten-year stretch, dividends advanced from $.09 to $.36, for a growth rate of 14.9 percent.
- The company is sound financially, since 76 percent of capitalization is in the form of shareholders' equity. The stock is rated A+ by Standard & Poor's and A by Value Line.
- The shares of Illinois Tool are heavily owned by the Smith family (37 percent) and officers and directors (5 percent). You can be sure these insiders have the shareholders' best interests in mind.
- ITW provides a wide variety of environmentally responsible products that improve the competitive positions of customers in many industries around the world.
- Illinois Tool maintains decentralized operating units, basing its production facilities in proximity to the markets they serve and building close working relationships with customers. Those strategies enable ITW to continuously enter into new industry niches, as well as increase penetration in markets currently served.
- Although characterized by decentralization, regional focus, and close customer contact, the company's operating units frequently collaborate on joint ventures targeted at specific industries. What's more, ITW maintains a technology center that serves as a focal point for intracompany research and new product development.
- Illinois Tool Works has a strong tradition of acquisitions, as exemplified in 1996. During that year, nineteen companies joined the ITW family. All of these were extensions of the various

core businesses and continued the company's strategy of penetrating its various worldwide markets. For example, Medalist Industries, a U.S. manufacturer of metal fasteners and specialty metal components and Comet, S.A., a French manufacturer of plastic fasteners, both expanded ITW's global presence in automotive markets.

Another example, Gerrard Strapping, a subsidiary of Australian-based Azon Limited, which produces industrial packaging consumables and equipment, enhanced the company's presence in Australasian packaging markets. And, of course, the acquisition of Hobart Brothers Company, headquartered in Troy, Ohio, was completed in January 1996 and brings the welding group up to full strength with regard to products and services for ITW's customers' welding needs.

Total assets: $4,806 million
Current ratio: 1.85
Common shares outstanding: 248 million
Return on 1996 shareholders' equity: 22.5%

	1996	1995	1994	1993	1992	1991	1990	1989
Revenues (millions)	4,997	4,152	3,461	3,159	2,812	2,640	2,544	2,173
Net income (millions)	486	388	278	207	192	181	182	164
Earnings per share	1.97	1.65	1.23	.92	.36	.82	.84	.77
Dividends per share	.36	.31	.28	.25	.23	.21	.18	.15
Price: High	48.7	32.8	22.8	20.3	18.2	17.4	14.4	11.9
Low	26.0	19.9	18.5	16.3	14.3	11.4	9.8	8.3

GROWTH & INCOME

Ingersoll-Rand Company

World Headquarters, 200 Chestnut Ridge Road, Woodcliff Lake, NJ 07675 ◻ Investor contact: Joseph P. Fimbianti (201) 573-3113 ◻ Dividend reinvestment plan available: (800) 524-4458 ◻ Listed: NYSE ◻ Ticker symbol: IR ◻ S&P rating: B+ ◻ Value Line financial strength rating: B++

Ingersoll-Rand, a leading diversified industrial manufacturer, produces primarily nonelectrical machinery and equipment under the company name, as well as a number of other brands. About 55 percent of IR's products are capital goods; the remaining 45 percent are expendables.

Ingersoll-Rand's nine operating segments market air conditioners, architectural hardware (hydraulic door closers, Schlage locks), bearings and components (Torrington), Club Car golf cars, construction and mining equipment (Blaw-Knox asphalt pavers), industrial pumps and tools, Bobcat skid-steer loaders, and production equipment.

For those who know its long history, Ingersoll-Rand is undoubtedly equated with construction equipment, as it should be. When Simon Ingersoll and the Rand brothers applied their ingenuity to rock drills in the 1870s, they hardly could have imagined that their names could grace a $6 billion enterprise 125 years later and be a leading manufacturer of not only rock drills, but of products as diverse as Schlage locks and Club Car golf cars.

Shortcomings to Bear in Mind

■ Tepid economic conditions in Europe, especially in France and Germany, are likely to keep sales growth there from outpacing growth rates in the more vibrant economies of North America, Latin America, and Asia. On the other hand, restructuring initiatives taken in the latter part of 1996 should help improve the company's European segment's operating margins. What's more, the company's divestiture of its Clark-Hurth unit in early 1997 should also give a lift to margins.

- In the 1986–1996 period, earnings per share performed well, advancing from $1.00 to $3.21, a compound annual growth rate of 12.4 percent. On the other hand, dividends did not keep pace. In the same ten-year stretch, dividends per share expanded from $.52 to $.78, a growth rate of only 4.1 percent.

Reasons to Buy

- Ingersoll-Rand is number one or number two in almost every market it serves. Here are some examples:
  - Bobcat skid-steer loaders, produced by Ingersoll-Rand's Melroe Operating Group, hold the top position in the worldwide market.
  - Blaw-Knox is the world's largest producer of asphalt road-paving equipment.
  - Club Car is a strong contender for world leadership in the golf car industry.
  - Torrington is North America's leading broad-line bearing manufacturer.
  - Ingersoll-Rand's Architectural Hardware Group, which includes such well-known brands as Schlage locks, Von Duprin exit devices, LCN closers, and Steelcraft steel doors, has the broadest line of door-related products in the United States.
- This leadership can partially be attributed to the company's commitment to research and development. IR consistently ranks among the top 100 U.S. corporations receiving patents and has

been issued more than 600 patents since 1990.

- For four years, IR has met or exceeded its goal of increasing earnings by 15 percent per year. Earnings of $358 million in 1996 were 32 percent higher than in 1995.
- The company has paid dividends on its common shares every year since 1910.
- Ingersoll-Rand follows a continuing strategy of pursuing acquisitions and joint ventures that extend the company's participation in markets throughout the world.
  - In 1996, two "bolt on" acquisitions, Zimmerman International and the Steelcraft Division of MascoTech, expanded the company's product lines and technology.
  - In January of 1997, the company proposed to acquire Newman Tonks PLC, a U.K.–based manufacturer of architectural hardware. The offer values the issued shares of Newman Tonks at about $376 million. IR noted that "the offer represents a premium over the cash alternative value of an unsolicited and hostile offer made by a British company." Tonks, based in Birmingham, England, is a maker, specifier, and supplier of branded architectural products for use in the building industry. In 1995, Newman Tonks had sales of about $417 million. No dilution from the acquisition is likely in 1997. Beyond that, the company should begin to contribute to IR's earnings.
  - The purchase of Clark Equipment in 1995 brought the Bobcat, Club Car, and Blaw-Knox brands under the Ingersoll-Rand umbrella. Clark's overall financial performance exceeded IR's projections in 1996, and the expectation is for further improvement in the future.

- About 40 percent of Ingersoll-Rand's sales are derived from abroad, and the percentage is expected to increase as the company penetrates growth areas in the Asia-Pacific region and Latin America.

  As part of its global strategy in 1996, the company established Ingersoll-Rand (China) Investment Company Limited. This holding company, the vehicle for IR's investments in China, already has equity in a joint venture established in January of 1996 for the production of industrial roller bearings and ball bearings in the country's Jiangsu Province. Ingersoll-Rand also entered a joint venture in India in 1996 for tool manufacturing.

- The company recently re-created three international organizations to better leverage Ingersoll-Rand's resources.

  Ingersoll-Rand Europe, Ingersoll-Rand Asia-Pacific, and Ingersoll-Rand Latin America have centralized regional administration for improved efficiencies and more responsive service to customers in those regions.

- More than half of the company's manufacturing facilities are outside the United States, providing a variety of bases from which to source key product lines and to participate in markets that would otherwise prove difficult to enter.

- Ingersoll-Rand is in its fourth year of a dramatic shift in how the company conducts its business. Management is fostering an environment of continuous change, in which work processes are constantly being improved.

  The most compelling example is a strategic sourcing initiative started in 1996. The company assembled sourcing teams to leverage and consolidate corporate wide purchasing power in such areas as motors, steel, castings, and indirect materials and services, which cost about $3 billion annually.

  In 1996, the effort saved more than $30 million; the figure is expected to save in excess of an additional $30 million in 1997, with even greater savings in the years to come.

  By working more closely with vendors during design phases of production, for example, Ingersoll-Rand will continue to help bring products to market faster and at better value. As a result, the company is poised to fulfill its vision of becoming the supplier and partner of choice for its customers.

- Ingersoll-Rand is also streamlining business processes to reduce cycle times in manufacturing, sales, and administration. For instance, drill-bit manufacturing cycle times have fallen by an average of 77 percent at Roanoke's Rock Drill Division plant, where order fulfillment times have fallen by about 48 percent.

  Over the past two years at Schlage, past-due orders for a master-keyed product fell by 80 percent, and shipment lead times fell by 75 percent. There are a number of other examples throughout the company.

- Ingersoll-Rand is committed to divesting businesses that don't fit the company's long-term profile, show limited growth potential, or cannot earn a return exceeding the cost of capital over the cycle.

Total assets: $5,622 million
Current ratio: 1.66
Common shares outstanding: 109 million
Return on 1996 shareholders' equity: 18.4%

	1996	1995	1994	1993	1992	1991	1990	1989
Revenues (millions)	6,704	5,729	4,508	4,021	3,784	3,586	3,738	3,447
Net income (millions)	344	270	211	164	148	145	185	202
Earnings per share	3.21	2.55	2.00	1.56	1.42	1.41	1.78	1.89
Dividends per share	.78	.74	.72	.70	.70	.66	.63	-.58
Price: High	47.6	42.4	41.6	39.9	34.3	27.5	30.3	25.1
Low	35.1	28.4	29.5	28.8	25.0	17.5	14.3	16.8

AGGRESSIVE GROWTH

International Business Machines Corporation

One Old Orchard Road, Armonk, New York 10504 ▫ Investor contact: H. Parke III (914) 765-5008 ▫
Dividend reinvestment plan available: (212) 791-4208 ▫ Listed: NYSE ▫ Ticker symbol: IBM ▫ S&P
rating: B- ▫ Value Line financial strength rating: A++

IBM is the largest manufacturer of data processing equipment and systems. Its products run the gamut, from personal computers to mainframes, as well as communications equipment.

A Breakdown of the Company's Lines of Business

• Hardware products include servers, which include System 390, AS/400, RS6000, and POWERparallel systems

• Personal computers and RISC System/6000 workstation products

• Display-based terminals, consumer and financial systems

• Storage

• Other peripherals

• OEM hardware

• Software, which includes consulting, education, systems development, managed operations, and availability services

• Maintenance represents separately billed maintenance services

• Rentals and financing is comprised of financing revenue associated with purchasing and leasing products

Recent Developments

• In mid-1995, IBM acquired Lotus Development Corporation for $3.2 billion.

• In 1994, IBM sold Federal Systems Company to Loral Corporation for a net gain of $248 million.

• In March of 1996, IBM completed the acquisition of Tivoli Systems, Inc., a provider of management software for client/server environments, for about $743 million in cash. Tivoli had revenues of $49.5 million in 1995.

• In late 1996, IBM acquired Edmark, a developer of consumer and educational software, for about $80 million.

• In September of 1996, IBM unveiled the next generation of its System 390 Server family and related software.

• Late in 1996, IBM introduced the IBM Network Station, a device priced under $700 intended for doing business on the Internet.

• Early in 1997, Lotus Development, a subsidiary of IBM, reported that SmartSuite 97 Edition for Windows 95 and Windows NT 4.0, the newest version of its desktop productivity suite, is available to the public.

- In early 1997, IBM announced a 2-for-1 stock split, to take effect in May. This is the first time IBM has split its stock since 1979.

Shortcomings to Bear in Mind

- While the trend toward the use of sophisticated technology is a favorable development, the industry is still dominated by intense competition that can quickly turn today's leaders into tomorrow's losers. The new computing paradigm demands that vendors constantly introduce new, more powerful, and cheaper versions of successful products, while keeping a tight rein on operating expense.
- Since the end of 1996, the dollar has strengthened against German mark, the French franc, and the Japanese yen. In particular, this creates a tough environment for IBM in Japan, since competitors may be more likely to gain share in areas such as high-end computer systems.
- To be sure, prospects for the industry remain bright, led by strengthening corporate demand for PCs and the continued build-out of the Internet/Intranet. Even so, some analysts expect shares of companies in the industry to remain volatile—at least in the short run—but have good prospects for the longer term. For this reason, I have placed IBM in the Aggressive Growth category.

Reasons to Buy

- IBM's services business is growing rapidly. The company's global reach helps it to win outsourcing contracts from companies with worldwide operations.
- IBM's expertise in networking is a plus in gaining contracts from the many businesses that are trying to tie together their vast computer resources.
- IBM is cashing in on the rapidly growing interest in electronic commerce to help businesses speed up the exchange of information with suppliers and customers.
- The fundamentals in the computer industry remain strong, mainly because of the growing global appetite for technology products that increase productivity. Worldwide competition is forcing companies to become more productive, a task being accomplished largely through the employment of technology.
- Analysts see strong demand for the relatively new CMOS-based (complementary metal oxide semiconductor) mainframes, given their good price/performance characteristics. Importantly, although the machines are cheaper than older models, they are also less expensive to manufacture, which means margins are wider.
- The company's hardware offerings are generally at good points in their product cycles. New families of mainframes and the midrange AS/400 line were rolled out in 1996; revamped workstations using IBM's PowerPC chip are due in 1997.
- IBM started the personal computer revolution in the early 1980s, and then was almost undone by it because it did not grasp the impact of what it had set in motion. When customers began to abandon their expensive IBM mainframes for clusters of cheaper personal computers, Big Blue was unprepared. Its revenues plunged, followed by its stock price. Now the company is determined to lead what its chairman, Louis V. Gerstner, Jr., believes is the next computing revolution.

    Its international data network is IBM's "hidden" jewel, according to Mr. Gerstner, who has been seeking new markets for IBM since he joined the company in 1993. Now he seems convinced that network computing will provide the revenue growth that IBM needs.

While various hardware and software companies are also seeking ways to parlay their strengths into some sort of Internet strategy, IBM—with offices in one hundred countries and an international voice and data network already serving over 25,000 customers and generating more than $2 billion—sees itself as uniquely positioned to become a provider of global corporate networks.

- IBM's personal computer operation has turned solidly profitable.
- In 1996, the ThinkPad 560 hit the market. At 4.1 pounds, it's one of the lightest notebook computers around, yet it sports one of the largest, sharpest screens.
- In 1996, IBM extended its Aptiva line of computers. The sculptural Aptiva S Series is the first home computer that lets people place the monitor and the media drives on their desk, and tuck the tower someplace out of the way.
- Louis Gerstner, Jr., has done a stunning job of proving that all those obituaries for the big computer were premature. Look at what has happened since he arrived at Big Blue in 1993. The company has replaced its aging line of water-cooled mainframes with smaller, faster, cheaper, but still immensely profitable mainframes.

At the same time, Gerstner has reduced IBM's bloated employment roster from 300,000 to less than 225,000, and lowered annual operating costs by $15 billion.

The hot item in IBM's catalog is a new line of System/390 mainframes based on so-called complementary metal-oxide semiconductor (CMOS) chips, designed to replace the older bipolar chips that ran faster and hotter and thus demanded messy water cooling. The new CMOS machines are so much cheaper, smaller, and easier to use that IBM has been overwhelmed by the demand. In 1996, IBM had a huge gross margin of 80 or 90 percent on its new CMOS hardware business and a 95 percent gross margin on a sister business, mainframe software.

- In the fall of 1996, IBM launched the world's first network computer, the IBM Network Station, a device streamlined and optimized for the Net. For about $700, it's the most affordable way for businesses to offer network access on a large scale.
- Major corporations increasingly want their employees to share documents, reports, and financial information across time zones and borders. Lotus Notes is the leading program that enables this kind of teamwork: a software category called *groupware*.
- The company's cost-control efforts should keep expenses in line.
- In October of 1996, IBM introduced VoiceType Simply Speaking, software that allows users to open an application, dictate a memo, or edit a document without touching a keyboard. Also in 1996, the company shipped more advanced versions of its speech recognition product for specific industries. The MedSpeak/Radiology technology, for instance, saves radiologists time and boosts their productivity.

Total assets: $81,132 million
Current ratio: 1.27
Common shares outstanding: 1,015 million
Return on 1996 shareholders' equity: 27.1%

	1996	1995	1994	1993	1992	1991	1990	1989
Revenues (millions)	75,947	71,940	64,052	62,716	64,523	64,792	69,018	62,710
Net income (millions)	5,429	6,334	2,965	13	1,435	2,112	6,020	5,251
Earnings per share	5.52	5.51	2.46	—	1.24	1.85	5.26	4.53
Dividends per share	.65	.50	.50	.79	2.42	2.42	2.42	2.37
Price: High	83.0	57.3	38.2	29.9	50.2	69.9	61.6	65.4
Low	41.6	35.1	25.7	20.4	24.4	41.8	47.3	46.7

INCOME

International Flavors & Fragrances Inc.

521 West 57th Street, New York, N. Y. 10019-2960 □ Investor contact: Thomas H. Hoppel (212) 765-5500 □ Dividend reinvestment plan not available □ Listed: NYSE □ Ticker symbol: IFF □ S&P rating: A □ Value Line financial strength rating: A++

Founded in 1909, International Flavors & Fragrances Inc. is the leading creator and manufacturer of flavors and fragrances used by others to impart or improve flavor or fragrance in a wide variety of consumer products.

Fragrance products are sold principally to makers of perfumes and cosmetics, hair and other personal care products, soaps and detergents, household and other cleaning products, and area fresheners.

Flavors are sold primarily to makers of dairy, meat, and other processed foods; beverages; snacks and savory foods; confectionery, sweet, and baked goods; pharmaceutical and oral care products; and animal foods.

IFF uses both synthetic and natural ingredients in its compounds. The company has a strong commitment to R&D; it spends 6 or 7 percent of sales on this endeavor each year.

Over the years, International Flavors & Fragrances has achieved steady sales and earnings, until 1996. In that year, IFF was hurt by slow customer ordering of fine fragrances. At the same time, flavor sales were limited by the impact of consolidation and downsizing among food customers. In addition, unseasonably cool summer weather had a negative impact on sales to beverage and ice cream industries. In short, 1996 is a year that IFF would like to forget.

Shortcomings to Bear in Mind

■ It should be borne in mind that the company's dividend payout ratio is not characteristic of a growth stock. In 1996, the dividend of $1.38 represents a payout ratio of 69 percent. That's one reason I have classified this stock in the Income category and not under Growth. On the other hand, I would not have included IFF in this book if I didn't think the company could shake off its present difficulties and resume its illustrious career as the leader in its field.

A Review of 1996

IFF's earnings per share in 1996, reflecting a one-time pretax charge of $49.7 million for streamlining the company's aroma chemical production facilities, amounted to $1.71, as compared to $2.24 the prior year. Excluding the one-time charge, earnings per share were $2.00.

The Good News

During the year, IFF's strongest sales growth was achieved for both flavors and fragrances in the Far East, Latin America, and the developing regions including Eastern Europe, India, the Middle East, and South Africa. Those encouraging results, once again, confirmed that growing economies and increased disposable incomes in such regions have an almost immediate, favorable impact on flavor and fragrance purchases.

The Bad News

While IFF maintained its market share of both flavors and fragrances in the developed countries of Europe and North America, the company's customers experienced moderated sales, which affected their inventory levels and reordering patterns.

The sluggish European economies and a reduction in new product introductions, both there and in North America, hurt fragrance sales. What's more, flavor sales felt the effects of restructuring programs with many of the company's food customers, as well as the impact of lower beverage, yogurt, and ice cream sales as a result of the coldest summer on record in both Europe and the United States.

Management is convinced that these factors are unusual and temporary and that flavor and fragrance sales will resume "their normal growth patterns" in the period ahead.

IFF Is Well Named "International"

The company's sales outside the United States were 70 percent of total sales, about the same as the prior year. Fragrance sales amounted to 57 percent of IFF's worldwide sales, compared with 43 percent for flavors. Here again, there was little difference in this breakdown from 1995.

Streamlining Should Help the Future

The streamlining of the company's worldwide aroma chemical production facilities, resulting in the nonrecurring charge to 1996 earnings, will achieve a $20 million increase in pretax earnings annually, beginning in 1998.

The closure of IFF's Union Beach, New Jersey, aroma chemical plant by the end of 1997 and the transfer of production to the company's new state-of-the-art facilities in Augusta, Georgia, as well as those of Benicarlo, Spain, and Haverhill, England, will result in the most globally integrated and cost-effective aroma chemical production complex in existence.

Reasons to Buy

- Despite lower earnings in 1996, International Flavors & Fragrances dutifully increased its dividend, as it has for the past thirty-six consecutive years—a record that few companies can match.
- IFF is strong financially, with a minimal amount of long-term debt. Its ratio of current assets to current liabilities, moreover, is exceptionally high, at well over 3 to 1.
- Growth of earnings per share has been steady and above average. In the 1986–1996 period, earnings per share expanded from $.76 to $2.00 (which does not take into account the one-time write-off to restructure operations), for a compound annual growth rate of 10.2 percent. In the same ten-year stretch, dividends per share climbed from $.39 to $1.38, a growth rate of 13.5 percent.
- While fragrance sales during the 1996 Christmas season in the United States were lackluster, independent market studies confirmed that half of the ten

leading fragrances sold in department stores were supplied by IFF. The remaining fragrances, supplied by various competitors, contained many ingredients supplied by International Flavors & Fragrances. A hallmark of IFF fragrances is their longevity in the marketplace, a critical advantage when one considers today's high cost of introduction and promotion.

- IFF has had particular success in flavors for snack foods, a growing market everywhere, but particularly in the U.S., where Americans consume eight times more savory snacks than the world average. Baked chips, for which IFF supplies a variety of flavors, were particularly successful in 1996.

- The company's capital spending in 1997 is expected to be about $85 million, or similar to the prior year. A major portion will be used to complete the final phase of IFF's aroma chemical plant investments in August, Georgia; Benicarlo, Spain; and Haverhill, England. In addition, flavor and fragrance facilities are scheduled to be expanded in Holland, Indonesia, Mexico, Brazil, and South Africa.

- International Flavors & Fragrances will spend $100 million on research in 1997, an increase of 7 percent over 1995. Management asserts that this R&D effort is the "key to our continued leadership and growth in providing new, innovative flavor and fragrance products for IFF's customers worldwide."

- As large consumer companies continue the trend toward consolidation, they are increasingly demanding fewer suppliers who can service them globally. No company is better able to meet their requirements than International Flavors & Fragrances. The company's creative and production facilities are strategically situated in all of the major international markets. The company also has the advantage of culturally diverse creative talent, drawing from a wide range of national and ethnic backgrounds. This enables IFF to provide unique and highly flexible responses to the demands of its leading customers in different marketplaces. Finally, the company's worldwide manufacturing capability and accessible raw material plants allows IFF to meet customer needs quickly and efficiently.

- Competition in the marketplace places a premium on new fragrances and ingredients. IFF scientists are continuously analyzing rare plants, flowers, and woods from around the world in its state-of-the-art greenhouse at its Research & Development Center in New Jersey. As the creator of Living Flower technology, IFF has led the way in identifying ingredients hidden by nature in remote parts of the world and previously unavailable for perfumery. These ingredients often impart a "signature" to a fine fragrance that enhances its identifiability and long-term success. The company has an unparalleled track record in creating fragrances with international appeal and proven longevity.

- In the beverage market, consumption of soft drinks continues to increase around the world. A large portion of IFF's flavors find their application in this growth area. Globally, cola, lemon-lime, and orange are consumer favorites, but there are local beverage preferences that impact the company's sales. In addition, sports drinks and beverages marketed to children continue to grow in popularity, with brightly colored drinks containing combinations of natural fruit flavors.

- IFF's flavor scientists have taken a fresh look at how nature composes the best-tasting citrus flavors, down to the molecular level. Using this knowledge, together with recently developed citrus knowledge, the company launched globally in 1996 a line of new citrus flavors called Citrue, which faithfully reproduces this organoleptic character of citrus products, from orange to grapefruit.

■ Fruit and vegetable juice beverages continue to hold wide consumer interest. In Asia, fruit juice consumption is on the rise. Juice favorites often come from local fruits such as mango, soursop, jackfruit, young coconut, and white radish. IFF has created flavors that replicate the authentic fresh, ripe taste of these local fruits and vegetables and combines them with its line of high-quality juice concentrates for beverages that provide satisfaction for the sophisticated palate.

Total assets: $1,507 million
Current ratio: 3.60
Common shares outstanding: 110 million
Return on 1996 shareholders' equity: 17.3%

	1996	1995	1994	1993	1992	1991	1990	1989
Revenues (millions)	1,436	1,440	1,315	1,189	1,126	1,017	963	870
Net income (millions)	221	249	226	203	190	169	157	139
Earnings per share	2.00	2.24	2.03	1.78	1.64	1.47	1.37	1.22
Dividends per share	1.38	1.24	1.12	1.00	.91	.83	.74	.66
Price: High	51.9	55.9	47.9	39.8	38.8	35.0	25.0	25.8
Low	40.8	45.1	35.6	33.0	31.5	22.9	18.2	16.1

GROWTH & INCOME

Jefferson-Pilot Corporation

P. O. Box 21008, Greensboro, NC 27420 ❑ Investor contact: John T. Still, III (910) 691-3382 ❑ Dividend reinvestment plan available: (800) 829-8432 ❑ Listed: NYSE ❑ Ticker symbol: JP ❑ S&P rating: A+ ❑ Value Line financial strength rating: A

Jefferson-Pilot has two business segments: insurance and communications. Within the insurance segment, JP offers individual life insurance products, annuity and investment products, and group insurance products through three principal subsidiaries: Jefferson-Pilot Life Insurance Company (JP Life), Alexander Hamilton Life Insurance Company of America (AH Life), and First Alexander Hamilton Life (FAHL).

Within the communications segment, JP operates television broadcasting stations (three) and radio broadcasting stations (seventeen) and provides sports and entertainment programming. These operations are conducted through Jefferson-Pilot Communications Company (JPCC).

JP's revenues are derived about 89 percent from life insurance, which consists of 44 percent from individual life products, 24 percent from group insurance products, and 21 percent from annuity and investment products, 9 percent from communications (3 percent from television, 3 percent from radio, and 3 percent from sports and entertainment), and 2 percent from the parent. This composition shifted toward life insurance in 1996 and 1995 as the result of acquisitions.

Jefferson-Pilot's sources of earnings have become better balanced, benefiting from a recent restructuring.

The company's individual life insurance business has grown from 48 percent to 57 percent of operating profits in 1996.

Annuities and investment products have increased from 17 percent to 24 percent. What's more, communications operations have remained meaningful, growing from 8 to 10 percent of earnings.

At the other extreme, group insurance has become less significant, dropping from 22 percent to 9 percent in 1996.

Life Insurance

Jefferson-Pilot distributes a broad line of individual life insurance products—traditional whole life, term, universal, and current assumption whole life—as well as specialized policies for the home service and payroll-deduction markets.

A Review of 1996

Jefferson-Pilot's operating earnings before realized investment gains grew 17.3 percent, to $263 million, from $224 million in 1995. Operating earnings on a per-share basis also increased 17.3 percent, to $3.66, from $3.12. The company's operating return on shareholders' equity increased to 15.2 percent, from 14.3 percent. Cash dividends in 1996 rose 12 percent, to $1.40, from $1.25.

Jefferson-Pilot outperformed the industry in an important way. With life insurance premium sales growth of almost 57 percent—$92 million in 1996, compared with $59 million in 1995—JP set a pace as one of the fastest-growing life insurance organizations in the nation in 1996.

This achievement was a product of both continued strong growth through Jefferson-Pilot Life's existing sales channels and successful integration of Alexander Hamilton Life into the company's marketing organization.

Alexander Hamilton also brought to Jefferson-Pilot a significantly expanded presence in the single-premium deferred annuity market. JP is now among the twenty largest writers of single-premium annuities, giving the company an important stake in the growing retirement savings market.

Shortcomings to Bear in Mind

- The outlook for the company's group business (25 percent of total sales) is clouded. This division has been burdened with price competition from other health insurers and managed-care companies. A recovery does not seem in sight. To cope with the problem, the company is reducing exposure to business with adverse claims experience. However, this doesn't help profitability. One possible cure: Sell the business.

- The industry is being subjected to powerful catalysts for change. The industry's life insurance premium sales are not growing, and, on the whole, the industry is losing share of consumer savings dollars to competitors.

  In addition, new products and distribution channels are blurring traditional industry product and distribution boundaries. Further, the industry also has committed too much capital to products and services with low returns on investment. Finally, profit margins and returns on capital are under pressure, resulting in a powerful trend toward mergers and consolidation.

Reasons to Buy

- Jefferson-Pilot is addressing these industry realities through constructive, creative, and disciplined strategies that are designed to set JP apart as an industry leader that can generate rising returns for shareholders. Specifically, the company has made impressive progress by:
  - Reducing units costs of producing and servicing a portfolio of solid, competitive life insurance and annuity products. Jefferson-Pilot is now one of the lowest-cost producers of life insurance in the nation.

- Enhancing existing distribution. Productivity among the company's career life agents increased over 200 percent from 1992 to 1996.
- Diversifying into new, rapidly growing distribution channels. JP has added over 10,000 new independent agents to the Jefferson-Pilot Life sales organization since 1992.
- Engaging in strategic acquisitions that enhance the company's geographic and demographic market diversification. Alexander Hamilton Life added 5,000 agents and a solid Midwestern market presence, while Chubb Life will give the company a strong position in the Northeast and in upscale markets.

■ On February 23, 1997, Jefferson-Pilot entered into a definitive agreement to purchase the life insurance operations of The Chubb Corporation for $875 million. This acquisition is the largest to date for Jefferson-Pilot and represents a major strategic step to enhance and build the company's core individual life insurance business to an industry leadership position.

Chubb Life Insurance Company of America and its subsidiaries offer a broad range of individual life insurance products and are leading producers of variable universal life products. The Chubb Life companies distribute their products through an independent network of more than 2,300 general agents and 9,000 agents.

This acquisition will provide a major boost to Jefferson-Pilot's market position:

- JP will become one of the three largest universal life underwriters, with $136 million of annualized UL premiums, based on 1996 results. Total combined life sales would have been $191 million in 1996, among the top ten in the industry.

- Chubb Life also will enhance Jefferson-Pilot's position substantially in several large states: Massachusetts, New York, New Jersey, and Illinois.
- Jefferson-Pilot's presence in higher-income markets will be strengthened, and the company will gain capability for variable universal life, a rapidly growing product segment.
- Chubb Securities, a well-regarded, full-service broker-dealer, will bring JP about 1,200 registered representatives.
- Jefferson-Pilot expects to gain access to sell life insurance products through the Chubb Corporation's strong property-casualty distribution system.
- JP expects this transaction to increase both its earnings and its return on equity after 1997. The company's assets will increase by nearly $5 billion, and its balance sheet will remain conservative, providing Jefferson-Pilot with financial flexibility to support its growth plans.

■ Successful integration of marketing, operational, and financial strategies depends on coordinated teamwork among experienced leaders. Jefferson-Pilot's record of growth is evidence of such teamwork. From 1992 through 1996, the company's assets more than tripled, life insurance premium sales quadrupled, operating earnings per share grew at better than annually. Finally, nearly a 19 percent total return for shareholders exceeded the average for the industry by a substantial margin.

■ Each of JP's business units has contributed to the company's growing profitability, except for group insurance. Operating profits from the company's core individual life insurance business have grown at close to a 16 percent compounded rate since 1992. In that same span, annuity and investment product earnings have expanded at a rate in excess of 20 percent per year. What's more, communications profits have grown by almost 19 percent annually.

- Jefferson-Pilot has been remolded in recent years. Since 1992, the company has shed noncore businesses, expanded its distribution capabilities, made or announced over $1.5 billion of acquisitions, and retired almost $200 million of its common shares. Management believes that its organization today possesses key resources and skills to maintain its strong growth record and to occupy a leadership position in the life insurance industry. Those resources and skills include:
  - A strong Southeastern brand, enhanced by its high-profile commu-

nications businesses, and accompanied by a growing national presence achieved through acquisitions.

- Superior financial resources, including a conservative balance sheet, strong risk-based capital levels, and high financial strength ratings.
- Critical mass and scale in its core life insurance and annuity businesses.
- Industry-leading expense management, allowing the company to produce highly competitive products on a common platform.
- Strong investment management capabilities, including specialized skills in asset classes such as private placements and commercial mortgages.

Total assets: $17,562 million
Common shares outstanding: 71 million
Return on 1996 shareholders' equity: 17.0%

	1996	1995	1994	1993	1992	1991	1990	1989
Prem. income (millions)	994	810	655	670	658	658	661	659
Net income (millions)	2,125	1,569	1,334	1,247	1,202	1,174	1,163	1,140
Earnings per share	4.09	3.55	3.15	2.91	2.66	2.29	1.96	1.62
Dividends per share	1.44	1.25	1.12	1.04	.87	.73	.66	.60
Price: High	59.6	48.3	36.8	38.6	33.0	26.1	19.9	20.2
Low	45.1	33.7	28.9	30.3	22.2	15.3	14.4	13.2

CONSERVATIVE GROWTH

Johnson & Johnson

One Johnson & Johnson Plaza, New Brunswick, N. J. 08933 ◻ Investor contact: David R. Sheffield (800) 950-5089 ◻ Dividend reinvestment plan available: (800) 328-9033 ◻ Listed: NYSE ◻ Ticker symbol: JNJ ◻ S&P rating: A+ ◻ Value Line financial strength rating: A++

Johnson & Johnson is the largest and most comprehensive healthcare company in the world, with 1996 sales of $21.6 billion.

JNJ offers a broad line of consumer products, ethical and over-the-counter drugs, as well as various other medical devices and diagnostic equipment.

Johnson & Johnson has more than 170 operating companies in 50 countries, selling some 50,000 products in more than 175 countries.

One of Johnson & Johnson's premier assets is its well-entrenched brand names, which are widely known in the United

States as well as abroad. As a marketer, moreover, JNJ's reputation for quality has enabled it to build strong ties to healthcare providers.

Its international presence includes not only marketing, but also production and distribution capability in a vast array of regions outside the United States.

One advantage of JNJ's worldwide organization is that markets such as China, Latin America, and Africa offer growth potential for mature product lines.

The company's well-known trade names include Band-Aid adhesive bandages; Tylenol; Stayfree; Carefree and Sure & Natural feminine hygiene products; Johnson's baby powder, shampoo and oil; and Reach toothbrushes.

More recently, through an acquisition, Johnson & Johnson now owns the Neutrogena line of skin care and beauty products. The company's stature in the skin and hair care market will greatly benefit from this acquisition. Renowned among consumers for its outstanding products for skin and hair care, Neutrogena enables JNJ to benefit from a broader access to this market. It follows smaller, but important, acquisitions in this field in recent years, including the acquisition of the RoC company in France in 1993.

The company's professional items include ligatures and sutures, mechanical wound closure products, diagnostic products, medical equipment and devices, surgical dressings, surgical apparel and accessories, and disposable contact lenses.

JNJ's sales in 1996 were almost evenly divided among pharmaceuticals, professional products, and consumer items. In the realm of profits, however, 58 percent came from pharmaceuticals, 28 percent from professional items, and 15 percent from the consumer sector. About one-half of JNJ's revenues come from abroad.

Shortcomings to Bear in Mind

- Because of its outstanding record and bright prospects for the future, JNJ generally sells at a premium to the market. If you are looking for a value stock, Johnson & Johnson is not for you. But if you are looking for a classic growth stock, you can't do much better than JNJ.

Reasons to Buy

- JNJ is experiencing robust growth in its pharmaceutical segment, paced by its newer products, such as Procrit (for anemia), Propulsid (a gastrointestinal drug), Risperdal (for schizophrenia), and Ultram (a pain reliever).

    At year-end 1996, the company obtained marketing clearance for a number of important new products and new indications for existing products. These include Levaquin (an anti-infective for use in certain respiratory tract infections), Topamax (for epileptic seizures), Procrit (to eliminate the need for blood transfusions in anemic patients undergoing certain surgical procedures), Floxin (for pelvic inflammatory disease), and the new use of Ortho Tri-Cyclen (for acne).

- Johnson & Johnson's broad range of products is one of the keys to its past success and its bright future. The company has dominant positions in a number of healthcare markets. It has been able to establish and enlarge leading market positions even in product areas in which it was not the innovator.

- JNJ has a good track record both in product development and in upgrading and repositioning its older products for additional applications and new markets.

- The company has a consistent record of growth. Earnings per share advanced from $.42 per share in 1985 to $2.17 in

1996, a compound annual growth rate of 16.1 percent. In the same eleven-year span, dividends climbed from $.16 to $.74, a growth rate of 14.9 percent. (In April of 1996, the board of directors boosted the dividend, the thirty-fourth consecutive yearly dividend increase.) The reason I used an eleven-year period is because earnings were temporarily depressed in 1986, which would have made the compound growth rate seem higher than it really was.

- One of the outstanding new developments in recent years is the rapid impact of the new Janssen drug for schizophrenia, Risperdal. The unique ability of this drug to treat the principal symptoms of schizophrenia with relatively few side effects has led to ready acceptance by physicians and patients.

- JNJ continues to benefit from the steady growth of the Ethicon Endo-Surgery line of products for minimally invasive surgery. Besides gaining market share, Ethicon Endo-Surgery is vigorously exploring the possibilities of medical conditions that can uniquely benefit from minimally invasive surgery. For example, it is working with doctors and hospitals to further the use of such procedures in conditions like gastroesophageal reflux and urinary stress incontinence.

- JNJ is the market leader in endoscopy, sutures, disposable contact lenses, and blood glucose monitoring; the demand for these products is robust.

- The company's drug portfolio is well protected from a patent standpoint, as no major drug comes off patent until 1999, when Hismanal's patent expires. However, Sporanox comes off patent in May of 1998, but the company hopes to have this date extended to 2000.

- Accelerated product development is central to JNJ's growth strategy. About 35 percent of 1996's revenues came from products that did not exist more than five years earlier. In 1990, by contrast, the comparable figure was about 30 percent. In 1997, Johnson & Johnson plans to spend 8.9 percent of sales on R&D.

In terms of total research spending—which amounted to $1.9 billion in 1996—these investments place the company among the top ten corporations (of any kind) in the United States. In recognition of JNJ's accomplishments in science and technology, the company was awarded the National Medal of Technology in 1996, the nation's highest technology honor.

- In 1996, net earnings climbed more than 20 percent, and earnings per share reached $2.17, a gain of 16.7 percent. These impressive results, moreover, were achieved despite intense competition, coupled with unfavorable current translation and a higher effective tax rate. What's more, virtually all of JNJ's sales increase came from real unit volume, since price increases were limited to about .1 percent worldwide.

- While internal development is Johnson & Johnson's preferred source of growth, the company views selective acquisitions as an appropriate mechanism for supplementing these efforts. Over the 1990–1996 period, JNJ made more than thirty acquisitions. Most of these were modest in size, but generally had two important characteristics—a proven technology lead and the lack of a worldwide presence or infrastructure, which Johnson & Johnson could provide very quickly.

Several of the company's acquisitions were substantial, including Cordis, Neutrogena, and Clinical Diagnostics.

During the same period, JNJ also divested fifteen companies or businesses that no longer met its growth criteria or were better off in someone else's hands.

- Realizing that technology is moving at a blinding rate of speed and that inventive groups, universities, start-up companies, and newly public companies are sources of great innovation, Johnson & Johnson is also entering into alliances of all types with organizations outside its sphere. In 1996 alone, the company entered into over 125 third-party transactions, including product licenses, equity investments, acquisitions, joint ventures, research and development agreements, and comarketing or distribution agreements.

  In the realm of equity investments, for example, the company invested over $100 million in 1996 in twenty-nine young companies trying to meet unsolved needs and problems.

- More than 22 years of experience in designing total knee implants led to the introduction of the P.F.C. Sigma Knee System from Johnson & Johnson's Professional, Inc. While retaining the very successful aspects of the original P.F.C. Knee, the new P.F.C. Sigma Knee System incorporates design modifications that address the most important clinical issue for patients and their orthopedic surgeons alike—implant longevity. This was achieved through careful analysis of both clinical outcomes data and extensive laboratory testing. It resulted in a new shape for the implant to increase contact area between key components and to reduce wear.

Total assets: $20,010 million
Current ratio: 1.95
Common shares outstanding: 1,332 million
Return on 1996 shareholders' equity: 29.0%

	1996	1995	1994	1993	1992	1991	1990	1989
Revenues (millions)	21,620	18,842	15,734	14,138	13,753	12,447	11,232	9,757
Net income (millions)	2,887	2,403	2,006	1,787	1,525	1,461	1,270	1,082
Earnings per share	2.17	1.86	1.56	1.37	1.23	1.10	.95	.81
Dividends per share	.74	.64	.57	.51	.45	.39	.33	.28
Price:　High	54.0	46.2	28.3	25.2	29.3	29.1	18.5	14.9
Low	41.6	26.8	18.0	17.8	21.5	16.3	12.8	10.4

GROWTH & INCOME

Kimberly-Clark Corporation

P. O. Box 619100, Dallas, Texas 75261-9100 □ Investor contact: Mike Masseth (214) 281-1436 □ Dividend reinvestment plan available: (800) 442-2001 □ Ticker symbol: KMB □ S&P rating: A □ Value Line financial strength rating: A++

Kimberly-Clark is a worldwide manufacturer of a wide range of products for personal, business, and industrial uses. Most of the products are made from natural and synthetic fibers, using advanced technologies in absorbency, fibers, and nonwovens.

The company's well-known brands include Kleenex facial and bathroom tissue, Huggies diapers and baby wipes, Pull-Ups training pants, GoodNites underpants, Kotex and New Freedom feminine care products, Depend and Poise incontinence care products, Hi-Dri household towels, Kimguard sterile wrap, Kimwipes industrial wipers, and Classic premium business and correspondence papers.

A Review of 1996

• Divestitures continued in 1996, almost all of them required by regulatory bodies as a result of the Scott Paper merger. These included the sale of certain consumer tissue businesses in the United Kingdom and Ireland, as well as KMB's tissue mill in Prudhoe, England. In the United States, Kimberly-Clark sold the former Scott Paper's baby wipes and facial tissue businesses, KMB's Lakeview tissue mill in Neenah, Wisconsin, and its tissue mill in Fort Edward, New York. These divestitures and the sale of Kimberly-Clark's remaining interest in Midwest Express generated about $450 million in cash in 1996. The final sale, driven by regulatory concerns, of the company's 50.1 percent stake in Canada's Scott Paper Ltd. took place in the first half of 1997.

• Kimberly-Clark's 1995 and 1996 divestitures reduced the company's sales base by nearly $1 billion.

• The company's personal care business had a strong showing in 1996. KMB now sells one out of every three diapers where it competes worldwide and one out of every four if you include the markets where the company does not compete.

• Despite the loss of earnings of the divested businesses, gross profit in 1996 improved 8 percent in absolute terms and from 34 percent to 37.3 percent as a percentage of sales. This was primarily because of higher sales volumes, the Scott Paper merger synergies, manufacturing efficiencies for personal care products, and lower pulp costs worldwide. Excluding the 1995 one-time charge, operating profit improved 24.2 percent in absolute terms, and from 12.4 percent to 15.6 percent as a percentage of net sales, due to higher gross margin, coupled with merger synergies.

• Excluding the divested businesses, 1996 operating profit increased more than 30 percent.

• Operating losses in the infant and child care business in Europe declined in 1996 as a result of higher sales volumes and improved operations. Partially offsetting these improvements were the lower selling prices and higher promotion costs to support the growth in sales volumes and to respond to competitive activity.

• Operating profit for the Tissue-Based Products business segment improved from 1995, helped by lower pulp costs and merger synergies.

Shortcomings to Bear in Mind

■ If Kimberly-Clark is to succeed, it must continually battle against the relentless, determined Procter & Gamble, one of the most innovative and skillful companies in the world.

Reasons to Buy

■ In the realm of professional healthcare products, the company has been achieving impressive results, much of it emanating from innovative surgical gowns, drapes, and wraps. The same is true of the performance of KMB's nonwoven materials segment, which supplies versatile fabrics to its consumer-products operations and other businesses at a cost advantage, compared with its competition.

■ Kimberly-Clark has been testing a reusable kitchen paper towel in Germany that absorbs more liquid than Procter & Gamble's premium-priced Bounty. KMB hopes that this new technology will eventually help the company overtake P&G's Bounty.

■ The diaper business may sound unexciting, but in fact technology plays a major role. In 1989, KMB came up with a whole new product line of so-called training pants: diapers for toddlers aged two and a half to four years. With a four-year head start on Procter & Gamble, and solid patents, Kimberly-Clark built a 74 percent share of what is now a $540 million market, compared with P&G's 8.5 percent. What's more, training pants sell for 39 cents—nearly twice as much as a conventional diaper. Kimberly has done the same innovative job with Depend in the growing adult incontinence market. In that realm, KMB has a 53.3 percent share, far overshadowing the mighty P&G, with 4.7 percent.

- In the 1986–1996 period, the company compiled a solid record of growth, as earnings per shares increased from $.73 to $2.49, a compound annual growth rate of 13.1 percent. In the same 10-year stretch, dividends expanded from $.31 to $.92, for a growth rate of 11.5 percent.
- One of Kimberly-Clark's strengths stems from the leadership position it holds in three core technologies: fibers, absorbency, and nonwovens. It also comes from the company's capacity in high-speed manufacturing and from its constant emphasis on innovation, productivity, and cost reduction.
- Kimberly-Clark has operations in 35 countries and products that are sold in 150. A great deal of the company's worldwide expansion can be attributed to the merger with Scott Paper, completed in December 1995. This represented a rare opportunity to bring together two companies with complementary product lines and geographic strengths. Management originally estimated that the merger would save the combined company $250 million in 1996 and $500 million annually by 1998. In fact, savings in 1996 totaled about $280 million, the result of the company integrating operations in Europe more quickly than expected.

On the other hand, Kimberly-Clark began charting its transformation long before the Scott Paper merger. In 1992, the company was widely diversified. It was a consumer products company, to be sure, but KMB also owned paper and forest products operations and an airline. All these businesses were profitable, but in mapping Kimberly-Clark's strategy for long-term sustainable growth, it concluded it lay in building on basic strengths: KMB's core technologies, its well-known trademarks, and its consumer product franchises.

Businesses that did not, or could not, build on those strengths would be candidates for divestiture. Conversely, those that fit into Kimberly-Clark's strategy would merit further investment and support. Finally, outside businesses that fit into the company's strategy became acquisition candidates.

Through 1995, this plan resulted in such acquisitions as the leading feminine care companies in China and the Czech Republic and majority ownership of the company's consumer products operations in Argentina and South Africa. Over the same period, KMB sold an in-house trucking operation, an envelope business, a label stock manufacturer, and a foot care and sports fitness business. What's more, Kimberly-Clark spun off its tobacco-related operations and sold 80 percent of Midwest Express Airlines in an IPO. In May of 1996, the company completed a secondary offering of the remaining 20 percent interest in Midwest Express, generating $40 million in proceeds.

- Looking at Kimberly-Clark as it is now constituted, it is a much more balanced company. Before the Scott Paper merger and other acquisitions, the company derived almost half of its revenues from diapers and other personal care products. That portion is now a third. Consumer tissue also accounts for about a third of revenues, with the balance coming from a combination of away-from-home and other products.

- Kimberly-Clark recently brought to market a super premium facial tissue line trademarked Kleenex ColdCare for cold and allergy sufferers.
- The company's Huggies Utratrim diapers now feature hook-and-loop fasteners from suppliers such as Velcro USA Inc. KMB also added a breathable outer cover to its Huggies Supreme brand.
- For Scott bathroom tissue, the company was able to increase softness and strength, even as it lowered costs. The improved product beat its predecessor, Scott 1000, two to one in consumer testing and has recaptured historical brand equity and market-share levels. In addition, the company also improved thickness and absorbency in Scott towels.
- In Europe, Kimberly-Clark has quickly become the leading tissue player with a rapidly expanding diaper business as well. Tissue products for the consumer and away-from-home markets account for about three-fourths of company revenues in the region. Additionally, Andrex bathroom tissue saw record shipment volumes in 1996, following improvements in thickness and absorbency.
- In 1996, the company more than doubled its diaper share in European markets in which KMB competes. Its market share in the United Kingdom, moreover, averaged 25 percent, up from 15 percent in 1995. With the acquisition of the Peaudouce brand in France, the company's market share in that country now exceeds 30 percent.
- In Central and Eastern Europe, Kimberly-Clark extended its line of consumer products in Russia, with the introduction of economy-priced diapers and feminine care products. The company also acquired Zisoft-Bobi, a Czech diaper and incontinence care products manufacturer, making Kimberly-Clark the largest personal care products company in that country. This presence provides a platform for offering products throughout Central and Eastern Europe. KMB has already introduced Kleenex and Scottex tissue products throughout the region and markets Huggies diapers in Russia, Romania, Croatia, Slovenia, and the Baltic states.
- Kimberly-Clark is the only multinational tissue producer operating in the Asia/Pacific region, with strong positions in Korea, Thailand, Taiwan, the Philippines, and Australia. In 1996, the company introduced Huggies baby wipes in Singapore, and in Malaysia it introduced Pull-Ups training pants. KMB also increased its ownership of Kimberly-Clark Malaysia from 51 percent to 100 percent. The company has begun shipping Kotex feminine care products and Scott bathroom and facial tissue to China. At present, consumption in these markets is low, but management sees a huge marketing opportunity as per capita income continues to grow.

Total assets: $11,846 million
Current ratio: 0.96
Common shares outstanding: 563 million
Return on 1996 shareholders' equity: 31.3%

	1996	1995	1994	1993	1992	1991	1990	1989
Revenues (millions)	13,149	13,789	7,364	6,973	7,091	6,777	6,407	5,734
Net income (millions)	1,404	1,104	535	511	517	508	476	424
Earnings per share	2.49	1.98	1.67	1.59	1.61	1.59	1.49	1.32
Dividends per share	.92	.90	.88	.85	.82	.76	.68	.65
Price: High	49.8	41.5	30.0	31.0	31.6	26.1	21.4	18.8
Low	34.3	23.6	23.5	22.3	23.1	19.0	15.4	14.3

Leggett & Platt, Incorporated

P. O. Box 757, No. 1 Leggett Road, Carthage, MO 64836-0757 ◻ Investor contact: J. Richard Calhoon (417) 358-8131 ◻ Dividend reinvestment plan not available ◻ Listed: NYSE ◻ Ticker symbol: LEG ◻ S&P rating: A ◻ Value Line financial strength rating: A

Founded in 1883, Leggett & Platt is the nation's leading manufacturer of furniture and bedding components used in homes, offices, and institutions. The company also produces some sleep-related finished furniture and other finished furnishings; it is also a significant producer of a variety of nonfurnishings products.

According to analysts, there are few companies that can match Leggett's impressive and steady returns. Since the company went public in March 1967, earnings per share have compounded in excess of 15 percent per year, and the stock has averaged an annual return of more than 17 percent.

In addition, Leggett has consistently increased its dividend. What's more, the company's strategy has remained consistent during this span. Leggett & Platt looks to increase sales of existing products, while pursuing an acquisition strategy that focuses on dominant companies in niche markets that can offer synergies and accretion once acquired.

The 1996 acquisition of Pace Industries is an excellent example of this strategy at work. By purchasing Pace, Leggett nearly doubled the size of its aluminum die-cast operations, while acquiring its dominant competitor.

Nor has the pace of acquisitions diminished. In early 1997, Leggett & Platt announced that it had recently acquired four businesses, two that manufacture and market commercial fixtures and displays and two that manufacture and market aluminum die castings. Combined, the four businesses will add about $80 million to Leggett's annual sales.

Customers who buy the company's broad lines of components for bedding and furniture include several thousand manufacturers of home, office, institutional, and commercial furnishings. Manufacturers of today's bedding sets can buy almost all of their mattress and boxspring components from Leggett & Platt. They also purchase some of the highly specialized machinery and materials-handling equipment that LEG designs and builds for their needs. Some of the company's machinery and equipment is sold in international markets, primarily to manufacturers of bedding and other furnishings. Leggett also offers a leading line of specialized components designed for customers that manufacture upholstered furniture and other types of furniture.

Leggett & Platt's finished furnishings include select lines of sleep-related furniture, carpet underlay and nonskid pads, metal and wire displays, and shelving and fixtures for various residential and commercial applications. The diversified nonfurnishings products the company manufactures are produced with technologies and processes very similar to those Leggett uses in making certain furnishings products or in producing some select raw materials.

Leggett & Platt maintains a strong emphasis on decentralized management responsibilities, coupled with centralized policies and controls and corporate services and support. Operations are organized in groups: Bedding and Furniture, Commercial Products, and Wire and Foam Components. There are several Leggett divisions within each group, and many operations produce products for sale in several niche markets.

Shortcomings to Bear in Mind

- The market is concerned about a future slowdown in the economy and the potential impact on the furniture business. To an extent, Leggett's business is tied to home-buying and new housing starts. The two years after a home is purchased are normally years of heavy furniture purchasing.

Reasons to Buy

- According to a U.S. Department of Labor Study, the age group that spends the most amount on furniture is the 45-to-54-year-old bracket. The second-highest amount is spent by those 35 to 44. The Census Bureau projects the number of consumers in the 45-to-54 age group will expand 14.1 percent from 1994 to 1999. The 35 to 44 age group will advance 7.3 percent. At the same time, the general population will increase only 4.7 percent.

  There are a number of reasons why middle-aged people spend more money on furniture:
  1. Their income is high during this span of their lives.
  2. They are more likely to be home-owners than are younger people.
  3. These more mature couples have sold their starter homes. Their new homes, moreover, are larger and may need a whole new set of more expensive furniture. In 1993, the average home had 2,100 square feet of living space, up 5 percent from 1988. It is projected that by 1998, the average home will increase to 2,200 square feet. Larger homes require much more furniture than smaller ones. For instance, a home with 3,000 square feet needs 2.5 times as much as one with 2,000 square feet.

- Leggett & Platt boasts a remarkable record of growth. In the 1986–1996 period, earnings per share climbed from $.47 to $1.85, a compound annual rate of 14.7 percent. In the same ten-year stretch, dividends per share expanded from $.10 to $.42, a growth rate of 15.4 percent.

- Leggett's commitment to research and development has kept pace with company growth. LEG has R&D facilities at both centralized and divisional locations. At those locations, engineers and technicians design and build new and improved products in all major lines and machinery. They also perform extensive tests for durability and function. Leggett's experience and accumulation of data in this highly specialized area of R&D are unmatched.

- Since 1967, acquisitions have been a key part of Leggett's growth strategy. Traditionally, the company pursues friendly acquisitions that fit with existing operations, either in marketing, technology, or both. Normally, Leggett's acquisitions broaden the company's product lines, providing entry into additional markets, or secure sources of select raw materials.

  The company uses cash, stock, or combinations of the two in making acquisitions.

- There are no comparable companies to Leggett & Platt in the public sector. However, since the company is in part a supplier to the furnishings industry, the market tends to view LEG as a furniture company. This is not a correct perception. Here is why I believe this to be so:
  1. Residential furniture (whether a finished product or a component) represents less than 30 percent of Leggett's revenue base. What's more, bedding components, a much more stable product line, accounts for nearly 30 percent of revenue; this is

a replacement business with just a minor decline in shipments during the last recession. The balance is composed of office, institutional, and commercial furnishings and fixtures (components and finished products) and the company's diversified non-furnishings products.

2. The risk/reward parameters of Leggett's business are quite different from that of a furniture manufacturer. Keep in mind that LEG's components go into making the "insides" of furniture (springs, frames, motion mechanisms, and construction fabric), thus making Leggett immune to the fashion risk inherent in the furniture business. Since most manufacturers buy components from Leggett, there is little, if any, fashion risk related to Leggett's products. This risk is borne by the manufacturer and the way the finished product is differentiated with style or fabric.

3. Leggett has opportunities to grow even if overall demand does not grow. This is accomplished through internal growth, driven by market share gains and aggressive new product development, plus an aggressive acquisition program that is responsible for two-thirds of the company's growth over the past fifteen years.

- Leggett & Platt has a proven strategy in place to expand its position in existing markets and to selectively approach a larger portion of the total market for furniture and bedding components. A strong financial position also provides substantial capital resources and flexibility to pursue future growth opportunities, both internally and through selective acquisitions.

- Through its leadership role in new product development, new manufacturing techniques, and technological improvements, analysts believe Leggett can gain market share vis-à-vis its smaller, less-well-financed competitors.

- Participation in such diverse furnishings categories as bedding and residential, office, and contract furniture gives Leggett & Platt the opportunity to spread new product developments into several sectors at all price points, while limiting its exposure to any one sector.

- Leggett & Platt has created a reputation for both innovation and confidentiality, often working with several larger manufacturers to develop exclusive components, giving each a competitive edge, while utilizing Leggett & Platt's massive manufacturing capabilities. Consequently, LEG can manufacture a broad range of distinctive, cost-effective components for any customer, whether large or small.

Total assets: $1,713 million
Current ratio: 2.52
Common shares outstanding: 91.8 million
Return on 1996 shareholders' equity: 20.1%

	1996	1995	1994	1993	1992	1991	1990	1989
Revenues (millions)	2,466	2,110	1,858	1,527	1,170	1,082	1,089	992
Net income (millions)	153	135	115	86	62	39	44	46
Earnings per share	1.85	1.59	1.39	1.045	.815	.545	.61	.645
Dividends per share	.42	.38	.31	.275	.225	.22	.21	.185
Price: High	34.8	26.9	24.8	25.0	17.7	9.6	9.4	8.7
Low	20.6	17.0	16.6	16.4	9.4	6.5	5.0	5.9

Eli Lilly and Company

Lilly Corporate Center, Indianapolis, Indiana 46285 ◻ Investor contact: Thomas W. Grein (317) 276-2506 ◻
Dividend reinvestment plan available: (800) 833-8699 ◻ Listed: NYSE ◻ Ticker symbol: LLY ◻ S&P
rating: A ◻ Value Line financial strength rating: A++

Eli Lilly is one of the world's foremost healthcare companies. With a solid dedication to R&D, Lilly is a leader in the development of ethical drugs.

It is well known for such drugs as Prozac (to treat depression), Ceclor (an antibiotic), insulin, and other diabetic care items. Some of its other important drugs include Keflex, Kefzol, Lorabid, Mandol, Nebcin, Vancocin Hcl, Tazidime, Darvon, Nalfon, and Axid.

In 1997, the company announced that four new major products (Gemzar, Humalog, ReoPro, and Zyprexa) had made strong contributions to results in the final quarter of 1996.

Lilly also has a stake in animal health and agricultural products.

Dow Elanco, 40 percent owned by Lilly and 60 percent by Dow Chemical, produces herbicides and other plant science products.

Like most drug companies, Lilly is active abroad and does business in 120 countries.

Shortcomings to Bear in Mind

- In the United States and elsewhere, cost-containment pressure is reducing prices on drug prices.
- The cost of developing new drugs, which was already high, is getting even higher. More emphasis is being placed on generic drugs by cost-conscious healthcare providers.
- The patent on one of Lilly's major antibiotic drugs, Ceclor, has expired. This means that generic versions are forcing the company to reduce prices.

Reasons to Buy

- Sales of Prozac (Lilly's biggest drug) hit $2.36 billion in 1996 (up 14 percent over the prior year), as it became the world's first prescription mental-health drug to have $2 billion in annual sales. By 1999, Prozac's annual sales could surpass $3 billion.

    Depression is a more serious and widespread illness than many realize. In the United States alone, one in five people will experience clinical depression at some time in their lives. Left untreated, depression can be dangerous. Discovered and developed by Lilly scientists, Prozac represented an important new treatment option: the first widely available product in a class of drugs called SSRIs (for selected serotonin reuptake inhibitors). In simple terms, SSRIs help the brain to maintain higher levels of an important natural substance called serotonin by selectively reducing its absorption of "reuptake."

- Lilly's own research into the brain and central nervous system (CNS) has led to the discovery and launch of additional important drugs, including Permax for the treatment of Parkinson's disease, and Zyprexa, the company's new product for the treatment of schizophrenia. Furthermore, Lilly is testing investigational compounds that may aid patients with Alzheimer's disease, migraine headaches, sleep disorders, epilepsy, and urinary incontinence.

- Late in 1995, Lilly filed an NDA with the FDA for an important new drug, Zyprexa (the generic name is olanzapine), to treat schizophrenia. Zyprexa, launched in the fourth quarter of 1996, had sales totaling $86.9 million after only three months on the market. As of early 1997, Zyprexa was already marketed in eleven countries throughout the world, with several additional launches pending. Analysts believe that annual revenues from Zyprexa could reach $1 billion in the year 2000.

There is reason for optimism; the drug appears not only effective but also free of most side effects. Some analysts contend that Zyprexa will be the number one treatment for schizophrenia. The market for drugs to treat this affliction is estimated at $7.5 billion per year. On the other hand, Lilly's new drug for schizophrenia faces a number of competitors, including Johnson & Johnson's Risperdal and Abbott's Serlect. Even so, analysts think Zyprexa has blockbuster potential, based on its efficacy, safety, dosing, and pricing.

- Several other new products are also doing well. Gemzar, launched in May of 1996, had worldwide sales of $61.9 million in 1996. Gemzar (for the treatment of pancreatic cancer) is marketed in thirty-one countries throughout the world. Gemzar is a new oncolytic compound that targets certain solid tumors. A natural enzyme converts this drug into an active agent that stops the production of DNA in some cancer cells.

ReoPro (currently authorized for use in angioplasty patients considered at high risk for suffering abrupt reclosure of the treated coronary artery) had sales of $149.3 million in 1996. ReoPro is a result of Lilly's collaboration with Centocor, Inc. ReoPro is used with angioplasty to prevent certain costly acute complications, such as heart attacks or the need for unplanned repeat angioplasty, in patients who are at high risk of having the treated blood vessels abruptly close. Of the more than 400,000 angioplasties performed in the United States each year, about 30 percent involve patients who run this risk.

Humulin (insulin made by recombinant DNA) had annual sales of $883.9 million in 1996, an increase of 11 percent over the prior year.

Finally, still another new drug holds great promise. Evista (its generic name is raloxifene) is a selective estrogen receptor modulator that may prove effective in treating osteoporosis. Evista is being sent to the FDA sometime in 1997, which means it may be commercially available by mid-1998.

Lilly is optimistic about the potential of Evista to treat and prevent osteoporosis, a disease that affects 60 percent of all Caucasian and Asian women over the age of 50.

Lilly's orally active compound xanomeline mimics the action of neurotransmitters thought to be involved in the cognitive impairment of people with Alzheimer's disease. This illness affects more than 15 million people around the world; the number is rising dramatically with the aging of world populations. Even more exciting, Lilly scientists, working with scientists at Athena Neurosciences, Inc., recently developed genetically altered mice that exhibit key features of this dreaded disease. That tool provides an important head start on screening potential Alzheimer's drug candidates.

- Lilly is leveraging its research and development resources by focusing them more sharply within five broad disease categories that match Lilly's strengths: central-nervous-system diseases, endocrine diseases, infectious diseases, cancer, and cardiovascular diseases. What's more, the company is seeking to be the world leader in each of those five categories.

- Diabetes, within the endocrine category, is a good example. As the developer of the first insulin product and one of the world's major suppliers of insulin, Lilly has long been a global leader in the field. But diabetes, which affects more than 100 million people worldwide, continues to cause severe long-term complications, suffering, lost productivity, and death.

  For many patients with this disease, diabetes is also inconvenient. Diabetics have to check their blood glucose several times a day. They may have to give themselves one or more shots of insulin. And they must take insulin at least 30 minutes before a meal or risk severe complications.

  Lilly believes that it has an answer that will give patients with diabetes a better quality of life and a good deal more convenience. More than 3,000 people in nineteen countries have taken Lilly's new insulin analog, Humalog, in clinical trials. The evidence from those trials shows that Humalog acts faster than traditional insulin to control blood-glucose levels. Patients take it right before a meal, compared with 30 to 45 minutes before with current products. Humalog provides them with more freedom, better health, and fewer complications.

- One of Lilly's strengths is in the field of biotechnology. Lilly is among the world's largest and most experienced biotech companies, with proven abilities to discover, develop, and manufacture both small organic molecules and large natural molecules.

- To treat a disease most effectively and efficiently, one must understand how it progresses; to avoid often serious and expensive complications, one must know precisely when and where to intervene; and to improve results, one must first be able to measure them. That takes information. And that's where Lilly's purchase of PCS Health Systems, Inc., comes in.

  PCS manages prescriptions for more than 55 million Americans. Using its electronic pharmaceutical-information databases, Lilly can improve communication among patient, doctor, pharmacist, and payer. Thus, the company can better administer cost-effective drug treatments; it can better analyze and understand how those treatments are working; and it can better educate payers, providers, physicians, and, especially, patients.

- The systematic antifungal market is the fastest-growing segment of the infectious diseases market, fueled by everything from toenail infections to the serious fungal infections that result from weakened immune systems, such as those in patients who have cancer or AIDS or those who have had organ transplants.

  Lilly's investigational antifungal compound ECB is a derivative of a new class of compounds that work by disrupting synthesis of the fungal cell wall.

- The rapidly growing resistance of bacteria to antibiotics is among the world's most urgent healthcare challenges. Some species of bacteria have even developed resistance to vancomycin, the first compound in the glycopeptide class. In laboratory studies, Lilly's investigational glycopeptide antibiotic has shown powerful activity. Whereas vancomycin inhibits stubborn Enterococcus bacteria, this glycopeptide kills them—something no drug now available is able to do.

Total assets: $14,307 million
Current ratio: 0.90
Common shares outstanding: 547 million
Return on 1996 shareholders' equity: 26.4%

	1996	1995	1994	1993	1992	1991	1990	1989
Revenues (millions)	7,346	6,764	5,712	6,452	6,167	5,726	5,192	4,176
Net income (millions)	1,524	1,307	1,269	1,347	1,393	1,315	1,127	940
Earnings per share	2.78	2.30	2.19	2.30	2.45	2.25	1.95	1.60
Dividends per share	1.38	1.31	1.25	1.21	1.10	1.00	.82	.68
Price: High	80.4	57.0	33.1	31.0	43.9	42.6	45.2	34.3
Low	49.4	31.3	23.6	21.8	28.9	33.8	29.4	21.2

GROWTH AND INCOME

Lubrizol Corporation

29400 Lakeland Boulevard, Wickliffe, Ohio 44092-2298 □ Investor contact: K. H. Hopping (216) 943-4200 □ Dividend reinvestment plan available: (800) 542-7792 □ Listed: NYSE □ Ticker symbol: LZ □ S&P rating: B+ □ Value Line financial strength rating: A

Lubrizol is the world's largest supplier of specialty chemical additives for lubricating oil used in transportation equipment.

Lubrizol manufactures over 250 individual chemical components in 117 production units around the world. Each component performs a specific function, such as dispersant, detergent, antioxidant, corrosion inhibitor, antiwear additive, viscosity modifier, friction modifier, deposit control, or extreme pressure agent.

Using this portfolio of components, the company's product-development formulators determine the optimum combination needed to meet the customer's specification for performance and cost. Formulation science is complex and requires thorough knowledge and experience in the performance and interaction of chemical components. This skill is then supported by comprehensive product testing capabilities to prove the performance of the additive package formulation.

Historically, component technology has been skewed toward engine oil additives, Lubrizol's largest business realm. While components may be developed at first for use in engine oils, they are used broadly in other business lines or markets. The company's line is diverse, with packages produced and sold into over twenty separate market sectors. However, all market segments are based on combining components into packages supported by testing. Chemistry, formulation, and performance testing expertise, service, and differentiation are common to all of Lubrizol's businesses.

Lubrizol ranks ahead of its principal competitors, which are divisions of larger corporations, including Exxon, Chevron, and Ethyl. Lubrizol is regarded as the premier research-testing-and-development company in the industry. Among the suppliers, Lubrizol is the most broadly based, serving both the automotive and nearly all industrial market segments. By contrast, Ethyl, Exxon, and Texaco largely serve the automotive market.

Chevron participates in both the industrial and the automotive lubricant market, but has targeted the diesel segment of the automotive engine oils market and the railroad diesel segment of the industrial engine oils market.

For its part, Shell (Royal Dutch Petroleum) is a broadly based multiline supplier in Western Europe, while in the United States it is beginning to make inroads marketing products beyond viscosity index improvers.

The largest market for lubricating oil additives is the domestic automotive engine oil segment. Over the past twenty years, this segment has experienced solid growth in the volume of oil additives it consumes. This growth has been a by-product of increasing lubricating oil specifications.

Lubricating oil standards are the products of trade associations, manufacturers, testing concerns, and additive suppliers, all working together to create better lubricant products.

The United States is the bellwether for industry specifications and, thus, for lubricating oil additive consumption. Analysts are convinced that the pace of specification change in the United States will increase. What's more, it seems likely that the rest of the world will eventually adopt similar specification standards.

Analysts believe that over the next five years, world lubricating oil additive volumes will expand as a result of the increased performance specifications demanded from lubricating oils. Although they project a decrease in the consumption of lubricating oils, the increase in additive content will more than offset the volume decreases in lubricating oil demand.

What's more, analysts point out that the improvements of operating efficiency and new engine design will result in a demand for better lubricants to lower operating costs. What it amounts to is this: Additives must increase high-temperature performance, neutralize acid materials generated by low-quality, high-sulfur-level fuels, reduce engine wear and deposit formation, and thereby continue to improve engine life.

Shortcomings to Bear in Mind

- Oil prices can have an effect on Lubrizol. Weak prices, for instance, tend to make Lubrizol's customers more resistant to price increases.
- In 1996, the industry standards for the level-of-performance additives used in domestic passenger car motor oil were lowered. The new level reduced industrywide demand for additives, which created an intensely competitive market where most companies struggled to maintain their market share. As a result, lower volume and prices hurt revenues in 1996. In the fourth quarter, however, volume picked up 2 percent.

Reasons to Buy

- To maintain its competitive edge, Lubrizol has always counted on its research laboratories, where workers test products in all types of engines to ensure that its additives meet accepted quality standards. They simulate such things as the effects of an engine pulling a trailer through a 64-hour desert trek on one oil change, or ten days of constantly shifting gears for an automatic transmission test.
- A number of factors have a positive impact on the demand for lubricating oil:
  - The number of automobiles in service correlates positively with lubricating oil consumption. The average age of the automobile population also drives lubricating oil consumption; older vehicles tend to use more lubricants.
  - The evolution of smaller, more efficient engines affects demand for lubricating oils. Modern engines have smaller crankcases that hold less oil. Accessories such as air conditioners and power steering put added strain on smaller engines, that, in turn, demand better operating characteristics from their lubricating oils.

- Improved manufacturing processes also enhance the demand for lubricating oils. Modern engines are machined with tighter tolerances between parts.

■ The company is strong financially, "with only a modest amount of long-term debt.

■ AMPS monomer is another interesting business that Lubrizol has been involved with over the past decade. This business segment manufactures a versatile monomer product. Applications include use as dye receptors in acrylic fiber, water-treatment chemicals, and oil recovery agents. The Bayport, Texas, facility was recently expanded to accommodate future growth. Analysts believe that this business should expand at a rate greater than Lubrizol's overall corporate growth rate.

■ Lubrizol has operated internationally for over fifty years and has both technical and production facilities in key global markets. The company sells its products extensively in North America, Europe, Asia-Pacific, Latin America, and the Middle East. Lubrizol has technical centers in Wickliffe, Ohio; Hazelwood, England; and Atsugi, Japan. It has twenty manufacturing plants around the world, including those of its affiliates and subsidiaries.

■ In 1996, Lubrizol announced an agreement to form a joint venture for the manufacture, marketing, and sale of lubricant additive packages in China. Lubrizol's partner in this venture is Sinopec Lanzhou Petroleum Processing Complex, which is the single largest producer of finished lubricants in China.

The joint venture will initially establish two blending operations scheduled to be online in mid-1997 for production of additive packages made from components supplied by the part-

ners. These performance packages will be sold to the Sinopec subsidiaries and other lubricant blenders, including major international lubricant producers, operating in China. The formation of this joint venture will provide Lubrizol with a strong position in this rapidly growing market and is an integral part of the company's overall strategy for the Asia-Pacific region. It will complement Lubrizol facilities in Japan, Singapore, India, and Australia.

■ Research, testing, and development capabilities provide a high barrier to entry for potential competitors. Lubrizol has demonstrated its commitment to the business by significantly expanding its research, development, and testing facilities in the United Kingdom, Japan, and the United States in recent years.

■ Another positive in Lubrizol's outlook for the next few years is the prospect of market share gains. Lubrizol believes that it can increase its share of the lubricant additive market from 35 percent currently to 40 percent by the year 2000. Simply maintaining market share while the industry consolidates would not be considered as a successful outcome. LZ does not plan to cut prices to increase market share. Rather, several other factors should enable it to increase its penetration:

- Upgrades in lubricant quality specifications represent an opportunity to introduce unique chemistry and gain a competitive advantage.

- Oil companies will want to reduce the number of additive suppliers that they can use, in effect forming partnerships or alliances with them. Lubrizol's technical strength would be a major attraction because the oil companies have downsized and reduced their in-house technical capabilities.

- Lubrizol plans to increase its share by expanding its product offering to include additional products such as viscosity index (VI) improvers, thereby becoming more of a full-line supplier. A key move in that direc-

tion was Lubrizol's acquisition of an acrylic-based VI improver business from Great Lakes Chemical. Sales of that product line have since grown rapidly.

Total assets: $1,402 million
Current ratio: 2.58
Common shares outstanding: 59 million
Return on 1996 shareholders' equity: 16%

	1996	1995	1994	1993	1992	1991	1990	1989
Revenues (millions)	1,598	1,658	1,599	1,518	1,545	1,468	1,445	1,220
Net income (millions)	170	133	149	114	119	124	134	94
Earnings per share	2.80	2.08	2.26	1.67	1.73	1.79	1.89	1.26
Dividends per share	.97	.93	.89	.85	.81	.77	.73	.69
Price: High	32.4	37.4	38.6	36.4	35.3	30.0	24.9	22.7
Low	26.5	25.5	28.5	26.6	23.4	21.3	16.3	16.9

INCOME

MDU Resources Group, Inc.

400 North Fourth Street, Bismarck, North Dakota 58501-4092 ◻ Investor contact: Warren L. Robinson (800) 437-8000 ◻ Dividend reinvestment plan available: (701) 222-7621 ◻ Listed: NYSE ◻ Ticker symbol: MDU ◻ S&P rating: B+ ◻ Value Line financial strength rating: A

MDU Resources Group, Inc., is a multidimensional natural resource company. The company's diversified operations, such as oil and gas and construction materials, should help MDU Resources grow at a better rate than electric utilities that depend entirely on their electric business.

However, investors should not ignore the increasingly competitive nature of the utility business. In this regard, MDU should fare better than utilities situated in more populated regions. It seems unlikely that a remote area such as Montana, Wyoming, and the Dakotas would entice low-cost competitors to invade their turf anytime soon.

Montana-Dakota Utilities Company, the public utility division of the company, distributes natural gas and propane. It also operates power generation, transmission,

and distribution facilities in North Dakota, eastern Montana, northern and western South Dakota, and northern Wyoming.

Business development activities throughout the four states served by Montana-Dakota have produced a healthy economic climate. At the same time, increasing competitiveness and improved operating efficiencies have been providing financial rewards to the utility division. Since 1994 (through 1996), earnings increased by 36 percent, while the work force was reduced by 14 percent.

Centennial Energy Holdings, Inc., a wholly owned subsidiary, owns all of the outstanding stock of Williston Basin Interstate Pipeline Company, Knife River Corporation, and the Fidelity Oil Group.

Williston Basin Interstate Pipeline Company operates an interstate pipeline system that provides underground storage, transportation, and gathering services. In addition, it operates about 500 producing natural gas wells.

Williston Basin owns and operates over 3,600 miles of transmission, gathering, and storage lines in the states of North Dakota, South Dakota, Montana, and Wyoming. Its system has links with five natural-gas-producing basins and interconnects with seven gas pipelines. Through three underground storage facilities located in Montana and Wyoming, storage services are provided to local distribution companies, suppliers, and other customers.

Aggressive marketing and increased demand by major midwestern markets resulted in the movement of a record 82.2 Mmdk in 1996. Proven natural gas reserves at December 31, 1996, about 133 billion cubic feet, with continued application of new drilling and completion technologies are expected to improve the investment performance of these reserves.

Williston Basin, through its wholly owned subsidiary (effective January 1, 1997), Prairielands Energy Marketing, Inc., seeks new energy markets while continuing to expand present markets for natural gas and propane.

Knife River Corporation, through its wholly owned subsidiary, KRC Holdings, Inc., and its subsidiaries, surface-mines and markets aggregates and related construction materials in Oregon, California, Alaska, and Hawaii. In addition, Knife River surface-mines and markets low-sulfur lignite coal at mines located in Montana and North Dakota.

Expansion of this business unit continued in 1996 with the acquisition of a construction materials firm that is a major supplier of aggregates, asphalt, and construction services located in northern California, as well as a ready-mix concrete and aggregates operation serving the southern Oregon market.

Growth continued early in 1997 with Knife River's acquisition of a hot-mix plant and aggregate reserves in northern California. As a result of this growth strategy, Knife River's revenues have grown from $41.2 million in 1991 to $167.2 million in 1996, when including the 50 percent ownership interest in the Hawaiian operations.

KRC Holdings, including its interest in Hawaiian Cement, has aggregate reserves of about 153 million tons. Economically recoverable coal reserves approximate 229 million tons, of which some 67 million tons are subject to existing long-term contracts or commitments.

The Fidelity Oil Group is involved in the acquisition, exploration, development, and production of oil and natural gas properties. Fidelity Oil's operations, which are located throughout the United States, the Gulf of Mexico, and Canada, vary from the acquiring of producing properties, to exploring development opportunities.

Two major acquisitions and a drilling success rate of 72 percent enhanced both production and reserves for 1996. By year-end, oil and natural gas reserves exceeded 27 million barrels of oil or its equivalent, while production approached the 4.5 million equivalent barrel mark.

The Economy of the Region

The company's traditional four-state service area is expected to experience moderate growth. The notable development of information processing and telecommunication operations, along with the population migration from small communities to metropolitan centers, are anticipated to result in continued growth in Montana-Dakota's customer base. The company's construction materials operation can expect continuation of the healthy regional growth experienced in Oregon and Alaska and improving economies in northern California and Hawaii.

Shortcomings to Bear in Mind

- Like most utilities, growth is rather drab. In the 1986–1996 period, earnings per share inched ahead from $1.27 to $1.57, a compound annual growth rate of 2.1 percent. In the same ten-year span, dividends per share expanded from $.93 to $1.10, a growth rate of only 1.7 percent. However, the dividend payout ratio is better than most utilities at a prudent 70.1 percent.

Reasons to Buy

- The company is financially sound, with a strong balance sheet. The equity portion is a healthy 54.5 percent. Coverage of bond interest is also solid, at 3.7 times.
- MDU's diversified operations are becoming increasingly important. Although the electric and gas operations are still significant, most of the company's growth will come from the construction materials and oil and gas segments.
- Acquisitions are a key part of MDU's strategy in these businesses. Since September of 1995, MDU has bought two construction materials companies and boosted its oil and gas reserves by 12 percent through another acquisition.
- Over the past four years, a period of sustained growth, earnings per common share have increased 30 percent. This performance has brought shareholders benefits both in the form of stock price appreciation and increasing annual cash dividends. In 1996, the company declared its sixth consecutive annual dividend increase.
- MDU Resources' common stock provided an excellent investment return in 1996, producing a 22 percent total shareholder return. Significantly, MDU kept pace with the Standard & Poor's 500 return of 23 percent. Interestingly, only a few years ago, the company's investment performance closely mirrored the electric utility industry, as measured by various indices. Obviously, the market is recognizing the value of MDU's growth efforts and the measurable results those efforts have provided.
- In 1996, the Fidelity Oil Group produced excellent earnings, as production increased by 12 percent and the company obtained the best oil and natural gas prices it has seen in some time. While production levels have more than doubled in the last five years, there has been a consistent growth in reserves.
- Two construction materials acquisitions in 1996 accelerated MDU's growth in that industry. Knife River Corporation's and mining materials businesses now operate in six western states. Knife River's revenues grew to $167 million, including the company's share of Hawaiian Cement, yielding an increase of over 300 percent in just five years.
- The company's dividend reinvestment plan has been improved. The plan now enables investors residing in North Dakota, South Dakota, Montana, and Wyoming to purchase initial shares of the company's common stock through the program without paying brokerage fees.
- Expansion of the construction materials operation continued in 1996. Through six acquisitions in five years, the company has built a significant presence in the construction materials industry. Currently, 81 percent of Knife River's revenues, including interest in Hawaiian Cement, come from construction materials and aggregate mining operations.
- Known collectively as KRC Holdings, Inc., the construction materials segment is composed of eight operating companies in four western states. Including its interest in Hawaiian Cement, KRC Holdings produced 4 million tons of aggregates, 694,000 tons of asphalt, and

499,000 cubic yards of ready-mixed concrete in 1996. In addition, the company sells significant cement volumes and provides asphalt laydown services.

Further evidence of KRC Holdings' investment value in the construction materials industry can be found in the company's aggregate reserves. Following its two 1996 acquisitions, KRC Holdings, including its interest in Hawaiian Cement, now has about 150 million tons of aggregate reserves, representing nearly forty years

of production at current production levels.

■ The *Oil & Gas Journal* now ranks Fidelity as the 94th largest publicly traded U.S. oil and natural gas firm out of the top 200. The ranking is up from 144th place only five years ago. Since 1986, Fidelity's reserves have more than doubled, while production has more than tripled. Fidelity's 1996 contribution to corporate earnings increased to 32 percent, up from 20 percent in 1995.

Total assets: $1,089 million
Current ratio: 1.16
Common shares outstanding: 28 million
Return on 1996 shareholders' equity: 13.0%

	1996	1995	1994	1993	1992	1991	1990	1989
Revenues (millions)	515	464	450	440	352	363	329	338
Net income (millions)	45.5	41.6	39.8	38.8	35.4	38.0	34.7	36.7
Earnings per share	1.57	1.43	1.37	1.33	1.21	1.31	1.19	1.26
Dividends per share	1.10	1.08	1.05	1.00	.97	.96	.95	.98
Price: High	23.5	23.1	21.4	22.0	17.9	16.6	15.3	15.3
Low	19.9	17.2	16.9	17.3	14.6	13.2	12.1	11.9

CONSERVATIVE GROWTH

Merck & Co., Inc.

One Merck Drive, P. O. Box 100, Whitehouse Station, New Jersey 08889-0100 □ Investor contact: Laura Jordan (908)423-5881 □ Dividend reinvestment plan available: (800) 613-2104 □ Listed: NYSE □ Ticker symbol: MRK □ S&P rating: A+ □ Value Line Financial Rating: A++

Up until recently, Merck had been the world's largest drug company. With the acquisition of Wellcome by Glaxo (both are British) Merck is now the second-largest, with total 1996 revenues of $19.8 billion.

Merck is a leading research-driven pharmaceutical products and services company. It discovers, develops, manufactures, and markets a broad range of innovative products to improve human and animal health.

Human health products include therapeutic and preventive agents, generally

sold by prescription, for the treatment of human disorders. Among these are:

● Elevated cholesterol products, which include Zocor and Mevacor; hypertension/heart failure products, which include Vasotec, the best-selling product among this group; Prinivil, and Vaseretic, as well as Cozaar and Hyzaar, both of which were launched in 1995.

● Anti-ulcerants, of which Pepcid is the largest-selling, succeeding Prilosec, the largest-selling prior to its 1994 transfer to the Astra Merck joint venture.

• Antibiotics, of which Primaxin and Noroxin are the best-selling.

• Ophthalmologicals, of which Timoptic, Timoptic-XE, and Trusopt are the best-selling.

• Vaccines/biologicals, of which M-M-R II, a pediatric vaccine for measles, mumps, and rubella; Recombivax HB (hepatitis B vaccine recombinant); and Varivax, a live virus vaccine for the prevention of chicken pox, are the largest-selling.

• Benign prostatic hyperplasia, which includes Proscar, a treatment for symptomatic benign prostate enlargement.

• Osteoporosis, which includes Fosamax, for treatment in postmenopausal women, launched in the United States in late 1995.

• Other Merck human health products include Crixivan, an HIB protease inhibitor, cleared for marketing in the United States by the U.S. Food and Drug Administration March of 1996, anti-inflammatory/analgesics, psychotherapeutics, and a muscle relaxant.

Merck-Medco Managed Care

The Merck-Medco Managed Care Division manages pharmacy benefits for more than 50 million Americans. Medco Containment Services markets pharmaceuticals through the mail and manages medical prescription and other benefits for patients, most of whom are in integrated plans.

Shortcomings to Bear in Mind

▪ The markets in which the company's business is conducted are highly competitive and, in many ways, highly regulated. Global efforts toward health-care cost containment continue to exert pressure on product pricing.

In the United States, government efforts to slow the increase of health-care costs and the demand for price discounts from managed-care groups have limited the company's ability to mitigate the effect of inflation on costs and expenses through pricing.

Outside of the United States, government-mandated cost-containment programs have required the company to similarly limit selling prices. Additionally, government actions have significantly reduced the sales growth of certain products by decreasing the patient reimbursement cost of the drug, restricting the volume of drugs that physicians can prescribe, and increasing the use of generic products. It is anticipated that the worldwide trend for cost containment and competitive pricing will continue for the balance of the 1990s and result in continued pricing pressures.

▪ In April of 1997, three analysts downgraded Merck, citing competition for Zocor. The new competitor is Lipitor, a statin (a cholesterol-lowering drug) co-marketed by Warner-Lambert and Pfizer. Since its launch earlier in 1997, Lipitor had captured a stunning 10 to 12 percent of new prescriptions for statins, a remarkable performance for any new drug, but even more impressive because Lipitor arrived on the scene as the fifth entrant in a hot but crowded market.

Despite this seemingly bad news, Chairman Raymond Gilmartin told shareholders at the company's annual meeting that a variety of new drugs under development for AIDS, heart disease, and arthritis, as well as formulations of existing cholesterol drugs, would allow Merck to maintain its high growth. What's more, new drugs introduced in 1995 and 1996 all accounted for about half of Merck's revenue growth in 1996. Merck executives said the company plans to market drugs in twenty-four major disease categories by the year 2000, up from fifteen in 1997.

Reasons to Buy

- Among the highlights of 1996 was the exceptional performance of Merck's new products, of which the company introduced eight since the beginning of 1995.
  - Cozaar and Hyzaar are the first class of a new class of cardiovascular drugs, and their market introductions represent the most successful launch of any antihypertensive medicine in this decade.
  - For its part, Fosamax is a breakthrough in the treatment of postmenopausal osteoporosis, reflected in its rapid acceptance by the medical community. After successful launches in forty-seven countries, more than 1.3 million patients are now being treated with Fosamax.

    Fosamax is meeting a serious medical need because at least one in three women over the age of fifty will fracture a bone due to osteoporosis. The most serious of these will be hip fractures, which require hospitalization and often lead to disability and sometimes premature death.
  - Trusopt is also doing extremely well as an important advance in treating glaucoma. After one year on the market, Trusopt has became the most widely prescribed anti-glaucoma medicine in the United States.
  - Varivax is the only vaccine against chicken pox available in the United States. It is recommended widely by government and pediatric medical authorities, resulting in the most rapidly accepted Merck vaccine in over thirty years.
  - Pepcid AC Acid Controller, sold by Merck's joint venture with Johnson & Johnson, was the first product in its class to be launched in over-the-counter markets. It quickly became the top-selling heartburn/acid indi-

gestion product and maintains this market leadership.
  - Among all of Merck's new products, none is more impressive than Crixivan, launched in 1996, for treating HIV infection. Resulting from a ten-year effort at Merck, Crixivan is already reaching more than 125,000 people and providing real hope that AIDS may become a manageable chronic disease.

    Crixivan is a potent inhibitor of the HIV protease enzyme that is critical to the replication of the virus that causes AIDS. It can be taken in combination with other anti-HIV therapies or alone. A Merck study in early 1996 showed that Crixivan, when used with two other anti-HIV drugs that both reverse transcriptase inhibitors, reduced the amount of HIV in the bloodstream so dramatically that no virus could be detected, within the limits of currently available tests, in six of the seven patients, or 86 percent.
- In mid-May of 1997, Novartis AG, the Swiss pharmaceutical and chemical giant, agreed to buy Merck's insecticide and fungicide business for $910 million. Analysts viewed this as a good move for Merck, since the price paid is more than four times annual sales of $200 million. Merck is shedding the unit as part of its broader strategy to focus on the more profitable human and animal health businesses.
- Merck-Medco Managed Care now provides pharmaceutical management services for about 50 million Americans. In 1996, Merck-Medco managed more than 235 million prescriptions, an increase of 38 percent in one year. These prescriptions represented more than $9 billion in prescription drug expenditures, compared with $6.6 bil-

lion managed by Merck-Medco in 1995, an increase of 39 percent.

Merck-Medco is the market leader in serving major corporate customers, health insurers, managed-care providers, and government-sponsored health plans. New corporate clients won in 1996 include Citibank, Mobil, and Sears. Other newly won customers include Maxicare, Preferred Care, and Blue Cross/Blue Shield of Vermont.

- Growth in earnings per share has been impressive. For instance, in the 1986–1996 period, earnings per share climbed from $.54 to $3.20, a compound annual growth rate of 19.5 percent. In the same ten-year span, dividends advanced from $.21 to $1.42, a growth rate of 21.1 percent.
- The company is sound financially, with 90 percent of capitalization in common equity. Value Line accords the stock a rating of A++ for financial strength, its highest rating.
- There are about 4 million babies born in the United States each year who would be candidates for Varivax. About 8 percent to 9 percent of unimmunized children get chicken pox each year. It is currently estimated that there are 3.5 million cases of chicken pox each year in the United States, primarily in children between the ages of five and nine years. Varivax has shown 93 percent efficacy in preventing the disease. Of the Varivax-vaccinated children, about 4 percent have gotten chicken pox, but with far fewer lesions than those experienced by unvaccinated children who get the disease.

The cost of Varivax to private physicians is $39 per dose. After discounts to various government-funded programs and larger institutional buyers, Merck realizes about $28 per dose.

- In looking at Merck strategically, Medco is expected to be extremely important to ensure a fast take off for new products, especially for Cozaar, by getting them into managed-care formularies quickly. This will enable Merck's sales force to concentrate on creating "pull-through" demand. Several years from now, analysts envision Merck's core sources of growth to be Cozaar, patented until 2009, and Zocor/Mevacor, to treat cholesterol, patented until 2005 and 2001, respectively. New therapeutic areas to Merck that are incremental sources of growth should be Fosamax, patented until 2008; Proscar, patented until 2005; and possibly MK-476 (brand name of Singulair), a potential advance to treat asthma by reducing the need for rescue medication and which is entering full-scale development.
- In an increasingly competitive environment, Merck is using every means possible to reduce by months the drug discovery, development, and application process. By identifying specific biochemical targets in a disease pathway, using robotics and high-volume automated screening strategies, and developing novel technologies, the company's multidisciplinary scientific staff can identify lead compounds rapidly for most programs. In 1994, Merck opened several new laboratories, including the Biological Support Laboratory and the Small Scale Organic Pilot Plant at the Rahway, New Jersey, site. What's more, the company is scheduled to open the Biological Support Laboratory in West Point, Pennsylvania, in 1995. Finally, additional projects for equipment and renovation are planned through the year 2000.
- Using its strong cash flow, along with proceeds from recent asset sales, Merck has paid off all the Medco purchase-related short- and long-term debt.

- Vasotec, Merck's flagship medicine for treating high blood pressure, asymptomatic left ventricular dysfunction, and heart failure, remains the most widely prescribed cardiovascular medicine in the world. Sales of Vasotec in 1996 exceeded $2 billion. It is the only angiotensin-converting enzyme (ACE) inhibitor indicated for the treatment of all three of these conditions. Due to several landmark clinical studies and more than ten years of clinical experience, Vasotec shows continued sales growth, particularly in the area of heart failure, where it is the only ACE inhibitor with combined indications for reducing mortality in patients with left ventricular failure.

  Sales of Prinivil, Merck's second ACE inhibitor for high blood pressure and heart failure, increased 34 percent in the United States and 30 percent worldwide.

- In 1997, two large-scale studies indicated that a drug under development at Merck can reduce deaths, heart attacks, and complications by one-third in patients suffering from severe chest pain.

  Researchers hailed the results as an important advance in treating the condition known as unstable angina, which can often be a precursor to a heart attack and causes about 1.2 million Americans to be admitted to the hospital a year.

  The findings, based on 4,800 patients, suggest that if widely used, the Merck drug Aggrastat could prevent 5,000 to 10,000 deaths and 30,000 to 40,000 heart attacks in the United States annually, researchers said.

Total assets: $24,293 million
Current ratio: 1.55
Common shares outstanding: 1,205 million
Return on 1996 equity: 30%

	1996	1995	1994	1993	1992	1991	1990	1989
Revenues (millions)	19,829	16,681	14,970	10,498	9,662	8,603	7,672	6,550
Net income (millions)	3,881	3,335	2,997	2,687	2,447	2,122	1,781	1,495
Earnings per share	3.20	2.70	2.38	2.32	2.12	1.83	1.52	1.26
Dividends per share	1.42	1.24	1.14	1.03	.92	.77	.64	.55
Price: High	84.2	67.3	39.5	44.1	56.6	55.7	30.4	26.9
Low	56.5	36.4	28.1	28.6	40.6	27.3	22.3	18.8

CONSERVATIVE GROWTH

Minnesota Mining & Manufacturing

3M Center, St. Paul, MN 55144 ◻ Investor contact: Jon Greer (612) 736-1915 ◻ Listed: NYSE ◻ Dividend reinvestment plan available: (800) 468-9716 ◻ Ticker symbol: MMM ◻ S&P rating: A+ ◻ Value Line financial strength rating: A++

Minnesota Mining & Manufacturing Company is an international manufacturer with a vast array of products (perhaps as many as 60,000). The company has a stake in such items as tapes, adhesives, electronic components, sealants, coatings, fasteners, floor coverings, cleaning agents, roofing granules, fire-fighting agents, graphic arts, dental products, medical products, specialty chemicals, and reflective sheeting.

The company's Industrial and

Consumer Sector is the world's largest supplier of tapes, producing more than 900 varieties. It is also a leader in coated abrasives, specialty chemicals, repositionable notes, home cleaning sponges and pads, electronic circuits, and other important products.

The Life Sciences Sector is a global leader in reflective materials for transportation safety, respirators for worker safety, closures for disposable diapers, and high-quality graphics used indoors and out. This sector also holds leading positions in medical and surgical supplies, drug delivery systems, and dental products.

Minnesota Mining, moreover, is making large investments to support growth in its businesses. In 1996, R&D spending totaled $947 million, or 6.7 percent of sales. This spending now has totaled nearly $4.3 billion over the last five years. Finally, capital expenditures totaled $1.1 billion in 1996, bringing the five-year total to more than $5 billion.

3M has a decentralized organization with a large number of relatively small profit centers, aimed at creating an entrepreneurial atmosphere.

3M is a highly diversified manufacturer of industrial, commercial, consumer, and health-care products that share similar technological, manufacturing, and marketing resources. Its business initially developed from its research and technology in coating and bonding.

MMM has many strengths:

• Leading market positions. Minnesota Mining is a leader in most of its businesses, often number one or number two in market share. In fact, 3M has created many markets, frequently by developing products that people didn't even realize they needed.

• Strong technology base. The company draws on more than thirty core technologies, from adhesives and nonwovens to specialty chemicals and microreplication.

• Healthy mix of businesses. 3M serves an extremely broad array of markets, from automotive and healthcare to office supply and telecommunications. This diversity gives the company many avenues for growth, while also cushioning the company from disruption in any single market.

• Flexible, self-reliant business units. 3M's success in developing a steady stream of new products and entering new markets stems from its deep-rooted corporate structure. It's an environment in which 3M people listen to customers, act on their own initiative, and share technologies and other expertise widely and freely.

• Worldwide presence. Minnesota Mining has companies in more than 60 countries around the world. It sells its products in nearly 200 countries.

• Efficient manufacturing and distribution. 3M is a low-cost supplier in many of its product lines. This is increasingly important in today's value-conscious and competitive world.

• Strong financial position. 3M is one of a small number of U.S. companies whose debt carries the highest rating for credit quality.

Shortcomings to Bear in Mind

▪ Even with its recent new-product successes, it's doubtful that Minnesota Mining & Manufacturing will ever duplicate its impressive growth of the 1980s. For one thing, the competition is intensifying. 3M's computer diskettes, for example, are under price pressure from Sony's products. On another front, the company's photography film unit is also feeling pressure from Eastman Kodak.

▪ Over the past ten years, the company's growth, although steady, has not been dynamic. In the 1986–1996 period, earnings per share increased from $1.70 to $3.63, an annual compound growth rate of 7.9 percent. In the same ten-year stretch, dividends expanded from $.90 to $1.92, a growth rate of 7.9 percent. Recent forecasts issued by management, however, are more upbeat. The company looks for growth to accelerate to a 10 percent annual pace.

Reasons to Buy

- With a presence in more than 200 countries, Minnesota Mining & Manufacturing still finds ways to exceed the pace of worldwide economic growth. One key to this success has been new-product development, made possible by an entrepreneurial corporate culture and heavy spending on research and development. The result: More than 30 percent of 3M's current sales are derived from products developed in the past four years.

- The company makes an effort to align its businesses around common markets, industries, and distribution channels. Individual 3M units—the sources of its product innovation—continue to identify customer needs and develop unique solutions. What's more, 3M's innovation and customer satisfaction efforts extend worldwide. In 1996, international sales reach $7.6 billion, representing 53 percent of total company sales. The company operates 3M companies in more than 60 countries outside the United States, providing the means to sell products in nearly 200 countries.

- Productivity gains play a significant role in the company's financial performance and competitiveness. In 1996, sales per employee in local currencies increased about 10 percent. This followed gains of 8 percent in 1995 and 9 percent the prior year.

- Minnesota Mining & Manufacturing leads the world in microreplication technology, which involves making ultraprecise patterns on the surfaces of materials. Drawing on this new 3M technology platform, the company is setting new standards for abrasives, reflective sheeting, electronic displays, closures for disposable diapers, computer mouse pads, and other products. Within five years, about one-fourth of 3M sales could come from products based entirely or partially on microreplication, up from 5 percent in 1996.

- Thanks to their unique construction, 3M Trizact abrasives last up to four times longer than conventional sandpaper and create a superior finish. They also can reduce the number of steps required to finish products, providing significant productivity gains.

  Trizact abrasives offer superior performance for polishing metals used in products such as surgical implants and instruments, jet engine turbine blades, and golf clubs.

- The Life Sciences Sector produces innovative products that improve health and safety for people around the world. In consumer and professional healthcare, 3M has captured a significant share of the first-aid market with a superior line of bandages. 3M Active Strips Flexible Foam Bandages adhere better to skin, even when wet, and 3M Comfort Strips Ultra Comfortable Bandages set new standards for wearing comfort. Under development are tapes, specialty dressings, and skin treatments that will reinforce and broaden the company's leading market positions and accelerate sales growth.

- In pharmaceuticals, 3M is a global leader in technologies for delivering medications that are inhaled or absorbed through the skin, and the company is expanding its horizons in new molecule discovery.

  In inhalation therapy, the company is continuing its tradition of innovation with the introduction of the world's first CFC-free, metered-dose inhaler, currently approved in more than thirty-five countries as Airomir (albuterol sulfate inhaler).

In transdermal drug delivery, 3M and Berlex Laboratories, Inc., a subsidiary of Schering AG, codeveloped the first once-a-week estradiol patch for treating menopausal symptoms. Introduced in 1995 as Climara (estradiol transdermal system), it already has captured more than 20 percent market share in the United States. The patch is also on the market in the United Kingdom and was launched in several other major European countries in 1997.

- In the dental field, 3M holds top positions around the world in orthodonitic brackets, restorative systems, and crown and bridge supplies. Using 3M adhesive technology, the company pioneered pre-coated orthodontic brackets, which offer improved bonding and removability. In 1996, Minnesota Mining launched Clarity Metal-Lined Ceramic Brackets, a new line of high-performance orthodontic braces enthusiastically received by both orthodontic specialists and patients.
- In closures for disposable diapers, 3M is a global leader in both tape and mechanical fastening systems. Its new hook-and-loop fasteners, based on 3M microreplication technology, improve diaper performance by ensuring a secure hold even when the fasteners are exposed to lotions, oils, and powders. The company's new fluted elastic materials for diaper waistbands, which expand the company's presence in the disposable diaper market, enable diaper manufacturers to eliminate bulky rolls of foam and increase manufacturing efficiency.
- In transportation safety, Minnesota Mining & Manufacturing leads the way in reflective sheetings that improve the visibility of signs, traffic lanes, vehicles, work zones, and license plates. What's more, 3M Scotchlite Diamond Grade Fluorescent Sheeting makes signs more visible during the day or night and in harsh weather, improving safety in pedestrian crosswalks, work zones, and other critical locations.
- The company is the world leader in systems and materials for premium durable graphics. Its graphics provide eye-catching logos, pictures, and markings on trucks, buses, signs, storefronts, and buildings. In addition, 3M FloorMinders Graphics provide an entirely new medium for important messages. Used in stores and plazas, the graphics are easy to apply and remove, and feature a durable, nonslip surface.

Total assets: $13,364 million
Current ratio: 1.71
Common shares outstanding: 416 million
Return on 1996 shareholders' equity: 24.4%

	1996	1995	1994	1993	1992	1991	1990	1989
Revenues (millions)	14,236	13,460	15,079	14,020	13,883	13,340	13,021	11,990
Net income (millions)	1,516	1,359	1,345	1,263	1,229	1,154	1,308	1,244
Earnings per share	3.63	3.23	3.18	2.91	2.82	2.63	2.96	2.80
Dividends per share	1.92	1.88	1.76	1.66	1.60	1.56	1.46	1.30
Price: High	85.9	69.9	57.1	58.5	53.5	48.8	45.7	40.9
Low	61.3	50.8	46.4	48.6	42.8	39.1	36.8	30.1

J. P. Morgan & Company, Inc.

60 Wall Street, New York, NY 10260-0060 ❑ **Investor contact: Ann B. Patton (212) 648-9446** ❑ **Dividend reinvestment program is available: (800) 519-3111** ❑ **Ticker symbol: JPM** ❑ **S&P rating: B+** ❑ **Value Line financial strength rating: A+**

J. P. Morgan, a holding company, owns Morgan Guaranty Trust, the fourth-largest bank in the United States. JPM emphasizes wholesale banking services to the largest corporations. In addition to lending services, Morgan provides corporate finance and capital market services, including bond, precious metals, and currency trading.

The company also provides investment and trust-management services, managing about $150 billion for individual and institutional investors. Operational services include securities custody, clearing, and settlement securities lending, among other services. International operations in thirty countries account for about 50 percent of consolidated assets.

Morgan's Business Sectors
Finance & Advisory

Morgan helps to structure and raise equity and debt capital as well as arrange credit to support clients' operating needs, counsels on business and financing strategy, and executes transactions—including mergers, acquisitions, divestitures, and privatizations—that advance strategic goals.

Market Making

Morgan provides clients with access to world financial markets. The bank deals in securities, currencies, commodities, and derivative instruments to help clients meet investment, trading, and risk management needs, supported by comprehensive research on market conditions and opportunities.

Asset Management & Servicing

Morgan manages financial assets entrusted to it by institutions and individuals, using separately managed portfolios and investment funds, striving to optimize performance. For private clients, the bank offers a range of investment, advisory, banking, brokerage, and fiduciary services. Morgan also operates the Euroclear System and acts as a futures and options broker on exchanges worldwide.

Equity Investments

Morgan manages its own diversified portfolio of equity investments, turning knowledge and experience around the world into a comparative investment advantage for stockholders. The bank invests in privately held growth companies, management buyouts, privatizations, and recapitalizations.

Proprietary Investing & Trading

Morgan actively manages market positions for its own account, with varying investment and trading horizons, diversified across a spectrum of markets and instruments. The bank uses global market knowledge and resources to manage the firm's capital and liquidity profiles.

How J. P. Morgan Differs from a Typical Bank

The average banking customer is not likely to do business with J. P. Morgan. Rather, this premier bank deals with huge corporations, wealthy individuals, and governments. To give you a flavor of what

J. P. Morgan does, here are some of its accomplishments in 1996:

- Advised Spain's Banco Bilbao Vizcaya on its acquisition of a 40 percent controlling interest in Banco Provincial, Venezuela's largest bank.
- Advised Ford Motor Co. on the sale of its commercial finance and leading subsidiary, USL Capital Corp., in a series of transactions worth $8.4 billion.
- Underwrote and syndicated an $800 million acquisition facility for Metro-Goldwyn-Mayer, Inc. The transaction moved Morgan into the top five arrangers of highly leveraged loans.
- Advised Mobil Corp. on its agreement with the British Petroleum Company p.l.c. to merge the companies' European fuels-and-lubricants operations, creating a refining and service-station concern with annual sales of $20 billion.
- Led the Royal Bank of Canada's debut offering in the Yankee debt market: a $300 million offering of subordinated notes.
- Advised on the creation of Peru's largest brewing company, Union de Cervecerias Peruanas Backus y Johnston S. A., through the merger of four leading Peruvian brewers.

Shortcomings to Bear in Mind

- Although J. P. Morgan has the strongest balance sheet of any bank and is very good at what it does, Wall Street has typically given it a lower multiple than other banks because its earnings are less predictable.
- J. P. Morgan relies for its profits not merely on loans and trust business, but far more than most banks, on income from worldwide securities trading activities and underwriting, which tend to be cyclical.

Reasons to Buy

- J. P. Morgan's worldwide activities are integrated and fall broadly into complementary categories: those that center on its clients and those the bank conducts for its own account. Both are integral to Morgan's comparative advantage and ability to produce superior returns over time for its stockholders.

  In 1996, the mix of earnings between the two shifted. The bank earned the greater part of income—about 60 percent, compared with 40 percent the prior year—from the advisory, capital-raising, market-making, and asset management services that Morgan provides for clients. This shift in the balance of earnings was the year's most significant financial milestone. It reflects more than a decade of investment in an expanded set of core capabilities and Morgan's growing ability to put more of them to work for clients.

- While J. P. Morgan's 1996 results were excellent, the bank continues to strive for the optimal mix of business and for increasingly productive use of resources and development of the firm's full earnings capacity. Incremental investment will be focused on areas of high potential:

  - *Equities.* Since launching Morgan's equities business six years ago, after regulatory hurdles were lowered, the bank developed fully competitive capability for clients and achieved rapid growth. But the firm has only begun to realize the economic benefits that its equities business has the potential to deliver with global leadership in underwriting, research, and equity derivatives.
  - *Asset management.* Morgan is a longtime leader in investment management, with more than $200 billion of assets under management. With the growth of retirement savings through a range of vehicles and

rising demand for professional investment management and global expertise, J. P. Morgan sees excellent opportunities to expand its services in the United States and abroad.

- *Service for private clients.* With a strong reputation and highly regarded capabilities in structuring and investing assets to meet the needs of individuals, the bank intends to expand the universe of private clients it serves, as the pace of wealth creation accelerates worldwide.
- *Emerging markets.* Building on leadership in Latin America, J. P. Morgan will continue to strengthen its presence in other regions, as growth and deregulation in emerging markets continue. Johannesburg, Lima, and Moscow are the latest additions to the bank's network.

■ Ten years ago, traditional financial intermediation—interest rate management and the extension of bank credit—generated half of Morgan's revenues. Today, it accounts for roughly a quarter. The bank's revenues are now spread across a broad range of highly complementary global activities, encompassed by the five business sectors. Many activities are characterized by lower risk than traditional intermediation, for example, investment management, corporate securities underwriting, and, contrary to common perception, making markets in swaps.

■ J. P. Morgan is a stronger firm than it was a decade ago, thanks to successful diversification and the bank's growing ability to manage risk dynamically. Today, J. P. Morgan is less dependent on any one source of revenue, has a broader global client base, and has engineered a measurable reduction in exposure to risk, especially relative to its substantial capital.

■ J. P. Morgan offers its clients many of the same risk management techniques that it uses itself, notably derivatives. As a derivatives dealer, Morgan is strongly oriented toward helping clients manage risk, not toward trading for its own account. The average credit quality of the bank's derivatives exposure is solidly above the high quality of its traditional loan portfolio.

■ J. P. Morgan's business activities are thoroughly integrated worldwide. In a global economic and market environment that offered plentiful opportunities, J. P. Morgan produced strong, balanced growth in 1996. Pretax income rose 22 percent, to $2.3 billion.

Total revenues of $6.9 billion were up 16 percent. The bank set and achieved a goal of generating a greater proportion of revenue from its business with clients. Client-related revenues reached $5.7 billion, growing by one-third from 1995. Revenues from activities conducted solely for Morgan's own account were $1.2 billion, down from $1.6 billion a year earlier.

Total assets: $222,026 million
Return on average assets: .71%
Common shares outstanding: 184.9 million
Return on 1996 shareholders' equity: 14.9%

	1996	1995	1994	1993	1992	1991	1990	1989
Loans (millions)	27,554	22,323	20,949	23,223	25,180	26,378	25,712	26,030
Net income (millions)	1,574	1,296	1,215	1,723	1,382	1,114	775	(1,275)
Earnings per share	7.63	6.42	6.02	8.48	6.92	5.63	3.99	(7.04)
Dividends per share	3.31	3.00	2.79	2.48	2.24	2.03	1.86	1.70
Price: High	100.1	82.5	72.0	79.4	70.5	70.5	47.3	48.1
Low	73.5	56.1	55.1	59.4	51.5	40.5	29.6	34.0

National City Corporation

P. O. Box 5756, Dept. 2145, Cleveland, Ohio 44101-0756 ◻ Investor contact: Julie I. Sabroff (800) 622-4204 ◻ Dividend reinvestment plan available: (800) 622-6757 ◻ Listed: NYSE ◻ Ticker symbol: NCC ◻ S&P rating: A- ◻ Value Line financial strength rating: A

National City Corporation is a $51 billion, diversified financial services company based in Cleveland, Ohio. NCC operates banks and other financial service subsidiaries, principally in Ohio, Kentucky, Indiana, and Pennsylvania.

National City subsidiaries provide financial services that meet a wide range of customer needs, including commercial and retail banking, trust and investment services, item processing, mortgage banking, and credit card processing.

Net income for 1996 was a record $736.6 million, or $3.27 per share; it was 23.9 percent higher than 1995. Return on equity was 17.7 percent on a capital base that is one of the strongest in the industry. Total revenues, excluding security gains, grew 8.8 percent, while overhead expenses, excluding one-time merger costs, were flat. Credit quality, long a National City hallmark, continues to be excellent, both in absolute terms and relative to the industry.

National City stock closed the year 1996 at $44.88 per share, representing a total return to investors (price appreciation plus dividends) of 40.7 percent for the year. Over the last five years, National City stock has outperformed both the banking industry and the general market, as measured by the S&P Regional Bank Index and the S&P 500 Index, respectively.

The reported numbers include the results of Integra Financial Corporation, a $14 billion Pittsburgh-based banking company that merged with National City in May of 1996 on a pooling-of-interests transaction.

As of June 1996, less than thirty days after closing, the new National City Bank of Pennsylvania made its debut, with all systems and procedures of the former Integra Bank converted to National City's single operating system.

By the end of 1997, National City should achieve the projected $85 million of cost reductions from consolidating the operations of Integra Financial with its own.

Retail Banking

The retail banking business includes the deposit-gathering branch franchise, along with lending to individuals and small businesses. Lending activities include residential mortgages, indirect and direct consumer installment loans, leasing, credit cards, and student lending.

The return on equity for this business was 25.2 percent in 1996, and earnings were $481.3 million. The 25.4 percent increase in net income was due to higher net interest income from consumer loan growth, wider spreads on deposit accounts, and increases in banking office and credit related fees.

Fee-Based Businesses

The fee-based businesses include institutional trust, mortgage banking, and item processing.

• Institutional trust includes employee benefit administration, mutual fund management, charitable and endowment services, and custodial services. Trust assets under management totaled $38 billion at year-end 1996, up from $35 billion a year earlier. Assets in the ARMADA mutual funds increased 50 percent to $5.1 billion, through new sales and a strong stock market.

• Mortgage banking includes the origination of mortgages through retail offices and broker networks and mortgage servicing. The servicing portfolio totaled $22.8 billion at the end of 1996.

• Item processing is conducted by National City's majority-owned subsidiary, National Processing, Inc. (NYSE:NAP) and includes merchant credit card processing, airline ticket processing, check guarantee services and receivables, and payables processing services.

The increase in net income in the fee-based businesses reflects growing revenues in all units.

Net Interest Income

On a tax-equivalent basis, NCC's net interest income was up 6.2 percent to $1,963.5 million in 1996. This compares with $1,849.5 million in 1995 and $1,811 million in 1994. Although average earning assets remained stable in 1996, net interest income growth was the result of an improved asset and funding mix.

Noninterest Income

Noninterest income increased 13.4 percent in 1996 to $1,164.9 million, from $1,026.9 million the prior year. All categories of noninterest income increased in 1996, with the highest growth coming from item processing, credit card fees, mortgage banking revenue, and brokerage revenue.

Noninterest Expense

Noninterest expense increased 3.7 percent to $2,010.7 million in 1996. This compares with $1,939 million the prior year. One-time charges associated with the Integra merger were the largest contributors to the increase. Excluding these charges, noninterest expense was essentially flat, compared to 1995.

Shortcomings to Bear in Mind

■ Despite its conservative lending policies, National City has not been immune to the nationwide rise in consumer loan losses (as evidenced by the credit card loss ratio of 4.38 percent), caused partly by rising personal bankruptcies. On the other hand, although consumer loan quality bears watching, the bank's credit card loans account for only 4 percent of total loans. What's more, NCC's loan loss reserve is more than twice the total of its problem assets and past-due loans, suggesting that higher charge-offs in the future won't seriously hamper earnings growth.

Reasons to Buy

■ National City's principal business strategy is to capture a greater "share of wallet" by selling more products to existing customers and therefore realizing the maximum long-term value of the customer relationship. In retail banking, for instance, NCC is using sophisticated information management techniques to better understand and predict customer needs and behaviors. In corporate banking, National City has automated the routine aspects of the credit administration process, and it is using a team selling approach to bring an impressive array of capital markets, cash management, and other corporate services capabilities to its large base of middle-market clientele.

■ To better serve the growing base of affluent individuals and households, NCC created the Private Client Group, which combines the former personal trust and private banking divisions into a single customer-driven entity.

The remainder of the former Trust Group, principally asset management, employee benefits, and corporate trust services, has been reorganized into Institutional Trust, focusing on corporate clients and providing investment management services to the Private Client Group.

- National City has long been an efficient and high-quality servicer of mortgages, but mortgage origination volume has been insufficient to maintain a critical mass of servicing. The bank has renewed its commitment to this business and is seeking ways to increase mortgage originations, including faster turnaround of applications and acquisitions. In early 1997, NCC announced the acquisition of a mortgage origination network that will augment annual origination volume by over 50 percent.

- National City has a solid record of growth. In the 1986–1996 period, earnings per share expanded from $1.61 to $3.27, a compound annual growth rate of 7.3 percent. In the same ten-year span, dividends per share climbed from $.53 to $1.47, a growth rate of 10.7 percent. Meanwhile, the payout ratio has remained at a prudent level: 45 percent, thus indicating that future dividend increases are likely.

Total assets: $50,856 million
Return on assets in 1996: 1.51%
Common shares outstanding: 223 million
Return on 1996 shareholders' equity: 17.7%

	1996	1995	1994	1993	1992	1991	1990	1989
Loans (millions)	35,830	25,732	22,566	20,843	18,354	15,216	15,699	14,965
Net income (millions)	733	465	429	404	347	231	234	263
Earnings per share	3.27	2.64	2.60	2.59	1.76	1.38	.65	1.74
Dividends per share	1.47	1.30	1.18	1.06	.94	.94	.94	.84
Price: High	47.3	33.8	29.0	28.1	24.8	21.1	19.9	20.8
Low	30.6	25.3	23.8	23.1	17.9	13.9	11.3	15.4

CONSERVATIVE GROWTH

Newell Company

29 E. Stephenson Street, Freeport, Illinois 61032 ◻ Investor contact: Ross A. Porter, Jr. (815) 969-6114 ◻ Dividend reinvestment plan available: (800) 317-4445 ◻ Listed: NYSE ◻ Ticker symbol: NWL ◻ S&P rating: A+ ◻ Value Line financial strength rating: B++

Newell Company manufactures and markets a variety of consumer products, primarily through volume retailers. The company operates in four main categories:

- Housewares (which includes such brand names as Mirro, Goody, Pyrex, WearEver, Ace, and Anchor Hocking). In 1996, this operation had revenues of $832 million. Newell defines housewares as "any transportable item used in the home for a given purpose, usually (but not limited to) use in the kitchen and where fashion or appearance play an important role in its function." In 1995, the company purchased the European operations of Corning as a vehicle to expand into that market.

- Hardware and Tools (Amerock, EZ Paintr, BernzOmatic, Bulldog). In 1996, Hardware had revenues of $383 million. Hardware and tools, as defined by Newell, are "a tool or part involved in another operation or system where functionality is the deciding feature in its design, usually for a single purpose, and the use is not limited to the home."

• Home Furnishings (Levolor, LouverDrape, Newell, Intercraft, Lee/Rowan, Dorfile, SystemWorks). In 1996, Home Furnishings had sales of $916 million. The company says that home furnishings include "any permanent or semipermanent item affixed to and/or found in the home where fashion is a major factor in its design, often coordinated in conjunction with other home fashion items and with a purpose to usually support some other item or theme."

• Office Products (Sanford, EF Eberhard Faber, Berol, Stuart Hall, Newell, Rogers, Keene). In 1996, Office Products had total revenues of $742 million. According to Newell, its office products are "items used in office productivity or used to enhance office productivity."

Newell Company manufactures high-volume lines of housewares, hardware, home furnishings, and office products to a diversified customer base including mass merchants, home centers, hardware stores, and warehouse clubs.

In 1996, Newell's sales to discount stores and warehouse clubs totaled $820 million. Included in this list were Wal-Mart, Kmart, Sam's, Price/Costco, and Target, among others.

In the home centers and hardware stores sector, the company's sales in 1996 totaled $450 million. Included here were Home Depot, Ace, Builder's Square, TruServ, and Lowe's.

Newell also does well with office suppliers, such as Office Max, Staples, and Office Depot. Sales to these stores totaled $600 million in 1996.

Finally, Newell does business with department stores, grocery stores, specialty stores, drug stores, and other retailers. This business was substantial in 1996; it totaled $1 billion.

Newell strives to penetrate high-volume mass merchandisers with moderately priced, branded consumer staples and is constantly expanding its multiproduct offering through acquisitions and by modifying existing lines to achieve maximum profit.

The company emphasizes high-quality, low-tech, recession-resistant, and highly recognized brand-name consumer products that generally hold leading shares in their respective markets.

Newell operates under the axiom that high-margined products are better than lower-margined items; therefore, it is constantly upgrading existing lines, adding products, and weeding out the less-profitable.

Shortcomings to Bear in Mind

■ Some analysts question whether Newell can continue its acquisition program at a rate that will enable the company to maintain its historic earnings growth. In 1996, for instance, the company made only two acquisitions, both in January. On the other hand, the pace seems to be picking up again in 1997.

Reasons to Buy

■ Thirty years ago, Newell was a small manufacturer of drapery hardware, with about $15 million in sales. Since then, the company has expanded sales and earnings about 20 percent per year to become an international consumer goods supplier with annual sales approaching $3 billion and net income of more than $250 million. This dramatic growth was largely the result of using acquisitions as the vehicle to execute a multiproduct strategy.

It was in the mid-1990s that Newell first noticed the beginnings of a consolidation trend in retailing. At that time, the typical retailer was the downtown variety store.

As America moved to the suburbs, those variety stores began evolving into today's mass retailers like Kmart and Wal-Mart. Recognizing this trend, the company began to focus on this new type of customer. As their sales grew, Newell's sales also grew.

Newell also recognized that to capitalize on growth with the mass merchants and other emerging channels, the company would need to move beyond a single product line. Rather than accepting the risk of developing new product lines from scratch, the company chose to use a focused acquisition program.

Under this strategy, Newell has acquired more than seventy companies in the last thirty years. In the last three years alone, the company's acquisitions include Eberhard Faber and Berol, which added more than $350 million in sales to Sanford's business and made it a world leader in pencils, as well as pens and markers.

In the same period, Newell also acquired Decorel and Holson Burnes, which added $200 million to Intercraft's sales and made this Newell division the supplier of the most complete line of picture frames, framed art, and photo albums in the world.

■ A strength of Newell is its exceptional frontline management, with extensive experience in the operating units and experience that often includes tenure at various Newell operating companies to oversee the Newellization process at acquired companies.

The typical company that Newell acquires has a history of under performance for a variety of reasons. For instance, they may have concentrated on increasing sales volume at the expense of profitability, or they may have lacked the size to compete successfully in a consolidated market. The under performance that Newell finds presents the company with untapped profit opportunities.

"Newellization" is the profit improvement and productivity enhancement process Newell applies to newly acquired companies to bring them up to the company's high standards of profitability.

Elements of Newellization include establishing a focused business strategy, eliminating corporate overhead by centralizing administrative functions, and tightening financial controls.

In the factory, Newellization means improving manufacturing efficiency, pruning nonproductive product lines, reducing inventories, increasing trade receivable turnover, and trimming excess costs.

Outside the factory, it includes improving customer service, building partnerships with customers, and improving sales mix profitability through program merchandising techniques.

Through Newellization (which usually takes about two years), acquired companies build a solid foundation for growth and become profitable, established members of the Newell family.

■ Throughout most of its history, Newell has sold its products primarily in the United States. This course was obvious, as the United States is the largest consumer goods market. Recently, however, several regions outside the United States, particularly Mexico, South America, and Europe, have seen changes in their consumer goods economies and retail structures similar to the changes that occurred in the United States during the last three decades. The evolution of these markets makes them attractive to Newell. By selling to these new, expanding markets, Newell vastly increases its growth opportunities.

Until a few years ago, the company's overseas effort was limited to a small export sales division. This

$60 million division, Newell International, has consistently increased sales since it was established more than two decades ago.

Then, in the fall of 1994, Newell began a major emphasis on overseas expansion with the acquisition of Corning's $130 million European consumer products business. Now known as Newell Europe, the acquisition included Corning's manufacturing facilities in England, France, and Germany. The purchase also included the trademark rights and product lines of Pyrex, one of the most recognized brands in Europe.

More recently, the 1995 acquisition of Berol, an international manufacturer and marketer of writing instru-

ments, provided Newell with international sales of more than $80 million and extensive foreign manufacturing facilities.

Recent acquisitions, combined with existing sales to foreign customers, have pushed Newell's international sales to nearly 15 percent of total sales. The company expects this percentage to increase in the years ahead.

- Newell has grown dramatically over the last decade; its current ten-year annual return is 19.6 percent, as of year-end 1996. In the same 1986–1996 period, dividends per share climbed from $.09 to $.56, a compound annual growth rate of 20.1 percent.

Total assets: $3,005 million
Current ratio: 1.74
Common shares outstanding: 158.8 million
Return on 1996 shareholders' equity: 20%

	1996	1995	1994	1993	1992	1991	1990	1989
Revenues (millions)	2,873	2,498	2,075	1,645	1,452	1,259	1,204	1,247
Net income (millions)	256	222	196	165	163	136	126	106
Earnings per share	1.62	1.41	1.24	1.05	1.05	.89	.84	.71
Dividends per share	.56	.46	.39	.35	.30	.30	.25	.21
Price: High	33.8	27.3	23.9	21.5	26.5	22.9	17.8	12.6
Low	25.0	20.3	18.8	15.4	16.5	11.5	8.9	6.4

INCOME

NICOR Inc.

P. O. Box 3014, Naperville, Illinois 60566-7014 ▫ **Investor contact: Randy Horn (630) 305-9500, ext. 2529** ▫ **Dividend reinvestment plan available: (630) 305-9500** ▫ **Listed: NYSE** ▫ **Ticker symbol: GAS** ▫ **S&P rating: A-** ▫ **Value Line financial strength rating: A+**

NICOR is a holding company. Its principal business is Northern Illinois Gas, one of the nation's largest gas distribution companies. Northern Illinois Gas delivers natural gas to more than 1.9 million customers, including transportation service, gas storage, and gas supply backup to about 21,000 commercial and industrial customers who purchase their own gas supplies.

The Northern Illinois Gas subsidiary operates in a 17,000-square-mile territory, covering 544 communities in northern Illinois, excluding Chicago.

The company operates seven underground gas storage facilities. On an annual basis, GAS (the company's ticker symbol) cycles about 130 Bcf in and out of storage. Having ample storage is particularly important during cold winter months when there is a huge demand on the pipelines. NICOR has one of the most extensive storage facilities in the industry.

The Northern Illinois Gas service territory has a stable economic base that provides strong and balanced demand among residential, commercial, and industrial natural gas users. Residential customers account for about 45 percent of deliveries, while industrial and commercial customers account for about 30 percent and 25 percent of deliveries, respectively.

NICOR also owns Tropical Shipping, which transports containerized freight between the port of Palm Beach, Florida, and twenty-six ports in the Caribbean and Central America. Tropical Shipping is recognized as a dependable, on-time carrier in its operating region.

To improve profitability, Tropical plans to increase vessel utilization and reduce costs. Future growth is anticipated, mostly from higher-margin services to existing and new markets. Tropical Shipping more than carries its own weight and accounts for almost 10 percent of NICOR's operating income.

Highlights of 1996

- The Illinois Commerce Commission authorized a 2.8 percent, $33.7 million general rate increase for Northern Illinois Gas, effective April 1996. Before that, the company had gone 14 years without a rate increase.
- Natural gas deliveries increased 5 percent due to weather that was colder than the prior year, demand growth among existing customers, and another good year of customer additions.
- Efforts to control operating and maintenance expenses and capital expenditures allowed Northern Illinois Gas to maintain its status as one of the most efficient gas distributors in the nation.

- At Tropical Shipping, a year of significant business expansion helped life revenues and volumes shipped to reach record levels for the fourth consecutive year.
- NICOR's annual dividend rate was increased to $1.32 per share, marking the ninth consecutive annual increase.
- A new $50 million common stock repurchase program was initiated in June of 1996. When the program is completed, the company will have purchased $280 million, or about 18 percent, of total common shares outstanding since year-end 1989.

Shortcomings to Bear in Mind

- By their very nature, public utilities are for conservative investors who are seeking above-average yield. However, growth is modest. In the 1986–1996, for instance, NICOR, like most utilities, did not enjoy explosive growth. In that stretch, earnings per share advanced from $1.48 to $2.42, a compound annual growth rate of 5 percent. On the other hand, this was better than many others in the industry. Unfortunately, NICOR chose to cut its dividend in 1986 when some of its nonutility segments fell on hard times. In the ten-year period since the cut, dividends per share inched up, from $.90 to $1.31.
- All public utilities are vulnerable to shifts in interest rates. In fact, interest rate changes are the most potent factor affecting the action of utility stocks. There are two reasons: For one thing, utilities borrow a lot of money and higher interest rates can hurt. Secondly, investors buy utilities for income. If they observe that they can do better elsewhere, they may be tempted to sell their utility shares, thus depressing them to lower levels.
- The weather has an impact on electric as well as natural gas utilities. Electric

companies like hot summers so they can sell more air conditioning. They like cold winters so they can sell more space heating. Natural gas utilities don't worry much about the summer, since they typically lose money during those months. But in the winter, they want plenty of cold weather. If they don't get it, their profits are hit hard.

Reasons to Buy

- Public utilities generally rely on a greater amount of debt in their balance sheets than industrial companies. For its part, NICOR is exceptionally strong, with 57.5 percent of capitalization in the form of shareholders' equity. At the other extreme, some utilities have only 35 percent in equity.

- One of the reasons Northern Illinois Gas has been able to increase gas deliveries in recent years is the upward trend in diversified uses of natural gas. The company continues to make steady inroads in such markets as electric power generation, cogeneration, and large-tonnage gas air conditioning.

- At Northern Illinois Gas, earnings growth will come from a combination of customer additions, increases in gas deliveries to existing customers, and efforts to minimize costs.

  Beyond the company's traditional gas distribution business, NICOR has developed several new sources of revenue. Examples include utilization of its transmission network and storage facilities to provide services to pipelines, gas distribution companies, and gas marketers. The company has also established several unregulated businesses that provide value-added services to NICOR's customers.

- Even with its recent rate increase, Northern Illinois Gas prices remain among the lowest in the nation. Low gas prices are important because con-tinued deregulation of the utility industry will likely result in more competitive pricing between natural gas and electricity. For Northern Illinois Gas's residential and small commercial customers, natural gas costs are currently about one-third the cost of using electricity, and the company expects to maintain a competitive advantage compared with electricity in the years ahead.

- Nicor has a flexible supply position. Northern Illinois Gas has interconnects with five interstate pipelines, providing access to most major gas-producing areas in North America. This allows for a diverse supply portfolio, which helps assure reliability and competitive pricing.

- Northern Illinois Gas's large and growing customer base continued to be a bright spot in 1996. The company added 29,500 customers in 1996 and has averaged over 30,000 customer additions a year for the past ten years.

- Minimizing operating and maintenance expenses is another high priority at Northern Illinois Gas. The company's ability to minimize these costs was one of the factors that enabled it to avoid filing for a rate increase for fourteen years. Operating and maintenance expenses increased less than 1 percent in 1996, and several initiatives have been implemented to help minimize expenses in future years.

  Northern Illinois Gas's focus on keeping costs low has made it one of the most efficient gas distributors in the nation. The company routinely ranks at the top in terms of many key efficiency measures when compared to other major gas distributors.

- Tropical Shipping's strengths also point the way to future opportunities. The company's attributes include its reputation for quality, on-time transportation services; the ability to establish and build close ties with customers; an experienced management team; and a fleet of vessels and customized equipment that is right for the Caribbean marketplace.

■ Tropical Shipping's growth strategy has been to take advantage of opportunities with the Caribbean region. During 1996, the company increased business in most of its established markets and expanded service to include:

• The Cayman Islands through the acquisition of Thompson Shipping Line's business;

• The Turks and Caicos Islands;

• Jamaica, Puerto Rico, and a second port in the Dominican Republic through alliances with other liners.

■ One of the most significant developments at Tropical Shipping in 1996 was an agreement to acquire the business of Thompson Shipping. These operations added 9,300, twenty-foot equivalent units (TEUs) to Tropical Shipping's volume growth in the second half of 1996. Tropical Shipping transported 119,200 TEUs in 1996, up from 96,900 the prior year. Thompson Shipping serves the Cayman Islands, a popular tourist attraction for cruise ships as well as for other visitors who stay at hotels.

Total assets: $2,439 million
Current ratio: 0.74
Common shares outstanding: 50 million
Return on 1996 shareholders' equity: 16.7%

	1996	1995	1994	1993	1992	1991	1990	1989
Revenues (millions)	1,851	1,480	1,609	1,674	1,547	1,457	1,472	1,559
Net income (millions)	121	100	110	109	95	100	102	111
Earnings per share	2.42	1.96	2.07	1.97	1.67	1.70	1.73	1.85
Dividends per share	1.31	1.28	1.26	1.22	1.18	1.12	1.06	1.00
Price: High	37.1	28.5	29.3	31.6	25.8	23.8	23.5	23.0
Low	25.4	21.8	21.9	24.1	19.0	19.5	17.4	14.9

CONSERVATIVE GROWTH

Nordson Corporation

28601 Clemens Road, Westlake, Ohio 44145-1119 ◻ Investor contact: Barbara T. Price (216) 892-9507 ◻ Dividend reinvestment plan is available: (216) 892-1580 ◻ Fiscal year ends about October 31 ◻ Listed: NASDAQ ◻ Ticker symbol: NDSN ◻ S&P rating: A ◻ Value Line financial strength rating: A

Nordson Corporation designs, manufactures, and markets systems that apply adhesives, sealants, and coatings to a broad range of consumer and industrial products during manufacturing operations.

Nordson's high-value-added product line includes customized electronic-control technology for the precise application of materials to meet customers' productivity, quality, and environmental management targets.

Nordson products are used around the world in the appliance, automotive, construction, container, converting, electronics, food and beverage, furniture, graphic arts, metal finishing, nonwovens, packaging, and other diverse industries.

Nordson markets its products through four international sales divisions: North America, Europe, Japan, and Pacific South. These organizations are supported by a network of direct operations in thirty-one countries. Consistent with this strategy, more than 60 percent of the company's revenues are generated outside the United States.

Nordson has manufacturing facilities in Ohio, Georgia, California, Connecticut, Germany, the Netherlands, Sweden, and the United Kingdom.

1996 Highlights

• The company introduced the Series 3000V adhesive-dispensing product line with advanced electronic controls that automate many packaging system functions such as startup and shutdown.

• Nordson strengthened its sales and service capabilities for liquid adhesive dispensing systems to support a growing base of domestic customers.

• The company enhanced the FoamMelt product line with improved system controls that increase materials output in demanding gasketing and sealing applications.

• Nordson expanded the product line of compact electrostatic coating systems used to apply protective coatings, adhesives, and lubricants to wire, cable, and other reel-to-reel products.

• The company developed a product line of extruders for applying high-performance compounds used to manufacture roll-to-roll insulating materials.

• Nordson expanded the product line of systems for bonding automotive upholstery in wide-web applications.

• The company installed the first ProLink adhesive systems that help manufacturers easily adapt to production changes and manufacturing innovations.

• Nordson developed a modular Control Coat adhesive applicator that gives manufacturers added flexibility in precisely applying small adhesive fibers to disposable products.

• The company installed a PluraFoam two-component dispensing system at a major automotive supplier.

• Nordson established a new business unit to develop technologies for manufacturing reinforced plastics used to make circuit boards, sporting goods, and other high-performance fiber glass products.

• The company opened a new 70,000-square-foot facility in Amherst, Ohio, to consolidate engineering, manufacturing, marketing, and customer service operations.

• Nordson introduced an automated system that applies adhesives used to reinforce steel body panels, helping to reduce denting, decrease weight, and lower labor costs.

• The company introduced the rotary powder applicator to improve the uniformity of finishes on horizontal automotive body surfaces such as trunk lids, roofs, and hoods.

Shortcomings to Bear in Mind

■ With well over half of its operations abroad, Nordson is vulnerable to a strong dollar. In fiscal 1996, for instance, the third quarter was hurt by a stronger U.S. dollar relative to the Japanese yen and weak conditions across several of the markets the company serves in the United States. Even though the company's sales momentum returned in the fourth quarter, annual revenues still fell short of Nordson's goal of increasing sales and profits by 15 percent.

Sales in Europe reached $229 million in 1996, a 14 percent increase over the prior year. In Japan, sales were up 13 percent in local terms. However, unfavorable currency offset this growth, bringing reported revenues to $86 million, down 1 percent from 1995.

On the plus side, Pacific South region (including Asia, Australia, and Latin America) maintained its pace of double-digit growth with sales of $57 million, a gain of 21 percent.

Reasons to Buy

- "Finishers of consumer and industrial products come to Nordson for the most efficient methods to apply liquid paints and powder coatings," says Sam Dawson, vice president of Nordson. "Spraying coating materials is the easy part...our ability to control their precise application is where we deliver real value to our customers."

  Nordson markets complete material application systems that help manufacturers improve product quality while lowering material usage.

  "Today, finishers want to reduce the environmental impact of their operations," says Dawson. "That's why Nordson focuses on providing systems that apply solvent-free powder coatings and low-solvent liquid paints. Finishers who convert to these finishes can meet environmental goals and reduce waste-disposal costs without sacrificing quality.

  "Proactive involvement in the industries we serve, through memberships in professional associations and relationships with coatings suppliers, is key to understanding our customers' needs," Dawson adds. "This involvement, combined with our experience base, gives Nordson two competitive advantages: the best equipment available and the fastest new-product cycle time."

- In 1996, Nordson again invested about 5 percent of its total annual sales in research and development activities focused on new technologies. The efforts of its scientific staff resulted in a total of thirty-five U.S. patents.

- In 1996, Nordson was active on the acquisition front. It acquired two companies whose technologies complemented and expanded the company's core businesses. In January, Nordson purchased Spectral Technology Group Ltd., a U.K.–based manufacturer of accelerated drying and curing systems with strong ties to the graphic arts industry.

  Later in 1996, the company added Asymtek of Carlsbad, California, to broaden Nordson's range of automated fluid dispensing systems for the fast-paced electronics industry. Both operations continue to be directed by the same management teams that paved the way to their strong market positions.

- In August of 1996, Nordson announced the establishment of Nordson India Private Limited, headquartered in Bangalore, India, which strengthens the company's position in South Asia. Nordson now has thirty-seven direct operations in addition to forty-three sales support offices in a total of thirty-one countries. In addition, Nordson maintains working relationships with more than 105 distributor organizations—expanding the company's worldwide presence to a total of fifty-two countries.

- In fiscal 1996, Nordson's worldwide sales expanded to $609 million, while earnings increased to $2.92 per share. Return on shareholders' equity was 23 percent, outpacing industry averages for the tenth consecutive year. At year-end, the board of directors increased Nordson's dividend by 11 percent, marking the thirty-third consecutive year of cash dividend increases.

- In the 1986–1996 period, Nordson's earnings per share climbed from $.67 to $2.92, a compound annual growth rate of 15.9 percent, which was right in line with its stated objective. Dividends during the same ten-year span expanded from $.23 to $.72, a growth rate of 12.1 percent. Meanwhile, the dividend payout ratio is low, at 25 percent, which gives the company funds to continue its future growth.

- Nordson has an exceptionally strong balance sheet, with only $17.1 million in long-term debt, compared with shareholders' equity of $245 million.

Coverage of bond interest, moreover, is a very healthy 17.1 times.

- Nordson stock is heavily owned by insiders and employees. For instance, officers and directors own 38.5 percent of the outstanding shares. Other employees own another 23 percent. It's logical to assume that these people have an interest in providing growth for shareholders.

Total assets: $510,493
Current ratio: 1.53
Common shares outstanding: 18 million
Return on 1996 shareholders' equity: 23%

	1996	1995	1994	1993	1992	1991	1990	1989
Revenues (millions)	609	581	507	462	426	388	345	282
Net income (millions)	53	53	47	41	40	34	29	34
Earnings per share	2.92	2.84	2.45	2.13	2.03	1.77	1.53	1.77
Dividends per share	.72	.64	.56	.48	.44	.40	.36	.32
Price: High	65.0	61.0	63.0	54.8	57.0	46.0	26.3	29.5
Low	45.5	53.8	52.0	38.3	43.0	22.1	16.8	22.0

CONSERVATIVE GROWTH

Norfolk Southern Corporation

Three Commercial Plaza, Norfolk, Virginia 23510-2191 ◻ Investor contact: Deborah Noxon (757) 629-2861 ◻ Dividend reinvestment plan available: (800) 524-4458 ◻ Listed NYSE ◻ Ticker symbol: NSC ◻ S&P rating: A+ ◻ Value Line financial strength rating: A+

Norfolk Southern Corporation is a Virginia-based holding company that owns all the common stock of and controls a major freight railroad, Norfolk Southern Railway Company; a motor carrier, North American Van Lines, Inc.; and a natural resources company, Pocahontas Land Corporation.

The railroad system's lines extend over more than 14,500 miles of road in twenty states, primarily in the Southeast and Midwest, and the province of Ontario, Canada.

North American provides household moving and specialized freight-handling services in the United States and Canada. It offers certain motor carrier services worldwide.

Pocahontas Land manages about 900,000 acres of coal, natural gas, and timber resources in Alabama, Illinois, Kentucky, Tennessee, Virginia, and West Virginia.

The Battle for Conrail

Since October of 1996, CSX and Norfolk were locked in an expensive bidding war for Conrail and control of its dominant East Coast route system. In March of 1997, however, Conrail agreed to a takeover for $10.5 billion, under which CSX Corporation and Norfolk Southern divided Conrail's 11,000-mile route system between them. The Northeast rail industry, after twenty years as a near-monopoly for Conrail, now is seeing competition reintroduced.

Norfolk Southern and CSX are expected to spend a total of at least $1 billion to modernize Conrail's facilities. Both companies have posted strong rail profits, allowing them to invest in new terminals, upgraded tracks, and more locomotives. What's more, by linking their own route systems with Conrail's, the two railroads will be able to keep freight moving for longer distances, reducing the slow connections and delays that have angered shippers, sending them into the arms of the trucking industry. In recent years, moreover, faster and more efficient trucks have built up their dominance in Conrail's territory, and today control 88 percent of freight revenues in the Northeast, up from about 80 percent in the early 1980s.

But with the Conrail issue resolved, the railroads in the region are expected to give truckers a run for their money. "Rail service will get better, and companies will use them more," one observer noted. Still another authority commented that the railroads could win back 15 to 20 percent of the freight business lost to trucks.

Strategic Position in Growth Markets

Norfolk Southern serves the growing Midwest and Southeast markets of the United States and through strategic agreements with other carriers is able to extend its reach into markets throughout the world. It works closely with connecting railroads and motor carriers to facilitate time-sensitive service, and with ocean shippers to move international freight through ports on the East, Gulf, and West Coasts.

In recent years, Norfolk Southern has enjoyed record revenues because of an aggressive, project-driven marketing approach designed to ensure growth in all markets. Norfolk Southern has succeeded in expanding existing markets and attracting new industry to its rail lines, capitalizing on the Southeast's burgeoning industrial development.

Working together, Norfolk Southern's Industrial Development and Marketing departments successfully attracted many new high-capacity woodchip mills, galvanizing plants, steel facilities, and feed mills to the Norfolk Southern rail service region.

The growth in the automotive markets has been particularly impressive, with eight of eleven new U.S. auto assembly plants located on Norfolk Southern's lines during the past ten years.

Railway revenues are diversely distributed among seven commodity groups. The largest of these, coal, accounts for 32 percent of revenues. Satisfying the needs of customers is at the heart of each division made every day by the coal, merchandise, and intermodal marketing groups.

Norfolk Southern's goal is to be every customer's lead logistics supplier. This goal has precipitated the expansion of new distribution networks and marketing initiatives. For example:

• In chemicals, new Thoroughbred Bulk Transfer terminals expedite transfer of commodities from rail to truck.

• In metals and construction, a new generation of coil-steel cars better protects lading.

• In paper and forest products, large cubic-capacity cars in rapid shuttle service enhance competitive advantage and increase profit margins.

• In agriculture, the "Pegasus Project" coordinates and speeds handling of grain trains, improving productivity and customer satisfaction.

• In coal markets, COLTtainer Service blends rail and truck transportation to generate business in short-haul markets, a first in the U.S. rail industry.

• On the intermodal side, strategic alliances with the Florida East Coast Railway, Conrail, and the Kansas City Southern Railway have provided Norfolk Southern's customers with new service into South Florida, the Northeast, and Texas, respectively. In addition, innovative service offerings such as the EMP domestic container network expand the traffic base to attract trucking assets as well as traditional intermodal freight.

Coal

Norfolk Southern is one of the nation's largest transporters of coal for domestic utility, steel, and industrial use and for export to nearly two dozen countries. It serves coal fields, primarily in West Virginia, Kentucky, and Virginia, that contain some of the world's best low-sulfur coal, both metallurgical and steam coal.

Coal is important to Norfolk Southern and constitutes about 30 percent of its revenues. This business is expected to improve because of the needs of electric utilities that are endeavoring to comply with the revised Clean Air Act. They have a choice of switching to low-sulfur coal or installing a device called a scrubber, which would remove noxious fumes. In either event, Norfolk Southern will benefit.

For one thing, the railroad owns some of its own low-sulfur coal through its Pocahontas Land Corporation. Norfolk Southern leases out this property to coal operators. In addition, the carrier also hauls low-sulfur coal originating from the Powder River Basin in Wyoming. After the coal is received in Memphis, it is shipped by Norfolk Southern to a utility in Alabama.

The Clean Air Act's Phase I rules kicked in at the beginning of 1995. Most of the coal currently being shipped by Norfolk Southern meets these more stringent guidelines, as well as the even stricter Phase II requirements that become effective in the year 2000.

To be sure, some utilities may elect to install scrubbers to eliminate the sulfur fumes. In this instance, however, their equipment would consume large amounts of limestone. Norfolk Southern believes that each plant would need between 100,000 and 200,000 tons of limestone each year. Fortunately, there are significant deposits of limestone along the carrier's lines.

About one-third of Norfolk Southern's coal traffic is export. Business has been depressed in recent years because of Europe's recession.

Besides coal, Norfolk Southern also has a stake in grain shipping, although it is less important than it is for western railroads. Chemicals are also of some importance and amount to about 14 percent of total rail revenues. Revenues from paper and forest products are also important.

Shortcomings to Bear in Mind

NSC's management faces a stiff challenge: how to take more costs out of a system that already carries less fat than most. Less efficient rivals are given a better shot at finding cost cuts that can fall straight to the bottom line.

Reasons to Buy

- Despite an extraordinary rise in fuel prices in 1996, Norfolk Southern ended the year on a high note, setting records across the board. Led by growth in automotive, coal, chemicals, and intermodal, railway operating revenues exceeded $4 billion for the second consecutive year. Thanks to vigilant attention to cost control and productivity improvements, the company's railway operating ratio improved more than one full point and was the best since the consolidation. Norfolk Southern's railway operating ratio—the percentage of revenues that goes into operating the railroad—is a key indicator of railway efficiency. It was 71.6 in 1996, compared with 72.7 (excluding the early retirement charge) in 1995.

- The outlook for the company's auto business is positive. Toyota's second plant at Georgetown, Kentucky, is now in production. BMW's Greer, South Carolina, plant came online in September of 1995. And in 1997, production at Mercedes' new Alabama plant began. Over the years, the company's region has been successful in attracting new auto plants. Of the last ten major domestic plants going into operation, seven facilities have been built in the NSC region. Several of these are so-called hybrids—plants that are run jointly by U.S. companies in cooperation with Japanese owners.

- Norfolk Southern's balance sheet is less leveraged than any of the other major railroads. At one time, in fact, the debt level was only 13 percent of capitalization. In recent years, however, this level has increased to a high of about 28 percent, primarily because of the company's share buy-back program. The level of debt is not likely to change much, once it reaches the low 30 percent range.

- A large portion of Norfolk Southern's grain and feed traffic moves out of the Midwestern heartland to the Southeastern poultry industry. During the past five years, the carrier's feed business has grown 21 percent.

- Intermodal traffic has been very successful for railroads in general. This involves moving truck trailers and containers that normally would be hauled over the highway. In the past, intermodal business did not apply to shorter hauls, those of 500 miles or less. More recently, railroads have even been competing successfully in this sector as well.

One reason for growth in intermodal is the problem that truckers have had in hiring drivers. Turnover among drivers has been high because drivers are averse to being away from home several weeks at a stretch. As a result, trucking firms such as J. B. Hunt and Schneider have signed contracts to cooperate in the carrier's intermodal business.

- Norfolk Southern has been eliminating some of its marginal lines. About 3,500 miles of less-profitable tracks were lopped off in the late 1980s. This is because the revenues produced were not sufficient to justify the maintenance requirements. Some of those lines were spun off to short-line railroads that now feed the Norfolk Southern system. Thus, this business is retained and is now profitable. Currently, the company anticipates reducing its track structure by about 500 miles per year.

- Norfolk Southern generates a large amount of free cash flow that it uses to enhance shareholder value. Its well-covered dividend has increased every year since 1986. What's more, the company has an aggressive buy-back program that has funded the repurchase of over 63 million shares since 1987. Even so, NSC has not neglected maintenance and investment in new equipment. Expenditures over this span have averaged over $655 million a year, and have accelerated since 1990 to about $700 million per year.

Total assets: $11,416 million
Current ratio: 1.21
Common shares outstanding: 375 million
Return on 1996 shareholders' equity: 15.7%

	1996	1995	1994	1993	1992	1991	1990	1989
Revenues (millions)	4,770	4,668	4,581	4,460	4,607	4,451	4,617	4,536
Net income (millions)	779	715	668	595	558	528	556	606
Earnings per share	2.03	1.82	1.63	1.42	1.31	1.19	1.14	1.16
Dividends per share	.75	.69	.64	.62	.60	.53	.51	.46
Price: High	32.2	27.2	24.9	24.1	22.5	21.9	15.8	13.8
Low	25.5	20.2	19.5	19.8	17.8	13.3	11.7	10.1

Pfizer Inc.

235 East 42nd Street, New York, New York 10017-5755 ◻ Investor contact: James R. Gardner, Ph.D. (212) 573-2668 ◻ Dividend reinvestment plan available: (800) 733-9393 ◻ Listed: NYSE ◻ Ticker symbol: PFE ◻ S&P rating: A- ◻ Value Line financial strength rating: A++

Pfizer traces its history back to 1849, when it was founded by Charles Pfizer and Charles Erhart. In those early days, Pfizer was a chemical firm. Today it is a leading global pharmaceutical manufacturer, creating and marketing a wide range of prescription drugs.

PFE also holds has an important stake in hospital products, animal health items, and consumer products.

Pfizer's growth over the past half century was paced by strategic acquisitions, new drug discoveries, and vigorous foreign expansion.

In 1996, prescription drugs accounted for 72 percent of revenues. Among the company's leading drugs are Norvasc calcium channel blocker heart drug (with sales of $1.8 billion); Zoloft, a drug to treat depression and obsessive/compulsive disorder ($1.3 billion); Procardia XL, a cardiovascular drug ($1.0 billion); Diflucan, an antifungal preparation ($910 million); Zithromax, a broad-spectrum quinolone antibiotic ($619 million revenues in 1996); and Cardura, a drug for hypertension and enlarged prostates ($533 million).

In 1996, the company's healthcare position was further strengthened through divestiture, acquisitions, and restructuring. During that year, the company sold the Pfizer Food Science Group, bringing to fifteen the number of operations the company has sold or closed in recent years because they did not meet Pfizer's goals or they were unrelated to healthcare.

Hospital Products added to the breadth of its product line by acquiring Leibinger, a leader in the manufacture and supply of implantable devices and instruments for skull and facial surgery; Corvita, which is developing proprietary stent-grafts; and Vesta, a developer of innovative specialty devices for women's health.

Shortcomings to Bear in Mind

- Like most stocks with bright prospects, Pfizer often sells at an elevated price/earnings ratio.
- During 1996 and 1997, many insiders were actively selling Pfizer stock. During this same period, the stock continued to climb to new highs. Could these insiders be wrong?
- The odds of discovering a new drug are staggering. Out of every 7 million compounds screened, only 1,000 hold promise. Of that 1,000, only 12 compounds actually become candidates for development. And of those 12, only 1 makes it to market.

Reasons to Buy

- The rapid growth in managed care is now viewed as a net positive for the drug industry. Despite the substantial discounts afforded to these providers, they tend to be heavily reliant on cost-effective pharmaceuticals that have the ability to prevent illnesses requiring expensive inpatient procedures.

Drug sales are also being boosted by the enrollment of Medicare patients into HMOs with prescription drug coverage. The growing influence of managed care, which now represents about 50 percent of the drug market, is expected to continue to spur demand for drugs and other cost-saving medical products in the years ahead.

- By every measure, 1996 was a banner year for Pfizer. For the forty-seventh consecutive year, the company's sales increased. For the first time in Pfizer's history, sales topped $11 billion—an increase of 13 percent over 1995. This 13 percent sales growth (15 percent in local currency) was virtually all volume-driven, as opposed to the result of price increases. Net income grew 23 percent, to nearly $2 billion, and earnings per share expanded by 20 percent.

- Pharmaceutical sales in 1996 increased by 16 percent, fueled by new product rollouts. Hospital sales grew by 8 percent as a result of strategic acquisitions and the growth of key product lines. Consumer Healthcare's sales rose 15 percent, reflecting, in part, the addition of two new brands during 1996: Cortizone, a leading over-the-counter anti-itch remedy, and Hemorid, a treatment for hemorrhoids. Despite adverse market conditions, Animal Health's sales were more than $1.2 billion—fueled by sales of Dectomax, which grew 36 percent.

- In January of 1997, the company raised the first-quarter dividend for 1997 by 13 percent, marking the thirtieth consecutive year of quarterly dividend increases by Pfizer.

- The company's focus on innovation resulted in unprecedented growth in 1996. The seven new drugs Pfizer launched in the early 1990s continued to perform well, accounting for more than two-thirds of Pfizer's total pharmaceutical sales in 1996. Sales of three of the company's products—Norvasc, Procardia XL, and Zoloft—each exceeded $1 billion.

- Norvasc, Pfizer's calcium channel blocker for hypertension and angina, became the best-selling product in Pfizer's history, with sales reaching nearly $1.8 billion. Norvasc's excellent record, coupled with the results of the recent PRAISE study, which found Norvasc to be safe for use in treating hypertension and angina in even the sickest heart patients, helped make it the leading drug in its class worldwide in 1996. The company also received approval for new uses for Zithromax, Zoloft, and Zyrtec, Pfizer's new antihistamine launched in the United States in February of 1996.

- In 1997, Pfizer introduced two new pharmaceuticals in development and marketing agreements with the discoverers of the drugs: Aricept, with the Eisai Company Ltd., and Lipitor, with the Warner-Lambert Company.

    Aricept is a safe and effective treatment for patients in the mild-to-moderate states of Alzheimer's disease.

    Lipitor is an innovative therapy that significantly reduces elevated levels of LDL cholesterol and triglycerides.

- At the end of 1997 or early 1998, Pfizer plans to launch Trovan, a powerful antibiotic discovered by Pfizer scientists that is effective against at least twelve different infections.

- To do justice to the unprecedented number and quality of the company's products, Pfizer has increased the size of its pharmaceutical field forces to more than 11,000 worldwide.

- Nowhere are the results of Pfizer's focus on innovation more evident than in the company's new-product pipeline. It has more than one hundred research projects under way, more than at any time in Pfizer's history. To fund the R&D necessary to support such a broad array of existing and potential products, the company invested almost $1.7 billion in 1996 and expects to invest about $2 billion in 1997.

■ *Fortune* magazine named Pfizer one of America's ten "Most Admired Companies." Headlined "Master of Innovation," the *Fortune* article cites innovation as "the force behind Pfizer, now known for having the best pipeline of new drugs coming to the market."

■ Pfizer's pharmaceutical operations have led the company's growth during the 1990s. Five years ago, Pfizer was the thirteenth-largest company in the worldwide pharmaceutical industry. Recent surveys rank the company as number six. In every year of this decade, Pfizer's worldwide pharmaceutical sales growth has significantly exceeded that of the industry as a whole; in recent years, the company's growth rate has been more than twice that of the industry.

■ Norvasc was again Pfizer's largest-selling product in 1996, with sales of nearly $1.8 billion in seventy-six countries. The product is distinguished by a smooth onset and long duration of action and steady blood levels that provide consistent around-the-clock control of blood pressure and angina with excellent toleration.

Norvasc is effective in treating a wide range of patient types, including the elderly and African Americans, who, according to clinical data, experience a greater propensity for hyperten-

sion. Norvasc is also safe in patients with concomitant conditions, such as diabetes and asthma.

■ Trovan, discovered by Pfizer scientists, is a new, once-daily, oral or intravenous broad-spectrum quinolone antibiotic. To accelerate clinical trials, Pfizer used a unique strategy, tracking the flu season around the world to test Trovan against the bacterial infections that follow.

• The U.S. filing in December 1996, covering twelve indications, was the largest New Drug Application Pfizer has ever filed with the FDA.

• Trovan has an outstanding safety profile, with no significant drug interactions.

• Its broad spectrum of activity includes many antibiotic-resistant bacteria.

• Its antimicrobial activity is highly effective against respiratory, surgical, urological, skin, and sexually transmitted infections.

• Trovan clinical trials, conducted in twenty-seven countries on five continents, involved 2,000 investigators and 13,500 patients.

• A trial in Nigeria during a meningitis epidemic demonstrated that easy-to-dispense oral Trovan was as effective as conventional treatment with older drugs given by injection.

Total assets: $14,667 million
Current ratio: 1.15
Common shares outstanding: 1,290 million
Return on 1996 shareholders' equity: 27.7%

	1996	1995	1994	1993	1992	1991	1990	1989
Revenues (millions)	11,306	10,021	8,281	7,478	7,230	6,950	6,406	5,672
Net income (millions)	1,929	1,554	1,298	1,180	1,094	917	801	727
Earnings per share	1.50	1.24	1.05	.92	.81	.68	.60	.54
Dividends per share	.60	.52	.47	.42	.37	.33	.30	.28
Price: High	45.6	33.4	19.8	18.9	21.8	21.5	10.2	9.5
Low	30.1	18.6	13.3	13.1	16.3	9.2	6.8	6.8

Philip Morris Companies Inc.

120 Park Avenue, New York, N. Y. 10017 □ Investor contact: Nicholas M. Rolli (212) 880-3460 □
Dividend reinvestment plan available: (800) 442-0077 □ Listed: NYSE □ Ticker symbol: MO □ S&P
rating: A+ □ Value Line financial strength rating: A+

Philip Morris is the largest cigarette manufacturer in the United States. It is also the fastest-growing tobacco company in the world and has doubled its worldwide market share in the last decade to 11 percent. At the same time, it is also the largest domestic food processor (Kraft) and is the second-largest brewer (Miller Brewing Co).

Realistically, however, Philip Morris is primarily a tobacco company, with such major brands as Marlboro (the top-selling brand in the United States), Merit, Virginia Slims (the best-selling women's cigarette), Benson & Hedges, and Parliament. Philip Morris has a 50.3 percent share of the domestic tobacco market. Outside the United States, the company also has well-known brands, such as L & M and Lark.

The company's other large operation is food, as a result of the prior acquisition of General Foods (1984) and Kraft (1988). Some well-known names include Jell-O, Shake 'n Bake, Lender's Bagels, Philadelphia Cream Cheese, Post cereals, Velveeta, Kool-Aid, Miracle Whip, Oscar Mayer, Cracker Barrel cheese, Tang, and Maxwell House coffee.

Ranking third was the company's beer business, featuring such brands as Lite, Miller, Molson, and Foster's Lager.

Finally, MO also has a stake in financial services (Philip Morris Credit Corp.) and real estate (Mission Viejo, a real estate developer in the West).

A Review of 1996
- In 1996, Philip Morris had its most profitable year ever, as net earnings

climbed 15.1 percent, to a record $6.3 billion. Net earnings per share soared 18 percent, to an all-time high of $2.56.

- In February of 1997, the company announced additional measures to continue to enhance shareholder value: a three-for-one split of common stock and a new, three-year, $8-billion share repurchase program.

- The dividend was increased 20 percent.

- In 1996, Philip Morris's worldwide tobacco operations sold a record 891 billion cigarettes, up 9.3 percent from the prior year. Of those, a record 458 billion cigarettes bore the Marlboro brand name.

- Philip Morris U.S.A. is the nation's leading cigarette manufacturer. For the fourteenth consecutive year, it had the highest revenues, income, volume, and share among U.S. tobacco companies.

Shortcomings to Bear in Mind

- As most investors are aware, Philip Morris is being besieged by the many pressures facing the U.S. tobacco industry: public smoking restrictions, possible excise tax hikes, the threat of FDA regulation, congressional hearings, negative media coverage, litigation. Still, we should remember that the company's tobacco segment has faced similar threats before and has overcome them. Finally, it important to note that over the past forty years, the tobacco industry has rarely lost or paid to settle a smoking-health product liability case.

In another realm is the problem of addiction. To be sure, most people have trouble quitting, and some apparently are unable to kick the habit. On the other hand, legal experts point out that deciding whether any particular individual is addicted is a highly speculative exercise and assumes that the definition of addiction can be established.

Despite all the evidence presented above, there is no question (at least in my opinion) that tobacco problems will continue to plague Philip Morris and cost it untold millions, which must be paid in legal fees and for the efforts of its throng of lobbyists who try to influence Congress not to put it out of business. The legions of anti-tobacco advocates—like many other feisty single-issue groups—are not about to give up their quest to legislate pristine air.

■ The company, along with its domestic tobacco peers, started preliminary discussions in the spring of 1997 with White House aides and attorneys general from several states. More than twenty states are suing the tobacco industry for medical costs, and there are at least fifteen additional class-action lawsuits pending. A recent court ruling granted the FDA partial jurisdiction over tobacco, a move vigorously opposed by the industry. Mounting litigation and attorney fees have pushed Philip Morris to the bargaining table, but the world's leading tobacco firm will work hard to get favorable terms before signing on the dotted line.

Reasons to Buy

■ Despite the never-ending strife against anti-smoking forces, Philip Morris has been a most successful company. Unlike many other huge companies, Philip Morris is growing at a consistent and impressive pace. In the 1986–1996 period, earnings per share climbed from $.52 to $2.56, a compound annual

growth rate of 17.3 percent. Similarly, dividends per share expanded from 21 cents to $1.47, a growth rate of 21.5 percent.

■ It goes without saying that the fear of anti-tobacco legislation haunts Philip Morris and has kept the stock at a low multiple. Even so, many big investors hold huge stakes in Philip Morris. For instance, MO is the largest position in a few billion-dollar mutual funds. In the words of one portfolio manager, "To buy a stock when other people worry is part of our investment discipline." Still another professional is unfazed by the furor over tobacco. He says he has seen it all before. "In 1985 and 1986," he points out, "there were great litigation concerns, and just as many negative stories. While 1985 was not a banner year for the stock, in 1986 it was up about 100 percent."

■ Analysts believe that Philip Morris is poised for earnings per share growth on the order of 18 percent per year over the next several years, as earnings are projected to increase in all major business units.

Key to the company's ability to achieve large EPS gains are the following factors:

● Strong earnings gains from the company's international cigarette business, with units estimated to grow at an 8 percent per year rate over the next few years.

● Further margin expansion in the company's domestic tobacco business.

● Large-scale share repurchases made possible by a high rate of excess cash generation.

■ Philip Morris's extensive worldwide network of manufacturing plants and distribution channels ensures that it can quickly meet shifting consumer demand in each of the more than 180 markets where it does business.

- Philip Morris's international operations, with $37 billion in operating revenues (54 percent of the total) and $5.3 billion in operating income (43 percent of the total), are larger and more profitable than those of any U.S.–based consumer packaged goods company. These figures include $6.5 billion of U.S. exports, making Philip Morris the largest exporter of consumer packaged goods in the nation.
- Philip Morris has the most valuable portfolio of premium brands in the consumer packaged goods industry. It includes sixty-eight brands that exceeded $100 million in 1996 sales, and among them, twelve—Marlboro, Kraft, Miller, L&M, Jacobs, Oscar Mayer, Post, Maxwell House, Merit, Philip Morris, Milka, and Virginia Slims—that each topped $1 billion. The Marlboro brand alone had almost $23 billion in sales in 1996, making it the world's best-selling consumer packaged product, hands down.
- Kraft is one of the largest coffee companies in the United States. Major brands include: Maxwell House, Yuban, Sanka, Maxim, and General Foods International Coffees.
- Kraft Foods International is among the largest food businesses in Europe, and the largest U.S.–based food company in the Asia/Pacific region.

Total assets: $54,871 million
Current ratio: 1.02
Common shares outstanding: 2,431 million
Return on 1996 shareholders' equity: 44.3%

	1996	1995	1994	1993	1992	1991	1990	1989
Revenues (millions)	69,204	66,071	65,125	60,901	59,131	56,459	51,160	44,759
Net income (millions)	6,303	5,478	4,725	3,568	4,939	4,202	3,540	2,794
Earnings per share	2.56	2.17	1.82	1.35	1.82	1.51	1.28	1.01
Dividends per share	1.47	1.22	1.01	.87	.78	.64	.52	.42
Price: High	39.7	31.5	21.5	25.9	28.9	27.3	17.3	15.3
Low	28.5	18.6	15.8	15.0	23.4	16.1	12.0	8.3

INCOME

Piedmont Natural Gas Company

P. O. Box 33068, Charlotte, NC 28233 □ Investor contact: Headen B. Thomas, (800) 532-0462 (within North Carolina); (800) 438-8410 (all other states) □ Dividend reinvestment plans available: (800) 532-0462 (Within North Carolina); (800) 438-8410 (All Other States) □ Fiscal year ends October 31 □ Listed: NYSE □ Ticker symbol: PNY □ S&P common stock ranking: A- □ Value Line financial strength rating: B++

Piedmont Natural Gas Company is a medium-sized local distribution natural gas utility serving over 567,000 customers in three states: North Carolina, South Carolina, and Tennessee. It also sells propane (bottled gas) to over 48,500 customers in areas where natural gas is not available, normally rural communities. Additionally, the company is engaged in acquiring, marketing, and arranging for the transportation of natural gas to large-volume purchasers and in retailing residential and commercial gas appliances.

Piedmont is the second-largest gas utility in the Southeast. Customer growth in all three states is well above the national average.

The Region Served

The region served by the company is a major center of commerce and one of the fastest-growing in the nation. The company's three-state service area consists of the Piedmont region of the Carolinas—Charlotte, Salisbury, Greensboro, Winston-Salem, High Point, Burlington, and Hickory in North Carolina; Anderson, Greenville, and Spartanburg in South Carolina; and the metropolitan area of Nashville, Tennessee.

In 1996, *Plant Sites and Parks* magazine named North Carolina number one for business relocation and expansion for the third consecutive year. The magazine named South Carolina number four and Tennessee number five. *Site Selection* magazine named North Carolina's business climate number one for the fourth consecutive year, South Carolina number four, and Tennessee number six.

The economic center of the Piedmont area is the Greater Charlotte urban region—sixth-largest in the nation—with over 6 million people within a 100-mile radius and an expanding manufacturing and service economy. Charlotte is the nation's second-largest financial center and headquarters city for NationsBank, the nation's fourth-largest bank, and for First Union National Bank, the sixth-largest. Wachovia Corporation, the nation's twentieth-largest bank, is headquartered in Winston-Salem.

Charlotte/Douglas International Airport, with over 500 flights per day and 21 million passengers annually, is the sixth-largest airline hub in the nation and the fourteenth-busiest airport in the world.

Nashville, the center of a retail trading area of over 2 million people, is world-renowned as an entertainment capital, but healthcare is its largest industry. Columbia/HCA, the world's largest healthcare company, relocated its corporate headquarters to Nashville in 1996.

The area is also home to major transportation, printing, financial, insurance, and communications companies and twenty colleges and universities. Nashville's new 20,000-seat downtown arena opened in December 1996, and the Houston Oilers NFL football team will soon move its franchise to a new stadium now under construction in Nashville.

Highlights for 1996

Net income increased 20.5 percent, to $48.6 million, and earnings per share 15.2 percent, to $1.67. Margin (revenues less the cost of gas) reached $291 million and revenues $685 million. All of these financial results were record achievements.

During the year, 31,200 new natural gas customers were added, surpassing the prior year's record results of 28,500 by 9.5 percent, for an annual growth rate of 6.2 percent—over four times the national average annual growth rate of 1.4 percent. The company now serves 567,000 natural gas customers.

In order to expand the company's distribution system to meet the needs of this customer growth, utility construction expenditures of $98.3 million were required, down slightly from the prior year's $100.8 million.

Shortcomings to Bear in Mind

- Piedmont's capital expenditures over the next few years will likely be higher in its efforts to keep pace with rapid customer growth. External financing will probably be required to support the company's cash flow. Management has indicated that this funding should come in the form of a secondary equity offering in late fiscal 1997 or early in 1998. This would help the company reduce the long-term debt-to-capital ratio.

Reasons to Buy

- The company has an exceptional CEO, John H. Maxheim, a graduate engineer, who served eight years as CEO of United Cities Gas prior to being selected as president of Piedmont Natural Gas in 1978. Since then, Piedmont's roster of customers has climbed from 183,000 to over 525,000, a compound annual rate of 6.4 percent, or close to triple the industry pace. In that same period, gross margin shot up from $44 million to $257 million, an annual growth rate of 10.9 percent. Finally, the company's earnings in those seventeen years have mushroomed from just over $5 million to $40 million, a compound growth rate of 13 percent. It would be difficult to find another gas distributor with such impressive statistics.

  During John Maxheim's years as the leader of Piedmont Natural Gas Company, he has divested a number of small subsidiaries and, at the same time, has managed a substantial merger with Tennessee Natural Resources, the parent company of Nashville Gas Company. He has also orchestrated Piedmont's growth in the propane gas business until today that business is among the twenty largest propane distributors in the country, serving over 48,500 customers.

- Piedmont increased its common stock dividend for eighteen consecutive years through 1996. In the 1986–1996 period, the per-share dividend climbed from $.60 to $1.15, a compound annual growth rate of 6.7 percent, an excellent record for a utility.

- A survey conducted for Piedmont in September of 1996 demonstrated that natural gas continues to gain market share over electricity. Consumer preference and customer loyalty survey results for natural gas heating and water heating were dramatic. Over 93 percent of homeowners who are natural gas customers consider it the best overall heating energy value and would choose it again for a new home.

- Piedmont Natural Gas continues to work with gas industry trade associations to foster the adoption of new uses for natural gas that offer more value than other forms of energy. New markets for natural gas include the year-round loads made possible by greatly improved natural gas cooling equipment for commercial structures, a natural gas heating and cooling unit for residential and small business applications, and natural gas-powered vehicles (NGVs).

  A wide variety of NGVs are now available from the major domestic vehicle manufacturers. NGVs are now a viable option for many fleet owners, such as school systems, transit systems, privately owned companies, and federal, state, and local governments that can refuel their vehicles at central locations.

  In the company's service area, NGVs are operating in the Charlotte-Mecklenburg school systems, the Charlotte branch of the Federal Aviation Administration, the U.S. Post Office in Nashville, and Charlotte/Douglas International Airport. In Greenville, natural gas-powered fork lifts are being utilized in industrial applications. In 1996, Charlotte-Mecklenburg added North Carolina's first school buses manufactured to run exclusively on natural gas to its existing fleet of NGVs that had been converted from gasoline. Finally, more NGV filling stations are opening around the country each year to serve natural gas-powered vehicles, which are predicted to become a more realistic alternative for the general public in the years ahead.

- Analysts view the Weather Normalization Adjustment (WNA) that was approved by all three of PNY's state utility commissions as a key ingredient in enabling the company to effectively manage its cash flow in order the meet the demands of its fast-growing service territory. The WNA formula permits the Company to increase its rates to recover margin losses due to warmer-than-normal weather and requires the company to decrease its rates to refund margin gains due to colder-than-normal weather. Because natural gas utilities are dependent on cold weather to meet their revenue projections, Piedmont has implemented the WNA to help protect it against mild winters. For example, margin increased by 9.5 percent for the six months ending April 1995, while the weather was 12 percent warmer than the same period a year earlier.

- The region's regulatory environment is highly regarded by analysts. This means that requests for rate increases are generally dealt with in a prudent and realistic manner. A good example of this fair-minded regulation is the WNA discussed above. All three states concurred on this concept.

Total assets: $1,064,916
Current ratio: 1.03
Common shares outstanding: 29.5 million
Return on 1996 shareholders' equity: 12.6%

	1996	1995	1994	1993	1992	1991	1990	1989
Revenues (millions)	685	505	575	553	460	412	404	421
Net income (millions)	49	40	36	38	36	21	26	25
Earnings per Share	1.67	1.45	1.35	1.45	1.40	.89	1.22	1.21
Dividends per Share	1.15	1.09	1.01	.95	.91	.87	.83	.79
Price: High	25.8	24.9	23.4	26.4	20.4	16.9	14.9	14.8
Low	20.5	18.3	18.0	18.8	15.4	12.9	12.8	11.5

AGGRESSIVE GROWTH

Pioneer Hi-Bred International, Inc.

700 Capital Square, 400 Locust Street, Des Moines, Iowa 50309 ◻ Investor contact: Dirck Steimel (515) 248-4893 ◻ Dividend reinvestment plan available: (800) 730-4001 ◻ Fiscal year ends August 31 ◻ Listed: NYSE ◻ Ticker symbol: PHB ◻ S&P rating: A- ◻ Value Line financial strength rating: A+

Pioneer Hi-Bred's business is the broad application of the science of genetics. Pioneer was founded in 1926 to apply newly discovered genetic techniques to hybridize corn. Today the company develops, produces, and markets hybrids of corn, sorghum, and sunflowers and varieties of soybeans, alfalfa, wheat, and canola.

Hybrids, crosses of two or more unrelated inbred lines, can be reproduced only by crossing the original parent lines. Thus, a grower must purchase new seed each year to obtain the original hybrid. Varietal crops, such as soybeans and wheat, will reproduce themselves with little or no genetic variation. Growers can save grain from the previous crop for planting. Growers are becoming increasingly aware of the advantages of purchasing "new" seed each year, although in times of cash-flow crisis, they may tend to forgo those advantages.

Pioneer maintains the ownership of and controls the use of inbreds and varieties through patents and the Plant Variety Protection Act. Within the United States, this essentially prohibits other parties from selling seed produced from those inbreds and varieties until such protection expires, usually well after the useful life of the seed.

Outside the United States, the level of protection afforded varies from country to country, according to local law and international agreement. Pioneer also applies for patents on new hybrids moving toward commercialization. The company believes it is vital that products developed by its research programs remain proprietary. They must remain so in order to provide the economic return necessary to support continued research and product development and to generate an adequate return to the company's shareholders.

The company's principal products are hybrid seed corn and soybean seed, which have accounted for about 89 percent of total net sales and substantially 100 percent of operating profits over the last five years. These products are expected to maintain a dominant role in the company's results of operations for the foreseeable future.

About 67 percent of total 1996 sales were made within the United States and Canada (the North American region) and 23 percent in Europe. Pioneer's goal within nonindustrialized nations is to aid the development of the existing seed markets and establish businesses that can grow and prosper.

In North America, the majority of Pioneer brand seed is marketed through independent sales representatives, most of whom are also farmers. In areas outside of the traditional corn belt, seed products are often marketed through dealers and distributors who handle other agricultural supplies. Pioneer products are marketed outside North America through a network of subsidiaries, joint ventures, and independent producer-distributors.

In the production of its commercial seed, the company generally provides the parent seed stock, detasseling and roguing labor, and certain other production inputs. The balance of the labor, equipment, and inputs are supplied by independent growers.

Pioneer brand microbial products include inoculants for high-moisture corn silage, hay, and other forages, and direct-fed microbial products for livestock. This product line is focused on the research and development products containing naturally occurring microorganisms.

The nutrition and industry markets (NIM) group is the worldwide focal point for addressing opportunities driven by the "end use" markets. The primary mission of the NIM group is to ensure that Pioneer is the premier seed supplier in this end-use market segment.

Shortcomings to Bear in Mind

- Two significant factors can determine the volume of seed sold and the related profit: government policies and weather. Government policies affect, among other things, crop acreage and commodity prices. Weather can affect commodity prices, product performance, the company's seed field yields, and planting decisions made by farmers. Compared to hybrid seed, sales and profits from nonhybrid seed are more heavily dependent on commodity prices and the competition from farmer-saved seed. As a result, the margins are narrower and contributions are subject to year-to-year fluctuations.
- The hybrid seed industry is characterized by intense competition. In 1996, Pioneer seed corn held an estimated market share of 44 percent in North America. The next six competitors held an estimated combined market share of

27 percent, with the closest competitor holding a 10 percent share. The remainder of the market is divided among more than 300 companies selling regionally. Pioneer's 1996 purchased soybean seed market share is at the 17 percent level, highest in the industry.

- In some instances, the company's products require government approval before they can be sold commercially. It is expected that a larger number of Pioneer Hi-Bred's future products will also be dependent on government approval.
- Because the seed business is highly seasonal, the company's interim results will not necessarily indicate the results for the full year. Substantially all seed sales are made from late second quarter through the end of the third quarter (February 1 through May 31) of the fiscal year (which ends August 31). Typically, the company operates at a loss during the first and fourth quarters. Varying climatic conditions can change the earnings pattern between quarters. These conditions affect the delivery of seed and can cause a shift in sales between quarters.
- Companies with good prospects often sell at an elevated price/earnings multiple. Try to time your purchase of Pioneer-Hi-Bred so that you avoid paying an excessive price. However, that it easier said than done, since this is an exceptional company.

Reasons to Buy

- Every new product begins with understanding the needs of Pioneer Hi-Bred's customers. After extensive interviews with customers on farms, livestock operations, and in research and test locations, the company is well aware farmers are looking for a corn hybrid with a specific insect resistance. Understandably, farmers want to con-

trol insects and reduce the amount of insecticides they apply.

- Pioneer Hi-Bred has a leading market share position in most countries outside North America in which it operates. Significant markets in which the company operates include: France, Italy, Germany, Hungary, Austria, Mexico, and Brazil. The company's market share within these countries ranges from near 10 percent to more than 60 percent.
- Competition in the seed industry is based primarily on product performance and price. Pioneer Hi-Bred's objective is to produce products that consistently outperform the competition and so command a premium price. The company has been successfully competing on that basis and expects to continue to do so though its extensive investment in research and product development.
- Pioneer Hi-Bred's research and product development activities are directed at products with significant market potential. The company believes that it possesses the largest single proprietary pool of germplasm (defined as hereditary material or genes, the cytoplasm of a germ cell) in the world from which to develop new hybrid and varietal seed products. The majority of the company's seed research is done through classical plant-breeding techniques. However, the use of biotechnology is expected to have an impact on future results, both for Pioneer and the seed industry at large.
- Success in the marketplace will require products that have a complete package of superior genetics. The most important quality in the past for a hybrid or variety has been yield. Pioneer Hi-Bred has been working to learn more about heterosis (hybrid vigor) and its effect on yield and quality. Even though significant yield improvements have been accomplished, the company's plant

breeders feel they are not close to the ceiling on yield. Adding value to a hybrid or variety by incorporating resistance to insects, diseases, or herbicides is also becoming increasingly important. Much effort is being placed on these traits by the company, as well.

- Pioneer Hi-Bred has introduced some 130 new seed corn hybrids and about 80 soybean varieties in North America since 1990. These have added to the company's ability to provide higher-yielding and more valuable products for customers. From 1990 to 1995, the company's seed corn hybrids in North America have out yielded the average of the company's competitors by about 6.5 bushels per acre.

- In addition to agronomic qualities, Pioneer is focusing on the end use of grain for nontraditional customers. With a majority of grain produced in North America fed to livestock, the company is taking steps to improve the value of its product for livestock producers by adding more functional and nutritional qualities, such as improved amino-acid profiles, oil profiles, and digestibility. What's more, Pioneer Hi-Bred also has programs in place pursuing opportunities to provide unique value-added traits for grain processors and food manufacturers, such as starch content, oil profiles, and milling quality.

- An estimated 152 million of the world's corn acres are planted with nonhybrids. Pioneer Hi-Bred already has a presence in most of these regions. China and the former Soviet Union are significant markets where Pioneer has a limited presence. However, the company is actively pursuing market opportunities in both of these markets.

Total assets: $1,422 million
Current ratio: 1.57
Common shares outstanding: 82 million
Return on 1996 shareholders' equity: 21.9%

	1996	1995	1994	1993	1992	1991	1990	1989
Revenues (millions)	1,721	1,532	1,479	1,343	1,262	1,125	965	867
Net income (millions)	223	183	187	138	152	104	73	73
Earnings per share	2.68	2.16	2.11	1.53	1.68	1.15	.78	.77
Dividends per share	.83	.71	.59	.50	.40	.39	.39	.36
Price: High	74.0	60.1	40.5	39.5	30.3	24.8	15.8	15.1
Low	49.3	32.5	29.5	24.1	19.8	11.8	10.4	11.2

GROWTH AND INCOME

Pitney-Bowes, Inc.

World Headquarters, 1 Elmcroft Road, Stamford, CT 06926-0700 □ Investor contact: Michael Monahan (203) 351-6349 □ Dividend reinvestment plan available: (800) 648-8170 □ Listed: NYSE □ Ticker symbol: PBI □ S&P rating: A+ □ Value Line financial strength rating: A

A pioneer and world leader in mailing systems (with an 87 percent share of the U.S. market), Pitney Bowes is a multinational manufacturing and marketing company that provides mailing, shipping, dictating, copying, and facsimile systems; item identification and tracking systems and supplies; mailroom, reprographics, and related management services; and product financing.

The key to Pitney Bowes will probably continue to be consistency rather than spectacular growth, in view of the maturity of its highly profitable postage meter rental business and the moderate growth of some of its other annuity revenues, such as service.

On the other hand, analysts believe that the stock has limited downside risk; it should appeal largely to long-term investors.

Pitney Bowes is best known as the worldwide leader in mailing systems. It markets a full line of mailing systems, shipping and weighing systems, addressing systems, production mail systems, folding and inserting systems, as well as mailing software.

Mailing Systems has a direct sales and service force of more than 6,600 people in fifteen countries, with dealers and distributors in more than one hundred countries. Mailing Systems develops and manufactures mailing products in the United States and the United Kingdom.

LPC, a division of Mailing System located in Illinois, offers a full range of advanced software and services for business communications, and marketing and mailing applications to *Fortune* 1000 companies. LPC changed its name to Pitney Bowes Software Systems in 1995.

Shipping and Weighing Systems (SWS) provides parcel and freight information and automation systems for the shipping and transportation management functions of the logistics market.

SWS's products are marketed through Mailing Systems' worldwide distribution channels, with particular emphasis on North America. Service is provided by specially trained service representatives and a National Remote Diagnostic Center.

Pitney Bowes Transportation Software, a division of Pitney Bowes located in Minnesota, markets and develops logistics management solutions and provides consulting services.

Other Businesses of Pitney Bowes

The company's other businesses are also important. A brief description of each follows.

Pitney Bowes Management Services (PBMS) is a leading provider of facilities management services for the business support functions of creating, processing, storage, retrieval, distribution, and tracking of information, messages, documents, and packages.

Using the latest available technology, PBMS manages mail centers, copy and reprographic centers, facsimile services, electronic printing and imaging services, and records management services for customers across the United States, as well as in Canada and the United Kingdom.

Pitney Bowes Facsimile Systems is a leading supplier of high-quality facsimile equipment to the business market. It is the only facsimile system supplier in the United States that markets solely through its own direct sales force nationwide.

Pitney Bowes' Copier Systems concentrates on serving larger corporations with multi unit installations of its full line of equipment.

Pitney Bowes Financial Services provides lease financing programs for customers who use products marketed by Pitney Bowes companies.

Shortcomings to Bear in Mind

■ There appears to be competition lurking in the wings. In the first nine months of 1996, for instance, Pitney-Bowes lost 2 percent of its customers to competitors. The bulk of the corporate migration to electronic machines is yet to come.

Even the U.S. Postal Service is stirring. For instance, profit-minded Postmaster General Marvin Runyon is beginning to get nervous. To hold and expand business in a digital world with aggressive private carriers like Federal Express and United Parcel Service—not to mention E-mail—Runyon needs more innovative postage equipment. To get the new technology into the marketplace quickly, Runyon wants electronic meters to replace all mechanical meters by March 1999. The Postal System, which processes some $20 billion of metered mail each year, hopes that the new computer-based approach will reduce fraud. Mechanical meters can be rigged to print unpaid postage—costing the agency as much as $100 million annually in lost revenue.

- Several small newcomers are racing to develop a computer-generated stamp that would replace the old, expensive system of stamping inky, eagle-adorned postmarks onto envelopes. The new "stamps" would include a bold, black bar code below the traditional postmark. Instead of going to the post office to purchase postage in bulk, users would save time by simply ordering and downloading stamps off the Internet and printing them onto envelopes.
- According to some observers, the company is facing the possibility of declining postal usage as more businesses switch their communications to the Internet.

Reasons to Buy

- Some observers are concerned that the volume of mail may be declining, as people rely more on the telephone and their connection with the Internet. Pitney's CEO, Michael Critelli, responds to this concern, "Outside experts confirm our internal findings that mail volumes worldwide will continue to increase for the next ten years. Lots of paper-based communication is going away, but it is more than being offset by growth engines."

According to Mr. Critelli, there is explosive growth in the direct mail marketing. To be sure, individual mailings are falling a couple of percent each year. On the other hand, direct mail is climbing at a far faster pace, between 6 and 8 percent a year. As a result, says the Pitney CEO, the overall volume of mail is going up each year. What's more, the same trend is visible in other developed markets. In the developing world, moreover, the growth of mail is even more explosive. China, for example, is registering increases of 25 percent a year.

- Still another development revolves around infrastructure. Along with the much-desired provisions of telephones, gas, water, or electricity come less-welcome bills for these services. This makes Michael Critelli respond enthusiastically, "The number of telephones in emerging markets is going to double over the next five years. We love the monthly billings."
- Deregulation is another growth engine for Pitney-Bowes. When governments sell off their ownership of businesses, private businesses step in and mail soars. Critelli points to Thailand, where government deregulation of the insurance market three years ago produced "astronomical" increases in the number of newly issued insurance policies, all involving regular billing.
- Operating profits at Pitney-Bowes' largest business, mail systems, should benefit from a host of new products, along with greater operating efficiencies. New software-driven equipment and systems utilize advanced digital technology, which, in turn, is derived from both its own research program and joint ventures with various partners, including IBM.
- In 1994, Pitney Bowes signed an important pact with the Chinese Ministry of

Telecommunications and Posts. Pitney Bowes will be the first company to help the Chinese modernize commercial mail processing. China is one of the fastest growing mail markets in the world.

- A recent Pitney Bowes/Gallup survey revealed that mail center expenditures account for more than 9 percent of *Fortune* 500 companies' total operating costs. PBI's new addressing and postal coding products provide cost-effective solutions by allowing mailers to increase productivity, improve efficiency, and take advantage of U.S. Postal Service work-sharing discounts.

- In the United States, 90 percent of businesses have 50 or fewer employees. Significantly, the vast majority do not have mailing systems. Pitney Bowes views this as an opportunity to bring cost-effective mailing solutions to the fastest-growing market in the country. As a consequence, in 1994, PBI introduced a series of new mailing products specifically designed for small businesses.

- Of the more than 2,500 stocks traded on the New York Stock Exchange, Pitney Bowes is one of only eighteen common stocks that have consecutive

double-digit dividend increases from 1983 through 1996.

- Pitney Bowes has a number of businesses that lag the economic cycle, but they should also resist a downturn. About two-thirds of total revenues come from annuity sources such as postage meter rentals, rentals of other mailing and business equipment, facilities management, rental, finance, service, and supply revenues.

- Pitney Bowes Management Services is expanding its existing business by incorporating technology-based services, such as on-demand document printing from electronic data provided by customers and services to enhance the processing and distribution of computer-generated mail, messages, and documents.

- In 1992, Pitney Bowes launched the Paragon mail processor as the high-tech cornerstone of its Mail Center 2000 state-of-the-art mailing system. This high-speed (240 pieces per minute) automated mail processor has no rival in sight and is a genuine cost-saver.

Total assets: $8,156 million
Current ratio: 0.69
Common shares outstanding: 148 million
Return on 1996 shareholders' equity: 21.0%

	1996	1995	1994	1993	1992	1991	1990	1989
Revenues (millions)	3,859	3,555	3,271	3,543	3,434	3,333	3,196	2,876
Net income (millions)	469	408	348	369	312	288	259	253
Earnings per share	3.12	2.68	2.21	2.32	1.96	1.80	1.62	1.59
Dividends per share	1.38	1.20	1.04	.90	.78	.70	.60	.52
Price: High	61.4	48.3	46.4	44.5	41.0	32.8	26.8	27.4
Low	41.9	30.0	29.3	36.3	28.0	19.0	13.5	20.4

PPG Industries, Inc.

One PPG Place, Pittsburgh, PA 15272 ◻ Investor contact: Douglas B. Atkinson (412) 434-3312 ◻ Dividend reinvestment plan available: (412) 434-3312 ◻ Listed: NYSE ◻ Ticker symbol: PPG ◻ S&P rating: A- ◻ Value Line financial strength rating: A++

PPG Industries, a diversified global manufacturer, is a leading supplier of products for manufacturing, construction, automotive, chemical processing, and numerous other world industries.

Established in 1883, the Pittsburgh-based company makes decorative and protective coatings, flat glass and fabricated glass products, continuous-strand fiber glass, and industrial and specialty chemicals.

PPG is a leading worldwide producer of chlorine and caustic soda, vinyl chloride monomer, and chlorinated solvents. Specialty chemicals include silica compounds, surfactants, photochromic lenses, and fine chemicals, such as optical resins, pool and water-treatment chemicals, phosgene derivatives, and flame retardants.

PPG operates seventy-four major manufacturing facilities in Australia, Canada, China, France, Germany, Ireland, Italy, Mexico, the Netherlands, Portugal, Spain, Taiwan, the United Kingdom, and the United States.

To benefit its customers through leadership in technology, the company conducts research and development at nine facilities throughout the world.

Over the past two decades, PPG has transformed itself from primarily a North American commodity producer to a global manufacturer of glass, coatings, and chemicals. Its international business contributed 33 percent of its sales and 21 percent of its operating profits in 1996. Sales and operating profits by group in 1996 were as follows:

	Sales	Profits
Glass	38%	32%
Coatings and resins	40	40
Chemicals	22	28

The company is one of the world's largest producers of flat glass and fabricated glass. Major markets include original and replacement glass for automobiles, commercial and residential construction, aircraft transparencies, furniture, and glass products for various industrial uses.

PPG is the world's second-largest producer of continuous-strand and chopped-strand fiber glass, including plastic reinforcement yarns and industrial and decorative yarns, for transportation, construction, electronics, recreational, and industrial uses.

PPG is the world's leading producer of original and refinish automotive and industrial coatings (used in appliance, container, and industrial equipment markets) and is a major North American supplier of architectural coatings. It also produces metal pretreatments and adhesives and sealants for the automotive industry.

PPG Industries is a leading worldwide producer of chlorine and caustic soda (used in a wide variety of industrial applications), vinyl chloride monomer (for use in polyvinyl chloride resins), and chlorinated solvents. These commodity chemicals are highly cyclical in nature. PPG has increased its chlor-alkali production for eleven consecutive years without significant new investment.

Specialty chemicals (about one-third of chemical sales) include silica compounds, surfactants, photochromic lenses and optical resins, and fine chemicals (pool and water-treatment chemicals, phosgene derivatives, and flame retardants). PPG continues to increase the proportion of specialty chemicals sales (which are generally less subject to cyclical business factors), with a long-term goal of equaling commodity sales.

Shortcomings to Bear in Mind

- Although PPG is less susceptible to the business cycle than it has been in the past, it is still vulnerable to vagaries of the automotive and housing markets.
- PPG is not a classic growth stock, with steadily increasing earnings. For instance, earnings fell from the prior year twice in the last ten years (in 1989 and 1991).
- PPG's earnings momentum lost steam in the fourth quarter of 1996. Reason: The price of natural gas, a major cost in the production of glass and chemicals, was dramatically higher.

Reasons to Buy

- PPG has had outstanding success in increasing productivity and cutting costs in the last ten years. Analysts anticipate continued positive impact from such factors during the next few years, in particular within the coatings and resins group.
- As compared with the last business cycle, PPG now has more international business and, through capacity expansion and acquisitions, coupled with the elimination of unprofitable and low-return businesses, a greater reliance on the high-margin fiber glass, specialty chemicals, and auto aftermarket businesses.
- The company has developed a broad portfolio of products with good growth potential. One of PPG's strategies is to increase the proportion of specialty chemicals it produces. A recent success

story is Transition eyewear lenses, which have experienced robust demand.

- PPG has increased its dividend for twenty-six consecutive years and has paid dividends without interruption since 1899. In the 1986–1996 period, moreover, the company increased its per-share dividend from $.47 to $1.26, a compound annual growth rate of 10.4 percent. During the same ten-year span, PPG's earnings climbed from $1.33 to $3.96, a compound growth rate of 11.5 percent. What's more, for the past thirty years, PPG has increased its earnings at an average rate of 10 percent, which compares favorably with that of the S&P 500, at only 7 percent.
- In 1996, an *Industry Week* magazine panel named PPG Industries as one of the world's 100 best-managed companies.
- Geographic expansion in 1996 was highlighted by business ventures in the Asia-Pacific region and Latin America. In the Asia-Pacific area, the company's participation is characterized by joint ventures in which PPG has limited its investment exposure. The company now has six manufacturing operations in China, including two world-class float-glass plants, as well as major facilities in Taiwan, South Korea, and Japan.

   Further, new growth opportunities have emerged in Latin America. In 1996, the company modernized its extensive coatings manufacturing operation in Mexico and entered the automotive original coatings markets in Argentina and Brazil.
- In automotive refinishes, PPG's emphasis continues to be on supplying high-volume collision centers. A key part of the company's marketing effort is to provide support services to help such centers improve their operating efficiency. Through PPG's certified collision center program, which ensures

professional competence, about 4,500 centers and 17,000 technicians have received certification.

In product development, the company concentrates on waterborne and lower volatile-organic-compound coatings because of their environmental benefits. In addition, PPG provided new, faster-drying Deltron coatings, which improve body shop productivity.

- To expand European operations, the company formed PPG Industries Poland to transfer technology to a Polish glass-maker and supply fabricated glass from that manufacturer to Fiat Poland for vehicles assembled in that country.

- Enhancing the company's prospects in automotive replacement glass is the new majority-owned company, LYNX Services from PPG, LLC. The service simplifies access to the insurance business for glass installers and gives them marketing support for insurance accounts, along with training and certification, electronic data processing services, and computer software to facilitate claims submission and billing.

- PPG Industries looks to technology to play a key role in its financial progress.

In 1996, the company spent $255 million on research and development, which has provided a constant stream of new products and improvements.

During 1996, among other new products for the consumer market, PPG introduced Transitions III variable-tint plastic lenses, which darken and lighten faster than the previous generation of lenses. New products also include Olympic stains for home interiors and, through a pressure-treated-wood provider, a wood treated with Olympic protection products for decks and other outdoor structures. Additionally, a unique PPG barrier coating to improve shelf life for carbonated beverages in plastic containers was recognized by a leading research journal as one of the 100 top developments of the year.

For industrial customers, the company's many new products included the Sungate antenna windshield for 1997 General Motors minivans, a highly dispersible silica to improve tread wear in tires, and a higher-purity chlorinated benzene going into a high-performance thermoplastic for numerous automotive and electronic uses.

Total assets: $6,441 million
Current ratio: 1.30
Common shares outstanding: 188 million
Return on 1996 shareholders' equity: 29.5%

	1996	1995	1994	1993	1992	1991	1990	1989
Revenues (millions)	7,219	7,058	6,331	5,754	5,814	5,673	6,021	5,734
Net income (millions)	744	748	566	377	342	201	475	465
Earnings per share	3.96	3.70	2.67	1.78	1.61	.95	2.22	2.09
Dividends per share	1.26	1.18	1.12	1.04	.94	.86	.82	.74
Price: High	62.3	47.9	42.1	38.1	34.2	29.7	27.6	23.0
Low	42.9	34.9	33.8	29.7	25.0	20.8	17.3	18.5

Praxair, Inc.

39 Old Ridgebury Road, Danbury, CT 06810-5113 ❑ **Investor contact: Joseph S. Cappello (203) 837-2073** ❑ **Dividend reinvestment plan available: (800) 524-4458** ❑ **Listed: NYSE** ❑ **Ticker symbol: PX** ❑ **S&P rating: Not rated** ❑ **Value Line financial strength rating: B++**

Praxair, Inc., serves a diverse group of industries through the production, sale, and distribution of industrial gases and high-performance surface coatings, along with related services, materials, and systems.

Praxair, which was spun off to Union Carbide shareholders in June 1992, is the largest producer of industrial gases in North and South America; it is the third-largest company of its kind in the world.

Praxair's major customers include aerospace, chemicals, electronics, food processing, healthcare, glass, metal fabrication, petroleum, primary metals, as well as pulp and paper companies.

As a pioneer in the industrial gases industry, Praxair has been a leader in developing a wide range of proprietary and patented applications and supply-system technology.

The company's primary industrial gases products are atmospheric gases (oxygen, nitrogen, argon, and rare gases) and process gases (helium, hydrogen, electronics gases, and acetylene). Praxair also designs, engineers, and supervises construction of cryogenic and noncryogenic supply systems.

Praxair Surface Technologies provides metallic and ceramic coatings and powders used on metal surfaces to resist wear, high temperatures, and corrosion. Aircraft engines are its primary market, but it serves others, including the printing, textile, chemical, and primary metals markets, and provides aircraft engine and airframe component overhaul services.

The company was founded in the United States in 1907 as Linde Air Products Company.

Praxair operates internationally, with 48 percent of sales in the United States; 14 percent in Europe; 22 percent in Latin America; and 16 percent in Canada, Mexico, Asia, and others.

The purchase of CBI Industries in early 1996 made PX the world's largest supplier of carbon dioxide. The acquisition significantly added exposure to more stable good markets and expanded Praxair's interest in South America and Asia.

Shortcomings to Bear in Mind

- The company's balance sheet is somewhat leveraged, since it has nearly as much debt as equity. As a consequence, the Value Line financial strength rating is only average, at B++. On the other hand, this an improvement over the rating given when I did my first edition. The rating then was only B.

Reasons to Buy

- Since the spin-off in 1992, Praxair has accomplished the following:
  - Almost doubled sales
  - Raised market capitalization from $2 billion to more than $7 billion
  - Expanded its geographic reach from fifteen countries to forty
  - Increased its dividend every year
  - Invested a record $3 billion in new plants, acquisitions, and geographic expansion
  - Strengthened its balance sheet and credit rating

- In 1996, Praxair received the U.S. Department of Energy's Best-in-Category Award in Industrial Technology for Energy Efficiency and Renewable Energy. This is the fourth DOE award Praxair has received in two years, recognizing the environmental and energy-efficiency benefits that Praxair's oxy-fuel combustion technology and advanced air separation systems have brought to the glass industry. Use of oxygen enhances productivity and reduces emissions of nitrogen oxides in glass-making. Acceptance of this technology by customers worldwide has grown substantially in only four years, yet significant additional growth potential remains, according to Praxair management.

- Praxair is also benefiting from a resurgence of commercial vitality in the steel industry, thanks in part to increased use of industrial gases. In December of 1996, Praxair received a patent for its oxygen-based, post combustion technology for electric-arc furnaces, which improves productivity while reducing energy consumption and hazardous emissions. Another technology, nitrogen slag-splashing, more than quadruples the refractory life of the basis oxygen furnace at integrated mills. Finally, argon increases the quality and yield of the continuous caster.

  Increases in unit consumption of oxygen per ton of steel produced are expected to continue since steel companies already have invested in technology that will expand oxygen use in both blast furnaces and electric-arc furnaces. Adoption of new technologies such as coal-based smelting processes and oxy-fuel-based re-heating offer potential for further significant growth beyond the year 2000.

- In 1996, Praxair started up the world's largest nitrogen membrane plant at S. A. Distrigas in Loenhout, Belgium. Its capacity of 19,100 cubic meters per hour compares favorably to the more typical 3,000 to 3,500 cubic meters per hour. Praxair operates and maintains more than 550 membrane nitrogen systems at customer sites worldwide.

- Acquisitions in 1996 strengthened packaged gases and surface technologies. Praxair's North American packaged gases business, Praxair Distribution, Inc., considerably strengthened its position during 1996, incorporating Liquid Carbonic's strong specialty gases business, and acquiring seven independent distributors with annual sales totaling $85 million. Included was Parry Corporation of Akron, Ohio, with $30 million in annual sales and fifteen locations, which enabled Praxair to establish a new hub in Ohio and western Pennsylvania. At year-end 1996, Praxair Distribution had more than 390 locations in the United States and Canada. Combined sales of majority- and minority-owned distributors was $838 million.

- The addition of carbon dioxide to Praxair's portfolio opens new avenues for growth in relatively noncyclical markets: food preservation, beverage carbonation, and water treatment. Looking ahead, increased demand for beverage carbonation and water treatment, particularly in emerging South American and Asian markets, promises to generate continued growth. Supplying global beverage-carbonation customers also leads to opportunities in new markets for other Praxair products and technology. Use of carbon dioxide in new food-preservation markets, such as bakery goods and dairy products, also is on the verge of rapid growth.

- The 1996 acquisition of Liquid Carbonic brought Praxair into Thailand for the first time, and the company expanded its strong position in Korea. In September of 1996, Praxair formed a joint venture that will build Praxair's first carbon dioxide plant in China. Located in Beijing, the plant will supply the beverage, food, medical, textile, environmental protection, and metals industries. Praxair holds a 60 percent share in the venture; a subsidiary of Beijing Chemical Industry Group Company holds the balance.

- Early in 1997, Shanghai Praxair Vidian, Inc., a joint venture between Praxair and Shanghai Maike Electronics, was selected to supply ultra-high-purity gases to a major new semiconductor manufacturing facility to be built by Shanghai Hua Hong Microelectronics Company Ltd. Praxair has four other joint ventures in China.
- In 1996, several agreements were reached to expand Praxair's business in India. The company is building and will operate a cryogenic air separation plant to supply oxygen to Kalyani Ferrous Industries' steel plant in Karnataka State by the fourth quarter of 1997. Praxair's other joint venture in India, Jindal Praxair Oxygen Company Ltd., is constructing another plant in Karnataka State that will supply oxygen to a Jindal steel plant beginning in late 1997. A second Jindal Praxair plant will start up in early 1999.
- Sales in Europe increased 10 percent in 1996, and operating profit increased 19 percent on a pro forma basis, excluding CBI integration charges. These results are due to continued cost reductions, acquisitions, and new business. Praxair entered a new geographic market by acquiring a majority interest in Maxima Air Separation Center Ltd., Israel's second-largest producer of industrial and specialty gases. The acquisition gives Praxair an opportunity to supply Israel's growing semiconductor industry.

Another new market is Poland, where Liquid Carbonic operated several plants and filling stations and enjoyed a strong market position.

- In recent years, Praxair has developed noncryogenic air-separation technology, which allows lower-cost delivery to customers who have smaller volume needs. By sacrificing a small amount of purity, these customers can purchase a gas that meets customer needs at a discount to the cost of traditional supplies of product in cryogenic liquid form. This product is less expensive for Praxair to produce and thus is higher-margined relative to "cryo" liquid. Demand for it is growing dramatically.
- The company has refocused strategies for the electronics market, which allows Praxair to capitalize on growth opportunities. Its packaged-gases strategies and geographic expansion enhance the company's ability to provide high-quality, total gas-management services to the worldwide electronics market.
- New developments in combustion and oxidation processes—with emphasis on steel, chemicals, glass, and pulp and paper markets—promise to increase the use of oxygen, much of which can be supplied through Praxair's state-of-the-art, noncryogenic supply systems.
- Producers of wine bottles, light bulbs, and construction glass use Praxair's oxygen. Praxair's argon, krypton, neon, and xenon also are used in the production of light bulbs.
- Metal fabricators use Praxair's blended shielding gases to increase productivity and decrease fume levels. Based on argon, helium, or hydrogen, these blends are used to produce a wide range of products, from ships and chemical plants to milk containers and motor cycles.
- By the end of the decade, Praxair estimates that noncryogenic oxygen and

nitrogen supply systems will achieve 40 percent penetration of liquid markets worldwide. In many markets, this will help optimize local business performance and moderate the need for new liquid capacity.

Total assets: $7,538 million
Current ratio: 0.65
Common shares outstanding: 156 million
Return on 1996 shareholders' equity: 22%

	1996	1995	1994	1993	1992	1991	1990	1989
Revenues (millions)	4,449	3,146	2,711	2,433	2,604	2,469	2,420	2,073
Net income (millions)	282	262	203	118	(60)	107	120	88
Earnings per share	1.77	1.82	1.45	1.06	.64	.84	.85	.62
Dividends per share	.38	.32	.28	.25	.125			
Price: High	50.1	34.1	24.5	18.6	17.5			
Low	31.5	19.8	16.3	14.1	13.6			

CONSERVATIVE GROWTH

The Procter & Gamble Company

One Procter & Gamble Plaza, Cincinnati, Ohio 45202 ◻ Investor contact: G. A. Dowdell (513) 983-1100 ◻ Dividend reinvestment plan available: (800) 742-6253 ◻ Listed: NYSE ◻ Fiscal year ends June 30 ◻ Ticker symbol: PG ◻ S&P rating: A ◻ Value Line financial strength rating: A++

Procter & Gamble markets a broad range of laundry, cleaning, paper, beauty care, healthcare, food, and beverage products, which are sold in more than 140 countries. Leading brands include Tide, Ariel, Crest, Pampers, Pantene, Crisco, Vicks, and Max Factor.

Nor is this the extent of its long list of well-known products. Others (among P&G's more than 300 brands) include Bounty, Charmin Ultra, Pert Plus, Head & Shoulders, Vidal Sassoon, Folgers coffee, Alldays Pantyliners, Camay soap, Prell, Secret, Cheer, Oxydol, Ivory, Zest, Comet, Safeguard, Dawn, Downy, Scope, Cover Girl, Noxema, Old Spice, Aleve, Pepto Bismol, Metamucil, Pringles, Cascade, Hawaiian Punch, and Bold.

Based in Cincinnati, the company has operations in fifty-eight countries and employs 99,200.

Procter & Gamble is a huge company, with 1996 sales of $35.3 billion. In the same fiscal year (which ended June 30, 1996), earnings per share advanced to $4.29. Dividends also climbed—as they have for many years—from $1.40 to $1.60.

Nor did P&G skimp on investment in its future in 1996. Capital expenditures totaled nearly $2.2 billion. Similarly, research and development costs climbed to more than $1.2 billion, its highest level ever. These are both key numbers and are indicative of a company that is not too content to rest on its laurels.

Such outstanding results tend to dispel the notion that large companies are only for widows and orphans. In my estimation, Procter & Gamble is a "core holding," a term used by my profession to indicate a stock you "must own."

Shortcomings to Bear in Mind

■ The company's new fat substitute, olestra, has been attacked by the Center for Science in the Public Interest, a Washington consumer group. It alleges consumers are experiencing "severe" gastrointestinal disturbances caused by olestra. The group wants olestra banned. In its defense, Procter & Gamble has asserted for years—and the Food and Drug Administration agrees—that olestra is safe for use in savory snacks. Even so, the FDA requires that products made with the new fat substitute carry the informational label saying it "may cause abdominal cramping and loose stools."

- The company's many attributes are no secret on Wall Street, which means the price of Procter & Gamble may be too high by historical standards.

Reasons to Buy

- In April of 1997, P&G announced the acquisition of Tambrands, Inc., for which it paid $1.85 billion. Tambrands has a 44 percent share of the international market, with $662 million in global sales in 1996, and close to a 50 percent share of the domestic market. The company sells Tampax in more than 150 countries. The CEO of Procter & Gamble said his company would look to increase Tampax sales in more countries, noting that Latin America and Asia account for less than 5 percent of the brand's volume. What's more, P&G wants to increase the U.S. market by developing new feminine hygiene products. Procter & Gamble's Always brand is the top sanitary pad in the United States (with a 36.3 percent market share).

- In mid-May of 1997, Procter & Gamble agreed to pay $135 million to Regeneron Pharmaceuticals, Inc., in a major new research effort to develop treatments for arthritis, cancer, and cardiovascular diseases. The pact provides a crucial cash infusion and deep-pockets partner for Regeneron, a biotech boutique known for an inability to bring products to the market despite cutting-edge science. For P&G, the ten-year pact represents a significant new step in the company's plan to become a major player in the pharmaceutical industry. Pharmaceutical sales now provide about $500 million of the company's $35 billion in annual sales.

- Procter & Gamble sees the importance of expanding its lineup of global brands. For example, in *Brandweek* magazine's ranking of "Super Brands," P&G led the list of companies in the categories in which it competes. *Brandweek* included seventeen P&G brands among its list of Super Brands. The next-closest competitor had eight.

- Tide detergent has been the U.S. market leader for nearly 50 years. It is now the leader in Canada, Saudi Arabia, and Morocco and moving toward leadership in Russia and China. What's more, Tide's future is bright. In 1996, the company introduced Tide Ultra 2—a new generation of Tide that represents the latest of more than sixty performance improvements since the brand was introduced. Tide is the company's single largest brand. In addition, Tide is the sixth-largest of all brand-name products sold in domestic grocery stores.

- Head & Shoulders shampoo has been the U.S. market leader virtually since it was introduced in 1961. Today, it is quickly becoming a global market leader as well, with growing businesses in nearly forty countries. Finally, there are many other P&G products that are on their way to becoming strong global brands, such as Oil of Olay and Old Spice.

- Procter & Gamble has a long history of being among the technology pacesetters. Today, the company has more than 250 proprietary technologies in the marketplace, technologies that provide a clear-cut advantage for brands like Bounty paper towels. What's more, P&G is accelerating its pace of innovation. In 1995, for example, the company filed for more than 17,000 patents worldwide—a 35 percent increase over 1994 and a 60 percent increase over 1993.

- In the realm of new developments, Procter & Gamble has come out with what could be the biggest potential blockbuster in the entire food industry—olestra, a fat substitute that was approved by the Food and Drug Administration after a twenty-five-year review. The company's trade name for olestra is Olean. P&G is predicting that within a few years, Olean will be a $1-billion ingredient in the $1.6 billion market for oils used in the snack-food industry. That estimate doesn't count possible revenue from the $1.2 billion in oil sold to U.S. restaurants for cooking french fries.

- On a worldwide basis, Procter & Gamble has reduced prices on many of its products while also building margins and improving overall product performance. Since 1992/93, for example, list prices (excluding coffee) have declined $1 billion.

  This price reduction largely reflects the move to value pricing, as the company has eliminated inefficient promotion costs by rolling them into lower list prices. Through this structural change, P&G has been able to significantly reduce the net price consumers pay for its products.

  In addition to price reductions on established brands, the company is introducing economy-priced brands in markets where consumer purchasing power is most restricted. Pampers Uni in Latin America is a good example.

  In Eastern Europe, the company's Feminine Protection business in Poland is up sixfold behind the introduction of Always Classic, a lower-priced feminine protection pad. And in India, P&G was able to triple its Bar Soap volume with new Camay Popular, an economy-priced version of Camay.

  Whether Procter is reducing prices on established brands or introducing new, economy-priced products, the strategy is the same: to offer superior performance at a competitive price. What's more, the strategy is working. In 1994/95, nearly three-fourths of the company's global categories worldwide maintained or expanded market share.

- Volume growth, driven by innovation and lower prices, is an important contributor to higher earnings. An essential element of this has been sharp cost control throughout the organization, which P&G has pursued aggressively for the past several years.

  For example, Product Supply, the company's purchasing, engineering, manufacturing, and distribution organization, has led a breakthrough effort to reduce the total delivered costs of P&G's products. Their goal, established in 1991, was to hold these costs flat on a per-case basis for four years.

  They exceeded this goal, not only offsetting inflation and the cost of products improvements, but actually reducing costs by over $1 per case, compared with the 1990/91 base. This equates to about $1.6 billion in savings, further enhancing the company's ability to price competitively while still building margins.

- Today, about half of P&G's sales come from North America, yet 95 percent of the world's population lives *outside* that region.

  According to CEO John Pepper, "If we can achieve these levels of success around the world in just our existing businesses, we'll more than double our current sales and profits."

  Durk Jager, P&G's chief operating

officer, points out, "Our laundry business is a good example of this growth opportunity. We're already the world's leader in this category, with a global market share of 24 percent. But in over a dozen countries, our laundry share is above 50 percent. If we can achieve that leadership level globally, we'll add an additional $6 billion in sales."

"This tremendous potential for growth exists in category after category," states Procter & Gamble's annual report. Capitalizing on this potential will not be easy, but the company will pursue it by staying focused on the company's key value and globalization strategies, while placing particular emphasis on three fundamental areas:

- Better products at more competitive prices
- Deeper, broader cost control
- Faster, more effective globalization

■ "Product innovation is driving the growth of our European business," says Harald Einsmann, a P&G executive vice president.

The company's European business has grown substantially over the past few years, with sales reaching $11 billion in fiscal 1995. The largest contributor to this growth has been a constant stream of product innovations on core brands.

Ariel laundry detergent is a good example. Ariel, the number one detergent brand in Europe, has been setting standards for cleaning performance since it was introduced in the late 1960s.

In recent years, several innovations, including Ariel Liquid, Ariel Color, and popular refill packs, have attracted new consumers to Ariel. What's more, Ariel has led the European market trend to more compact products, most recently with the introduction of Ariel Futur, a reduced-dosage product that uses a completely new ingredient system to deliver improved cleaning performance.

Today, Ariel's volume and share are at their highest levels ever in Europe, and the brand is growing elsewhere in the world as well. Ariel is now sold in more than thirty countries and, along with Tide, has established P&G as the leader of the global laundry detergent category.

■ P&G's Asia region, which includes the Pacific Rim and Japan, is the most densely populated area in the world, with over 3 billion people. Procter's brands are sold to nearly 95 percent of those consumers, reaching more than a billion in China alone.

■ Procter & Gamble is entering new categories and introducing new brands throughout the world. From new categories like fine fragrances to new brands such as Olay Body Wash and Olay Bath Bar, new P&G businesses are building a foundation for future growth.

Total assets: $27,730 million
Current ratio: 1.41
Common shares outstanding: 682 million
Return on 1996 shareholders' equity: 26%

	1996	1995	1994	1993	1992	1991	1990	1989
Revenues (millions)	35,284	33,434	30,296	30,433	29,362	27,026	24,081	21,398
Net income (millions)	3,046	2,645	2,211	2,015	1,872	1,773	1,477	1,206
Earnings per share	4.29	3.71	3.09	2.82	2.62	2.46	2.07	1.78
Dividends per share	1.60	1.40	1.24	1.10	1.03	.98	.88	.75
Price: High	111.0	81.6	64.6	58.9	55.8	47.7	45.6	35.2
Low	79.4	60.6	51.3	45.3	45.1	38.0	20.9	21.1

Russell Corporation

P. O. Box 272, Alexander City, Alabama 35011 □ Investor contact: K. Roger Holliday (205) 329-4832 □
Dividend reinvestment plan available: (205) 329-4832 □ Listed: NYSE □ Ticker symbol: RML □ S&P
rating: B+ □ Value Line financial strength rating: B+

Russell is a vertically integrated manufacturer of activewear, athletic uniforms, knit shirts, leisure apparel, licensed sports apparel, sports and casual socks, as well as a comprehensive line of lightweight, yarn-dyed, woven fabrics. Over 90 percent of the company's total revenues are derived from completed apparel, with the balance from woven fabrics. The company's products are sold in ninety countries.

The company's manufacturing operations include the entire process of converting raw fibers into finished apparel and fabrics.

The company's products are marketed under various trade names, including Russell Athletic, Jerzees, Cross Creek, The Game, Chalk Lines, and Locker Line.

Apparel is marketed to sporting goods dealers, department and specialty stores, mass merchants, golf pro shops, college bookstores, distributors, screen printers, and mail order houses.

Under the Russell Athletic label, the Athletic Division, believed to be the largest U.S. manufacturer of athletic uniforms, supplies uniforms nationwide to professional, collegiate, high school, and other teams, as well as individuals.

In addition, this division markets activewear.

Under the Jerzees label and private labels, the Knit Apparel Division produces a wide variety of knitted apparel, including fleece sportswear, such as sweatshirts, sweatpants, and lightweight sportswear.

Cross Creek Apparel (acquired in 1988) designs and markets high-quality knit products, including placket, turtle-neck, and rugby knits.

Russell Corp. U.K. (1989) produces fleece garments and T-shirts for the United Kingdom and Europe.

The Game, Inc., is a wholesale distributor of high-quality, licensed collegiate and professional caps and apparel.

A Review of 1996

For the twenty-first consecutive year, sales reached a new high, $1.24 billion, which represents nearly an 8 percent increase. Net income climbed to $81.6 million, or $2.11 per share, up 53 percent from the previous year on a per-share basis.

Gross margins increased to 32 percent from 29.1 percent in 1995, primarily due to lower prices for raw materials and benefits from cost reductions. The annual dividend rate increased 8 percent, to 13 cents per quarter, the twenty-first increase in the past twenty-four years.

While Jerzees and Russell Athletic enjoy top fleece market positions in their respective categories, these leading brands are constantly pushing for more. Jerzees, for instance, increased its commanding 34 percent share of the men's fleecewear at the mass merchant level to 39 percent during 1996. Similarly, Russell Athletic did an excellent job of maintaining its leading men's fleecewear share in the face of aggressive competition from footwear companies.

Shortcomings to Bear in Mind

■ The Russell Athletic and Licensed Products divisions (about 25 percent of total revenues) could continue to face tough competition and industrywide overcapacity.

- Some analysts are concerned that RML may not be able to generate strong revenue gains. Most of the profit improvement in 1996 came from improved margins. They contend that companies that manufacture basic apparel, such as Fruit of the Loom and Russell, will likely experience only moderate demand. However, sales advanced a respectable 7.9 percent.
- The apparel retail business is a mature one. Over the longer term, some analysts are convinced that the industry will show selected growth. Only companies that are innovative will be able to do well. They also point out that Americans seem content to sacrifice major apparel purchases so that they can spend more on their homes, travel, entertainment, or their families. Additionally, there is a demographic factor to bear in mind: The population is aging and gaining weight, which tends to make clothes shopping less interesting. These older folk may elect to stay home and dress comfortably.

Reasons to Buy

- *Apparel Industry* magazine recently awarded Russell Corporation its 1996 Gold Star Award in recognition of superior manufacturing with innovative technology and excellent management.
- Russell has become known for its efficiency in distribution and quick response to customer needs. In fact, RML can ship a new uniform to a traded player within forty-eight hours. This gives the company a distinct advantage over international competitors.
- There has been a recent trend worldwide toward a less formal approach to living. Russell's products reflect this lifestyle of comfort and practicality.
- Despite industrywide overcapacity and increased competition, Russell's margins have been improving from the

depressed levels of 1995. Factors causing this improvement include higher volume, manufacturing efficiencies, increased overseas outsourcing (which is cheaper than domestic outsourcing), and stable raw material prices. What's more, margins are expected to continue to improve in 1997 on further cost-cutting efforts.
- A distinct positive for the domestic apparel business was the passage of NAFTA. Not only does this agreement create a huge new market for apparel makers, it also will enable manufacturers to give retailers shorter lead times by sourcing production in Mexico instead of the Far East.
- Russell expects to achieve a 30 to 35 percent annual revenue growth internationally for at least the next two years.
- Like other leading brand name producers of basic apparel, RML should see greater market penetration, especially with its largest customer, mass merchandiser Wal-Mart, at the expense of lesser-known and undercapitalized companies.
- Analysts contend that sales growth could be bolstered by acquisitions and increased penetration into European markets. What's more, Latin America should also contribute to sales growth.
- As U.S. apparel markets reach maturity, domestic market share and international growth become critical success factors. Developments such as NuBlend, Russell's 50-50 blend of fleece fabric that virtually eliminates pilling, have aided the company's domestic gains in activewear.
- Russell has made significant inroads into Europe, the company's major international market, with both manufacturing and marketing. Russell's European production operations include knitting, dyeing, finishing, cutting, and sewing; the European distribution

facilities are in and around Livingston, Scotland. What's more, Russell has developed a European sales infrastructure with offices in Alicante, Spain; Brussels, Belgium; Frankfurt, Germany; Paris, France; Prague, Czech Republic; and Prato, Italy.

- As a volume producer, vertical integration allows Russell to realize the massive economies of scale that are only enjoyed by major textile companies. The company's capital expenditure program has made and continues to make the necessary technological investments to keep facilities state-of-the-art for maximum capacity utilization and operating efficiency. Russell is obsessed with "finding a better way." This frequently results in the creation of proprietary products and processes that lead to improved quality, new cost savings, or

quicker turnaround. Furthermore, total management of the supply chain allows Russell to respond quickly to changing market conditions and satisfy customer needs faster than competitors more reliant on others for their products.

- Globally, activewear is estimated to be a $125 billion market. Today, international sales represent just over 10 percent of Russell's total sales. Increasing this percentage is a top priority with RML management. It is the company's single biggest growth opportunity, but also the most complex. In 1996, the International Division's growth slowed to 13 percent from more than 30 percent the prior year. This setback was caused by intense competition in Europe. Management is confident, however, that international sales will accelerate in 1997.

Total Assets: $1,195 Million
Current ratio: 3.20
Common shares outstanding: 38 million
Return on 1996 shareholders' equity: 12.4%

	1996	1995	1994	1993	1992	1991	1990	1989
Revenues (millions)	1,244	1,153	1,098	931	899	805	714	688
Net income (millions)	82	54	79	73	82	57	68	65
Earnings per share	2.11	1.38	1.96	1.79	1.99	1.38	1.65	1.57
Dividends per share	.50	.48	.42	.39	.34	.32	.32	.28
Price: High	33.8	31.3	32.6	36.9	40.4	36.3	31.0	26.5
Low	23.1	22.0	24.0	26.0	27.8	19.8	16.0	15.6

CONSERVATIVE GROWTH

Sara Lee Corporation

Three First National Plaza, Chicago, Illinois 60602-4260 ◻ **Investor contact: Leigh Ferst (312) 558-4966** ◻
Dividend reinvestment plan available: (312) 558-8450 ◻ **Fiscal year ends about June 30**
Listed: NYSE ◻ **Ticker symbol: SLE** ◻ **S&P rating: A** ◻ **Value Line financial strength rating: A+**

Sara Lee Corporation is a global manufacturer and marketer of high-quality, brand-name products for consumers throughout the world. With headquarters in Chicago, Sara Lee has operations in nearly 40 countries. It markets branded products

throughout North America, Europe, and the Asia-Pacific region. All told, its products are sold in over 140 countries.

Fully 40 percent of Sara Lee's sales and 45 percent of operating income are produced by its international operations—

double the percentage of foreign sales and profits only ten years ago.

The company's global strategy expressly recognizes that growth rates in developing markets are now exceeding gains in the developed world. This is especially so in Asia and South America, where discretionary consumer income is growing rapidly, and where consumer desire for U.S. branded goods is accelerating.

Sara Lee markets over 100 well-known consumer brands around the globe. Twelve of the company's largest brands (including Hanes, Douwe Egberts, Sara Lee, Hillshire Farms, and Playtex) had sales exceeding $250 million in fiscal 1996, which ended about June 30, 1996.

Sara Lee's portfolio of brands and products is as diverse as it is far-reaching. Sara Lee is the largest manufacturer and marketer of women's hosiery in the world. Sara Lee is strong in the following business areas:

• A leader in the domestic retail packaged meats industry

• The leader in the U.S. intimate apparel markets

• The second-largest retail coffee company in Europe

• A leader in U.S. and European underwear and activewear markets

• The world's largest marketer of shoe-care products

• And, of course, Sara Lee's bakery business enjoys the number one position in the domestic retail frozen baked goods market.

Sara Lee breaks its products down into 4 categories:

Sara Lee Packaged Meats and Bakery

Sara Lee Packaged Meats holds a leading position in the domestic retail packaged meats category with brands such as Hillshire Farm, Ball Park, and Jimmy Dean; ventures in Europe and Mexico strengthen the company's international commitment. In fiscal 1996, this segment was responsible for 35 percent of sales and 23 percent of profits.

Sara Lee Bakery is number one in the U.S. retail frozen baked goods market and holds strong market positions in Australia, the United Kingdom, and Mexico. PYA/Monarch is the nation's third-largest full-line food service company.

Coffee and Grocery

Sara Lee's Coffee and Grocery business reaches consumers throughout Europe, North America, and Australia. The flagship coffee brand is Douwe Egberts, with other leading names including Maison de Café, Marcilla, and Merrild. In the Netherlands, Belgium, and Hungary, Sara Lee has a number one position in retail roasted coffee, and a number two share in France, Spain, Australia, and the Czech Republic. Pickwick tea has a growing share of the $2.9 billion European tea market. This segment of SLE in 1996 represented 15 percent of sales and 24 percent of overall profits.

Personal Products

Consumers in North America, Europe, South Africa, and the Asia-Pacific region recognize Sara Lee's leading brands of hosiery, bras, panties, activewear, and underwear under the Abanderado, Bali, Champion, Dim, Hanes, Hanes Her Way, L'eggs, Playtex, Princesa, Rinbros, and Wonderbra brands. In fiscal 1996, the operation was responsible for 40 percent of the company's sales and 41 percent of profits.

Sara Lee holds the number one position in the United States for women's hosiery, women's and girls' panties, bras, and fleecewear, and a strong number two position in men's and boys' underwear.

In Europe, Sara Lee is the market leader for sheer hosiery. The company holds leading positions in the bra markets in France, Italy, Spain, and the United Kingdom, and in men's and women's underwear markets in Spain, France, and Italy.

Household and Personal Care

Sara Lee's most global business focuses on core strategies of shoe care, body care, and insecticides. Kiwi shoe care products are sold in 118 countries. Sanex, Duschdas, Badedas, Zwitsal, and other body care products hold leading positions in several European markets. In 1996, this segment accounted for 10 percent of revenues and 12 percent of profits.

Insecticide brands Vapona, Catch, and Ridsect are marketed in Europe and the Asia-Pacific region. The company also manufactures and markets air fresheners, detergents, deodorants, and oral care, skin care, furniture care, and lavatory care products. The direct selling operations of House of Fuller, House of Sara Lee, and Avroy Shlain distribute cosmetics, fragrances, toiletries, jewelry, and personal products in Mexico, the Philippines, Indonesia, and South Africa.

Reasons to Buy

- In fiscal 1997, Sara Lee acquired Finnegans Famous Cakes Ltd., a leading privately owned food service company based in the United Kingdom. Finnegans manufactures high-quality food service cakes, cheesecakes, pies, and snack cakes.
- Helping to establish the Playtex brand in the world's second-largest intimate apparel market, Sara Lee entered into a strategic co-branding alliance with Amway Japan Limited to market an exclusive Playtex line in Japan. The exclusive collection of Playtex intimates are sold through more than 1 million Amway Japan distributors.
- Sara Lee's management is committed to the principle of decentralized management. The company is organized into a large number of discrete profit centers, each led by an operating executive with a high degree of authority and accountability for the performance of that business.
- Sara Lee pursues multichannel distribution for many of its major product lines. Its apparel products are sold through mass merchandisers, department stores, supermarkets, and catalogs.

The company's food products are sold through both retail and food service channels and, for both food and apparel, SLE even has its own stores.

Sara Lee's direct selling operations, currently situated in Mexico, South Africa, the Philippines, and Indonesia, enable the company to reach millions of new consumers in those developing countries.

In fact, through its own stores, catalogs, and direct selling ventures, over $1 billion of Sara Lee's fiscal 1996 revenues resulted from sales directly to consumers. SLE intends to build this part of the company to significantly greater levels in the future. Going directly to the consumer, finding them in the workplace, at restaurants, shopping malls, watching cable networks, or on the Internet, is the best way to ensure that Sara Lee's brands achieve leadership positions in their markets.

- Over the past ten years (1986–1996), Sara Lee has been on a roll. Earnings per share climbed from $.51 to $1.83, for a compound annual growth rate of 13.6 percent. Moreover, there were no dips along the way. In the same period, dividends advanced at a similar pace, from $.20 to $.74, a growth rate of 14.0 percent.
- The world leader in shoe care, Sara Lee's Kiwi brand is found in 120 countries and is the company's most global brand. In fiscal 1996, Sara Lee further

leveraged the strength of the Kiwi name through product enhancements and brand extensions. A major strategic initiative for Kiwi is development of shoe accessories, such as inner soles and laces, as well as cleaning products for nontraditional footwear, such as canvas, patent leather, and suede shoes.

- Sara Lee maintained its number one position in the intimate apparel markets of the United States, Canada, and Mexico. For fiscal 1996, Sara Lee's dollar share of the $3.2 billion U.S. bra market increased 2 points to 29 percent, reflecting an expanded array of styles, features, and benefits for customers.

- Sara Lee moved into the number one market position in the $2.3 billion U.S. men's and boys' underwear market during 1996, increasing its unit market share more than 2 points to 35 percent.

- Sara Lee's growing international meats business now includes Holmeat, the parent company of Imperial Meats Group, based in Lovendegem, Belgium.

    Imperial Meats manufactures and distributes processed meats in Belgium, France, Germany, and the Netherlands under the Imperial Cornby and Marcassou brand names. The company has 384 employees. Its annual sales are about $100 million.

    Sara Lee's European meats business includes the Stegeman brand in the Netherlands, Dacor in Belgium, Argal in Spain, and Nobre in Portugal. In other international markets, Sara Lee is part of a joint venture with Kir Alimentos, Mexico's second-largest packaged meats company and a leading manufacturer of hot dogs, luncheon meat, sausage, and ham under the Kir and Duby brands.

- Targeting the "better-for-you" market, while capitalizing on the popularity of rotisserie-flavored poultry, Bil Mar introduced a line of fat-free Mr. Turkey Rotisserie Flavor lunch meats.

    Smoked turkey and smoked chicken are offered in pre-sliced or deli-cut varieties. The rotisserie-flavor turkey is also being marketed in quarter-breast packages. The luncheon meats have 10 calories per slice.

- Coffee lovers in Spain are enjoying a new choice in the premium market: the Marcilla Mocca brand. Sara Lee's newest variety of roasted coffee, Marcilla Mocca coffee is made from 100 percent Arabica beans, enhanced through a unique roasting process.

- Sara Lee is still seeking to stimulate hosiery demand with innovative new products. It introduced a longer-wearing sheer hosiery called Hanes Resilience. This hosiery is engineered to wear better than conventional pantyhose through the use of more durable yarns.

    More important, the company's strategic emphasis has moved from building unit volume to managing the business for healthier profits. To that end, it has reduced excess capacity, taken a more aggressive stance on pricing, and cut back on promotions.

- In late 1996, Sara Lee announced a 20-million-share-repurchase plan. On top of the 12 million shares remaining on the existing plan, this represents the repurchase of 7 percent of the company's stock. Studies show that when stock is repurchased by a company, the share price is likely to outperform the market.

- In the fall of 1996, Sara Lee increased its dividend by 11 percent. It was the twenty-first consecutive annual dividend increase.

- Sara Lee operates internationally. In fiscal 1996, foreign sales were 39 percent of the total (31 percent Western/Central Europe; 6 percent Asia Pacific/Latin America; 2 percent other).

- Sara Lee has been putting increasing emphasis on raising its return on invested capital by curtailing capital-intensive projects. This program should bolster excess cash flows, allowing for a more aggressive level of stock repurchases.
- Sara Lee Packaged Meats maintained a leading position in the $23 billion domestic packaged meats industry

during fiscal 1996, continuing its focus on high-margin, value-added products that satisfy consumer demand for convenient and "better-for-you" selections. Sara Lee's Packaged Meats brands held number one positions in the hot dog, smoked sausage, and breakfast sausage categories and in several specialty categories, including corn dogs, cocktail links, and breakfast sandwiches.

Total assets: $13,099 million
Current ratio: 1.03
Common shares outstanding: 486 million
Return on 1996 shareholders' equity: 21.5%

	1996	1995	1994	1993	1992	1991	1990	1989
Revenues (millions)	18,624	17,719	15,536	14,580	13,243	12,381	11,606	11,718
Net income (millions)	916	804	729	704	620	535	470	399
Earnings per share	1.83	1.62	1.47	1.40	1.24	1.08	.96	.85
Dividends per share	.74	.67	.63	.56	.61	.46	.41	.35
Price: High	40.5	30.4	26.0	31.1	32.5	29.1	16.7	16.9
Low	29.9	24.3	19.4	21.0	23.3	14.8	12.1	10.7

CONSERVATIVE GROWTH

Sherwin-Williams Company

101 Prospect Avenue, N. W., Cleveland, Ohio 44115-1075 □ Investor contact: Conway G. Ivy (216) 566-2102 □ Dividend reinvestment plan available: (800) 542-2140 □ Listed: NYSE □ Ticker symbol: SHW □ S&P rating: A+ □ Value Line financial strength rating: A+

Sherwin-Williams' shares are particularly suitable for investors seeking consistency of earnings growth, an exceptionally strong balance sheet, coupled with astute management. The company has displayed its ability to prosper through two full business cycles since Jack Breen and his management team took control.

Sherwin-Williams, which was founded some 130 years ago, is the largest architectural coatings company in the United States and the third-largest coatings company in the world. The company is a vertically integrated, multibrand, multichannel distributor.

Company Background
Sherwin-Williams has 2,156 company-operated paint and wall covering stores that sell Sherwin-Williams-labeled architectural coatings, industrial finishes, and associated supplies. These stores are situated in forty-nine states, Puerto Rico, and Canada.

The company manufactures and sells Dutch Boy, Martin-Senour, Kem-Tone, Dupli-Color, Cuprinol, and Krylon brands, plus private-label brands for mass merchandisers and home-improvement centers.

Sherwin-Williams also produces coatings for original equipment manufacturers

(OEMs) and special-purpose coatings for the automotive market, industrial maintenance, and traffic paint markets.

The Paint Stores Segment exclusively distributes Sherwin-Williams branded architectural coatings, industrial maintenance products, industrial finishes, and related items produced by the Coatings Segment of the company and others.

Paint, wall coverings, floor coverings, window treatments, spray equipment, and other associated products are marketed by store personnel and direct sale representatives to the do-it-yourself customer, professional painter, contractor, industrial and commercial maintenance customer, property manager, architect, and manufacturer of products requiring a factory finish.

The five divisions within the Coatings Segment (Coatings, Consumer Brands, Automotive, Transportation Services, and Specialty) participate in the manufacture, distribution, or sale of coatings and related products.

The Coatings Division manufactures paint and paint-related products for the do-it-yourselfer, professional painter, contractor, industrial and commercial maintenance account, and manufacturer of factory-finished products.

The Consumer Brands Division is responsible for the sales and marketing of branded and private-label products by a direct sales staff to unaffiliated home centers, mass merchandisers, independent dealers, and distributors.

The Automotive Division develops and manufactures motor vehicle finish and refinish products that are marketed under the Sherwin-Williams and other branded labels in the United States and Canada, through a network of 135 company-operated branches, jobbers, and distributors.

The Transportation Services Division provides warehousing, truckload freight, pool assembly, freight brokerage, and consolidation services primarily for the company and for certain external manufacturers, distributors, and retailers throughout the United States. This division provides the company with total logistics service support that allows increased delivery schedules, lower field inventory levels, and fewer out-of-stocks.

The Specialty Division competes in three areas: custom and industrial aerosols, paint applicators, and retail and wholesale consumer aerosols. This division participates in the retail and wholesale paint, automotive, home care products, institutional, insecticide, and industrial markets. A wide variety of aerosol products are filled, packaged, and distributed to regional and national customers.

The Other Segment is responsible for the acquisition, development, leasing, and management of properties for use by the company and others. Obtaining real estate in the proper location at the appropriate cost is a critical component for achieving the desired operating success, particularly for paint stores and distribution centers.

Shortcomings to Bear in Mind

- Margins were hurt in 1996 because of the integration of Pratt & Lambert into core operations, but these costs were less in 1997. However, profitability has been hurt by increases in the cost of titanium dioxide (the key white pigment). Higher raw material costs put pressure on margins that are not easily offset by price increases.
- The lead liability concern periodically surfaces for former pigment manufacturers like Sherwin-Williams. The most noteworthy cases involving Sherwin-Williams have been dismissed. On the other hand, visibility of cases and actions can periodically affect the stock price.

Reasons to Buy

■ Early in 1997, Sherwin-Williams acquired Thompson Minwax Holding Corporation. Minwax is the dominant manufacturer of exterior stains used for cabinets, woodwork, and furniture. Thompson sealants, which include the well-known Thompson's Water Seal brand, dominate the clear-coat sealant market.

Sherwin-Williams paid $830 million for Thompson, which was financed with cash and debt. This was the fourteenth acquisition made by the company in a twelve-month period. There are a number of positive aspects from the purchase of Thompson Minwax:

● Thompson Minwax's U.K. operation provides Sherwin-Williams a base from which to sell its other paint lines.

● A broadened product line will enable the company to increase shelf space at home centers, mass merchandisers, and independent paint stores.

● Increased sales to the do-it-yourself channel provides Sherwin-Williams with a more balanced mix.

● Thompson Minwax's product-development capabilities should enhance Sherwin's proven ability to introduce new products.

● The acquisition of Thompson Minwax gives Sherwin a leading position in the $900 million domestic interior and exterior stain and sealant markets. In the past, SHW had been underrepresented in these sectors.

■ In 1996, the company broadened its horizons with the acquisition of Pratt & Lambert United, Inc., for $400 million in cash and the assumption of Pratt & Lambert United's debt. Already the nation's biggest paint company, the acquisitive Sherwin-Williams purchased a Buffalo company that is the eleventh-largest manufacturer.

According to analysts, the deal expands Sherwin-Williams' standing in three key markets: independent dealers, which are smaller, privately owned paint stores; mass merchants; and industrial coatings.

For its part, the company said, "Pratt & Lambert has been a great quality brand for independent dealers since 1849." Sherwin-Williams, which will continue to use the Pratt & Lambert brand name, currently has only a small position in the independent dealer market, which it supplies with its Martin-Senour brand.

■ The architectural coatings business is a fairly stable one, with a cyclicality much less pronounced than that of other building products. The reason for this consistency is that about 90 percent of demand for paint comes from the remodeling market, not from the new construction market. Moreover, the low cost of paint relative to other remodeling costs makes purchase of it less subject to delay in economic downturns.

■ Sherwin-Williams is exceptionally strong financially, with 98 percent of its capitalization in shareholders' equity. Standard & Poor's and Value Line both give the company high marks for financial strength: A+ and A+, respectively.

■ The company should benefit from operating leverage in manufacturing, as sales and distribution grow. What's more, its distribution will benefit from new or acquired products, product lines. and brand names.

For example, the acquisition of DeSoto's manufacturing assets in 1990 brought state-of-the-art manufacturing and the capacity to more aggressively pursue the retail channel.

Krylon, purchased in 1990, expanded the company's participation in aerosol paints; Cuprinol, a well-recognized Northeastern and Northwestern regional stain brand acquired in 1991, was expanded geographically through Sherwin-Williams distribution.

- During 1995, Sherwin-Williams made an unsuccessful attempt to acquire Grow Group, which also makes paints. It lost because it was unwilling to outbid the other company. While this was a disappointment, it is characteristic of

Sherwin-Williams that it is unwilling to make dilutive acquisitions. Over the past fifteen years, SHW has been disciplined in valuing and pursuing acquisitions.

- Although somewhat sensitive to interest rates, the company's overall business is not significantly affected by new home construction.

Total assets: $2,995 million
Current ratio: 1.24
Common shares outstanding: 171 million
Return on 1996 shareholders' equity: 18.9%

	1996	1995	1994	1993	1992	1991	1990	1989
Revenues (millions)	4,133	3,300	3,100	2,949	2,748	2,541	2,267	2,124
Net income (millions)	229	201	187	165	145	128	123	109
Earnings per share	1.33	1.17	1.08	.93	.82	.73	.71	.63
Dividends per share	.35	.32	.28	.25	.22	.21	.19	.18
Price: High	28.9	20.8	17.9	18.8	16.4	13.9	10.5	8.9
Low	19.5	16.0	14.8	14.9	12.7	8.8	7.5	6.3

INCOME

SIGCORP, Inc.

20 NW Fourth Street, Evansville, Indiana 47741-0001   ◻ Investor contact: Timothy L. Burke (800) 227-8625   ◻ Dividend reinvestment plan available: (800) 227-8625   ◻ Listed: NYSE   ◻ Ticker symbol: SIG   ◻ S&P rating: A   ◻ Value Line financial strength rating: A

SIGCORP is an investor-owned holding company. Its core gas and electric utility business is conducted through Southern Indiana Gas and Electric Company, which serves ten counties in southwestern Indiana.

SIGCORP is also the parent company of a number of nonregulated subsidiaries, which provide services closely related to the core utility business and also advance SIGCORP's preparation for the coming competitive energy market.

The company's goal is to derive 20 percent of pretax income from nonutility operations by the year 2000, compared with 4 percent in 1996.

Southern Indiana Gas and Electric Company (SIGECO) is SIGCORP's primary subsidiary. Providing some of the lowest-cost utility service in the United States, SIGECO utilizes its $850 million in assets to serve 122,000 electric and 106,000 natural gas customers in southwestern Indiana and provide wholesale electric service in a multistate region.

SIGECO Strengths
- A growing service area and healthy economic climate.
- Low production costs, which are 25 percent lower than the average for all investor-owned utilities.

• Generation that complies with all major Clean Air Act requirements.

• No "stranded investment" in facilities.

Other Subsidiaries

Southern Indiana Properties invests in leveraged leases of real estate and equipment and participates in other structured finance opportunities. It has assets of nearly $90 million.

Energy Systems Group provides energy-savings solutions, primarily through guaranteed-performance contracts, to businesses and institutions throughout the region.

Southern Indiana Minerals was established to market coal combustion by-products for use in many industrial applications.

ComSource offers communications solutions to businesses and individual users through Internet access and other services.

SIGCORP Energy Services was created to market natural gas and provide related energy management services to utilities, industrial users, and other large-volume natural gas consumers in the region.

SIGCORP Power Marketing has been formed to market electricity to regional utilities and power marketers.

SIGCORP Capital provides financing and cash management services for SIGCORP's nonregulated subsidiaries.

SIGCORP Fuels was established to procure low-cost fuel supplies, potentially including coal-producing properties.

Highlights of 1996

• The company achieved record earnings per share (before nonrecurring items) despite a very cool summer (which hurt air conditioning revenues).

• Increased the common stock dividend in January of 1997 for the thirty-eighth consecutive year. In the past ten years, the dividend climbed from $.73 to $1.15, a compound annual growth rate of 4.6 percent, easily outpacing the march of inflation.

• Played a key role in bringing new industries and businesses to the area.

• Enhanced its position as one of the lowest-cost suppliers of electric power in the nation. In the period ending June 30, 1996, the company's retail rates—in cents per kilowatt hour—compared favorably with other major cities in the United States:

	Retail Rates (cents/kilowatt-hour)
Chicago	8.31
Buffalo, NY	8.13
Hammond, IN	6.37
St. Louis, MO	6.27
Cincinnati, OH	6.03
Milwaukee, WI	5.55
Fort Wayne, IN	5.53
Indianapolis, IN	5.11
Evansville, IN	4.97
Terre Haute, IN	4.57
Lexington, KY	4.12

• SIGCORP continued to prepare for competition by streamlining the operation and maintenance of the company's power production facilities. This entailed the purchase of state-of-the-art customer information and billing systems and the revamping of demand side management and the large customer marketing structure.

• SIGCORP achieved record-breaking safety performance while decreasing the number of employees through attrition.

• The company more than doubled total pretax margin from spot sales of electricity to other utilities and power marketers.

• SIGCORP formed subsidiaries to supply low-cost coal, market electricity and natural gas, and provide working capital and long-term financing for nonregulated businesses.

Shortcomings to Bear in Mind

- In 1996, the company was hurt by a number of items:
  - Increased operating expenses related to the additional costs of post-retirement benefits other than pensions.
  - Higher full-year operating expenses of SIGECO's new Culley sulfur dioxide removal facility, which began operations in 1995.
  - Fewer sales to Alcoa Generating Corporation.

  On other hand, there were some offsetting developments that helped earnings in 1996:
  - Increased sales to retail gas and electric customers.
  - Higher sales margins resulting from approved increases in gas and electric rates.
  - Lower maintenance expenditures.
  - Record high sales to other electric utilities and power marketers.
- Electric and natural gas utilities are both subject to a sharp earnings impact from the weather. If the summer is hot, electric utilities benefit, since they sell more power for air conditioning. In the winter, both types of utilities enjoy robust profits when the weather is cold. This is particularly true for natural gas distributors, since the bulk of their sales are for space heating. A mild winter can hurt earnings severely. Unfortunately, the weather is extremely difficult to forecast.

Reasons to Buy

- SIGECO is strong financially. For instance, the company has a solid AA financial strength rating from three major credit-rating agencies. Very few other electric utilities have higher ratings. What's more, the average interest rate on the company's $300 million of long-term debt is 6.6 percent, compared to an industry average of about 8 percent. Of the 119 utilities in a recent comparison, only 6 had average interest rates lower than SIGECO.
- Since public utilities are virtual monopolies, it is necessary that they be regulated. Without regulation, a company without competitors might be tempted to charge whatever the traffic would bear.

  Unfortunately, regulators are often more interested in rate payers than they are in utilities. Each state has its own regulation; federal regulation is rarely a factor. Some states select commissions by the electoral process. This is particularly true in several southern states, among others.

  More often, commissioners are chosen by the governor and normally have to be ratified by the legislature. Brokerage houses often rate these regulators as to how well they treat the utilities within their borders. For its part, Indiana is generally accorded high marks. Of course, the utility itself can make a difference as well. In a sense, it's a matter of salesmanship. SIGECO has a history of cooperation and a straightforward approach that has allowed the company to settle major regulatory issues without the expense of protracted legal hearings.
- The health of the service territory should not be ignored when you are evaluating an electric utility. If power sales are to grow, it's necessary to have a thriving economy. Many public utilities play a key role in achieving this end, as they help to bring new businesses to the region.

  The utility's headquarters city, Evansville, is the largest city in the territory. It continues its rapid development as a service center. Educational, medical, retail, cultural, and other activities are expanding to meet the growing demand.

At the end of 1995, the company's service territory had an unemployment rate below 4 percent, with no sign of slowed economic activity. Because of the region's solid midwestern work ethic, the productivity of workers in manufacturing companies in Evansville exceed the national average by 90 percent.

- SIGECO's ratio of dividend payout to earnings is about 65 percent, compared to the industry average of over 80 percent. SIG's management is convinced that a conservative dividend payout results in greater value for long-term investors. A low payout ratio enables the company to continue to raise dividends even when earnings are flat. It also gives management more capital to plow back into the business without resorting to outside financing.

- The low-cost energy that the company provides, coupled with its aggressive economic development efforts, have played a large role in the area's significant growth. Major manufacturers such as Toyota, ConAgra, Bristol-Myers Squibb, Waupaca Foundry, and AK Steel are pouring billions of dollars of new investment and creating thousands of new jobs in southwestern Indiana.

- SIGECO remains a low-cost producer of electricity, with rates among the most competitive in the country. The company's fuel costs are low. Its plants meet all major Clean Air Act of 1990 requirements for the year 2000. According to most industry analysts, SIGECO has little or no "stranded," or unrecoverable, investment in its generating plants. What's more, the company does not face an immediate need to spend money to build additional generating capacity.

Total assets: $952,653,000
Current ratio: 0.84
Common shares outstanding: 23.6 million
Return on 1996 shareholders' equity: 12.5%

	1996	1995	1994	1993	1992	1991	1990	1989
Revenues (millions)	373	339	330	328	306	323	312	313
Net income (millions)	43	49	41	40	37	38	38	36
Earnings per share	1.83	1.63	1.69	1.63	1.51	1.58	1.51	1.41
Dividends per share	1.15	1.13	1.10	1.07	1.04	1.00	.95	.90
Price: High	24.7	24.3	22.6	23.7	22.7	22.5	16.7	16.1
Low	21.9	17.6	16.0	21.3	20.3	15.6	13.9	13.7

CONSERVATIVE GROWTH

Snap-on Inc.

P. O. Box 1430, Kenosha, Wisconsin 53141-1430 ◻ Investor contact: Lynn McHugh (414) 656-6488 ◻ Dividend reinvestment plan available: (800) 524-0687 ◻ Listed: NYSE ◻ Ticker symbol: SNA ◻ S&P rating: B+ ◻ Value Line financial strength rating: A

Snap-on is a leading developer, manufacturer, and distributor of tool and equipment solutions for professional technicians, motor service shop owners, specialty repair centers, original equipment manufacturers, and industrial tool users worldwide. Snap-on (formerly Snap-on Tools) manufactures a line of 15,000 high-quality professional mechanic tools, diagnostic equipment, and tool chests.

In the past, most customer needs in the industry centered around the turning of a wrench. Basic mechanical repair, to be sure, still represents a considerable portion of automotive service and remains a growth opportunity for Snap-on.

Today, however, customers face new vehicle systems, new regulations, and a new competitive challenge at every turn. In a time of dramatic change, people look to the industry leader, Snap-on Incorporated.

The Snap-on Product Line

Hand tools include wrenches, screwdrivers, sockets, pliers, and similar items. Power tools include pneumatic impact wrenches, air ratchets, power drills, sanders, and polishers. Tool storage refers to tool chests and roll cabinets. Electronic tools and shop equipment include automotive diagnostic equipment, wheel balancing and aligning equipment, and battery chargers.

Snap-on's products are sold to mechanics, industrial accounts, and foreign distributors for use in automotive service, manufacturing, and other repair and maintenance. Special customer tools are also made.

The company manages mobile van sales to automotive technicians who are serviced by more than 5,000 (mostly franchised) dealers throughout the world.

Industrial products are sold by more than 500 company salesmen. Dealers operate out of walk-in vans that carry an inventory of products. Snap-on Diagnostics employs a company sales force to sell equipment, diagnostics, and software to repair shops and original equipment manufacturers.

Snap-on Financial Services provides financing to facilitate the sale or lease of products, with a particular focus on more expensive electronic equipment.

1996 Acquisitions

During 1996, SNA acquired three new businesses.

John Bean is a leading producer of wheel and brake service equipment, including wheel aligners and balancers, tire changers, and brake lathes. Its products are sold in North America, Europe, and other parts of the world. The acquisition extends the company's reach in the global market for under-car service. It also provides greater access to original equipment manufacturers, national service chains, and other service repair providers through John Bean's traditional distribution channel.

Automotive Data Solutions (ADS) is a tele-diagnostics company that offers over-the-phone diagnostics service for automotive technicians. With a custom-designed computer program, ADS master technicians guide technicians through repairs, and supply the appropriate solutions for the specific vehicle model and system.

Snap-on Tools/PST Africa is a mobile van distributor of tools to professional users in South Africa. The acquisition represents the company's first operation in that country, which can be used as a base for the region.

Early in 1997, Snap-on acquired a 50 percent interest in the Thomson Corporation's Mitchell Repair Information business. Snap-on will purchase the remainder of the newly formed Mitchell Repair Information Company, LLC within the next five years.

The new company is the largest provider of print and electronic versions of vehicle mechanical and electrical system repair information to repair and service establishments throughout North America. The acquisition will enable Snap-on to offer a complete package of integrated information and business services to vehicle repair centers around the world. The integration of the vehicle repair database into the company's diagnostics equipment is also an important benefit of the relationship.

Shortcomings to Bear in Mind

- Excluding Europe, sales in other nondomestic markets declined 1.1 percent in 1996, after an increase of 22.9 percent in 1995. Growth in tool and equipment sales in Australia were more than offset by a decline in sales in Japan. The strength of the U.S. dollar against the yen and general weakness in the Japanese economy were primarily responsible for the 1996 decrease. On the other hand, excluding the net effects of foreign currency, 1996 sales increased 5 percent. In 1995, strong sales were recorded by most of the countries in this geographic category. What's more, 1995 results also benefited from a weak U.S. dollar relative to the Japanese yen.

- Snap-on does not have a particularly impressive record of growth. In the 1986–1996 period, earnings per share advanced from $1.06 to $2.16, a compound annual growth rate of 7.4 percent. Dividend growth has also been lackluster. In the same ten-year stretch, dividends moved from $.41 a share to $.76, a growth rate of only 6.4 percent. What's more, dividends have not advanced at a steady pace. In the 1990-to-1995 period, the same dividend ($.72) was paid every year.

Reasons to Buy

- In August of 1996, Snap-on agreed to provide car care and maintenance equipment for more than 800 Penske Auto Centers located in Kmart store locations.

  Penske Auto Centers is equipping and updating its automotive service centers located at Kmart stores across the country. As it had done with tires, automotive parts, and lubricants, Penske was seeking a single supplier for all of its equipment needs. After an extensive review of all those in the industry, it chose Snap-on.

  "Snap-on is recognized throughout the industry for quality," said Roger S. Penske, Jr., chief executive officer of Penske Auto Centers. "Its products represent an image that is consistent with that of the Penske name. Snap-on is also the leader in service technology. Using its equipment in our auto centers strengthens our position as a premier service provider in the automotive repair industry."

  In addition to the equipment, Snap-on conducts automotive systems training for all Penske technicians. "Snap-on was the only supplier able to provide the complete package, including training and product support," Penske said.

- An important development with good prospects is the expected beginning of automotive emissions-testing programs, both at home and abroad. To date, however, only a few of the fifty states and a handful of European nations have implemented these programs. For its part, Snap-on, which has been broadening its diagnostic equipment lines since the early 1990s, stands to benefit when these programs begin to kick in.

- In 1996, Snap-on expanded its line of ergonomically designed, pistol-shaped pliers, cutters, and screwdrivers. Designed with the special challenges of the automotive service technician in mind, these tools deliver considerable power, while helping the technician conserve energy and limit strain.

- In both tools and equipment, Snap-on's global presence grows. Nondomestic sales now contribute 30 percent to total revenues. The company is following the vehicle manufacturers' entry into new markets and is preparing to meet their needs, as well as those of others in the automotive service environment. Snap-on has new van operations in Singapore and Malaysia and has completed a joint venture in South Africa. At the same time, the company continues to expand operations in Southeast Asia, while pursuing opportunities in China.

- Sales in Europe increased 46.7 percent in 1996, following a decline of 4.4 percent from the prior year. The year was helped from contributions from the 1995 acquisition of Herramientas Eurotools, S.A., of Spain ("Eurotools") and the 1996 acquisition of John Bean, higher sales through the dealer channel,

and equipment sales related to the start-up of an emissions-testing program in the United Kingdom.

- Sales per employee, a common measure of productivity, increased 11 percent in 1996 over the prior year. Since 1992, moreover, sales per employee have grown 28 percent.
- Snap-on moved up two slots to number five in *Entrepreneur* magazine's annual rating of the Top 500 franchises. Snap-on was ranked number one "home-based franchise in America" in *Entrepreneur*'s September 1996 issue. Snap-on was also recognized as one of the best franchise businesses in America in *Success* magazine's Franchise Gold 100. Finally, the company was selected from among 2,500 franchise companies.

Total assets: $1,521 million
Current ratio: 2.98
Common shares outstanding: 61 million
Return on 1996 shareholders' equity: 16.7%

	1996	1995	1994	1993	1992	1991	1990	1989
Revenues (millions)	1,485	1,292	1,194	1,132	964	882	932	891
Net income (millions)	132	113	98	86	66	73	101	105
Earnings per share	2.16	1.84	1.53	1.34	1.04	1.17	1.63	1.70
Dividends per share	.76	.72	.72	.72	.72	.72	.72	.69
Price: High	38.3	31.5	29.6	29.7	26.7	23.0	25.3	27.9
Low	27.3	20.7	19.3	20.3	18.0	18.3	17.5	19.3

INCOME

Texaco Inc.

2000 Westchester Avenue, White Plains, New York 10650-0001 □ Listed: NYSE □ Investor contact: Ms. Elizabeth P. Smith (914) 253-4478 □ Dividend reinvestment plan available: (800) 283-9785 □ Ticker symbol: TX □ S&P rating: B □ Value Line financial strength rating: A

Dating back to 1902, Texaco is one of the world's largest integrated oil companies. The company has extensive international interests, including 50 percent ownership of Caltex (Chevron holds the rest). Caltex operates in fifty-eight countries, including some of the world's fastest-growing economies.

In 1988, Texaco and Saudi Arabian Oil Company (the world's largest oil company) formed Star Enterprises, a U.S.–based joint venture that refines, distributes, and markets Texaco-brand petroleum products in twenty-six East and Gulf Coast states and the District of Columbia.

Chemical operations were sold in 1994. A brief glimpse of Texaco follows:

Texaco

Operating in more than 150 countries, Texaco and its affiliates help supply the world's needs. The company finds and produces crude oil and natural gas; manufactures and markets high-quality fuel and lubricant products; operates transportation, trading, and distribution facilities; and produces alternate forms of energy for power and manufacturing.

Strengths

Texaco has a solid asset base and a strong balance sheet. Backing one of the world's best-known brands are some 29,000 employees, coupled with sophisticated technology. Texaco, moreover, has profitable, growing business partnerships and enjoys a presence in the world's leading production areas and energy markets.

1996 Performance

Increased production and market share, coupled with higher commodity prices and the benefits of cost-containment, yielded excellent results in 1996. Total net income was more than $2 billion, with a 14.9 percent return on average capital employed. A sharp rise in Texaco's stock price and higher dividends brought a 30 percent total return to shareholders.

Strategies

Texaco's success does not hinge on high energy prices. The company is continuing to make its own margins with increased production and sales volumes and with persistent strategies for cost reduction. Technology, alliances, and new markets all help Texaco extract more value from its oil and natural gas resources.

Exploration and Production

Texaco finds and produces oil and natural gas from a global portfolio of new and mature fields. Newer prospects in the U.K. North Sea, China, West Africa, and Latin America complement established operations in the United States, Indonesia, and the Middle East and exploration activities in the Asia-Pacific region and the deepwater Gulf of Mexico.

Strengths

Texaco's core upstream assets around the world provide solid cash flow and earnings. The company's teams apply the most advanced technology to find, develop, and produce oil and natural gas. At a five-year average of 112 percent, Texaco's worldwide reserve replacement rate places the company among the leaders in the industry.

Texaco intends to move nimbly to extract maximum value from its existing assets around the world and to accelerate development of reserves in emerging core areas. Texaco's 1997 upstream capital and exploratory budget is 22 percent higher than in 1996, and the company has financial flexibility to pursue a number of new growth opportunities.

1996 Performance

Strong oil and gas prices and increased production raised total upstream operating earnings 153 percent, to $1.6 billion worldwide, including a record $1.1 billion in the United States. Worldwide production rose 3 percent, primarily from applying technology to bring new fields onstream faster and to raise production at maturing fields.

Marketing, Manufacturing, and Distribution

Texaco and its affiliates own or have interests in twenty-five refineries in United

States and around the world. Equity crude processing capacity is 1.5 billion barrels a day. With the company's affiliates, Texaco markets automotive fuels through some 22,000 service stations worldwide. Through its global businesses, the company sells lubricants, coolants, and marine and aviation fuel.

Strengths

The Texaco brand is well-known and respected worldwide. With its affiliates, Texaco is a leading marketer of refined products in the United States, and the company holds a significant market share in the world's growth areas. Texaco's marketing efforts are supported by an increasingly efficient and technologically advanced manufacturing system.

1996 Performance

Total downstream operating earnings in 1996 were $657 million. Sales of Texaco-branded gasoline were strong in the United States, and Latin American operations posted gains in volumes, market share, and earnings. In Europe and the Pacific Rim, industry overcapacity continued to pressure margins and profits.

Strategies

Texaco is committed to creating its own downstream margins, even under challenging industry conditions. Texaco's Global Brand Initiative enhances the strength of its brand and the quality of its facilities. What's more, through alliances, such as the proposed venture with Shell Oil Company in the United States, Texaco is creating more value from its core downstream assets.

Global Businesses

Texaco's companywide realignment, effective January 1997, created this unit to coordinate an array of worldwide operations with opportunities for new revenue growth. They include Global Gas and Power, the company's interest in Caltex, Worldwide Lubricants, Fuel and Marine Marketing, International Aviation Sales, and the Technology Division.

Strengths

The unit gives Texaco a focused presence in business activities in which a global strategy can unlock greater value for the company and its shareholders. This allows Texaco to leverage its partnerships, products, and technology with other Texaco businesses in both the upstream and downstream.

1996 Performance

Operating separately in 1996, several of the company's global businesses felt the impact of downstream pressures. Yet there were bright spots: an increase in earnings from Texaco's natural gas and gas liquids business; gains in U.S. and European sales of Texaco's long-life coolants; and Caltex's introduction of a new brand image throughout its operating area.

Strategies

Texaco's natural gas reserves play a key role in the Texaco's drive for success as an energy company. Its ability to leverage these assets with the company's expertise in power generation and gasification technology positions Texaco to benefit from the global demand for clean power generation and the opportunities it expects to result from deregulation of the U.S. power industry.

Shortcomings to Bear in Mind

■ Although Texaco has an above-average dividend yield, the growth of its dividend in the past ten years has not been impressive. In the 1986–1996 period, the dividend advanced from $3.00 to $3.30, a compound annual growth rate of less than 1 percent. In the same span, earnings per share performed better, rising from $2.53 (which was down from $4.62 the prior year) to $6.07, a growth rate of 9.1 percent. On the other hand, if you start with the EPS figure of $4.62 in 1985, the eleven-year growth rate is much less: 2.5 percent.

Reasons to Buy

■ Texaco enjoyed considerable success in 1996:

- Total return to shareholders was 30 percent.
- Net income before special items increased 45 percent over 1995.
- The reserve replacement rate was 113 percent.
- Return on capital employed before special items increased from 9.5 percent to 12.8 percent.
- Texaco's debt-to-total-capital ratio improved from 33.6 percent from 38 percent.
- The quarterly dividend was increased by 6.25 percent.

■ Texaco's strong balance sheet and a 1997 capital and exploratory budget of $4.5 billion—30 percent higher than in 1996—will continue to afford the company the financial flexibility to act decisively on new opportunities. In 1996, TX accelerated its deep-water Gulf of Mexico program with aggressive lease acquisitions. What's more, the company moved swiftly to acquire an interest in Venezuela's Hamaca heavy-oil project when that significant hydrocarbon region opened to private investment.

■ Beyond the Continental Shelf in the Gulf of Mexico, Texaco is appraising and developing Petronius, Gemini, and Fuji—three deep-water discoveries announced in late 1995. The company also moved from fifth to third place in deep-water lease-acreage position versus its competitors. With 1996 acquisitions of 149 new leases in water depths greater than 1,300 feet, Texaco now has 271 exploratory leases and 87 undrilled prospects in the Gulf.

Total assets: $26,963 million
Current ratio: 1.26
Return on 1996 equity: 20.4%
Common shares outstanding: 264 million

	1996	1995	1994	1993	1992	1991	1990	1989
Revenues (millions)	45,500	35,551	32,540	33,245	36,812	37,271	40,899	32,416
Net income (millions)	2,018	1,152	915	1,132	1,128	1,243	1,535	1,186
Earnings per share	7.52	4.20	3.19	3.98	3.96	4.36	5.38	4.31
Dividends per share	3.30	3.20	3.20	3.20	3.20	3.20	3.05	3.00
Price: High	107.1	80.5	68.1	69.5	66.9	70.0	68.5	59.0
Low	75.5	59.8	58.1	57.6	56.1	55.5	55.0	48.5

CONSERVATIVE GROWTH

Textron Inc.

40 Westminster Street, Providence, RI 02903 ◻ Investor contact: Mary F. Lovejoy (401) 457-6009 ◻ Listed: NYSE ◻ Dividend reinvestment plan available: (201) 324-0498 ◻ Ticker symbol: TXT ◻ S&P rating: A ◻ Value Line financial strength rating: B++

Textron, a pioneer in the conglomerate sector, focuses on five core businesses:

- Aircraft (29.1 percent of 1996 sales and 24.9 percent of operating income)

- Automotive (17.5 percent and 13.4 percent)

- Industrial (23.7 percent and 21.4 percent)

- Systems & Components (7.0 percent and 5.2 percent)
- Finance (22.6 percent and 35.1 percent)

Aircraft

Bell Helicopter is a leading international helicopter company, serving the commercial and military markets. Cessna Aircraft is the world's largest light and midsize business jet company. Revenues in 1996 were $2.7 billion, up 7.3 percent over the prior year.

Automotive

Textron Automotive Company is a leading, global, full-service supplier of automotive interior and exterior plastic components. Products include instrument panels, interior and exterior trim, lighting, and functional components.

In partnership with original equipment manufacturers (OEMs), Textron Automotive provides modular assembly of components for delivery in sequence on a just-in-time basis. In 1996, Automotive had revenues of $1.6 billion, up 6.1 percent over 1995.

Industrial

The Industrial segment is composed of three major business groups: fastening systems, golf and turf-care equipment, and diversified products. The products are sold under a number of worldwide brand names. Global leadership in these products is supported by a worldwide distribution network in nearly fifty countries. In 1996, Industrial revenues were $2.2 billion, up 40.8 percent over the prior year.

Systems and Components

The Systems and Components businesses manufacture various products and components, primarily for the commercial aerospace and defense industries. The segment has aggressively met reduction in industrywide demand by consolidating operations. In 1996, this operation had revenues of $653 million, down 23.6 percent, compared with the prior year.

Finance

Avco Financial Services is a multinational consumer finance company with nearly 1,200 branches in seven countries. Textron Financial Corporation is a diversified commercial finance company that finances the sale of Textron and third-party products. In 1996, it had revenues of $2.1 billion, a gain of 5.5 percent over the prior year.

Solid Management Team

Textron, under a strong hands-on management team, led by James F. Hardymon, works to improve productivity, costs, and assets. The veteran executive came to Textron after a long career as chief operating officer at Emerson Electric, well known for its string of uninterrupted earnings growth over a thirty-seven-year span.

Hardymon has lowered costs via significant operating improvements, which include higher inventory turns and shorter product manufacturing lead times. Management emphasizes strong core businesses where it can add value and achieve attractive returns on invested capital.

Shortcomings to Bear in Mind

The Financial Services unit—even without the drag from faltering Paul Revere—had a mediocre year in 1996, reflecting the rising number of bankruptcies in the United States. As a result, the provision for loan losses increased considerably.

Reasons to Buy

- Textron's presence in diverse industries helps achieve balance and stability in a variety of economic environments by providing insulation from business and industry cycles.

What's more, the company's multi-industry structure also allows it to balance the long and short-cycle characteristics of Textron's businesses. It takes about ten months to produce a Bell Helicopter, but only one day for 700,000 fasteners to roll off a manufacturing line at Camcar. Blending these characteristics generates consistent cash flow and permits steady investment in new technology and markets.

- Textron is making tough decisions to bring underperforming businesses up to standard: improving the businesses that can meet its requirements, selling those that do not, and managing businesses for cash when divestiture is not appropriate.

  Over the past five years, the company has restructured eleven commercial aerospace and defense businesses, closing or selling twenty-four plants to meet profitability goals in the face of continued weakness in the defense and commercial aviation markets. Textron also sold two divisions in 1994, Homelite and Textron Lycoming Turbine Engine, that did not promise attractive returns on investment.

- Textron is benefiting from the outsourcing trends in the domestic auto industry. To bolster its relationship with the Big Three, Textron relocated its automotive operations to Detroit. The company is the number one independent supplier of interior components in the United States.

- Textron emphasizes strong core businesses where it may add value and achieve attractive returns on capital invested (examples are Avdel and Acustar acquisitions, Homelite and Lycoming dispositions).

- Bell Helicopter is the world's leading manufacturer of commercial helicopters, with 50 percent of the 1995 market.

Through customer surveys and interviews, the company has learned that customers want helicopters with expanded flying capabilities, a larger cabin size, and improved quietness—all at no extra cost.

Bell responded in 1993 with a new 206LT TwinRanger and, in 1994, the 230 executive twin. Two new models were delivered in 1996—the 430 expanded executive twin and the 407 single-engine light.

- Two impressive new products from Textron's Aircraft segment were showcased at the Paris Air Show in June 1995. Cessna Aircraft Company's Citation X, the world's fastest business jet and the largest jet built by Cessna, made its first appearance outside the United States.

  What's more, the V-22 Osprey, a revolutionary tiltrotor aircraft developed by Bell Helicopter and the Boeing Company for the U.S. military, made its public debut in Paris.

- Textron fastener companies sell solutions. The company spends time on their customers' manufacturing lines and taking products apart to find better ways to put them back together. As a consequence, Textron fastener responds with products like the TORX PLUS Drive System. A fastening system developed by Camcar, TORX PLUS Drive delivers higher assembly-line speeds and increased durability for reduced downtime, improved productivity, and cost savings for the customer.

- Textron Automotive's partnership with OEM customers extends from initial product design through manufacturing and installation. Its work as interior appearance integrator for the 1995 Chrysler Minivan led to a larger role as full interior coordinator for the 1998 replacement for Chrysler's Intrepid, Concorde, Vision, and LHS models.

- With more than 60 percent market share, Cessna is the world's leader in the growing market for light and mid-size business jets. Their secret is a commitment to listening carefully to the firm's customers and understanding their requirements for technology, value, reliability, and service. For example, Cessna's new Citation Excel, a light jet with the largest cabin in its class, is set for certification in 1997. The Excel was designed with extensive input from Cessna's customer-based Citation Advisory Council.
- Seeking growth opportunities on a global basis, Avco Financial Services (AFS) has opened operations in New Zealand, Spain, and Hong Kong within the past three years. Its newest market, Hong Kong, provides access to a large middle class and a vibrant economy. AFS's success in international markets is enhanced by employing local managers and personnel who are intimately familiar with local cultures, customs, and operating environments.
- Textron is on the acquisition trail. For instance, in 1996, the company bought eight companies, four of them in Europe. According to CEO James F. Hardymon, "International expansion is a critical element of our growth strategy. In 1996, we achieved our goal of gener-

ating at least 35 percent of our revenues from non–U.S. sources. In the spirit of continuous improvement, we've now raised the bar to 40 percent by 2001."

One of Textron's acquisitions was Germany's Kautex Werke Reinhold Hagen, the world's largest producer of plastic automotive fuel tanks. That should bolster annual revenues by $500 million and gradually make Textron's automotive unit less dependent on the automakers in Detroit. Chrysler alone accounted for over 60 percent of the division's revenues in 1996.

- In 1997, Textron's Cessna unit will ship 20 of its $15 million Citation X jets, up from seven in 1996. Its new Citation Excel light-business aircraft is sold out through the year 2000.
- The company's 83-percent-owned Paul Revere operation was sold early in 1997 to Provident Companies for $1.2 billion. This troubled insurance company proved to be an albatross, mainly because of the unexpectedly high number of claims by physician policyholders.
- Early in 1997, Textron split its stock two for one. It was the first stock split for the company in the past ten years. The dividend was raised by 14 percent, its sixth increase in as many years.

Total assets: $18,235 million
Current ratio: 2.84
Common shares outstanding: 166 million
Return on 1996 shareholders' equity: 15.8%

	1996	1995	1994	1993	1992	1991	1990	1989
Revenues (millions)	7,179	6,468	6,678	6,271	5,617	5,210	5,471	5,272
Net income (millions)	479	479	433	379	324	300	283	269
Earnings per share	2.80	2.76	2.40	2.11	1.83	1.71	1.59	1.51
Dividends per share	.88	.78	.70	.62	.56	.52	.50	.50
Price: High	48.9	38.7	30.3	29.4	22.4	19.8	13.8	14.7
Low	34.6	24.3	23.3	20.2	16.8	12.5	9.7	11.3

TRW Inc.

1900 Richmond Road, Cleveland, Ohio 44124-3760 ◻ Investor contact: Thomas A. Myers (216) 291-7506 ◻ Dividend reinvestment plan available: (216) 291-7654 ◻ Listed: NYSE ◻ Ticker symbol: TRW ◻ S&P rating: B+ ◻ Value Line financial strength rating: A+

Founded in 1901, TRW provides high-technology products and services primarily to the automotive, space and defense, and information markets.

Automotive products include steering, suspension, and occupant restraint systems, engine valve train parts, electromechanical assemblies, fasteners, car and truck accessories, as well as car care products.

The space and defense segment designs and manufactures spacecraft and related equipment as well as software and systems engineering support services.

TRW has 119 automotive operations in twenty-four countries.

TRW's future looks bright. Growing safety concerns no doubt will lead to greater air bag usage throughout the world and increase use of side-impact air bags in the United States.

A Review of 1996

• Sales grew 3 percent, earnings increased 8 percent, and fully diluted earnings per share rose 9 percent.

• The company strengthened its position as the worldwide leader in occupant restraints with the purchase of 80 percent of Magna International's air bag and steering wheel operations, TRW's largest acquisition ever.

• TRW sold the information services business for $1.1 billion.

• The company won two major allocations for new electrically assisted steering systems.

• The dividend was increased by 13 percent—it was the twenty-fifth consecutive annual increase.

• The company repurchased 7.9 million shares of its stock.

• In 1996, automotive sales increased to a record $6.5 billion. Space and defense sales increased to a record $3.4 billion.

Shortcomings to Bear in Mind

▪ TRW's record of growth is not outstanding. In the 1986–1996 period, earnings per share advanced from $1.62 to $3.26, a compound annual growth rate of only 7.2 percent. In the same ten-year stretch, dividends per share inched ahead from $.78 to $1.14, a modest growth rate of 6 percent. However, its low payout ratio (35 percent in 1996) is an offsetting bright spot, since it indicates the company is reinvesting in its future.

Reasons to Buy

▪ The company is maintaining strong research and development programs to sustain its technological superiority. In the last five years, TRW doubled its automotive research and development spending as a percent of sales. Over a ten-year period, the company substantially increased research and development levels in its space and defense business, despite a very difficult environment.

▪ In the automotive business, TRW is the world leader in occupant restraints, steering systems, engine valves, and certain vehicle electronics markets. What's more, the company has been successful in a tough marketplace characterized by intense pricing pressure, strict quality requirements, and continued industry consolidation.

- In information systems and services, TRW has reached new highs in quality and performance. The company has improved credit file accuracy and put renewed emphasis on customer satisfaction, which is enabling TRW to differentiate itself in the highly competitive financial services arena.

- Technologically, TRW continued to evolve as a systems supplier, developing "smart restraints" and side-impact air bag systems, new products in automotive radar, vehicle electronics, advanced integrated occupant safety systems, electrically assisted steering, and lightweight engine valves and suspension systems.

- A program to watch is the Odyssey telecommunications satellite, a large new commercial undertaking. Odyssey is TRW's answer to Motorola's Iridium project. What's more, the Odyssey system is one-third cheaper than Iridium and is scheduled to be in place before Iridium. Odyssey would add another 50 percent to TRW's backlog, raising the space and defense backlog to the highest level since the mid-1980s.

- In February of 1997, TRW announced the acquisition of a majority interest in Magna International's air bag and steering wheel businesses. As part of this action, the company acquired seven manufacturing facilities employing about 2,500 and generating annual sales of about $550 million. The acquisition further solidifies TRW's number one position as a supplier of occupant safety systems and establishes the company as a leading independent steering wheel supplier. In addition, TRW and Magna agreed to form a 50/50 joint venture to provide vehicle manufacturers with total safety systems integration. This alliance, unique in the industry, will provide new products that improve the safety performance of vehicles.

- In 1996, the company added new automotive operations or joint ventures in France, China, Poland, Brazil, Turkey, India, Thailand, and the United States. In all, ten agreements in eight countries. TRW's space and defense segment won important contracts in the United Kingdom, Jamaica, South Africa, and Korea, as well as the United States.

- The company's activity in China was not limited solely to automotive ventures. TRW signed a memorandum of understanding with China Aerospace Company to collaborate on space systems and systems integration programs. Meanwhile, the company continues to be committed to the Odyssey project, a satellite-based personal communications system. An agreement with China Telecommunications Broadcast Satellite Corporation provides the opportunity to offer Odyssey services throughout that country.

- In 1996, TRW made important strides in electrically assisted steering, metallurgy for engine components, gallium arsenide electronic chips for defense and telecommunications needs, and lasers for missile defense.

These and other technologies flow across TRW's businesses to boost its competitiveness and customer satisfaction. To further its research effort, the company invested a most impressive $2 billion in 1996, a figure matched by few companies, regardless of size.

TRW's technical excellence enabled the company to deliver several large space and defense systems that enhance its ongoing role as a major U.S. defense resource. Superior technology also led TRW's diversification beyond defense programs, with nondefense projects now totaling 35 percent of the company's space and defense segment sales, up five percentage points from 1995, and up 25 points from just a few years ago.

Typical of these efforts is a pilot

project the company has started in Jamaica for a nationwide electoral and enumeration system. Another example is the company's enhanced emergency communications system contract for the Los Angeles Police Department. That system could become one of the world's most highly advanced public safety systems.

- In 1997, TRW passed a critical test of the graphite spacecraft structure that the company developed for NASA's Advanced X-ray Astrophysics Facility satellite. TRW has begun integrating this satellite, which is one of the first to use an all-graphite spacecraft bus. Another milestone was achieved in February of 1997 with the launch of the latest in the series of TRW-built Defense Support Program satellites, which provide early warning of strategic and tactical ballistic missile launches and nuclear explosions. With this launch, TRW has achieved a series of fifty-one consecutive missions without an on-orbit failure, a record unmatched in the industry.

- The company is seeing solid demand for side-impact air bags, which reflects strong consumer demand. The side-impact accident is the second leading cause of injury in a car and, crash-for-crash, the most lethal.

Worldwide, TRW expects application rates for side-impact air bags to grow quickly, with market demand of almost 30 million bags by 2000. TRW provides both the air bag and the side-impact crash sensor. The company has fifty-five production or development programs for side-impact air bags and thirty-four production or development programs for sensors. So, in both of these products, which TRW integrates into systems, the company is the market leader.

- TRW is the world's foremost manufacturer of power rack-and-pinion steering gears, commercial vehicle steering systems, and engine valves. The company operates sixty-three plants in twenty countries. While the company has had operations in every region of the world for many years, it wasn't until January of 1996 until the group reorganized to establish a truly global structure. TRW now has four global product lines:
  - Passenger car steering systems
  - Linkage and suspension systems
  - Engine components and value train systems
  - Commercial steering systems

This global approach enables TRW to improve financial controls and performance and allows the company to standardize products and processes throughout the world.

TRW's customers are virtually all the major car makers. Volkswagen, Ford, and Chrysler are the largest. The company also produces 100 percent of the steering gear systems for Fiat. What's more, TRW sells to the Japanese vehicle makers in Japan, as well as to their transplant operations in North America.

Total assets: $5,899 million
Current ratio: 1.29
Common shares outstanding: 126 million
Return on 1996 shareholders' equity: 22%

	1996	1995	1994	1993	1992	1991	1990	1989
Revenues (millions)	9,857	10,172	9,087	7,948	8,311	7,913	8,169	7,340
Net income (millions)	434	446	333	220	170	122	208	263
Earnings per share	3.26	3.31	2.53	1.70	1.55	.99	1.70	2.11
Dividends per share	1.14	1.05	.99	.94	.91	.90	.88	.86
Price: High	52.0	41.3	38.7	35.1	30.1	23.1	25.9	24.9
Low	37.4	30.9	30.5	26.3	20.5	17.3	15.4	20.6

United Technologies Corporation

One Financial Plaza, Hartford, CT 06101 ◻ Investor contact: Angelo J. Messina (203) 728-7575 ◻
Dividend reinvestment program is not available ◻ Ticker symbol: UTX ◻ S&P rating: B ◻ Value Line
financial strength rating: A+

United Technologies provides high-technology products to the aerospace, building systems, and automotive industries throughout the world. UTX's companies are industry leaders and include Pratt & Whitney, Carrier, Otis, UT Automotive, Sikorsky, and Hamilton Standard.

United Technologies posted strong revenue and earnings performance in 1996. Earnings per share jumped 21 percent, to $3.45; net income increased 21 percent, to $906 million.

The commercial businesses, Carrier, Otis, and UT Automotive, generated 63 percent of total revenues in 1996. International operations contributed 56 percent of revenues.

Pratt & Whitney
Products and Services

Pratt & Whitney manufactures large and small commercial and military jet engines and provides spare parts and product support, specialized engine maintenance, and overhaul and repair services for airlines, air forces, and corporate fleets. They also manufacture rocket engines and space propulsion systems, and industrial gas turbines.

Primary Customers

Primary customers include commercial airlines and aircraft leasing companies; commercial and corporate aircraft manufacturers; the U.S. government, including NASA and the military services; regional and commuter airlines.

Financial Results

Revenues in 1996 were $6.2 billion, up 1 percent from 1995; operating profit was $637 million, up 20 percent from 1995.

Carrier
Products and Services

Carrier's products and services include heating, ventilating, and air conditioning (HVAC) equipment for commercial, industrial, and residential buildings; HVAC replacement parts and services; building controls; commercial, industrial, and transportation refrigeration units.

Primary Customers

Carrier's primary customers include mechanical and building contractors; homeowners, building owners, developers, and retailers; architects and building consultants; transportation and refrigeration companies; shipping operations.

Financial Results

In 1996, revenues were $5.96 billion, up 9 percent over the prior year; operating profit was $422 million, up 19 percent over 1995.

Otis
Products and Services

Otis manufactures elevators, escalators, moving walks, and shuttle systems and provides related installation, maintenance, and repair services as well as modernization products and services for elevators and escalators.

Primary Customers

Primary customers include mechanical and building contractors; building owners and developers; homeowners; architects and building consultants.

Financial Results

In 1996, revenues were $5.60 billion, up 6 percent over the prior year. Operating profit was $524 million, a gain of 3 percent over 1995.

UT Automotive
Products and Services

UT Automotive manufactures automotive electrical distribution systems, including wire harnesses, terminals, connectors, and junction boxes; DC electric motors and actuators; motor-driven cooling fan modules; electromechanical and electronic controls, switches, and components; automotive interior trim systems and components, including instrument and door panels, consoles, and headliners; insulation and acoustical materials and systems; and automotive exterior trim.

Primary Customers

Original equipment manufacturers of automobiles, trucks, and sport-utility vehicles.

Financial Results

Revenues in 1996 were $3.23 billion, a gain of 6 percent over the prior year. Operating profit was $196 million, up 9 percent over 1995.

Flight Systems
Products and Services

The Flight Systems group provides the following products and services: military and commercial helicopters and maintenance services; engine and flight controls; propellers; environmental controls for aircraft, spacecraft, and submarines; space life support systems; fuel cells; microelectronics.

Primary Customers

Primary customers include the U.S. government, including NASA, FAA, and the military services; non–U.S. government-

ments; aerospace and defense prime contractors; commercial airlines; aircraft and jet engine manufacturers; hospitals; and oil and gas exploration companies.

Financial Results

Revenues in 1996 were $2.65 billion, down 10 percent from 1995. Operating profit was $234 million, a gain of 12 percent over the prior year.

Shortcomings to Bear in Mind

- In the past fifteen years, United Technologies has normally sold at a price/earnings ratio of less than the market. In 1997, it sells at a P/E higher than the market. It also has a dividend yield below the level of the past fifteen years.

Reasons to Buy

- A startling 76 percent of the world's wealth is concentrated in just 14 percent of the population. With the opening of formerly closed societies over the last decade, the world's economies are in massive transition. In just ten years, global trade has nearly tripled, to more than $6 trillion. Foreign direct investment flows are compounding in excess of 15 percent annually. Deregulation and privatization are increasing. In years ahead, the management of United Technologies sees global wealth creation unforeseen a decade ago and with it unprecedented opportunities for leading multinational companies like UTX.

  As an infrastructure company, United Technologies will benefit especially from urbanization in Asia, the source of more than half of the company's revenues twenty years from now. By 2015, according to the United Nations, more than 700 million people will have migrated from rural to urban areas in just seven Asian countries: the People's Republic of China, India,

Indonesia, Pakistan, Vietnam, the Philippines, and Thailand.

To put these migrations into perspective, one needs to note that European postwar urbanization moved one person in five, or only 60 million people. And on the force of that change, Otis and Carrier created their modern European presence, expanding sales more than 100-fold, to nearly $4 billion.

- United Technologies' revenues in Asia exceeded $4.5 billion in 1996, or 19 percent of the company's worldwide total. The company's revenues in China and Hong Kong exceeded $1 billion annually. Otis has four joint ventures in China; the sale of $17 million worth of escalators to the Shanghai Metro in 1996 was one of the many highlights.

- Carrier has eight China ventures. Most recently, Shanghai Carrier Transicold introduced the first air conditioned bus in that city of 15 million people. But China is not alone in Asia. Asia's geography is substantially equatorial, and weather patterns are hot and humid. The Indian air conditioning market, to name a second example, is growing in excess of 20 percent annually. Carrier Aircon India, a 1986 startup, already has 26 percent share. A highlight of 1996 was the $5 million order for the air conditioning of the new Sahar International Airport in Bombay, now Mumbai.

- United Technologies is now at the tail end of a sweeping reorganization that has cut costs at all of its units. Earnings have been climbing for several quarters. Even the jet-engine business, which had been posting losses because of a slump in aircraft orders and shrinking defense markets, is now profitable.

- Management believes that over the next several years, United Technology's increasing liquidity will give the company the flexibility to continue share repurchases and pursue strategic investments in its core businesses, more than ever before.

- In recent years, United Technologies has purchased several small elevator and air conditioning manufacturers and entered into joint ventures around the world. Management expects to do the same in the jet-engine business, where a shrinking defense industry and a slump in the commercial-airline business are causing a shakeout among the second-tier aerospace and aircraft engine companies.

- Cycle times at Pratt & Whitney have been pared dramatically as a result of the company's restructuring. New engines are now being developed in two and a half years, rather than five years. The time between order and delivery of new engines has been compressed to seven months from two years. Final engine assembly, a process that used to take three months, now is accomplished in ten days, a span that is on its way down to just three days.

- Improvements in UT Automotive's electrical business took root in 1996. Sales of $2.4 billion were a record high, product quality and performance rose, and UTA won new business from a key customer, General Motors. Simplified design and manufacturing processes for inherently complex wire harnesses helped lower reported defects. Product problems fell 40 percent for North American electrical systems and defect rates for connectors dropped to nearly zero. Overseas, UT Automotive broke ground on a new engineering center in Cebu, the Philippines, to serve its growing customer base in the Asia-Pacific region.

Total assets: $16,745 million
Current ratio: 1.30
Common shares outstanding: 243.6 million
Return on 1996 shareholders' equity: 17%

	1996	1995	1994	1993	1992	1991	1990	1989
Revenues (millions)	23,512	22,802	21,197	21,081	21,641	20,840	21,442	19,532
Net income (millions)	906	750	585	487	486	319	751	702
Earnings per share	3.45	2.85	2.20	1.65	1.80	1.16	2.76	2.60
Dividends per share	1.10	1.03	.95	.90	.90	.90	.90	.80
Price: High	70.5	48.9	36.0	33.1	28.9	27.3	31.3	28.7
Low	45.2	31.1	27.5	21.9	20.8	21.1	20.1	19.9

AGGRESSIVE GROWTH

Varian Associates, Inc.

3050 Hansen Way, Palo Alto, CA 94304-1000 ◻ Investor contact: Wayne Somrak (415) 424-5553 ◻ Dividend reinvestment plan available: (617) 575-2900 ◻ Fiscal Year ends September 30 ◻ Listed: NYSE ◻ Ticker symbol: VAR ◻ S&P rating: B+ ◻ Value Line financial strength rating: A

Varian Associates is a diversified, international electronics company that manufactures high-technology systems and components.

Major products lines include:

• Radiation therapy and planning equipment for cancer treatment

• Wafer fabrication equipment for the semiconductor industry

• Analytical instruments and vacuum equipment for science and industry

• Electron tubes for communications, radar, electronic countermeasures, science, medicine, and industrial uses.

The company has manufacturing sites in Arizona, California, Illinois, Massachusetts, South Carolina, and Utah, as well as seven countries outside the United States. More than eighty sales and services offices provide customer support throughout the world.

Healthcare Systems

Varian is the world's largest supplier of equipment for treating cancer with radiation. Products include linear accelerators that generate high-energy electron and photon beams for treatment; simulators for therapy planning and verification; brachytherapy systems for the internal irradiation of tumors; and ancillary equipment and software aimed at improving both therapeutic and administrative efficiency. The company also is a leading supplier of x-ray tubes for the diagnostic imaging industry.

More than 80,000 cancer patients are treated each day by healthcare professionals using Varian Clinac medical linear accelerators and Ximatron simulator systems at more than 2,700 locations worldwide. While the United States currently leads the world in the application of medical technology, Varian expects demand abroad to accelerate as other countries increasingly employ radiation as a cost-effective treatment.

Instruments

Varian is a leading supplier of analytical instrumentation and related equipment for studying the chemical composition of myriad substances. It also manufactures vacuum products and accessories for industrial and scientific applications.

The company's instruments are used in environmental monitoring and analysis; biological and biochemical research; quality control and research in such industries as pharmaceuticals, foods, metals, chemicals, and petroleum; and in independent laboratories.

Its vacuum products and helium leak detectors are utilized in such applications as semiconductor manufacturing, high-energy physics, surface analysis, space research, and petrochemical refining.

Semiconductor Equipment

Varian is among the world's largest producers of semiconductor fabrication equipment, with leadership positions in ion implantation and thin-film-coating systems.

The company's equipment is used by virtually every major semiconductor manufacturer in the United States, Japan, Korea, and Europe. Varian Korea Ltd., a joint venture, provides manufacturing and customer support in this fast-growing market. A joint venture with Tokyo Electron Ltd. enhances Varian's strength in Japan through research and development, sales, and customer support efforts.

Electron Devices

Varian is a major manufacturer of microwave and power grid tubes and related equipment, such as satellite communications amplifiers and power supplies. It also fabricates circuit boards and subassemblies for customers both inside and outside the company at its Tempe Electronics Center.

Global markets served include communications, industry, defense, and energy research. Varian tubes and amplifier systems are used by more satellite communications stations worldwide than those of any other manufacturer.

Shortcomings to Bear in Mind

- Varian does not have a particularly impressive record of growth. In the 1986–1996 period, earnings per share were volatile, but they have stabilized in more recent years. EPS rose from $.01 in 1986 to $3.81 in 1991, which makes calculating a growth rate impractical. In the same period, dividends moved ahead at a moderate pace, rising from $.13 to $.31 in the ten-year span, a growth rate of 9.1 percent. The same story prevailed for book value growth during the 1986–1996 span; it inched ahead from $9.58 to $15.27, a growth rate of 4.8 percent.

Reasons to Buy

- For analytical laboratories, sample handling can be a time-consuming and costly bottleneck. Varian has developed several innovative solutions to address this challenge, including automated solid-phase microextraction for gas chromatography, which slashes preparation times from hours to minutes while eliminating the use of costly solvents.

  In 1997, the company introduced the revolutionary Mercury, a nuclear magnetic resonance (NMR) spectrometer that combines high performance and ease of use in the smallest, most affordable package on the market today. With this introduction, Varian has redesigned its entire NMR product line in less than three years, refreshing its offerings with key technological advances. The products, moreover, also incorporate significant reductions in manufacturing costs to enhance operating margins.

- Demand for the company's chip-making systems has been broad-based, with particularly strong orders received from Pacific Rim customers, accounting for over one-half of the total volume. With over forty new chip-production facilities planned or under construction around the world, demand for Varian systems should remain healthy.

- Under the leadership of CEO J. Tracy O'Rourke, Varian devoted the last several years to tuning its internal engine to achieve greatly enhanced efficiency and cost-effectiveness. Now those investments are beginning to pay off.

- The company's Healthcare Systems business has been expanding into important markets, including those outside the United States, where the potential for growth is promising. The acquisition of Eureka X-ray Tube Corporation added several low- and mid-tier tubes to Varian's product offerings. The new lines complement current high-tier product lines and are used in diagnostic applications in both the original equipment and replacements markets.

- The purchase of Sopha Eurotube Services provides Varian with its first healthcare systems facility in France. Its radiation oncology distribution and x-ray tube loading station activities will be conducted under its new name, Varian Medical, France.

- Oncology Systems received permission from the U.S. Food & Drug Administration (FDA) to market its Varis computer-based oncology management system during 1995. Varis software and hardware combinations enable clinicians to more effectively plan and safely deliver a course of radiation therapy. They also automate many administrative tasks so healthcare providers can focus on patient needs.

- The company's newly introduced VariSource brachytherapy cancer treatment system has been winning acceptance, particularly in Latin America. The FDA granted permission for Varian to market its VariSource, which is manufactured at Varian-TEM Ltd. in the United Kingdom. This cancer-treatment system is expected to be well-received by U.S. hospitals for its cost-effectiveness and ability to treat cancers in difficult-to-reach areas, such as the bronchial lobes.

- In 1996, Varian introduced products designed for integrated cancer care: medical information systems, accessories to facilitate and enhance treatment, and services to assist medical institutions in realizing more cost-effective operations. What's more, the x-ray tube business negotiated agreements with key original-equipment manufacturers, including a $90-million, three-year contract with Toshiba. The company also introduced a new component for medical imaging that is expected to increase the efficiency of diagnostic imaging while decreasing costs. In addition, Varian Biosynergy, Inc. was launched to develop technologies and products that target energy at specific regions of the body and work in combination with novel biological and chemical modifiers to fight disease.

- Varian's multiyear program to broaden international distribution uniquely positions the company to capitalize on burgeoning demand outside the United States. In the cost-conscious United States, integrated cancer-care solutions and productivity enhancement should continue to be in demand. The company expects to expand its capabilities through acquisitions and partnerships that extend existing product lines. At the same time, it will continue to invest in promising new technologies such as solid-state imaging components and the application of focused energy in developing new treatments.

- Another customer-focused product, Varian's new Star+gas chromatography (GC) system, is the fastest GC system in the world. Using two new Varian technologies, Star+ analyzes samples at least ten times faster than conventional units. It also reduces overall costs and is solvent-free. The Star+ is proving to be a time- and cost-saving product for laboratories where high-speed analysis and improved process control are critical.

- Varian's Semiconductor Equipment's newest product, the VIISion high-cur-

rent ion implanter, is gaining widespread acceptance among chip manufacturers because of its high-volume output and superlative performance. Expected to become the leading production workhorse in ion implantation, the system provides higher verification, outperforming all other current systems.

Total assets: $1,019 million
Current ratio: 1.59
Common shares outstanding: 31 million
Return on 1996 shareholders' equity: 28.8%

	1996	1995	1994	1993	1992	1991	1990	1989
Revenues (millions)	1,599	1,576	1,553	1,311	1,288	1,378	1,265	1,344
Net income (millions)	122	106	79	46	39	58	45	32
Earnings per share	3.81	3.01	2.22	1.26	1.02	1.48	1.13	.77
Dividends per share	.31	.27	.23	.20	.18	.16	.13	.13
Price: High	62.9	57.4	39.3	30.0	22.4	25.1	17.4	15.3
Low	40.5	34.5	28.3	19.0	16.8	14.9	10.0	9.9

AGGRESSIVE GROWTH

VF Corporation

1047 North Park Road, Wyomissing, PA 19610 ▫ **Investor contact: Cynthia F. Knoebel, CFA (212) 782-0276** ▫ **Dividend reinvestment plan available: (215) 378-1151** ▫ **Ticker symbol: VFC** ▫ **S&P rating: A-** ▫ **Value Line financial strength rating: B++**

Unlike most other apparel stocks, the shares of VF Corporation, the largest publicly traded apparel company, have maintained strength since dipping in late 1993. Thanks to aggressive growth strategies, including acquisitions, wider distribution, and strong brand management, as well as conservative financial management, VF has reported sales and earnings growth over the past few years, despite the ups and downs of the apparel industry. Combining its several brands of jeans, VF has a 30 percent share of the domestic market.

VF's apparel business falls into these categories:

- The Jeanswear business group produces denim products sold under such names as Riders, Rustler, Lee, and

Wrangler in the United States as well as in international markets. Also included is the Girbaud Division, which designs and markets licensed products in the United States under the Marithe & Francois Girbaud label.

VF owns three of the top four jeans brands in the United States, with a total unit market share of about 30 percent.

Shortcomings to Bear in Mind

- VF operates in the apparel industry, which is well known for its volatility and uncertainty.

Reasons to Buy

- VF seeks a return on average common shareholders' equity of 17 percent to 20 percent. In 1996, the company just missed this target, since return on equity was 16.2 percent.

- VF does not consider itself a pioneer. In other words, it doesn't try to be the first company to introduce a new idea. It tends to wait until the innovator shows the way.

    For instance, when Sara Lee introduced its new Wonderbra in the United States in New York in the spring of 1994, it did so after the trendy cleavage-builder took the British market by storm. On the sidelines, VF kept a watchful eye on Sara Lee's introduction to the American shopper, to make sure she would follow in the footsteps of her British counterparts. When it became evident that she liked the new product, VF quickly entered the fray with it own version, It Must Be Magic.

    But once VF decided to move, it moved swiftly. Using state-of-the-art distribution, it surged ahead with a nationwide rollout five months ahead of Sara Lee, which itself is an accomplished marketing machine.

- Adhering to a set of core strategies has enabled VF, a global apparel industry leader, to demonstrate steady, consistent growth despite the challenges of a dynamic and often unpredictable industry environment. In summary, these are the company's core strategies:
  - Build strong brands that deliver value to consumers.
  - Focus on high-volume basic fashion apparel categories.
  - Target specific brands to specific channels of distribution.
  - Lead the industry in responsive service.
  - Expand its international presence.
  - Maintain conservative financial policies.
- At the end of 1996, VF's financial position was extremely strong. The com-

pany's debt-to-capital ratio reached a thirteen-year low, while cash flow from operations reached an all-time high. VF's cash flow outlook remains positive, giving the company the flexibility to pursue acquisitions, repurchase shares, maintain conservative debt levels, and increase dividends.

- While image-driven brands fight to capture the passing fashion whims of consumers, and others rely on rock-bottom pricing to attract shoppers, VF remains true to a strategy of "functional fashion" by designing products that meet discernible, functional needs.

    Creating a more active, continuous link between consumer research and new product development is one of VF's most important consumerization initiatives. This link, which the company calls its Consumer Response System (CRS), will move VF from a series of project-based research efforts to a more formalized, ongoing process. With CRS, VF is embarking on the most extensive consumer research program in its nearly one-hundred-year history.

    For example, in 1996, the company launched the VF Consumer Monitor, a quarterly survey of apparel purchases by thousands of consumers. Through this Monitor, the company is building a powerful set of indices to track market share and consumers' awareness of the company's brands, their purchases and intent to purchase, on a consistent basis across all VF brands.

- When the company introduced its Market Response System (MRS) over seven years ago, VF set the industry standard for customer responsiveness. Today, the company is able to replenish retail inventories with its products automatically, based on actual sales information received electronically from its customers.

Now, VF Corporation is taking MRS to a new level of excellence by actually "micromarketing" its products to consumers on a store-by-store basis. Essentially, this means the company can tailor product assortments in specific stores to respond to the requirements of specific consumer segments. Through a combination of data mining techniques, store-specific consumer profiles, and customized in-store presentations, VF intends to break new ground in consumer responsiveness. The company began to test this program on a limited basis in 1997.

- In 1996, the members of VF's Operating Committee worked with the company's division managers to analyze VF's markets and brands to determine where best to direct the company's investments. They concluded that four key categories—jeanswear, intimate apparel, workwear, and daypacks—presented the areas of greatest strength and opportunity for the company. Strong, established brands and leading market shares give VF a distinct competitive advantage. And over the next several years, the company is committed to investing an additional quarter of a billion dollars to realize this potential.

The Wrangler and Rustler brands, for example, hold a dominant share in the men's jeanswear category in discount stores. Through the company's Wrangler for Women and Riders jeans programs, VF seeks to capture a similar position on the women's side.

- Department stores also offer opportunities to expand the company's market share in jeans. Continuing its aggressive marketing program, Lee is determined to become the women's brand of choice for casual dressing. Its new Lee Riveted line had an outstanding first year in 1996 and will serve as a cornerstone for the brand's new product efforts in 1997.

- VF's international jeans sales have more than doubled over the past five years, but the company's market shares are still well below those it enjoys in the United States, representing a considerable opportunity for growth. Most of the company's expansion has occurred in Western Europe, but growth is accelerating in newer markets such as Eastern Europe and Asia.

- In intimate apparel, Vanity Fair Intimates has emerged from a period of restructuring and consolidation, primed for renewed growth. Working together, Vanity Fair, Vassarette, and Private Brands have developed a pipeline of new products for each business segment, which are slated for rollout in 1997. Already firmly established in France and Spain, with a number of European brands, VF will also continue to explore new global opportunities in intimate apparel.

- The acquisition of Bulwark Protective Apparel, Inc., a premium brand of flame-resistant apparel, capped 1996 for the company's workwear company, Red Kap. Long the market leader in occupational apparel, Red Kap's low-cost manufacturing base and service capabilities are helping to fuel expansion in service, safety, and executive appeal.

- In February of 1997, the company announced a restructuring effort that will shed between 2,000 and 3,000 employees over a four-year period. This move will also entail a consolidation of manufacturing and administration, as well as an updating of product lines. Prior to this announcement, the company employed 65,000.

The restructuring is expected to cost a total of $400 million and yield about $150 million in annual savings by the year 2000. A VF spokesman said the company would account for the restructuring as expenses and didn't plan to take any charges against earnings.

Total assets: $3,450 million
Current ratio: 1.94
Common shares outstanding: 64 million
Return on 1996 shareholders' equity: 16.2%

	1996	1995	1994	1993	1992	1991	1990	1989
Revenues (millions)	5,137	5,062	4,972	4,320	3,824	2,952	2,613	2,533
Net income (millions)	300	244	274	246	237	161	105	176
Earnings per share	4.64	3.76	4.20	3.80	3.97	2.75	1.78	2.72
Dividends per share	1.44	1.38	1.30	1.22	1.11	1.02	1.00	.91
Price: High	69.9	57.1	53.8	56.4	57.5	41.5	34.3	38.4
Low	47.6	46.8	44.3	39.5	38.5	17.6	11.6	27.8

GROWTH AND INCOME

Vulcan Materials Company

P. O. Box 530187, Birmingham, Alabama 35253-0187 ◻ Investor contact: E. Starke Sydnor (205) 877-3206 ◻ Dividend reinvestment plan available: (201) 324-0498 ◻ Listed: NYSE ◻ Ticker symbol: VMC ◻ S&P rating: A- ◻ Value Line financial strength rating: A

Vulcan Materials is the largest domestic producer of construction aggregates (a product category that includes crushed stone, sand, and gravel). The company does not materially depend upon sales to any one customer or group of customers. Its products are mostly sold to private industry. However, most of VMC's construction materials are ultimately used in public projects.

From 127 permanent crushed stone plants and 93 other production and distribution facilities, Vulcan provides a diversified line of aggregates, other construction materials, and related services to all parts of the construction industry in seventeen states. Vulcan's principal product, crushed stone, is used in virtually all forms of construction.

Vulcan's Chemicals segment is a significant producer of basic industrial and specialty chemicals. Through its Chloralkali Business Unit, it produces chlorine, caustic soda, hydrochloric acid, potassium chemicals, and chlorinated organic chemicals. The food and pharmaceutical markets provide stable demand for several of Chloralkali's chemical products.

Through its Performance Systems Business Unit, it provides process aids for the pulp and paper and textile industries, and chemicals and services to the municipal, industrial, and environmental water-management markets. It also has a stake in the custom manufacture of a variety of specialty chemicals.

A Review of 1996

Construction Materials had record sales for the fourth consecutive year. Sales were $962 million, up 9 percent from 1995. Record aggregates shipments of about 158 million tons in 1996, including shipments by affiliated companies, were up 7 percent from the prior year's level.

Shipments of crushed stone, the segment's principal product, increased 7 percent. Excluding the impact of freight to remote distribution yards, the average price of crushed stone increased 3 percent.

Segment earnings, before interest expense and income taxes, of $197.3 million also were at a record level and increased 9 percent from 1995's level of $181.5 million.

Sales for the Chemicals segment in 1996 were at a record level of $607 million, up 5 percent from the prior year. Chemicals reported record earnings of $94.7 million, up 8 percent from the prior year.

Chloralkali earnings were even with results reported in 1995. Chloralkali operating results in 1996 were hurt by a decline in caustic soda prices, particularly during the second half of the year, as well as by somewhat higher costs referable to energy and plant maintenance. These negative operating impacts were partly mitigated by higher earnings from chlorinated organic products.

A Look at the Industry

Aggregates account for about 95 percent of the weight of each ton of asphalt that is used to pave highways and parking lots. Aggregates account for 85 percent of the weight of ready-mix concrete used for such projects as dams, highways, and foundations.

Vulcan quarries and processes the stone to various sizes, so that it conforms to specific engineering standards. Independent truckers or customer trucks haul the stone to the construction site, typically no more than twenty or thirty miles away.

There are two major exceptions to this rule. The first exception is the Reed quarry, which ships a large portion of its production great distances, mainly by barge on the Mississippi River system. A much smaller portion is shipped by rail.

The company's so-called Crescent Market Project is the second exception to the local-market rule of thumb. Because aggregate deposits along the Gulf Coast are limited, most aggregates are supplied from inland sources seventy or more miles away. Consequently, transportation costs increase the product's delivery prices substantially.

Vulcan participates in a venture that produces crushed limestone at a quarry near Cancún, Mexico, ships the product to the U.S. Gulf Coast, and markets the stone in a number of cities, including Houston, Galveston, New Orleans, Mobile, and Tampa. The economics of the project work because ocean shipping costs much less than truck or rail transportation, even though the distance is much greater.

The largest end-use for aggregates is highway construction and maintenance. Crushed stone is used as a highway base material and as the major portion of the asphaltic concrete and ready-mixed concrete used as a surface material.

Crushed stone is the company's largest product; it accounts for three-fourths of Construction Materials sales. Vulcan also produces sand and gravel, asphaltic and ready-mix concrete, and numerous other, less-significant products.

Shortcomings to Bear in Mind

- The company's Chloralkali unit is part of its commodity chemicals business. A commodity differs from a proprietary product in that it is not differentiated from the products of its competitors. In order to survive in a commodity business, you should be a low-cost producer or offer a unique service, such as quick delivery.
- Demand for aggregates is both cyclical and mature.

- Caustic soda prices tend to be volatile. For instance, prices peaked in April 1991 at nearly $300 per ton; then they plummeted to $61 in March of 1994. In the spring of 1997, the price was about $130 per ton—or well below earlier levels. The reason for the decline was too much of the chemical in the marketplace. Vulcan sells nearly all of the caustic soda it produces. As a consequence, any price change can impact earnings significantly.

Reasons to Buy

- Earnings per share have moved ahead steadily in recent years, with only one significant drop (in 1991, EPS slid to $1.38 from $3.10). In the 1986–1996 period, earnings per share expanded from $2.10 to $5.36, a compound annual growth rate of 9.8 percent. In the same ten-year stretch, dividends per share climbed from $.74 to $1.68, a growth rate of 8.5 percent.
- The aggregates industry has undergone significant ownership and concentration changes in recent years. In 1985, the top ten producers in the United States accounted for about 13 percent of total domestic sales.

    By 1995, the top ten producers shipped about 22 percent of the U.S. market. Vulcan, the industry leader with an estimated 6.4 percent of the U.S. aggregates market and an estimated 10.6 percent of the crushed stone market, currently serves geographic markets with about 25 percent of the U.S. population. Notwithstanding the recent consolidation, the aggregates industry remains highly fragmented and contains significant growth opportunities.
- Adequate deposits of high-quality stone reserves in strategic locations are essential to the long-term success of the Construction Materials segment.

Vulcan has pursued an aggressive strategy to maintain and increase its level of reserves. In the past decade, reserves increased by over 88 percent, from about 4.3 billion tons in 1986 to some 8.1 billion tons in 1996.

In addition to new reserves associated with acquisitions and green-field sites, reserves at operations owned by the company since 1986 actually increased during the past decade, despite production of nearly one billion tons. Vulcan continues to control the largest quantity of stone reserves in the industry by a wide margin.

- Construction began in 1996 on a major capacity expansion for the Chloromethanes II facility at the company's Geismar, Louisiana, chemical manufacturing complex. The expansion will enable Vulcan to better serve customers in the growing refrigerant, fluoropolymer, and silicones markets.
- Historically, Construction Materials enjoys good results when housing starts are strong. Conversely, Chemicals enjoys its best results when caustic soda prices are high. The inverse relationship between changes in housing starts and caustic prices has been almost perfect for the last twenty-five years.

    The relationship occurs because the demand for chlorine is heavily dependent upon economic activity, especially construction. Demand for caustic is much less cyclical because of the diverse nature of its end-use markets. Hence, when economic activity is strong, chlorine demand increases sharply, putting caustic in an oversupply situation.

    However, when the economy is slack, chlorine production is curtailed, thus reducing caustic production and creating a shortage of caustic.
- Vulcan manufactures sodium chlorite at a world-class facility at the company's

Wichita, Kansas, chemical complex. Vulcan is the largest North American producer of sodium chlorite and the world's second-largest. Sodium chlorite is used in a variety of applications, including drinking and industrial water treatment, air scrubbing, and paper, textile, and electronics manufacturing.

- Late in 1996, Vulcan Chemicals Company, a subsidiary of Vulcan Materials, acquired the food-processing business of Savolite, Inc., a sister company of Savolite Corporation of Canada. Savolite's food-processing business is concentrated in the U.S. Pacific Northwest. Its major markets include meat processing, fruit juice, vegetables, dairy, prepared salads, and other food-processing operations.

- In mid-1996, Callaway Chemical Company, a subsidiary of Vulcan Materials, acquired Mayo Chemical Company. Mayo makes specialty chemicals for niche markets in the water-treatment, textile, industrial cleaning, mining, and pulp and paper industries.

- Vulcan Materials has a low beta coefficient, which means it fluctuates less than the market. A beta of 1.0 is indicative of a stock that fluctuates at the same rate as the market. A lower beta indicates the stock will hold up well in a bear market. Vulcan's beta (according to Value Line) is only 0.60—about the same as a public utility. Interestingly, Standard & Poor's gives Vulcan a beta of a minuscule 0.33.

Total assets: $1,321 million
Current ratio: 2.02
Common shares outstanding: 34 million
Return on 1996 shareholders' equity: 22.4%

	1996	1995	1994	1993	1992	1991	1990	1989
Revenues (millions)	1,569	1,461	1,253	1,134	1,078	1,008	1,105	1,076
Net income (millions)	189	166	98	88	91	53	120	133
Earnings per share	5.36	4.63	2.67	2.39	2.41	1.38	3.10	3.30
Dividends per share	1.68	1.46	1.36	1.26	1.20	1.20	1.12	.98
Price: High	66.5	60.4	56.5	56.1	49.6	40.0	46.8	48.5
Low	53.1	48.1	44.0	40.3	36.0	30.4	29.4	40.5

INCOME

Wachovia Corporation

P. O. Box 3099, Winston-Salem, NC 27150 ◻ Investor contact: James C. Mabry (910) 732-5788 ◻ Dividend reinvestment plan available: (800) 633-4236 ◻ Listed: NYSE ◻ Ticker symbol: WB ◻ S&P rating: A ◻ Value Line financial strength rating: A+

Wachovia Corporation is an interstate bank holding company. It has dual headquarters, in Atlanta, Georgia, and Winston-Salem, North Carolina. The company's properties are situated in the Southeast and include operations headquartered in Atlanta, Winston-Salem,

Columbia, South Carolina, and Wilmington, Delaware.

At the end of 1996, Wachovia (pronounced wuh-KOVE-ee-uh) had assets of $46.9 billion, making it the twentieth-largest banking company in the United States.

However, the bank's return on common shareholders' equity of 17.6 percent gives it a rank of eighth. It has a similar rank for its 1.43 percent return on assets. WB's average common equity to assets places it ninth among the nation's banks. Finally, Wachovia is financially sound; the corporation's senior debt is rated AA by Standard & Poor's and Aa3 by Moody's.

At the end of 1996, Wachovia had 220 banking offices in North Carolina, 123 in Georgia, and 145 in South Carolina.

Major corporate and institutional relationships are managed by Wachovia Corporate Services, Inc., through banking offices in Georgia, North Carolina, and South Carolina and through representative offices in Chicago, London, New York City, and Tokyo. The corporation maintains foreign branches at Grand Cayman through its banking subsidiaries and an Edge Act subsidiary in New York City.

Wachovia Trust Services, Inc., provides fiduciary, investment management, and related financial services for corporate, institutional, and individual clients.

Discount brokerage and investment advisory services are provided by Wachovia Investments, Inc., to customers primarily in Georgia, North Carolina, and South Carolina.

Wachovia Operational Services Corporation provides information processing and systems development for Wachovia's subsidiaries. Finally, WB is involved in other financial services activities, in other financial services, including residential mortgage origination, state and local government securities underwriting, sales and trading, foreign exchange, corporate finance, and other money market services.

Wachovia is fortunate to have extensive branch banking networks in three of the nation's most vibrant states. By several economic measures, the Southeast is growing faster than the nation, and the bank's three home states are outpacing the region as well. Wachovia's markets within each state are expected to accelerate more quickly than the states as a whole. The combined three-state population is 17.8 million, with 6.6 million total households. WB now has relationships with about 2.1 million of them.

Business growth continues to be strong within the three states. North Carolina, Georgia, and South Carolina are among the top fifteen states nationally in the announcement of new and expanded manufacturing facilities. In these vibrant markets, Wachovia covers a broad business spectrum, serving over 7,000 corporate clients, in addition to some 130,000 small and medium-size businesses within primary markets and contiguous states.

Shortcomings to Bear in Mind

- The total return on Wachovia's common stock, including price appreciation and dividends, was 27.6 percent for 1996. By contrast, the Keefe, Bruyette & Woods Index of fifty money-center and regional banks was 41.5 percent.
- In its home state of North Carolina, Wachovia's market share of deposits has remained stable at about 15 percent. However, the bank has dropped to number three in deposit share from number two in 1995. In Georgia, Wachovia's market share has also remained steady at about 10 percent, but other banks have zoomed ahead.

Reasons to Buy

- For years, Wachovia has enjoyed a reputation as a "banker's bank." It consistently generates a high return on equity. Its discipline in keeping overhead costs low puts it among the elite of efficient banking institutions. What's more, Wachovia's conservative stance when granting credit helped it sidestep the loan losses that bedeviled rivals in the past.

- The bank's stripes may be changing, under the leadership of a new CEO, Leslie "Bud" Baker, Jr. Since the fifty-four-year-old president, who has been with Wachovia since 1969, took the reins in 1994, he has launched a quiet revolution, which some analysts contend is now beginning to bear fruit.

  According to one analyst, "When Bud Baker came in, he was really faced with a pretty monumental task. He had to spend hundreds of millions of dollars to bring technology up to par."

  Mr. Baker carefully examined every part of the bank's operations and has been taking steps to discover the best way to proceed. For one thing, Wachovia is closing as many as 10 percent of its branches and reorganizing its trust operation. It is updating and converting its computer systems and plans a $40 million charge in 1997 to cover these costs.

  Mr. Baker says he believes that Wachovia will be able to exceed its historical target of 10 percent to 12 percent a year growth in earnings per share. The bank also plans to boost fee income to 50 percent of total revenue, up from only 32 percent by introducing fee-based products and raising current charges.

- Some investors might complain that Wachovia has a low yield. However, it is well above average. But, more important, WB has a fine record of growth, which means dividends are likely to move smartly ahead over the years. In the 1986–1996 period, earnings per share expanded from $1.50 to $3.81, with only one dip during those years. The compound annual growth rate for earnings per share is a solid 9.8 percent. Dividends, moreover, climbed at an even better clip in this ten-year stretch, rising from $.44 to $1.52, a compound growth rate of 13.2 percent.

- Wachovia is the industry leader when it comes to credit quality. Among the twenty-five largest American banks, WB has the lowest nonperforming assets-to-loans and foreclosed property ratio.

- Banks traditionally have focused on acquisitions of other commercial banks to expand geographic reach or deepen consumer deposits or branch banking market share. To be sure, such transactions may continue to have appeal. On the other hand, Wachovia is not obsessed with size nor attracted to transactions that dilute shareholder value. Rather, WB is convinced that strategic acquisitions or combinations should enhance product capabilities, increase the scale of existing businesses, provide access to a larger base of customers, and increase shareholder value.

- Wachovia's share of market in its home states has outpaced branch share for some time. The bank's national corporate presence belies the organization's asset size by a wide margin. However, Wachovia intends to strengthen its ability to sell both through the core branch network and by exploring new initiatives outside the traditional branch structure.

- Wachovia has long been recognized for its credit quality. While there are some who believe credit issues are now less important, Wachovia's commitment to being a sound bank is unwavering. But risk management today encompasses practices that go well beyond sound credit administration. It includes the operational service delivery and general market risks associated with all aspects of the bank's business. For example:

  • Wachovia has been using interest-rate swaps and other off-balance-sheet derivative instruments for a number of years. These instruments are used principally to help manage interest-rate risk and are generally designed to neutralize the balance sheet from the adverse impact of external forces.

• Wachovia is one of the leaders in addressing the growing issue of check fraud. WB's check fraud task force, with representatives from operations, product management, legal, and security, is helping bring industry associations together to focus on common loss-prevention initiatives, conducting seminars to educate companies on risks and prevention measures, and seeking ways to leverage image processing and other technology capabilities to combat the problem.

• Credit quality and expense management ratios have been strong at Wachovia. At the end of 1996, for instance, nonperforming assets were .25 percent of loans and foreclosed property, the best among the twenty-five largest bank holding companies.

The corporation's reserve coverage of nonperforming loans was 681 percent, the second-best among this peer group. WB's overhead, or efficiency ratio, was 52.2 percent, also ranking second-best among these twenty-five banks.

Total assets: $46,905 million
Return on average assets: 1.43%
Common shares outstanding: 164 million
Return on 1996 shareholders' equity: 17.6%

	1996	1995	1994	1993	1992	1991	1990	1989
Loans (millions)	31,283	29,261	25,891	22,416	19,642	20,257	16,433	15,102
Net income (millions)	645	602	539	492	433	230	297	269
Earnings per share	3.81	3.50	3.13	2.83	2.51	1.34	2.13	1.94
Dividends per share	1.52	1.38	1.23	1.11	1.00	.92	.82	.70
Price: High	60.3	48.3	35.4	40.5	34.8	30.0	22.4	22.7
Low	39.6	32.0	30.1	31.9	28.3	20.3	16.2	15.5

CONSERVATIVE GROWTH

Walgreen Company

200 Wilmot Road, Deerfield, Illinois 60015 □ **Investor contact: John M. Palizza (847) 914-2972** □
Dividend reinvestment plan available: (312) 461-5535 □ **Fiscal year ends August 31** □ **Listed: NYSE** □
Ticker symbol: WAG □ **S&P rating: A+** □ **Value Line financial strength rating: A+**

Dating back to 1901, Walgreen opened its first drugstore on Chicago's South Side. Its 2000th store was opened ninety-three years later, in Cleveland, Ohio, on November 4, 1994. Walgreens now enjoys first or second place in thirty-five of its top fifty-three markets—all of which rank in the largest one hundred drugstore markets in the United States.

Walgreen Company is the leader of the domestic chain drugstore industry in sales, profits, store growth, and technology use. Walgreen fills more prescriptions than any other American retailer.

The company's strategy is to be the nation's most convenient healthcare provider.

Sales for 1996 reached $11.8 billion, produced by 2,193 drugstores in thirty-four states and Puerto Rico. Walgreen drugstores serve 2.2 million customers daily and average $5.2 million annual sales per unit. That's $520 per square foot, among the highest in the industry.

Shortcomings to Bear in Mind

- Although Walgreen prospects are bright, the stock is rarely priced low enough to entice a value investor. More often than not, the P/E ratio is above the general level of the market. In May of 1997, for instance, it traded at 30 times earnings. At the same time, a number of insiders (such as officers and board members) were selling part of their holdings.

Reasons to Buy

- Walgreen has an impressive growth record. In the 1986–1996 span, earnings per share climbed from $.42 to $1.50, for a compound annual growth rate of 13.6 percent. In the same ten-year stretch, dividends per share advanced from $.13 to $.44, a growth rate of 13 percent.
- Per-capita use of medications is heaviest among people over fifty-five and under five. These are the most rapidly growing segments of the American population. These are the people who patronize Walgreen stores. Not only do they buy drugs, they also buy a lot of other items that are commonly found in a Walgreen store, such as toothpaste, stationery, vitamins, magazines, books, toys, light bulbs, hair coloring, and cosmetics.
- A large portion of Walgreen's sales is derived from "must-have" items, which consumers are unlikely to forgo no matter what the economic climate.
- Walgreen's management has not relaxed its intensity to excel. It's continually opening new stores in new markets and spending heavily on technological improvements and remodeling.

- Walgreen tends to avoid locating its stores in malls. Rather, it prefers freestanding units that are highly visible. A typical store is 14,000 to 15,000 square feet in size.
- With or without healthcare reform, the United States is rapidly moving toward managed care. Walgreen's is in excellent position to benefit from this because of the following characteristics:
  - National, interconnected store presence
  - Market share penetration
  - Technologically advanced systems
  - Nursing home and durable medical equipment businesses
  - Pharmacy mail service
  - Walgreen retail and mail service prescription capabilities, combined with its already large and growing national store presence, make Walgreens especially attractive to managed care plans.
- Walgreen's share of the pharmacy market continues to grow, solidifying the company's position as the largest filler of prescriptions in the country. Beyond that, Walgreen is experiencing the most robust pharmacy growth in the past ten years. The number of Walgreen-filled prescriptions has risen nearly 60 percent since 1989—double the industry average.
- In just six years, 82 million Americans—almost 30 percent of the population—will be over fifty years old. By 2010, that number approaches 100 million. That's good news for drugstores— average prescription use rises rapidly after age 50, doubling between the ages of 45 and 65.
- New Walgreen stores are about 10 percent larger than five years ago. The prototype store is 13,500 square feet. Pharmacy waiting areas, consultation windows, fragrance bars, food departments, and clerk-served photo-finishing

departments enhance customer convenience and traffic flow.

One-hour photo finishing is now offered in more than one hundred stores, chiefly in new markets. This service generates strong volume. More importantly, stores that open with "one-hour" service show higher sales in total photo department volume.

- The company relocated seventy-five stores to freestanding sites in 1997. A relocated store, on average, sees sales volume rise more than 30 percent in the first year. However, profitability remains flat during this initial year, before it increases significantly in succeeding years.
- Walgreen is now first or second in thirty-five of its top markets—all of which rank in the largest one hundred drugstore markets in the United States. Expanding market share is especially advantageous because of the rapid growth of managed care prescription sales, which now account for two-thirds of all retail prescriptions in the United States. Combine that number with estimates that 95 percent of the U.S. population will be in managed care by the year 2000, and you'll understand why Walgreen takes this business seriously. Convenient drugstores with strong market share presence are especially attractive to managed care providers, who want accessible pharmacy locations for their patients.
- Walgreen 1997 capital-spending budget is more than $400 million. Despite this level of expenditure, the company is virtually debt-free, has a strong balance sheet, and is in excellent financial condition.
- Installation of SIMS (Strategic Inventory Management System) autoreorder system chainwide is helping to push down operating costs. The company's inventory investment-to-sales ratios continues to improve in markets where Walgreen has had SIMS the longest. In the distribution centers, SIMS has already saved more than $100 million in inventory investment, while increasing inventory turns by two. SIMS also adds to sales by reallocating inventory—basically, getting the right items to the right stores at the right times, thus enhancing the company's in-stock condition.
- Walgreen is a leader in drugstore technology. Its proprietary Intercom Plus pharmacy system should be installed throughout the entire chain by the end of fiscal 1997. This leading-edge system should significantly improve the pharmacy department's (46 percent of total volume) overall productivity by reducing the time required to fill prescriptions.
- Skeptics might be concerned that Walgreen will soon saturate the market with its stores. Management doesn't share this concern, however. For one thing, the number of independent pharmacies declines every year. Fifteen hundred independents closed in 1994, many driven out of business by the nation's rapid move toward lower-margin, third-party pharmacy business.

   Conventional drugstore chains and deep discounters are also consolidating. Since January 1994, fourteen drug chains, which operated 2,500 stores, have disappeared. There is tremendous pressure on weak regional chains lacking the resources to update stores and lower costs through technology.
- Prescription sales increased 18 percent in 1996, 19.8 percent in 1995, and 18.9 percent in 1994. Comparable drugstores were up 13 percent, 13.8 percent, and 12.1 percent in those same years. Prescription sales were 45.2 percent of total sales for fiscal 1996, compared with 43.4 percent in 1995, and 40.8 percent in 1994.
- In 1996, sales were boosted by the growing number of freestanding

locations. The company has found the more convenient its stores are, the less they need to advertise. Average sales per store have climbed almost 30 percent since 1991.

- In 1996, operating expenses had dipped to 22.6 percent of sales, the lowest in Walgreen's history. Management credits the improvement to technology, distribution efficiencies, lower advertising costs, strict attention to payroll control, and healthy sales volume.

- Walgreen's strong market share, geographic dispersion, and the full line of services offered through its pharmacy benefits manager (WHP Health Initiatives) provide the leverage that increased third-party prescription sales 25 percent in 1996. Nearly 75 percent of Walgreen pharmacy business is now third-party.

Total assets: $3,949 million
Current ratio: 1.57
Common shares outstanding: 246 million
Return on 1996 shareholders' equity: 19.4%

	1996	1995	1994	1993	1992	1991	1990	1989
Revenues (millions)	11,778	10,396	9,235	8,295	7,475	6,733	6,048	5,380
Net income (millions)	372	321	282	245	221	195	175	157
Earnings per share	1.50	1.30	1.14	.99	.89	.79	.71	.64
Dividends per share	.44	.39	.34	.30	.26	.23	.20	.17
Price: High	43.6	28.5	22.7	22.3	22.3	19.3	13.3	12.6
Low	29.1	21.6	16.9	17.7	15.2	12.3	10.0	7.5

INCOME

Washington Gas Light Company

1100 H Street N. W., Washington, D. C. 20080 ◻ Investor contact: Maria T. Frazzini (202) 624-6410 ◻
Dividend reinvestment plan available: (202) 624-6558 ◻ Listed: NYSE ◻ Fiscal year ends September 30 ◻
Ticker symbol: WGL ◻ S&P rating: A ◻ Value Line financial strength rating: A

Washington Gas Light is a natural gas distributor serving the Washington, D.C., metropolitan area as well as sections of Virginia, Maryland, and Martinsburg, West Virginia. The company's franchise service area covers 6,648 square miles. The gas system contains over 20,000 miles of gas lines.

Meter growth on the Washington Gas system averaged 3.2 percent annually during the past five years, compared to an industry average of 1.7 percent. Residential and firm commercial customers provide a stable financial base, accounting for 78.8 percent of the company's therm deliveries in fiscal 1996.

Washington Gas has service agreements with eight interstate pipelines and connects directly to four. The company purchases gas from over sixty suppliers. This portfolio approach enables the company to benefit from competition among gas suppliers.

Shortcomings to Bear in Mind

- Rising interest rates are generally bad news for utilities. There are two reasons: Public utilities borrow money for expansion and are hurt by higher interest rates. Investors tend to seek higher yields and may sell their utilities

if they can find better income elsewhere.

- A growing customer base has one draw-
back: It means that the company has to
invest in new mains and other facilities
to serve the new customers. In 1995,
Washington Gas Light spent $112.7 mil-
lion on capital expenditures. This
climbed to $124.4 million in 1996.

Reasons to Buy

- The Washington metropolitan area is
among the fastest-growing regions in the
nation; its work force enjoys the highest
household income and is the most educated. With its concentration of service,
information, and technology industries,
the region also enjoys economic stability.
These qualities give Washington Gas
Light a highly stable customer base with
firm residential and commercial load
accounting for 70 percent of therms
delivered. Its lack of reliance on cyclical
industrial customers is an important
reason to favor this stock.

- Metropolitan Washington area homeowners prefer natural gas heating 4-to-1
over the electric heat pump.

- Natural gas is abundant and not materially dependent on foreign supply; 95
percent of the nation's consumption of
natural gas is produced domestically.

- Sales to natural gas vehicles have begun
to contribute to sales growth. Various
provisions of the Clean Air Act and
local D.C. regulations have resulted in
increased use of natural gas in fleet
vehicles. The number of gas vehicles
not owned by WGL is increasing on an
annual basis and now totals in excess of
1,000. Natural gas fueling stations num-
bered thirty-four at year-end.

- WGL has an exceptionally strong balance sheet, with 58.9 percent of its capitalization in shareholders' equity. This
compares favorably with an industry
average of 52 percent. Coverage of bond

interest is also high, at 5.6 times. Its
financial strength is also evident in its
bond rating, AA-, which is higher
than nearly any other gas utility. A
strong balance sheet makes it easier for
the utility to finance its construction
program.

- As noted above, Washington Gas Light
serves a growing territory. Most of the
utility's new customer additions are new
homes where gas is favored by four out
of five, allowing it to achieve a market
share of 90 percent. The remaining new
customers are normally those switching
from electric or oil heat to gas heat.

- In recent years, Washington Gas Light
has steadily sold off its various minor
nonutility businesses. Analysts view this
strategy as favorable from an investor's
point of view. For one thing, most
public utilities have not fared well with
their diversified operations. They've
done better by concentrating on
what they know best—expanding the
market share of natural gas within their
territory.

- Washington Gas Light is aware that
competition is heating up, but it
believes that it can succeed effectively.
The company brings a number of
strengths to the competitive arena:

  - *Market leadership.* In a recent nine-
  year period, the company more than
  tripled its market share of new
  residential construction to over 90
  percent.

  - *Exceptional reputation.* Employees
  and services are highly rated by consumers in monthly surveys; the company enjoys excellent relationships
  with builders, contractors, and appliance dealers.

  - *Premium product.* Washington area
  consumers prefer natural gas heat
  more than 4 to 1 over electric.

  - *Innovative approaches.* The company
  was among the first to offer flexible

pricing and margin sharing for alternate fuel customers (larger customers who can switch back and forth from fuel oil to natural gas, depending on price), to purchase natural gas in the open market and to employ extended meter supply lines.

- *Experienced competitor.* The company has prospered while competing with some of the lowest-cost electric companies in the nation.

■ The outlook for continued growth is exceptionally bright. Home construction and local economic growth, fueled by population increases, are expected to create steady demand for energy services. In some outlying counties, population increases of up to 50 percent are forecast for the current decade. Loudoun and Prince William counties in the company's Virginia service territory were cited by a *Wall Street Journal* article as among the ten fastest-growing areas in the nation.

■ Washington Gas Light offers operating and life-cycle cost advantages over electric competitors in commercial heating, water heating, cooking, and drying.

By introducing technology to reduce the amount of gas piping the builder or contractor must install, the company has also significantly lowered initial costs.

■ Washington Gas is active in coalitions to advance clean fuels for automotive use and oppose attempts to weaken clean air legislation. The real potential of this market, however, will not become apparent until 1998/99, when the first federal mandates for fleet conversions to clean fuels are scheduled to go into effect.

A study released by the Gas Research Institute showed that, considering full cycle energy use, NGVs are unsurpassed in overall environmental cleanliness, even when compared to electric vehicles.

■ Customer convenience is important to Washington Gas. Its most significant improvements have come from installing encoder-receiver-transmitters (ERTs) on customer meters, enabling the company to read meters without entering the premises. Radio signals from the ERTs transmit meter readings to vehicle-based computers driven past homes and businesses.

With this technology, meters can be read quickly and estimated bills eliminated. The result is higher productivity and more satisfied customers.

■ Today, more than 95 percent of new homes sold by the top builders in the Washington market use natural gas, compared with 82 percent five years ago. What's more, a number of communities, built at a time when gas service was unavailable, are lined up to convert.

■ In 1996, the company raised its dividend to $1.14 per year. This was the twentieth consecutive year of dividend increases. WGL has paid dividends for 145 years, a record equaled by fewer than 1 percent of companies listed on the New York Stock Exchange.

Total assets: 1,464.6 million
Current ratio: 1.00
Common shares outstanding: 44 million
Return on 1996 shareholders' equity: 15.0%

	1996	1995	1994	1993	1992	1991	1990	1989
Revenues (millions)	970	829	915	894	746	698	736	756
Net income (millions)	82	63	61	55	52	46	50	47
Earnings per share	1.85	1.45	1.42	1.31	1.27	1.14	1.26	1.22
Dividends per share	1.14	1.12	1.11	1.09	1.07	1.05	1.01	.97
Price: High	25.0	22.3	21.3	22.9	19.6	17.3	16.3	15.9
Low	19.1	16.1	16.0	18.1	15.6	13.7	13.3	11.8

GROWTH AND INCOME

Weyerhaeuser Company

Tacoma, WA 98477 ◻ Investor contact: Richard J. Taggart (206) 924-2058 ◻ Dividend reinvestment plan available: (800) 851-9677 ◻ Listed: NYSE ◻ Ticker symbol: WY ◻ S&P rating: B+ ◻ Value Line financial strength rating: B++

Dating back to 1900, Weyerhaeuser is primarily engaged in the growing and harvesting of timber and the manufacture, distribution, and sale of forest products. It is also in real estate development and construction, as well as financial services, which are businesses that are being down-sized.

The company's wood products businesses produce and sell softwood lumber, plywood, and veneer; composite panels; oriented strand board; hardboard; hardwood lumber and plywood; doors; treated products; logs; chips; and timber.

These products are sold primarily through the company's own sales organizations. Building materials are sold to wholesalers, and industrial users.

Weyerhaeuser has the following pulp, paper, and packaging businesses:

• Pulp—manufactures chemical wood pulp for world markets.

• Newsprint—manufactures newsprint at the company's North Pacific Paper Corporation mill and markets it to West Coast and Japanese newspaper publishers.

• Paper—manufactures and markets a range of both coated and uncoated fine papers through paper merchants and printers.

• Containerboard Packaging—manufactures linerboard and corrugating medium, which is primarily used in the production of corrugated shipping containers, and manufactures and markets corrugated shipping containers for industrial and agricultural packaging.

• Paperboard—manufactures bleached paperboard that is used for production of liquid containers and is marketed to West Coast and Pacific Rim customers.

• Recycling—operates an extensive wastepaper collection system and markets it to company mills and worldwide customers.

• Chemicals—produces chlorine, caustic, and tall oil, which are used principally by the company's pulp, paper, and packaging operations.

Shortcomings to Bear in Mind

■ The major markets, both domestic and foreign, in which the company sells its products are highly competitive, with numerous strong sellers competing in each realm.

Many of Weyerhaeuser's products compete with substitutes for wood and wood fiber products. The real estate and financial services subsidiaries, moreover, also compete in highly competitive markets, competing with numerous regional and national firms in real estate development and construction and in financial services.

Reasons to Buy

■ Weyerhaeuser is uniquely positioned in its industry. It manages more privately owned timber than any other company.

Likewise, Weyerhaeuser leads the industry in private forestry, having launched, nearly a generation ago, a program to maximize timber yield on every acre of planted forest land.

■ To build on the timber asset and increase shareholder value, Weyerhaeuser is following a strategy that contains three elements:

• Sell or dispose of nonstrategic assets

- Work assiduously to upgrade the company's portfolio of land, mills, and other facilities
- Ally strategically with domestic and international partners
- Emphasize value-added products
- Continually improve product quality and the cost-efficiency of production.

■ Weyerhaeuser has been narrowing its business focus since 1990. The company divested its milk carton, personal care products, insurance, nursery products, and gypsum wallboard businesses. What's more, over the past year, WY reduced its investments by selling selected real estate assets, and the company has signed agreements to sell Weyerhaeuser Mortgage Company and Shemin Nurseries, Inc.

■ WY is continuing to adjust its core business portfolio through asset acquisitions and sales. In the past five years, Weyerhaeuser acquired an additional 1.1 million acres of domestic timberland and 5.4 million acres of Canadian timber licenses, plus two pulp mills, eight sawmills, nine corrugated packaging plants, and fifteen recycling centers—an investment of $1.5 billion.

■ Portfolio adjustments to the company's major businesses also include divesting assets that are not an optimum strategic fit. As a result, in the last five years, Weyerhaeuser has sold 800,000 acres of timberlands, including 1996's sale of 600,000 acres near Klamath Falls, Oregon. The company also sold two sawmills, one plywood mill, and two composite panel plants. These actions yielded $500 million in proceeds.

■ Weyerhaeuser's management believes that the amount of capital needed to maintain its current asset base will decline. In 1997, for instance, the company expects spending to maintain and enhance productivity of its current facilities will be about $750 million, or sig-

nificantly less than the amount spent in 1996.

Strategic ventures with both domestic and international partners are one way the company has grown, while controlling capital outlays. Through such arrangements, WY can leverage its own core competencies, team with those who have complementary capabilities, and pool financial resources.

As a matter of fact, the company has a number of such ventures. They include a newsprint joint venture with Nippon Paper Industries Co. Ltd., which manufactures newsprint primarily for export, and the Cedar River Paper Company, a joint venture containerboard plant. Other joint ventures are in the formative stages.

In 1996, the company entered into a joint venture agreement with SCA Packaging Europe BV for the purpose of serving packaging markets in Asia. In December of 1996, WY announced the initial closing of a joint venture partnership that will make investments in timberlands and related assets outside the United States. The partnership between Weyerhaeuser Forestlands International and UBS Resource Investments International completes one stage in the company's long-term strategy to pursue international investments.

■ Extensive restructuring, carried out by CEO John W. Creighton, Jr., since he took the reins in 1991, has transformed Weyerhaeuser—a one-time laggard—into one of the industry's most profitable players. In years past, investors scorned Weyerhaeuser as unwieldy and paternalistic. It was loaded down with outdated mills. What's more, it was hobbled by a host of noncore subsidiaries making everything from milk cartons to disposable diapers. Besides jettisoning these businesses, Creighton led his managers through an eighteen-month re-engineering in which each mill and tree farm had to redesign the way it worked. Creighton's goal: to add $700 million to operating earnings by 1995—a goal he achieved a year earlier than planned.

- In 1996, the company reached the thirtieth anniversary of its decision to develop high yield forestry. During these three decades, sustained investments in forestry research, reforestation, and silviculture have dramatically increased the amount of wood growing in the company's private forests. Weyerhaeuser expects its annual harvest from U.S. fee timberlands to increase about 70 percent above present levels over the next twenty years.

- Combined earnings for the Real Estate and Financial Services sectors of Weyerhaeuser increased from $13 million in 1995 (before a special charge) to $43 million in 1996, primarily the result of Weyerhaeuser Real Estate Company realizing benefits from its business restructuring efforts.

   The real estate company improved results from its primary businesses and markets while continuing to make significant progress liquidating marginal assets identified in 1995. With home building and land development activities in Southern California, Las Vegas, Houston, Maryland, Virginia, and the Puget Sound area, the company remains one of the top twenty home builders in the nation.

Total assets: $13,596 million
Current ratio: 1.64
Common shares outstanding: 198 million
Return on 1996 shareholders' equity: 9.5%

	1996	1995	1994	1993	1992	1991	1990	1989
Revenues (millions)	11,114	11,788	10,398	9,545	9,219	8,702	9,024	10,106
Net income (millions)	463	983	589	463	372	182	394	601
Earnings per share	2.34	4.83	2.86	2.26	1.83	.90	1.87	2.83
Dividends per share	1.60	1.50	1.20	1.20	1.20	1.20	1.20	1.20
Price: High	49.9	50.4	51.3	46.5	39.3	30.6	28.4	32.8
Low	39.5	36.9	35.8	36.3	26.6	20.1	17.4	24.5

CONSERVATIVE GROWTH

Winn-Dixie Stores, Inc.

P. O. Box B, Jacksonville, Florida 32203-0297 ▢ Investor contact: Richard P. McCook (904) 783-5000 ▢ Dividend reinvestment plan available: (904) 783-5433 ▢ Listed: NYSE ▢ Fiscal year ends last Wednesday in June ▢ Ticker symbol: WIN ▢ S&P rating: A+ ▢ Value Line financial strength rating: A++

Winn-Dixie, which dates back to 1925, is the nation's fifth-largest retail food chain, with 1,178 supermarkets in fourteen states and in the Bahama Islands. In all, it does business in 700 communities. Winn-Dixie is the Sunbelt's largest food retailer.

   The company also operates a network of distribution centers, processing and manufacturing plants, and a fleet of trucks, providing a comprehensive support system. The fleet consists of 1,300 tractors, 2,100 trailers, and 1,500 drivers. They travel a total of 74 million miles a year.

   An average store in the Winn-Dixie network has square footage of 38,800. The new units have 50,000 square feet of space.

Winn-Dixie operates supermarket and Marketplace superstores throughout Florida, Georgia, North and South Carolina, Alabama, Mississippi, Louisiana, Kentucky, Tennessee, Indiana, Virginia, Texas, Ohio, and Oklahoma.

The company's retail support centers are located in Jacksonville, Miami, Orlando, and Tampa, Florida; Raleigh and Charlotte, North Carolina; Montgomery, Alabama; New Orleans, Louisiana; Atlanta, Georgia; Louisville, Kentucky; and Fort Worth, Texas.

Winn-Dixie also operates twenty-two facilities to produce or process company products such as coffee, tea, and spices; carbonated and noncarbonated drinks; grocery bags; crackers, corn snacks, and cookies; frozen pizza; detergents and soap products; sausage; luncheon and smoked meats; mayonnaise and salad dressing; preserves and peanut butter; eggs and dairy products.

The quality of all company-manufactured products, as well as those produced by Winn-Dixie suppliers, is maintained by a staff of qualified food technologists in a modern testing laboratory in Jacksonville.

Shortcomings to Bear in Mind

■ Winn-Dixie is not an aggressive growth stock, since its record of earnings and dividends, while well above average, is far from spectacular. In the 1986–1996 period, earnings per share advanced from $.71 to $1.69, a compound annual growth rate of 9.1 percent. There were two years in which earnings declined (1987 and 1994). In the same ten-year span, dividends per share expanded from $.44 to $.89, a growth rate of 7.3 percent, which, of course, is still much better than the rate of inflation. Finally, book value per share during these years moved ahead from $4.26 to $8.85, a growth rate of 7.6 percent.

Reasons to Buy

■ Winn-Dixie places considerable emphasis on the autonomy of its store managers, giving them freedom and greater responsibility for merchandising to meet the needs of each store's customers.

Today's customer prefers one-stop shopping. In response, Winn-Dixie continues to its move to larger stores in centralized locations.

With increased square footage, WIN is able to surround the customer with more departments and more time-saving choices from service centers such as seafood, service meat, nutrition, floral, pharmacy, deli-bakery, international wines and cheeses, banking, photo processing, postage stamps, and money orders. In addition, the chain is expanding general merchandise, health and beauty care, and frozen food sections.

■ Winn-Dixie's store-opening and remodeling program has been moving ahead at a brisk pace. Fiscal 1995 marked the first year since 1987 that, in addition to increasing its square footage, the chain increased store count as well. In 1996, moreover, WIN opened and acquired 60 additional stores (averaging 48,500 square feet), closed 58 older and less-productive units (averaging 29,400 square feet), and enlarged or remodeled an additional 128 stores. At the end of fiscal 1996, the company's stores averaged 38,800 square feet.

Inside these stores, the company features more pharmacies, banks, One-Hour Photo Labs, and dry cleaning operations than ever before. To provide added convenience, nearly 1,000 stores are open twenty-four hours a day.

To support these stores and the growing number of customers, Winn-Dixie is making a number of improvements in its facilities. In 1996, the company enlarged its warehouse in Orlando, built a new warehouse for perishables in Montgomery, and built a new warehouse and distribution facility for its Raleigh Division.

- Winn-Dixie has completed the installation of its satellite communications network, which currently is the largest satellite network of any grocery chain. This network enhances WIN's capability to provide more ATMs, facilitate faster check-approval, and transmit data internally with greater efficiency.

One of the system's first applications was the establishment of Winn-Dixie's own network of automated teller machines. Over 1,000 ATMs have been installed, providing cardholders with the ability to make withdrawals, fund transfers, and balance inquiries—all with the convenience and security found inside a Winn-Dixie store. Winn-Dixie Network ATMs accept cards from a wide range of systems, including Alert, Cirrus, Gulfnet, Honor, Jeanie, Mac, Plus, and Pulse. Winn-Dixie ATMs also accept Visa, MasterCard, Discover, and American Express. Today, Winn-Dixie is one of the largest owner/operators of ATMs in the country.

- The company is ever alert to expansion. For instance, in 1995, Winn-Dixie acquired Thriftway, Inc., a twenty-five-store chain based in Cincinnati, Ohio. While continuing to operate these stores under the Thriftway banner, the company has combined their unique strengths with Winn-Dixie's hallmarks of U.S. Choice Beef and low-price leadership. The Thriftway chain consists of twenty-three combination (food and drug) stores and two conventional supermarkets.

In another move to expand, Winn-Dixie will enter the Chattanooga market in 1996. The company now has eight new stores planned for this new market, with the first store scheduled to open in September 1995.

- Winn-Dixie boasts a long string of sales increases: sixty-two years in a row.
- Incredible as it may seem, Winn-Dixie has boosted it dividend for fifty-three consecutive years.
- In 1991, Winn-Dixie adopted a strategy that focuses on low prices. The company now calls itself "the largest Everyday Low Price supermarket in America." In 1992, the company permanently lowered the prices of over 1,000 health and beauty care products in the majority of its stores.

Total assets: $2,649 million
Current ratio: 1.30
Common shares outstanding: 151 million
Return on 1996 shareholders' equity: 19.9%

	1996	1995	1994	1993	1992	1991	1990	1989
Revenues (millions)	12,955	11,788	11,082	10,832	10,337	10,074	9,744	9,151
Net income (millions)	256	232	216	236	196	171	153	135
Earnings per share	1.69	1.56	1.45	1.56	1.28	1.10	.97	.84
Dividends per share	.89	.78	.72	.66	.60	.54	.50	.48
Price: High	39.0	28.9	33.9	39.9	22.3	20.6	17.0	12.8
Low	31.0	21.3	21.8	20.8	17.3	14.5	12.0	9.4

Worthington Industries

1205 Dearborn Drive, Columbus, Ohio 43085 ◻ **Investor contact: Jeff Bradley (614) 438-3133** ◻ **Dividend reinvestment plan available: (617) 575-3170** ◻ **Fiscal year ends May 31** ◻ **Listed: NASDAQ** ◻ **Ticker symbol: WTHG** ◻ **S&P rating: A-** ◻ **Value Line financial strength rating: A**

Worthington Industries, founded by John H. McConnell in 1955, is a leading manufacturer of metal and plastic products. Worthington, a $1.5 billion global company, operates fifty-five facilities in twenty-one states, Canada, Mexico, China, and France.

At the outset, you should understand that Worthington is no ordinary steel company. For one thing, Worthington respects the judgment of its workers. They can refuse to ship product if they feel the quality is below standard—a decision normally left to management. Thus, Worthington's product rejection rate from customers is less than 1 percent, compared with 3 percent for competitors.

What's more, there is no room in the company's scheme of things for the M.B.A. mentality. At Worthington, factory workers can become managers. For instance, Worthington's current president, Donal Malenick, started as a general laborer, as did many of its vice presidents.

Worthington's business is made up of these segments: processed steel products, custom plastics, and precision metals.

Processed Steel Products
Steel Processing

Worthington Steel is the country's premier intermediate steel processor of flat-rolled steel, offering more products and services than any of its competitors. Specializing in close-tolerance, cold-rolled strip steel, Worthington processes over 3 million tons of steel annually, ranging in thickness from .006 inches to over .5 inches. The company serves more than 1,700 customers who produce a variety of products in the automotive supply, appliance, electrical, communication, office equipment, machinery, and leisure-time industries.

Pressure Cylinders

Worthington Cylinders is the largest North American producer of low-pressure cylinders for L.P. and refrigerant gases. The company also manufactures high-pressure acetylene, industrial, medical, halon, and electronic gas cylinders. Additional products include recovery and recycling tanks for refrigerant gases and helium balloon kits.

Metal Framing

Dietrich Industries is the country's largest manufacturer of steel framing for the commercial and residential construction industries. Dietrich processes over 400,000 tons of framing and operates eighteen facilities located throughout the United States.

Custom Products
Custom Plastics

Worthington Custom Plastics provides a wide variety of both functional and decorative custom-made injection-molded plastic products for the automotive, appliance, lawn and garden, and recreational industries. These products may be as small as air-conditioning louvers for automobiles or as large as entire dashboard assemblies. The company's capabilities include painting, foam-in-place molding, vacuum forming, intricate assembly, silk screening, vacuum metalizing, hot stamping, roll foiling, and appliqués.

Precision Metals

Worthington Precision Metals supplies extremely close-tolerance critical parts to the automotive industry for use in automatic transmissions, power steering, and antilock braking systems.

Joint Ventures

WSP-*Worthington Specialty Processing*
This joint venture with USX processes wide sheet steel primarily for the automotive industry.

London Industries

This joint venture with Nissen Chemitec and Sumitomo manufactures injection-molded plastic parts and assemblies, with a focus on foreign transplant automakers.

WAVE-Worthington Armstrong Venture

This joint venture with Armstrong World Industries is one of the largest producers of metal ceiling grid systems in the world.

TWB Company

This joint venture with Thyssen Stahl of Germany produces tailor laser-welded steel blanks for the auto industry.

Acerex

This joint venture with Hylsa in Monterrey, Mexico, is Worthington's first steel-processing operation outside the United States.

From its inception, Worthington's core business has been steel processing. Through the construction of new plants and by acquisition, the steel-processing operation has spread from its headquarters in Columbus, Ohio, to twelve facilities, including joint ventures located throughout the eastern half of the United States and including the recently opened joint venture Acerex, in Monterrey, Mexico.

The company has continually increased its capacity and capabilities to meet the growing needs of its customers and to take advantage of market opportunities. Worthington offers the widest range of processing capabilities and services available in its market, including slitting, annealing, rolling, cut-to-length, pickling, coating, and blanking. Today, the company does virtually everything necessary to prepare steel for over 1,700 customers in the automotive, appliance, electrical, communication, construction, office equipment, machinery, and leisure-time markets.

Shortcomings to Bear in Mind

- The primary risks are general economic conditions and a potentially declining contribution from Rouge Steel, as steel prices weaken. Analysts are looking for a "soft landing" rather than a recession. However, if they are wrong, a weaker economy would most likely be reflected in lower sales and somewhat lower margins, although margin erosion is mitigated by Worthington's reliance upon incentive compensation for all employees and the direct relationship between steel purchase costs and selling prices. However, income from Rouge Steel would not be insulated in the same way, and analysts have assumed a decrease in earnings from this source.

Reasons to Buy

- Worthington Industries pays its employees a salary instead of hourly wages and promises not to lay them off in bad times—a real benefit in a cyclical industry like steel processing. No one at the company has ever been laid off just because business was slack. While few of Worthington's thirty plants are unionized, wherever it operates, its wages are in the top quartile for its area.

■ Dividends have been increased for twenty-eight consecutive years.

■ Worthington's success is evidenced by its inclusion in both editions of the best-selling book *The 100 Best Companies to Work for in America.*

■ Perhaps the key factor in Worthington's success is its philosophy and the unique partnership it has forged with its employees. There has been nothing more vital to this link than the company's profit-sharing plan. Each quarter, a fixed percentage of earnings is shared and distributed to all nonunion employees, regardless of position.

A typical employee can expect to get 35 percent to 70 percent of his compensation, depending on his job responsibility, from profit sharing. When the company suffers, of course, the workers suffer, too, since a significant part of their compensation is profit sharing. That means Worthington's labor costs decline automatically when business is weak, eliminating the wage rigidity that forces unionized companies to resort to layoffs at every drop in the order book. On the other hand, employees can become owners. Since workers often own a chunk of the stock, they are less resentful when there is a slump in business. They know the decline in their compensation is helping protect their investment.

■ Most Worthington plants have councils made up of nonsupervisory workers who serve two-year terms. One of the council's important functions is to vote on whether to give regular status to temporary employees. When someone is first employed, they are told that they are going to get a 40-hour workweek. On the other hand, they are not immediately granted permanent status. Rather, the employees vote in those who are to become regular employees. In other words, this determination is not made by management. A candidate must receive a majority vote to join the company full-time.

To be sure, not all of Worthington's plant are nonunion. What's more, labor relations with these four union shops have sometimes been a bit contentious.

■ Worthington is again broadening its market coverage. Specifically, the steel finisher recently built a large processing plant next to the BHP/Northstar thin-slab mini-mill. The processing facility, which cost $70 million, has both pickling and slitting capabilities and provides Worthington with an entrée into the hot-dipped galvanizing market. The WTHG plant can to pickle 900,000 tons annually of hot-rolled steel sheet; it has 400,000 tons of coating capacity from the minimill next door. A supply agreement with BHP Northstar gives Worthington a ready market for its steel and ensures a degree of success for the new facility. The new enterprise was completed in the fall of 1996. Analysts believe the company will feel the full impact of this new facility in 1998. While the company originally announced that this venture will generate sales in excess of $250 million, analysts contend this number is "extremely conservative" relative to what the plant should generate in a short time. They believe that the new project will produce annual revenues of as much as $300 million within the third year of operation.

Total assets: $1,220,125
Current ratio: 2.66
Common shares outstanding: 90.8 million
Return on fiscal 1996 shareholders' equity: 14.9%

	1996	1995	1994	1993	1992	1991	1990	1989
Revenues (millions)	1,478	1,484	1,285	1,113	971	872	914	934
Net income (millions)	91	117	85	68	58	48	56	62
Earnings per share	1.01	1.29	.94	.70	.65	.54	.62	.69
Dividends per share	.45	.41	.37	.33	.30	.27	.25	.20
Price: High	22.5	23.5	21.7	19.7	17.6	11.6	11.1	10.8
Low	17.5	17.5	16.7	12.6	10.9	8.6	9.1	9.2

Index

About the Author

A graduate of the University of Buffalo, John Slatter started his investment career as a registered representative in Rome, New York, with Hugh Johnson & Company. During these same years, he wrote scores of articles for *Barron's Financial Weekly*, while still acting as a broker.

He then moved to Buffalo, New York, to edit an investment magazine published by Hugh Johnson & Company. After some experience as a securities analyst, he moved to Cleveland to become a full-time analyst with a firm that now calls itself Everen Securities. He specialized in the analysis of public utilities and pharmaceutical stocks. During this same seventeen--year period, he devoted time to analyzing and restructuring the portfolios for major investors and was editor of two publications put out by Everen Securities.

This experience led to his joining a Cleveland-based investment advisor, a firm that manages portfolios for investors on a fee basis. Four years later, John Slatter and his wife moved to Vermont, where he owns his own firm that manages portfolios for serious investors. He also publishes a market letter, *John Slatter's Investment Commentary*. He has continued his freelance writing, and his articles often appear in *Physician's Management*. He may be reached by calling (802)872–0637 or writing him at 70 Beech Street, Essex Junction, VT 05452.